National Survey of State Laws

National Survey of State Laws

FIRST EDITION

Richard A. Leiter,
Editor

 Gale Research Inc. • *DETROIT* • *WASHINGTON, D.C.* • *LONDON*

Richard A. Leiter, *Editor*

Gale Research Inc. Staff

Carol DeKane Nagel, *Developmental Editor*
Lawrence W. Baker, *Senior Developmental Editor*

Mary Kelley, *Production Assistant*
Evi Seoud, *Assistant Production Manager*
Mary Beth Trimper, *Production Director*

Arthur Chartow, *Technical Design Services Manager*
Cynthia Baldwin, *Art Director*

Eastword Publications Development, Inc., *Typesetters*

Library of Congress Cataloging-in-Publication Data

National survey of state laws / edited by Richard A. Leiter
   p.   cm.
   ISBN 0-8103-8406-X : $49.95
     1. Law—United States—States. I. Leiter, Richard A.
KF386.N38 1993
349.73—dc20
[347.3]   92–13519

♾ This book is printed on acid-free paper that meets the minimum requirements of American National Standard for Information Sciences—Permanence Paper for Printed Library Materials, ANSI Z39.48-1984.

ISBN 0-8103-8406-X
Printed in the United States of America

Published simultaneously in the United Kingdom
by Gale Research International Limited
(An affiliated company of Gale Research Inc.)

10 9 8 7 6 5 4 3 2

IP

The trademark **ITP** is used under license.

To Nana and Harry Leiter and Mark and Grace Laevsky, my grandparents, who are no longer with me but are still sources of great inspiration.

CONTENTS

PREFACE

National Survey of State Laws provides an overall view of forty-two of the most-asked about and controversial legal topics in the United States. Presented in chart format, this reference allows users to make basic state-by-state comparisons of current state laws. The subjects featured fall into eight general legal categories:

Business and Consumer Laws
Criminal Laws
Education Laws
Employment Laws
Family Laws
General Civil Laws
Real Estate Laws
Tax Laws

The types of topics covered range from Abortion to the Right to Die, Gun Control to Prayer in Public Schools, Personal Income Tax to Right to Work, and Lemon Laws to Leases and Rental Agreements. The information presented is culled from laws on the books as of March 1, 1993.

Arrangement

National Survey of State Laws is divided by legal category into eight sections. Within each section each topic is arranged alphabetically and is presented in its own subsection, which begins with a general overview of that law followed by a table briefly describing each state's and the District of Columbia's stances on particular aspects of that law.

The salient points of each law appear at the top of each column. Beneath, brief statements provide the core points of the state law. References to each state's statute or code section covering that law are also presented, enabling users who are interested in reading the original text to find it in the state's code of law. The appendix comprises a list of **Statutory Compilations Used in This Book** and provides the abbreviations and full names of each state code.

Selection of Topics

Aside from being controversial and sought-after, the topics presented in *National Survey of State Laws* must meet another criterion: state statutes covering that topic must be available. In many cases, there are no statues; here the common law, or the law of the courts, which is determined by many cases taken together, forms the single rule of law pertaining to that topic.

There are also a few instances where state statutes have been rendered ineffectual by the states' adopting uniform acts or by U.S. Supreme Court decisions. Therefore, comparisons for these types of laws are not included here. However, because two situations in which the Supreme Court has seized jurisdiction over state laws—Prayer in Public School and Abortion—remain so controversial, we've included them in *National Survey of State Laws* for state-by-state comparison.

Editor's Note

Always consult an attorney before making decisions of any legal consequence. Never use a reference such as this, which is not meant to be an exposition of the law but a source for comparisons, as a definitive statement of the law.

Comments and suggestions regarding future editions of *National Survey of State Laws* are welcome and should be addressed to:

Editor, *National Survey of State Laws*
Gale Research Inc.
835 Penobscot Bldg.
Detroit, MI 48226-4094
Phone: (313)961-2242
Fax: (313) 961-6741
Toll-free: 1-800-347-GALE

ACKNOWLEDGMENTS

Very specially, I thank my wonderful wife Wendy for her hard work keying in every word of this book and for her patience, organization and support throughout the whole project. I also thank my children, Maddie, Annie and Becky, for their patience. Hey, kids! Daddy's back! (Mommy, too!)

I want to thank my parents, Labe and Lois Leiter, for their support, encouragement and love over all these years. It may have been rough sometimes, but it was always interesting. Thanks for not giving up.

Great appreciation must be expressed to my head research assistant, Cheri (soon to be Duggan) Carlson, who has performed at the highest levels of care and professionalism. Cheri is also responsible for a significant part of the Abortion chapter overview, which came from research she did for an article being published in the *Regent University Law Review.*

I wish to thank my other research assistant, Cathy McClean, for her diligence and hard work. Appreciation also goes out to Patrick Robbins and Julie Adams for being willing to step in in a pinch to help with the compiling of the information for various chapters. I also thank Anna Dinkins, our Public Services supervisor, for allowing me to borrow her staff when the need arose.

My staff at Regent University Law Library were also very supportive and patient with me throughout this project, and I appreciate each one of them. Thank you, Joyce Jenkins, for tolerating my distraction; Linda Muckelroy, for your quiet, firm support in the day-to-day things; and Jan Beard, for your great support, friendship and help. And thanks to my professional staff, Jack Kotvas, Eric Welsh and Kathleen Miller, for your understanding and flexibility as I routinely missed my few reference hours. I also wish to express my appreciation for my colleagues on the law faculty, especially the terrific leadership of Dean Herbert Titus: Thank you for your support and guidance.

Thanks also needs to be expressed to Cathy White and Louise Lieb for their introducing me to the profession of law librarianship; to Frank Houdek for his early instruction and inspiration; and to Roy Mersky for his training, support, encouragement and friendship. Special thanks also to professional colleagues and friends who had significant influence on the book in its initial stages: Mitch Fontenot, who worked on some of the preliminary compilation of material for the Abortion chapter; Mark Mackler, a terrific counselor and friend in general and, in particular, as I was agonizing over the planning and contract for the project; and Jackie Grossman, a fine librarian, friend and colleague, during the initial planning for the project; thanks for covering for me.

I also wish to express my appreciation to Gale Research editors Carol Nagel for her excellent editing and firm encouragement and Barb Beach for her kindness and positive outlook. Thanks, too, to Charles Bodnar, my copy editor, for his diligent work. Great appreciation also goes out to Bob Thomas for his original encouragement of this project.

Above all, thanks be to God, through whom and by whom all things are possible, for the opportunity, the resources and the skills to undertake this task. If the book is useful at all, it is due to His grace and goodness; if it fails, it is I. "Unless the Lord built the house [book] those who build it labor in vain."—Ps 127

I. BUSINESS AND CONSUMER LAWS

1. ANTITRUST

Antitrust violations are "crimes" committed by business entities that injure both competing businesses and the consumer by artificially inflating or fixing prices.

Antitrust laws came into national prominence in the late nineteenth century with the rise of the giant industrial monopolies. Two types of monopolies, horizontal and vertical, were felt to be particularly harmful to competition. In a horizontal monopoly, a single entity owns all or an unreasonable percentage of the firms competing in the same business, such as all the telephone or oil companies. In a vertical monopoly, a single entity owns all or an unreasonable percentage of all levels of business within a single industry, for example, all the forests, logging firms, mills, printing plants, and newspapers.

Through the exercise of its power to regulate interstate commerce, Congress has enacted the most sweeping of antitrust regulations in the Sherman Antitrust Act. Because of the great size of the businesses engaged in antitrust or anti-competitive practices as well, the federal government has taken the lead in enforcing against these types of unfair business practices.

Most antitrust statutes are enforced in two ways: the state attorney general can sue on behalf of the state in order to correct the unfair practice, either by obtaining an injunction prohibiting the offensive practice or by ordering fines or other redress to be paid or otherwise addressed to the consumers; the other way is by a private right of action, whereby consumers themselves or competing businesses sue to recover for damages or injuries suffered as a result of the offending behavior.

Table 1: Antitrust

State	Code Section	Private Action	Statutes of Limitation	Attorney's Fees
FEDERAL	Tit. 15 §§4, 15(a-b), 21	Yes	4 yrs.	No
ALABAMA	6-5-60	Yes	Not specified	No
ALASKA	45.50.562 to 588	Yes	4 yrs.	Yes
ARIZONA	44-1401 to 1415	Yes	4 yrs.	Yes
ARKANSAS	4-75-301, *et seq.*	No prerequisite; it is the duty of the attorney general to enforce the status	Not specified	Attorney general receives costs
CALIFORNIA	Bus. & Prof. §§16700, *et seq.*	Yes	4 yrs.	Yes
COLORADO	6-2-101, *et seq.*; 6-4-101, *et seq.*; *13-80-101*	Yes	6 yrs. for actions brought by attorney general; 3 yrs. for other actions	No
CONNECTICUT	35-24, *et seq.*	Yes; attorney general also enforces	4 yrs.	Yes
DELAWARE	Tit. 6 §§2101, *et seq.*	Yes	3 yrs.	Yes
DISTRICT OF COLUMBIA	28-4501, *et seq.*	Yes	4 yrs.	Yes
FLORIDA	542.15, *et seq.*	Yes	1 yr. (plus period for attorney general action)	Yes
GEORGIA	13-8-31, *et seq.*; 16-10-22 Specific provisions according to subject of agreement	Yes		
HAWAII	480-13, 20, 24	Yes	4 yrs.	Yes
IDAHO	48-101, *et seq.*	Yes	Not specified	Yes
ILLINOIS	Ch. 38 §§60-1 to 60-11	Yes	4 yrs.	Yes
INDIANA	24-1-1-1, *et seq.*; 24-1-2-1, *et seq.*; 24-1-3-1, *et seq.*	Yes	4 yrs.	Yes
IOWA	553.1, *et seq.*	Yes	4 yrs.	Yes for individual plaintiff but not for state
KANSAS	50-101, *et seq.*; 50-112, *et seq.*	Yes	Not specified	Yes
KENTUCKY	365.020, *et seq.* (Unfair Trade Practices)	Yes	Not specified	No
LOUISIANA	51.121, *et seq.*	Yes	Not specified	Yes
MAINE	Tit. 10 §§1101, *et seq.*	Yes	Not specified	Yes
MARYLAND	Com. Law II §§11-201, *et seq.*	Yes	4 yrs.	Yes
MASSACHUSETTS	Ch. 93 §§1, *et seq.*	Yes	4 yrs.	Yes

(Continued)

Table 1: Antitrust—Continued

State	Code Section	Private Action	Statutes of Limitation	Attorney's Fees
MICHIGAN	445.772, *et seq.*	Yes	4 yrs.	Yes
MINNESOTA	325D.49, *et seq.*	Yes	4 yrs.	Yes
MISSISSIPPI	75-21-1, *et seq.*	Yes	Not specified	No; $500 penalty
MISSOURI	416.011, *et seq.*	Yes	4 yrs.	Yes
MONTANA	30-14-201, *et seq.*	Yes	Not specified	No
NEBRASKA	59-801, *et seq.*	Yes	Not specified	Yes
NEVADA	598A.010, *et seq.*	Yes	4 yrs.	Yes
NEW HAMPSHIRE	356:1, *et seq.*	Yes	4 yrs.	Yes
NEW JERSEY	56:9-1, *et seq.*	Yes	4 yrs.	Yes
NEW MEXICO	57-1-1, *et seq.*	Yes	4 yrs.	Yes
NEW YORK	Gen. Bus. §§340, *et seq.*	Yes; no prerequisite for administrative action but private party plaintiff must notify the attorney general	4 yrs. (suspended during pendancy of federal action based in whole or in part on same matter)	Yes
NORTH CAROLINA	75-1, *et seq.*	Yes	4 yrs.	Yes
NORTH DAKOTA	51-08.1-01, *et seq.*	Yes	4 yrs. or 1 yr. after conclusion of action by state	Yes
OHIO	1331:01, *et seq.*	Yes	None	No
OKLAHOMA	Tit. 79 §§1, *et seq.*	Yes	4 yrs.	Yes
OREGON	646.705, *et seq.*	Yes	4 yrs. or within 1 yr. after conclusion of any proceeding based on the same matter	Yes; individual and state win reasonable attorney's fees and expert's fees
PENNSYLVANIA	Tit. 73 §§201, *et seq.*	Yes	Not specified	No
RHODE ISLAND	6-36-1, *et seq.*	Yes, but private party plaintiff must notify attorney general of his complaint and file proof of service.	4 yrs.	Yes
SOUTH CAROLINA	39-5-10, *et seq.*	Yes	3 yrs.	Yes
SOUTH DAKOTA	37-1-3.1, *et seq.*	Yes	4 yrs.	Yes
TENNESSEE	47-25-101, *et seq.*	Yes	Not specified	No
TEXAS	Bus. & Com. §§15.21, *et seq.*	Yes	4 yrs. or 1 yr. after conclusion of action based on the same act	Yes
UTAH	76-10-911, *et seq.*	Yes	4 yrs.	Yes
VERMONT	No statutory provisions			
VIRGINIA	59.1-9.1, *et seq.*	Yes	4 yrs.	Yes

(Continued)

Table 1: Antitrust—Continued

State	Code Section	Private Action	Statutes of Limitation	Attorney's Fees
WASHINGTON	19.86.010, *et seq.*	Yes	4 yrs., except when attorney general brings action in whole or in part; in matter of private action, the private action's statute of limitations is suspended	Yes
WEST VIRGINIA	47-18-1, *et seq.*	Yes	4 yrs., unless one civil action is brought, then any other is suspended during the first's pendancy and one year after.	Yes
WISCONSIN	133.01, *et seq.*	Yes	6 yrs. Statute begins running upon discovery of a cause of action by an aggrieved party. Other actions have suspended statute of limitations during pendancy of any civil or criminal action and for one year afterward.	Yes
WYOMING	40-4-101, *et seq.*	Yes	Not specified	No

2. ATTORNEYS

Legal Education and Admission to the Bar

When the American Bar Association (ABA) was founded a little more than one hundred years ago, its first priority was to set standards for legal education. Its Section on Legal Education and Admission to the Bar immediately set out to accredit law schools and monitor the quality of the legal education each school provided. The purpose was to guard against widely varying levels of preparedness and education and, thus, professionalism, among attorneys.

What has become a near-universal requirement for becoming a lawyer is possession of a diploma from an ABA-accredited law school, which allows a law school graduate to take the bar examination in any state. Few states permit graduates of non-ABA accredited law schools to sit for their own bar exams, though California allows individuals who have not attended law school but have diligently and in good faith studied law for at least four years to sit for its bar exam. New York, Vermont, Washington, and Wyoming also have conditions under which individuals who have not graduated from law school may sit for the bar exam. But by and large a law degree is necessary to take the bar exam, and in most cases it must be from an ABA-accredited school.

Many states allow reciprocity to attorneys already admitted to the bar in other states, while some place various restrictions upon attorneys admitted outside their jurisdictions, such as requiring attorneys admitted elsewhere to have actively been in practice for a certain number of years before s/he can be admitted without an examination. States that do not permit attorneys from other jurisdictions to be admitted without examination require them to take a special or abbreviated exam. These states have a large number of attorneys and maintain that the requirement of the bar exam limits the numbers of attorneys coming into the state.

Many states have responded to the lack of practical skills among some members of the bar by requiring every attorney to take a required number of continuing legal education courses each year. Mandatory Continuing Legal Education (MCLE) generally focuses on areas of the law that are undergoing rapid, dramatic changes or on areas that strengthen practical skills. Though only about two-thirds of the states have MCLE requirements to date, the trend is clearly to require such ongoing education and MCLE is likely to be a universal requirement in the future.

Table 2: Attorneys

State/Code Section	Education	Age	Exam	Reciprocity	MCLE	Admitting Body	Residency
ALABAMA S.Ct. Rule for Mandatory C.L.E. 1, *et seq.*; 34-3-1, *et seq.*; Admin. R. 1, *et seq.*	Law school: graduation after at least 3 yrs. of 30 wks. each from ABA or AALS approved school or graduation after 4 yrs. of 30 wks. each from Birmingham School of Law, Jones Law Inst. or Miles College School of Law; Undergraduate: graduation from any accredited college or university or 96 sem. hrs. or 144 quarter hrs. if legal education at accredited school	19	MBE, including MPRE, and state exam; multistate score from another jurisdiction accepted for 20 mos. if equal or better than national median	None for foreign attorneys; certain professors who have taught for 3 yrs. at accredited Alabama law schools and who are admitted in another state may apply for admission without exam	12 hrs. each calendar year	Supreme Court	
ALASKA 08.08.200, *et seq.*	Law school: ABA or AALS accredited law school or graduate of non-accredited school who has practiced in another jurisdiction for at least 5 yrs; one may register as law clerk to qualify as applicant without completing law school by presenting proof of bachelor's degree and completion of first year of law school; must have regular fulltime employment with Alaska judge or attorney, tutor, and meet other specified study requirements	18	2 ½ days, includes MBE and essay on Alaska law and Alaska practicum; MPRE administered separately also required; MBE scores from other jurisdictions not transferable		No	Board of Governors	
ARIZONA Sup. Ct. Rules 31-80	Law school: ABA accredited or actively practiced 5 of last 7 yrs. in another state	21	MBE and MPRE and essay; MBE scores accepted from another jurisdiction if within last 13 mos.	None	15 hrs. each educational year, including minimum 2 hrs. professional responsibility	Supreme Court	None

(Continued)

Table 2: Attorneys—Continued

State/Code Section	Education	Age	Exam	Reciprocity	MCLE	Admitting Body	Residency
ARKANSAS 16-22-2-1; Ark. Rule for CLE 3; Rules Governing Adm. to Bar	Law school: approved by ABA	21 unless graduate of accredited, recognized, or Class A law school	MBE and essay	None	Resident: 12 hrs. annually; Nonres-ident: must comply to require-ments of their state and file annual cer-tificate of completion	Courts of state	None
CALIFORNIA Bus. & Prof. §§6060, *et seq.;* §§6070, *et seq.*	Law school: Graduate from law school accredited by examination committee full-time for 3 yrs. or part time for 4 yrs. or proof applicant has otherwise diligently and in good faith studied law for at least 4 yrs; students at unaccred-ited law school must take preliminary bar exam at end of first year of law school; undergraduate: 2 yrs. or apparent intellectual ability equivalent to 2 yrs. of college work	18	MBE, essay, and MPRE	Must: (1) meet age and moral charac-ter requirements; (2) be admitted before highest court in sister state or foreign country; (3) have actively engaged in practice of law 4 of last 6 yrs.; (4) may have to take exam	36 hrs. every 36 months, 8 hrs. of which must be law prac-tice man-agement or legal eth-ics, of which 4 hrs. must be legal ethics	Supreme Court	None
COLORADO CRCP Rules 201, 260; 12-5-101	Law school: Class A: First professional degree from ABA-approved law school; Class B: ABA-approved or state-approved or common law English speaking nation, if portion of legal education from foreign jurisdiction, must graduate from ABA-approved school or, if graduate of state accredited school, then applicant must be admitted in state and have practiced law 5 of 7 yrs.		Class A applicant: admitted in another jurisdic-tion and actively practiced for 5 of last 7 yrs. or scored 152 (scaled) on MBE within last 2 yrs.; Class B appli-cant: all others, must take written exam	Class A: no exam required; Class B: MBE and addi-tional subjects; Full-time commis-sioned officer and U.S. judge advo-cate stationed in Colorado may be admitted tempo-rarily	45 units every 3 yrs., 2 units must be ethics	Supreme Court	

(Continued)

Table 2: Attorneys—Continued

State/Code Section	Education	Age	Exam	Reciprocity	MCLE	Admitting Body	Residency
CONNECTICUT Rules of Prac. for Sup. Ct. §§16.21, *et seq.*	Law school: graduate of school accredited by committee or Master of Laws from accredited school; must have passed professional responsibility exam or course	18	2 day exam, MBE, and essay; MBE scores not transferable	(1) Practiced court of original jurisdiction (10 yrs. if ever failed Conn. Bar Exam); (2) meets other requirements; (3) passed course or exam in professional responsibility; (4) intends that major portion of practice shall be in Connecticut shall be given temporary license for 1 year; if after 1 year s/he intends to continue practice in Conn., temporary license may be made permanent	None	Superior Court	
DELAWARE Sup. Ct. Rules 52, 70; Rules for Mandatory CLE 4; Board of Bar Examiners Rules BR-52.4, 52.5	Law school: baccalaureate law degree or equivalent from ABA approved law school; Undergraduate: baccalaureate degree or equivalent or pass exam determined by board	21	MBE, essay, and Delaware Professional Conduct Examination	None	30 hrs. every 2 yrs.	Supreme Court on recommendation of board of 12 examiners	5 mos. clerkship in Delaware required for admission
DISTRICT OF COLUMBIA D.C. Ct. App. Rule 46	Law school: ABA approved law school or if not, 26 semester hrs. at accredited school		MBE, essay, and MPRE; MBE scores from other jurisdictions may be transferred	(1) Active member in good standing of other jurisdiction immediately preceding, or (2) J.D. or LL.B. from accredited school, admitted to any state or territory with at least 133 scaled score on MBE, and passed MPRE; must apply within 25 mos. of MBE	None	D.C. Court of Appeals	
FLORIDA Rules Re Fla. Bar 6-10.3	Law school: graduate of ABA approved law school; Undergraduate: bachelor degree from regionally accredited school	18	MBE, essay, and MPRE; MBE scores not transferable	None	30 credit hrs. every 3 yrs., 2 in ethics	Supreme Court	

(Continued)

Table 2: Attorneys—Continued

State/Code Section	Education	Age	Exam	Reciprocity	MCLE	Admitting Body	Residency
GEORGIA 15-19-30, *et seq.*; State Bar Rules & Regs R.8-104; Rules Governing Adm. to Prac. of Law §4	Law school: must complete requirements approved by ABA, AALS, or GA Board of Examiners, requiring 3 yrs. of classroom attendance at 400 hrs./yr.; Undergraduate: degree from accredited school or passed CLEP test		MBE, essay, MPRE; MBE scores not transferable	None	12 hrs. minimum per year	Superior Court	
HAWAII Sup. Ct. Rules 1	Law school: graduate of ABA approved school or unaccredited and 5 of last 6 yrs. practice; LL.M. not satisfactory substitute for J.D. or LL.B.		MBE, essay, including legal ethics; MBE scores not transferable	Full-time faculty of U. of Hawaii Law School who meet citizenship and education requirements and admitted in another jurisdiction admitted for 3 yrs.; after 3 yrs. may be given permanent license	None	Supreme Court	3 mos. prior to admission and must be in state 75% of said 3 mos.
IDAHO 3-401, *et seq.*	Law shool: graduate of ABA approved school; attorney applicants must be admitted to highest court of another state and practiced 5 of last 7 yrs.	Age of majority	MBE, essay; attorney applicants licensed for more than 5 yrs. need not take MBE		30 credit hrs. every 3 yrs.	Board of Commissioners of State Bar	
ILLINOIS ILCS S. Ct. Rule 701	Law school: First law degree from ABA approved school; Undergraduate: must be graduate of 4 yr. high school or prep school and successfully completed at least 90 semester hrs. at college or university approved by Board of Law Examiners; in lieu of college or preliminary work, Board may accept satisfactory completion of program or curriculum of particular college or university	21	Professional responsibility and academic exam; after fifth exam failure, permission of board or Supreme Court is required before admission to another exam	Practiced in another jurisdiction 5 of last 7 yrs.; passing grade on MBE in last 5 yrs.	None	Board of Law Examiners	

(Continued)

Table 2: Attorneys—Continued

State/Code Section	Education	Age	Exam	Reciprocity	MCLE	Admitting Body	Residency
INDIANA Admin. & Discipline of Atty. §§ 1, *et seq.*	Law school: graduation from ABA approved school or approved list of Indiana Supreme Court or agency thereof	21	Conducted by Board of Law Examiners usually in Indianapolis; does not use MBE	1 yr. conditional admission to members in good standing of another bar who are 21, residents of Indiana, of good moral character, and practiced for 5 of last 7 yrs.; may be received for 5 one-year periods after which admission shall be permanent	No less than 6 hrs. each calendar year and no less than 36 hrs. each 3-year educational period	Supreme Court	
IOWA 602.10101, *et seq.*; Sup. Ct. Rules 101, *et seq.*	Law school: LL.B. or J.D. from reputable law school		25 questions on various areas of federal and Iowa law, including ethics and professional responsibility; MBE not used; may take exam before degree if graduating within 75 days of exam	Member of any other U.S. bar who is resident may be admitted without exam if practiced 5 of last 7 yrs.	Minimum 15 hrs. during each calendar year and 2 ethics credits during every 2-year period	Supreme Court	Required for admission
KANSAS Rules 7-101, *et seq.*	Law school: degree from ABA accredited law school; Undergraduate: bachelor's degree from accredited college		Essay questions on local law, MBE, MPRE; MBE scores may be transferred from another jurisdiction if within 13 mos. of current exam and if applicant passed entire bar exam of other jurisdiction	Temporary license granted if: (1) attorney passed written bar exam in some other jurisdiction more than 5 yrs. ago; (2) has or intends to become Kansas resident to accept employment other than practice of law; (3) will perform legal services only for single employer; (4) of good moral character	36 hrs. every 3 yrs. including at least 12 hrs. per year except: (1) during first year of practice; (2) retired or inactive; (3) federal and state judges; (4) others exempted for good cause	Supreme Court	

(Continued)

Table 2: Attorneys—Continued

State/Code Section	Education	Age	Exam	Reciprocity	MCLE	Admitting Body	Residency
KENTUCKY Supreme Ct. Rules 2.070; 3.661; 3.665[1]; 3.666;	Law school: graduate of ABA or AALS approved law school		MBE; written exam on 14 topics; must receive 75% or more; may take exam 3 times	Citizen of U.S. admitted in D.C. or state and has practiced 5 of last 7 yrs. provided qualifications were equal or higher than those required for admission in Kentucky	15 hrs./yr.; at least 2 hrs. of legal ethics	Supreme Court	
LOUISIANA Supreme Ct. Rules 30, *et seq.*; CLE Rule 1, *et seq.*; State Bar Art. of Inc. Art. 14 §7	Law school: ABA approved law school	18	MBE not used, but all applicants must pass MPRE	No	15 hrs. per year, including not less than 1 hr. legal ethics, professional responsibility, and rules of conduct	Supreme Court	Citizen of U.S. or resident alien
MAINE Tit. 4 §§801, *et seq.*	Law school: ABA accredited; Undergraduate: at least 2 yrs. at accredited school		MBE; MPRE and general examination; MBE score from other jurisdiction transferable if taken at same time as ME exam or score over 155	No; foreign attorney may be admitted temporarily on motion	None	Supreme Court	
MARYLAND Bus. Occ. §§10-101, *et seq.*; Bd. of Law Examiners Rule 4, *et seq.*	Law school: J.D. or equivalent at school recognized by Board of Law Examiners; Undergraduate: 90 semester hrs. college work and adequate academic work to enter ABA approved school	18 to be admitted to bar but not to take exam	MBE, essay test; MBE scores transferable from another jurisdiction if score of 140 or better	If practiced 5 of last 7 yrs. and proof of good, moral character and intent to practice or teach	None	Court of Appeals and State Board of Law Examiners	
MASSACHUSETTS Ch. 221 §§37, *et seq.*; SJC Rule 3:01, *et seq.*	Law school: ABA approved or authorized foreign law school; Undergraduate: bachelor's degree	18	State law and MBE; must pass MPRE within 2 years of passing bar exam	Admitted elsewhere and satisfactory moral character and legal ability	None	Supreme Judicial Court and Superior Court	

(Continued)

Table 2: Attorneys—Continued

State/Code Section	Education	Age	Exam	Reciprocity	MCLE	Admitting Body	Residency
MICHIGAN 600.901, *et seq.*; State Bar Rules 17 §1	Law school: reputable and qualified law school in U.S. or its territories; Undergraduate: at least 2 yrs. of study	18	MBE, no additional local bar examination requirements; out-of-state MBE scores accepted if within preceding 3 yrs. and person meets all other requirements for admission and other state grants reciprocal right to elect to use score on MBE administered in Michigan	Admitted to highest court of another state and practiced or taught 3 of last 5 yrs.	12 hrs. in first year; 12 in second and 12 in third year of practice	Supreme Court or any circuit court	
MINNESOTA 481.01, *et seq.*; S. Ct. Admis. Rules 2, *et seq.*; Legal Cert. Plan Rule 6	Law school: J.D. or LL.B. from ABA approved school	18	MBE, MPRE, additional questions	Engaged in law 5 of last 7 years; passed exam in other state within last 2 yrs. and scored at least 145 on MBE; good moral character	45 hrs. every 3 yrs.; if specialized, 20 hrs. must be in area of specialty	Supreme Court	Must be resident or designate Clerk of Appellate Courts as agent for service of process or maintain office in state
MISSISSIPPI 73-3-2, *et seq.*	Law school: 3 yr. law course at ABA approved school; Undergraduate: bachelor's degree or 3 yrs. of college work	21	MBE, additional subjects; MBE scores from other jurisdictions not transferable	Must have practiced at least 5 yrs.; other state must reciprocate with Mississippi; must meet other requirements for admission	12 hrs. per year	Supreme Court	
MISSOURI CR 8.03, *et seq.*; 484	Law school: J.D. or LL.B. from ABA approved school; Undergraduate: ¾ of bachelor's work	21	MBE, MPRE, essay questions on local law; MBE scores may be transferred from another jurisdiction if taken within last 19 mos., score was at least 128 and applicant passed bar in other state	Member of bar of another state and has practiced or taught for preceding 5 yrs.	15 hrs. of which 3 must be on professionalism, legal/judicial ethics, or malpractice	Supreme Court	

(Continued)

Table 2: Attorneys—Continued

State/Code Section	Education	Age	Exam	Reciprocity	MCLE	Admitting Body	Residency
MONTANA 37-61-101, *et seq.*, Montana S. Ct. Rule 4	Law school: ABA accredited law school approved by Montana Supreme Court	21	MBE, MPRE, and essay; MBE scores from another jurisdiction admissible if taken within 2 yrs. of examination date	Certain attorney applicants may be admitted without examination or by abbreviated examination	15 hrs./yr.	Supreme Court	Must be resident of state
NEBRASKA 7-101, *et seq.*	Law school: LL.B. or J.D. from reputable law school, law school with similar entrance requirements and course of study at U. of Neb. Law School and AALS member; Undergraduate: at least equivalent to 3 yrs. of high school course	21	MBE, Nebraska law	Admission upon showing that admission in another state required equal qualification and has practiced 5 full years	None; except county attorneys must complete continuing education hours established by the NE County Attorney Standards Advisory Council, not to exceed 36 hours annually (§23-1216); and public defender shall take at least 10 hrs. of continuing education annually (23-3406)	Supreme Court	
NEVADA S. Ct. Rules 48, 51, 52-53, 54, 64-66, 77, 98	Law school: Bachelor of Laws or equivalent from ABA approved school; Undergraduate: at least 3 yrs.	Age of majority	MBE, additional exam; MBE scores from other jurisdictions not admissible	None	10 hrs. per year	Supreme Court	

(Continued)

Table 2: Attorneys—Continued

State/Code Section	Education	Age	Exam	Reciprocity	MCLE	Admitting Body	Residency
NEW HAMPSHIRE Ch. 311 §§2, 5, 8, 13; S. Ct. Rule 42, *et seq.;* S. Ct. Rule 53.1	Law school: graduate of 3-year full-time or 4-year part-time program from ABA approved school or foreign law school of common law country Undergraduate; 3 yrs. of work required for bachelor's degree	18	MBE, additional essay questions; MBE scores from other jurisdictions not admissible	None	12 hrs./yr. at least two hrs. must be in legal ethics, professionalism, substance abuse, or attorney-client disputes	Supreme Court	
NEW JERSEY Rule 1:21, *et seq.*	Law school: bachelor's degree or equivalent from ABA approved law school	18	MBE, additional subjects	In certain instances teachers at New Jersey law schools may be admitted without examination	None	Supreme Court	
NEW MEXICO R. 15-103, *et seq.;* SCRA 18, App. A	Law school: graduate of law school fully accredited by ABA	21	MBE, MPRE, additional subjects; no provision for transfer of MBE scores from other jurisdictions	None; all applicants must take exam	15 hrs., at least 1 hr. ethics; newly admitted members must take 10 hrs. practice skills in first 2 yrs. of practice	Supreme Court	
NEW YORK 22 NYCRR 520 ; JL §90[6]; 465	Law school: graduation from approved law school or 4 years of study in office of practicing attorney and at least one year in approved law school or approved study of law in foreign country	21	MBE, additional subjects	Over 26 and admitted to practice in highest court of another state, territory, D.C., or common law country and has practiced for 5 years	None	Appellate Division of Supreme Court	
NORTH CAROLINA 84-24; Rules Governing Admission to the Practice of Law §0501, *et seq.*	Law school: degree from law school approved by Council of the North Carolina State Bar	18	MBE, state examination; MBE scores not transferable from another jurisdiction	Must be in good standing, practiced or taught for 4 of last 6 yrs., and state from which s/he comes must grant reciprocity to N.C.	12 hrs. per year, at least 2 on professional responsibility and during first 3 yrs. of admission, 9-12 hrs. in practical skills courses	General Court of Justice upon recommendation from Board of Law Examiners	

(Continued)

Table 2: Attorneys—Continued

State/Code Section	Education	Age	Exam	Reciprocity	MCLE	Admitting Body	Residency
NORTH DAKOTA 27-11-02; Admin. Rule 1, 4; USDC Rule 2; CLE Rule 3	Law school: J.D. or equivalent from law school approved or provisionally approved by ABA	18	MBE, MPRE, additional subjects; scores from other jurisdictions accepted if taken same year as N.D. exam	Meets educational requirements, is admitted to bar in another state, has practiced or taught for at least 5 yrs. and 4 of immediate last 5 yrs.	45 hrs. in each 3-year period	Supreme Court	Non-resident eligible for admission but must designate clerk of court as agent for service of process
OHIO Supreme Court Rules for Government of Bar of Ohio Rule I, *et seq.*	Law school: degree from ABA approved law school; Undergraduate: bachelor's degree from approved school	21	MBE, additional subjects; MBE scores from other jurisdictions not accepted	Meets educational requirements, is admitted to bar in another state, has practiced 3 of last 5 yrs.; applicant who has ever failed Ohio Bar may not be admitted without exam	24 hrs. every 2 yrs. of which at least 2 hrs. must relate to legal ethics	Supreme Court	Must be resident of Ohio or intent to establish permanent Ohio residence
OKLAHOMA Tit. 5 §1, *et seq.;* OK St. Bar Rules Art. 13 §1, *et seq.;* OK St. Admis. Rule 1, *et seq.*	Law school: graduate of law school accredited by ABA or Board of Bar Examiners	18	MPRE, essay	Ex-judges of other states and attorneys who have practiced for at least 5 yrs. immediately preceding	12 hrs. per calendar yr., 1 hr. must be professional responsibility or legal ethics or legal malpractice	Supreme Court	Resident of Oklahoma
OREGON 9.005-9.755; 9.990; Rules Reg. Adm. to Practice Law 1.10, 2.10, 3.05; State Bar Rules 1-2	Law school: degree from ABA approved law school	18	MBE, MPRE, additional subjects; MBE scores from other jurisdictions not accepted	All applicants must pass exam	45 hrs. over 3-year period including 6 hrs. of legal ethics. New admittees: 15 hrs., inc. 10 hrs. of practical skills and 2 hrs. of ethics	Supreme Court	Non-resident must designate Oregon resident for service of process

(Continued)

Table 2: Attorneys—Continued

State/Code Section	Education	Age	Exam	Reciprocity	MCLE	Admitting Body	Residency
PENNSYLVANIA Pa. B.A.R. 103, 203, *et seq.*; P.A.R. CLE Rule 105	Law school: LL.B. or J.D. from accredited law school; Undergraduate: degree from accredited school or equivalent education		MBE, additional subjects; MBE scores from other jurisdictions not accepted	Member in good standing of bar of reciprocal state; must have practiced or taught 5 of past 7 yrs.; if ever failed Pa. bar, must take exam	5 hrs. each fiscal year on Rules of Professional Conduct and on subject of professionalism generally	Court Administrator of Pennsylvania	
RHODE ISLAND SCR 33, *et seq.*	Law school: graduate of school approved and accredited by ABA and Board of Bar Examiners	21	MBE, additional subjects; no person may take exam more than 3 times except by court order	If in practice or teaching 5 of last 10 years, applicant must take only essay portion of exam	None	Supreme court	
SOUTH CAROLINA SC App. Ct. Rules 400 *et seq.*	Law school: graduate of law school approved by ABA or S.C. Supreme Court	21	MBE, additional subjects; MBE scores from other jurisdiction accepted only if taken immediately before essay portion of this exam and for this exam only		12 hrs. per year plus 6 hrs. of legal ethics or professional responsibilities every 3 yrs.	Supreme Court	
SOUTH DAKOTA 16-16-1, *et seq.*; 16-17-1, *et seq.*; 16-18-1, *et seq.*	Law school: graduation from ABA accredited law school	18	MBE, MPRE, additional subjects; MBE scores from other jurisdictions accepted	None	None	Supreme Court	Must be resident, maintain office in state or designate clerk of Supreme Court as agent for service of process
TENNESSEE 23-1-101, *et seq.*; 23-2, *et seq.*; 23-3, *et seq.*; Rules of Sup. Ct. Rule 6, Rule 7 §1.01, *et seq.*; Rule 21 §3.01, *et seq.*	Law school: graduate of ABA accredited law school; Undergraduate: bachelor's degree from regionally accredited school	18	MBE, other subjects; MBE scores from other jurisdictions not accepted	Meets educational requirements; admitted in another state; has practiced at least 5 yrs; has passed equivalent exam	12 hrs. each calendar year and 3 additional hrs. per year ethics and professionalism	State Board of Law Examiners supervised by Supreme Court	Citizen of Tennessee

(Continued)

Table 2: Attorneys—Continued

State/Code Section	Education	Age	Exam	Reciprocity	MCLE	Admitting Body	Residency
TEXAS Gov. §§2.024; 81.061, *et seq.*, Art. 12 §6; Rules Gov. Adm. to Bar. Rule 1, *et seq.*	Law school: graduate of approved law school	18	MBE, MPRE, additional subjects; MBE scores from other jurisdictions not accepted	Supreme Court will make rules governing foreign attorneys, however, they must be of good, moral character	15 hrs. per reporting period, at least 1 hr. of which is devoted to legal ethics and professional responsibility	Supreme Court	
UTAH 78-51-10	Law school: graduate of ABA accredited law school	21	MBE, MPRE, other subjects; MBE scores from other states not acccepted	None	27 hrs. during each 2-year period, at least 3 hrs. legal ethics	Supreme Court	U.S. citizen or intends to become one
VERMONT Tit. 12, App. I, Pt. II; CLE Rules §3; Adm. to Bar §§5, *et seq.*	Law school: degree from ABA approved law school, 6 mos. internship with Vt. attorney or study under supervision of Vt. attorney who has been admitted for at least 3 yrs.; Undergraduate: at least ¾ of bachelor's work	18	MBE, additional subjects; MBE scores of 137 or greater may be transferred from another jurisdiction	Must have practiced 5 of preceding 10 yrs.	20 hrs. during each 2-year period, at least 2 hrs. legal ethics	Supreme Court	
VIRGINIA 54.1-3925, *et seq.*; Rules of S. Ct. of Va. 1A:1, *et seq.*	Law school: graduate of ABA approved law school or 3 yrs. study under conditions prescribed by Board of Bar Examiners	18	MBE, MPRE, other subjects	Any lawyer entitled to practice before highest court of any other state or territory for not less than 5 yrs. may be admitted without exam	12 hrs. per year, at least 2 hrs. legal ethics or professionalism	Supreme Court	
WASHINGTON 2.48; Admissions to Practice Rules 1, *et seq.*	Law school: graduate of approved law school or completion of law clerk program; Undergraduate: not specified if law school graduate; if law office study, must have bachelor's degree from approved college or university		MBE not used	No admission without exam	15 hrs. per year except year of admission and following year; 45 hrs. per 3 yrs.	Board of Governors, but Supreme Court has ultimate responsibilities	
WEST VIRGINIA Ch. 30, Art. 2; Admission to Practice of Law Rule 3.0	Law school: graduate of ABA and AALS accredited law school or equivalent; Undergraduate: degree from accredited college or university	18	MBE, MPRE, additional subjects; MBE scores from other jurisdictions admitted if passing score within last 13 mos.	Applicant's state of bar membership must be reciprocal with W. Va.; must have practiced for preceding 5 yrs.	24 hrs. every 2 fiscal years, at least 3 hrs. in legal ethics or office management	Supreme Court of Appeals	

(Continued)

Table 2: Attorneys—Continued

State/Code Section	Education	Age	Exam	Reciprocity	MCLE	Admitting Body	Residency
WISCONSIN SCR 40.02, *et seq.*; 31.02	Law school: graduate of ABA accredited law school within last 5 yrs.	Age of majority	MBE, other subjects; MBE scores from other jurisdictions may be transferred; graduates of ABA approved law schools in Wisconsin may be admitted without exam upon production of diploma and certificate showing satisfactory completion of requirements relating to Wisconsin law	Must have actively practiced for 3 of last 5 yrs.	30 hrs. every 2 years	Supreme Court	
WYOMING 5-2-118; 33-5-100, *et seq.*	Law school: 3 yrs. in law school approved by state board of examiners or 1 yr. in law school and 2 yrs. in office of judge or member of bar, or 2 yrs. law school and 1 yr. in law office or judge	21	MBE, other subjects; MBE scores from other jurisdictions accepted	Attorneys from other states may be admitted without examination upon showing they are still in good standing in other state and of good moral character	15 hrs. per year	Supreme Court	

Note: ABA = American Bar Association; AALS = American Association of Law Schools; MBE = Multistate Bar Examination; MCLE = Mandatory Continuing Legal Education; MPRE = Multistate Professional Responsibility Examination.

3. DECEPTIVE TRADE PRACTICES

A deceptive trade practice is an activity in which an individual or business engages that is calculated to mislead or lure the public into purchasing a product or service. False advertising and odometer tampering are two of the most blatant examples of this commercial lying. Such activities are given special status as offenses against the citizenry in general and are therefore accorded by law special enforcement status.

Deceptive trade practices result in criminal prosecution in some states; in others, statutes provide for private enforcement, whereby a citizen is entitled to sue a business for violating deceptive trade practice laws and may be able to recover punitive damages and/or statutory fines. The attorney general of the state may also bring a lawsuit against an offending business enterprise.

Because a deceptive trade practice may affect individuals or businesses from more than one state, a number of states have adopted the standardized Uniform Deceptive Trade Practices Act. The Uniform Act does not add or detract from the law of any one state; rather, it is inclusive and tends to cover, in general terms, all the prohibitions and issues addressed in state law in this area. For example, the Uniform Act prohibits making deceptive representations in connection with commercial goods. This obviously covers odometer tampering, but it also addresses all forms of deception in the marketing or advertising of goods and services.

There is little controversy among the states over what activity amounts to a deceptive trade practice. However, there is a great deal of variety concerning the remedies available for the violations and who may sue for those violations. There are two main purposes of the statutes providing for remedies for businesses engaging in unlawful activity: (1) injunctions or restraining orders forbidding the continued deceptive trade practice and (2) punishment via fines, damages, and imprisonment. But because businesses are generally in violation of deceptive trade practice laws, and because it is difficult to determine whom to punish in the violating business, fines are generally the most effective method of extracting restitution.

Table 3: Deceptive Trade Practices

State	Uniform Deceptive Trade Practices Act Adopted	Auto Odometer Tampering Forbidden	False Advertising Forbidden	Who May Bring Suit	Remedies Available
ALABAMA	Similar act	Yes (§8-19-5; 15)	Yes, but won't apply if advertiser didn't know it was false, cooperates with attorney general, and discontinues the ad (§13A-9-42 Criminal Code for False Advertising)	Private parties, attorney general, district attorney (§8-19-8)	Restraining orders (§8-19-8); actual damages or $100, whichever is greater, or in court's discretion up to three times actual damages (§8-19-10); willful violation is Class A misdemeanor (§8-19-12); civil penalty up to $2,000 per violation (§8-19-11)
ALASKA	No	Yes (§45.50.471; 18)	Yes (§45.50.471)	Attorney general (§45.50.501); private or class action suites (§45.50.531)	Injunction; $200 or actual damages, whichever is greater; treble damages or equitable relief (§45.50.531)
ARIZONA	No	Yes; Class 1 misdemeanor (§44-1223)	Yes (§44-1522); unlawful practice (§13-2203); Class 1 misdemeanor	Attorney general; consumer (§44-1524)	Subpoena; injunction, civil damages (§44-1524); if willfully violated: $10,000 civil penalty (§44-1531); violating injunction: $25,000 penalty (§44-1532).
ARKANSAS	No	Yes; license may be denied or revoked for violation (§23-112-308, 13)	Yes (exception for those falsely advertising unknowingly) (§4-88-107)	Petition consumer protection (§4-88-110 to 111); attorney general	Injunction and return any money for purchased good to consumer; suspend corporate charter or business permit; possible $10,000 fine per violation if violation willful (§4-88-113)
CALIFORNIA	No	Yes (Veh. C. §28050.5, 28051); misdemeanor (Veh. §40000.15)	Yes (Bus. & Prof. §17500 *et seq.*)	Class action suits; attorney general; district attorney or other prosecuting attorney may bring suit for injunctive and civil penalties (Bus & Prof. §17535); any individual may bring suit for injunction or restitution (Bus. & Prof. §17203)	

(Continued)

Table 3: Deceptive Trade Practices—Continued

State	Uniform Deceptive Trade Practices Act Adopted	Auto Odometer Tampering Forbidden	False Advertising Forbidden	Who May Bring Suit	Remedies Available
COLORADO	Adopted with modifications	Yes (§42-6-206)	Yes (§6-1-105)	Class action; attorney general; private citizens; district attorney (§6-1-113)	Enjoin practice and sue for civil penalty; individuals may receive damages and attorneys fees; treble damages or $250, whichever is greater (§6-1-113)
CONNECTICUT	Fed. Trade Comm. Act (§§42-110a to 42-110q; 42-144 to 42-149)	Yes (§14-106b)	None generally but §42-110b describes "unfair or deceptive acts" in trade, defined as including advertising by §42-110a4	Private parties; attorney general; class action; Commissioner of Consumer Protection (§§42-110d, g)	Willful violation: $2,000 for each offense; costs; attorney's fees; injunctive or equitable relief
DELAWARE	Yes (Tit. 6 §§2531, *et seq.*)	Yes (Tit. 21 §§6401, 6404)	Unlawful (Tit. 6 §2513)	Attorney general and victims of deceptive trade practices (Tit. 6 §2514)	Violation of Tit.6 §2501 is $100 (Tit. 6 §2503); enjoin practice or other appropriate relief (Tit. 6 §§2522 to 2524); actual damages (Tit. 6 §2524); treble damages (Tit. 6 §2533[c]); injunction, attorney's fees (Tit. 6 §2533)
DISTRICT OF COLUMBIA	Yes (§28-3904)	No	Unlawful (§28-3904)	Director of Department of Consumer and Regulatory Affairs; consumer	Appropriate civil penalties: injunction, actual and treble damages, attorney's fees; consumer redress remedies; punitive damages (§28-3905)
FLORIDA	No (§§501.201, *et seq.*)	Yes; guilty of felony in third degree if violated (§319.35)	Yes; insurance (§641.441); fairs, public expositions (§616.091); food (§500.032); "deceptive acts" (§501.204)		Criminal penalty (§817.45)

(Continued)

Table 3: Deceptive Trade Practices—Continued

State	Uniform Deceptive Trade Practices Act Adopted	Auto Odometer Tampering Forbidden	False Advertising Forbidden	Who May Bring Suit	Remedies Available
GEORGIA	Yes (§10-1-370 to 375; 390 to 407)	Yes (§40-8-5); violator liable for three times actual damages or $1,500, whichever is greater, costs and attorney's fees	Yes (§§10-1-420, 421)	Administrator; private party (§§10-1-397, 398)	Injunction (§10-1-423); enjoining practices (§10-4-404); treble damages for intentional violation, limited to actual damages if bona fide error (§10-1-399, 400); fine over $100 but less than $1,000 or prison for up to 20 days or both (§10-1-421); exception for ignorance (§10-1-396)
HAWAII	Yes (§481A)	Yes (§486-77)(1) and (4)	Yes (§481A-3; 708.871 Criminal Code)	Consumer Protection Agency (§487); private parties (§481A-4)	Injunction; costs to prevailing party; attorney's fees
IDAHO	Yes, with modifications (§48-601)	Yes (§49-1629); revocation of license	Insurance policies (§41-1303); generally (§41-1235; §18-3112); food, drugs, and cosmetics (§37-131)		
ILLINOIS	Yes (§815 ILCS 510/1 *et seq.*)	Class A misdemeanor (§720 ILCS 5/17-11)	Deceptive ad is Class A misdemeanor (§720 ILCS 295/1a)	State attorney or attorney general may enjoin	Enjoinment from false advertising (§720 ILCS 295/1b)
INDIANA	No (§24-5-0.5-1 to 10)	Yes (§9-19-9-2)	(§24-5-0.53)	Consumer or consumer class; attorney general	Actual damages; attorney's fees; attorney general may seek injunction, costs and up to $15,000 for violating injunction (IC §24-5-0.5-4, 8); penalty up to $500 for incurable deceptive act
IOWA	No. Consumer fraud (§714.16)	Yes (§321.71)	Food, drug, and cosmetics (§§203B.16; 1904.6; criminal: §714.16)		
KANSAS	No (§§50-623, *et seq.*)	Injured customer may void sale and recover penalties and attorney's fees (§21-3757) based on 15 U.S.C. §§1981, *et seq.*	Yes (§50-626)	Attorney general investigates and enforces (§§50-628, 631); consumer may bring individual or class action (§50-634)	Obtain declaratory or injunctive relief and actual damages (§50-632); individuals may get attorney's fees (§50-634); civil penalties available (§50-636); restraining order (§50-634)

(Continued)

Table 3: Deceptive Trade Practices—Continued

State	Uniform Deceptive Trade Practices Act Adopted	Auto Odometer Tampering Forbidden	False Advertising Forbidden	Who May Bring Suit	Remedies Available
KENTUCKY	No	Yes; license may be revoked and civil penalties of $5,000 per violation (§367.990; 190.270)	Yes (§367.170)	Attorney general, consumer (§§367.190, 200)	Injunction, $2,000 to city per violation (§367.990(2)); any order necessary to restore a person in interest (§367.200); any violation of Act is also a Class C felony (§367.170)
LOUISIANA	Yes (51:1401 to 1418)	Yes; misdemeanor with fine up to $500 and/or up to 90 days prison (§726.1)	Yes (§1405)	Attorney general (§1404); individual who has suffered ascertainable loss	Actual damages, and if willful, violator must pay treble damages plus attorneys fees and costs; injunctive relief (§1407); additional relief as necessary to compensate (§§1408, 1409)
MAINE	Yes (Tit. 10 §§1211 to 1216; Tit. 5 §§206 to 214)	Yes (Tit. 29 §365)	Unlawful (Tit. 10 §1212)	Attorney general, person likely to be damaged by practice may get an injunction (Tit. 10 §1213)	Injunction, possible to get attorney's fees and costs; also available are common law and other statutory remedies (Tit. 10 §1213)
MARYLAND	No (Com. Law §§13-301, *et seq.*)	Yes (Transp. 22 §415); fine of up to $500 and/or prison for 2 months	Unlawful (Com. Law §13-301)	Consumer Protection Division; attorney general; consumer (Com. Law §13-401)	Violator of false advertising: up to $1,000; injunction; actual damages; possibly attorney's fees (Com. Law §§13-401, *et seq.*)
MASSACHUSETTS	Yes (Ch. 93A §21(a))	Yes, liable for three times actual damages or $1,500, whichever is greater (Ch. 266 §141); attorney's fees	Unlawful (Ch. 93A §2)	Attorney general; private parties (Ch. 93A §9)	Injunction, double or treble damages, attorney's fees and costs (Ch. 93A §11)
MICHIGAN	No (MCL §§445.901 to 922	Yes (§257.233a)	Yes (MCL 445.903)	Attorney general, prosecuting attorney, or private citizen; class action by attorney general (MCL 445.910)	Injunction, civil penalty to state up to $1,000 for first offense and $5,000 for second; actual damages or $250, whichever is greater, plus attorney's fees (MCL 445.55)
MINNESOTA	Yes (§§325D.43-48)	Yes (§325.E.14)	Yes (§325.F.67)	Attorney general, county attorney (§325.F.67); any person likely to be damaged (§325.D.46)	Injunction (§325.F.70); attorney's fees (§325.D.46)

(Continued)

Table 3: Deceptive Trade Practices—Continued

State	Uniform Deceptive Trade Practices Act Adopted	Auto Odometer Tampering Forbidden	False Advertising Forbidden	Who May Bring Suit	Remedies Available
MISSISSIPPI	Yes; (§§75-24-1, *et seq.*)	Yes (§63-7-203); violation is misdemeanor and punishable by fine up to $500 and/or prison up to 6 months (§63-7-209)	Yes (§75-24-5)	Attorney general, district attorney, county attorneys; injured consumers; no class actions (§75-24-15)	Restoration of money or property: civil penalty up to $500 for willful violations; individual may recovery attorney's fees; injunction
MISSOURI	No	Yes; liable in civil damages (§407.546); injunction (§407.521); odometer fraud in the first degree is a Class A misdemeanor (§407.516); in the second degree, Class D felony	Yes (§407.020); misdemeanor penalty (§570.160, 170)	Consumer, class action	For odometer tampering: civil, criminal, and injunctive remedies available; for false advertising: court may award punitives, attorney's fees, injunction (§407.025)
MONTANA	Montana Unfair Trade Practices and Consumer Protection Act of 1973 (§§30-14-101 to 224)	Yes (§61-3-607); fine up to $5,000 and/or prison up to 10 years	Yes (§30-14-103)	County attorney; attorney general; individuals but not class actions (§30-14-133)	Recovery of out-of-pocket losses (§30-14-132); the greater of $200 or actual damages, treble damages; injunction (§30-14-133)
NEBRASKA	Yes with modifications (§§87-301 to 306) (Sections 2(a)(12) and 7 not adopted)	Yes (§60-2301)	Yes (§87-302)	Person likely to be damaged (§87-303)	Criminal penalties for violating Act; costs, perhaps attorney's fees, plus other common law and statutory remedies (§87-303)
NEVADA	Revised Uniform Act adopted with significant variations (§§598.360 to 598, 640)	Yes (§484.6062); tamperor is guilty of misdemeanor; person selling a tampered-with vehicle guilty of gross misdemeanor	Yes (§598.410; Criminal Code §§207.171 and 207.174, 175)	Attorney General; consumer advocate; consumer if he is victim of deceptive trade practice (§§41.600; 598.512)	Injunctions; return of money or property; penalties up to $10,000 for each violation possible and willful violation is misdemeanor, second is gross misdemeanor, third is a felony (§598.640); suspension of right to conduct business or dissolution of corporation possible (§598.005); criminal and civil penalties (§§207.174 and 175)

(Continued)

Table 3: Deceptive Trade Practices—Continued

State	Uniform Deceptive Trade Practices Act Adopted	Auto Odometer Tampering Forbidden	False Advertising Forbidden	Who May Bring Suit	Remedies Available
NEW HAMPSHIRE	Yes (§358A:2)	Yes (§262.17)	Yes (§358A:2)	Attorney General, consumer protection (§358A:4); private and class actions (§358A:4)	Misdemeanor penalty (§358A:6); injunctive; equitable relief; attorney's fees
NEW JERSEY	No (§§56:8-2.2, *et seq.*)	Yes (§2C:21-8)	Yes (§56:8-2)	Attorney general, private party (§56.8-10)	Penalty as Attorney General deems proper (§56.8-3.1); injunction; penalty up to $2,000 for first offense and $5,000 for second (§56:8-13)
NEW MEXICO	Yes (§§57-12-1, *et seq.*)	No specific statute against tampering, although provisions for auto sellers, etc. to include odometer statement with car (§66-3-10, 101)	Yes (§§57-15-1,2)	Attorney general (§§57-15-6, 8) and any private person likely to be damaged may seek injunctive relief or damages (§57-12-10); attorney general (§57-15-3); district attorney	Injunctive relief, actual damages, treble damages, and attorney's fees (§57-12-10); restitution; prevailing party may also receive costs and attorney's fee; civil penalties up to $500
NEW YORK	No	Yes (Gen. Bus. §392-e)	Yes (Gen. Bus. §356)	Attorney general (Gen. Bus. §350); private litigation (Gen. Bus. §350-a) for party injured	Restitution for defrauded consumers (Gen. Bus. §396y); civil penalty up to $500; actual damages or $50, whichever is greater (Gen. Bus. § 350d); possibly treble damages; possibly attorney's fees
NORTH CAROLINA	No	Yes (§20-343)	Yes (§§75-1.1; 75-29)	Attorney general; consumer (§§75-15.2, 16)	Civil penalties: up to $5,000; treble damages for one injured (§75-16); attorney's fees (§75-16.1)
NORTH DAKOTA	No	Yes; violation is a Class C felony if prior conviction; otherwise Class B misdemeanor (§39-21-51)	Yes (§§51-12-01; 15-12-08)	Attorney general, state's attorney (§51-12-13)	False advertising is a misdemeanor (Class B); injunction (§51-12-14)
OHIO	Adopted with modifications (Ch. 4165); (overlaps with Uniform Consumer Sales Practice Act (§1345.01-13)	Yes (§§4549.42, 46, 49)	Yes (§4165.01)	Attorney general; class actions; person likely to be damaged (§4165.03)	Civil penalty of not more than $25,000 if practice found to be unfair, deceptive, etc. (§1345.07(01)); injunction; other remedies as available at common law and other statutes

(Continued)

Table 3: Deceptive Trade Practices—Continued

State	Uniform Deceptive Trade Practices Act Adopted	Auto Odometer Tampering Forbidden	False Advertising Forbidden	Who May Bring Suit	Remedies Available
OKLAHOMA	Yes (Tit. 15 §§751 to 765)	Yes (Tit. 12 §503)	Yes (Tit. 15 §753)	Attorney general; district attorney (Tit. 15 §756.1); consumer (Tit. 15 §761.1)	Declaratory judgment, enjoin, restrain, actual damages (Tit. 15 §756.1); violator liable to aggrieved consumer for actual damages and litigation costs (Tit. 15 §761.1); civil penalty: if violation is unconscionable, penalty of up to $2,000 (Tit. 15 §761.1)
OREGON	Main provisions adopted with significant variations (§§646.605 to 656)	Yes; Class C felony (§815.410)	Yes (§646.607)	State, consumers	Civil actions may be brought to recover actual damages or $200, whichever is greater; punitive and equitable relief also (§646.638); injunction; attorney's fees
PENNSYLVANIA	No (Tit. 73 §§201(1) to (9))	Yes; license denied or revoked; constitutes deceptive practices (Tit. 75 §7132); three times actual damages or $1,500, whichever is greater, and attorney's fees (Tit. 75 §7138); criminal penalties (Tit. 75 §7139)	Yes (Tit. 73§201 (2) and (3))	Private actions, attorney general, district attorney, consumer-purchaser suffering ascertainable loss (Tit. 73 §201-9.2)	Private actions for treble damages (Tit. 73 §201 (9.2)); civil penalty up to $1,000 (Tit. 73 §201-8); suspend right to do business (Tit. 73 §201.9)
RHODE ISLAND	No (§§6-13.1-1 to 12)	Yes (§§31-23.2-4; 31-23.2-7); prison up to 5 years or fine up to $10,000 or $1.00 per mile mileage fraud; revocation of license	Yes (§6.13.1-1)	Attorney general (§6-13.1-5); consumer with ascertainable loss (§6-13.1-5.2)	The greater of actual damages or $200; punitives or equitable damages; injunction; attorney's fees, costs (§6-13.1-5.2)
SOUTH CAROLINA	No (§§39-5-10, *et seq.*)	Yes (§§56-15-350, 180)	Yes (§39-5-10)	Attorney general (§39-5-50); any person suffering ascrtainable loss (§39-5-140)	Treble damages (§39-5-140); civil penalty up to $5,000; actual damages; costs and attorney's fees

(Continued)

Table 3: Deceptive Trade Practices—Continued

State	Uniform Deceptive Trade Practices Act Adopted	Auto Odometer Tampering Forbidden	False Advertising Forbidden	Who May Bring Suit	Remedies Available
SOUTH DAKOTA	No (§37-24)	Yes (§32-15-33); violator is guilty of Class 1 misdemeanor	Yes (§37-24-6); class 2 misdemeanor	Attorney general; any individual	False advertising punishable criminally (§§22-41-10, 11, 12); injunction; civil penalty up to $2,000 (§37-24-27); actual damages (§37-24-31)
TENNESSEE	No	Yes (§47-18-104, (16))	Yes (§47-18-104); Class B misdemeanor	Attorney general; individual for damages and injunction	False advertising punishable by up to $100 and 6 months in prison; injunctive relief, damages for injured customers; revocation of violator's license; willful violators fined up to $1,000 (§§47-18-106, 108, amended 1991, Ch. 468); also possibly treble damages for willful violator (§47-18-109)
TEXAS	No (Bus. & Com. §§17.41 to 505)	Yes (Bus. & Com. §17.46(16))	Yes (Bus. & Com. §17.46)	Attorney general; consumers; consumer protection division, district attorney	Actual and treble damages (Bus. & Com. §17.50); injunctive relief, restitution, attorney's fees and costs, plus remedies available in other laws (Bus. & Com. §17.43); restraining order (Bus. & Com. §17.47)
UTAH	No (§13-11a-1, *et seq.*)	Yes (§41-1-173); second degree felony	Yes (§13-11-4)	Enforcing authority; consumer; class action	Declaratory judgment, enjoin, greater of $2,000 or actual damages; actual damages (§§13-11-17, 19); costs and attorney's fees; no injunction without a correction notice to defendant and 10 day wait for defendant to comply (§13-11a-4); remedies are in addition to remedies available for same conduct under state or local law

(Continued)

Table 3: Deceptive Trade Practices—Continued

State	Uniform Deceptive Trade Practices Act Adopted	Auto Odometer Tampering Forbidden	False Advertising Forbidden	Who May Bring Suit	Remedies Available
VERMONT	No (Tit. 9 §2453)	Yes (Tit. 46.2 §112); civil liability; treble damages or $1,500, whichever is greater; up to $10,000 fine and/or up to 12 months in jail	Yes (Tit. 9 §2453)	Attorney general, state attorney (Tit. 9 §2458); damaged consumer (Tit. 9 §2461)	Injunction; civil penalty up to $10,000 (Tit. 9 §2458); equitable relief, actual damages, attorneys fees, exemplary damages (Tit. 9 §2461)
VIRGINIA	No (§§59.1-196, *et seq.*)	Yes (§46.2-112)	Yes (§§59.1-196, *et seq.*)	Attorney general; commonwealth attorney (§59.1-203); harmed individual (§59.1-204)	Enjoin violations, actual damages or $100, whichever is greater (§59.1-204); penalty for willful violation is fine up to $1,000; attorney's fees and costs
WASHINGTON	No (§19.86)	Yes (§46.37.540); civil suit may recover costs and attorney's fees	Yes (§19.86.020)	Any injured person, attorney general (§§119.86.090, 095)	Civil penalties; injunctive degrees; treble damages, including costs and attorney's fees (§19.86.090); (treble damages may not exceed $10,000); actual damages; injunctive relief
WEST VIRGINIA	No	Unlawful practices generally (§46A-6); odometer disclosure requirements (§174-3-12a); no specific provision against tampering	Yes (§46A-6-102)	Consumer with ascertainable loss (§46A-6-106)	The greater of actual damages or $200; injunction (§46A-6-106); equitable relief
WISCONSIN	No (§423.301); Wisconsin Consumer Act (§§421 to 427)	Yes (§347.415)	Yes (§423.361)	Class actions; individuals (§426.110)	Monetary awards (§425.305); actual damages; unenforced obligations; attorney's fees; fine up to $2,000; injunction (§426.110)
WYOMING	Yes (§§40-12-101 to 112)	Yes (§31-16-119)	Yes (§40-12-105)	Attorney general (§40-12-102); class actions, actual damages, consumers (§40-12-108)	Restraining order; injunction; actual damages for consumer; costs and fees (§40-12-108); other common law remedies not barred

4. INTEREST RATES

Every state has very specific limits on the amount of interest that may be charged on consumer contracts, ranging anywhere from 5 to 15 percent. But because parties may always agree to interest rates that are above the legal limit, most consumer contracts include interest rates that are above that limit.

Thus few states have limits on what can be expressly agreed to in a contract. For example, Alaska limits express contract terms to 5 percent over the legal rate, while the District of Columbia has the highest stated ceiling, at 24 percent. A number of states allow the limit to be pegged to the rate set by the Federal Reserve Board; most of these states have limits of 5 percent above the Federal Reserve. Potentially, these may be much higher than the District of Columbia's 24 percent. Overall, it appears that the more rural the state, the lower the limits. Presumably, farmers are protected and are more secure with lower interest rates than citizens of generally urban states with larger economies.

Usury is an unconscionable and exorbitant rate or amount of interest which exceeds those permitted by law. There is a great variety of statutory remedies for usury. A few states class usury as a crime and prescribe prison for violations of its usury laws. The majority of states provide for economic remedies such as forfeiture of all interest paid, recovery of double the usurious amount, payment of a fine, or making the contract unenforceable. Some states even specify that banks or savings and loans pay penalties. North Dakota has one of the more extreme usury penalties: it requires payment of all interest plus 2.5 percent of the principal.

For the most part there are myriad exceptions to the legal interest rate, which may be tied to the character of the lender, borrower, loan amount, the nature of the contract, or the matter that is the subject of the contract. Effectively, legal interest rates are no more than general guidelines for all transactions rather than the specific limits placed on them. There are so many exceptions in many states that it is often necessary to find a different rate for every conceivable situation.

Table 4: Interest Rates

State	Legal Maximum Rate of Interest	Usury Penalty	Judgments	Exceptions
ALABAMA	If agreed upon in writing, up to 8% per year, otherwise 6% per year (§8-8-1)	Forfeiture of all interest and interest paid deducted from principal (§8-8-12)	Other than costs, dollar judgments bear interest from date of entry at 12%; judgment on contract action bears interest at rate in contract (§8-8-10)	Loans over $2000 (§8-8-5); debts under National Housing Act (§8-8-6); Veterans' Benefits acts; industrial development boards and medical clinic boards (§11-54-97, 11-58-15); bonds issued by public or non-profit organizations (§8-8-7); public housing bonds, State Board of Education Securities (§§24-1-32; 16-3-28); public hospital corporations (§22-21-6)
ALASKA	Absent contract: 10.5%; express contract agreement: 5% over legal rate (§45.45.010)	One paying usurious interest may recover double amount thereof within 2 years (§45.45.030)	10.5% interest unless contract action, then use contract rate (§09.30.070)	Contract where principal amount exceeds $25,000 (§45.45.010)
ARIZONA	10% per year; any rate may be agreed and contracted upon (§44-1201)	Forfeit all interest (§44-1202); usurious payments deemed to be made toward principal; if payments exceed principal, judgment may be given in favor of debtor with interest at rate of 10% (§§44-1203, 1204)	At allowable rate or as agreed upon as long as not in excess of that permitted by law (§44-1201)	Loans under $1,000 (§6-652)
ARKANSAS	Consumer and nonconsumer rate is 5% above Federal Reserve discount rate (consumer rate is capped at 17%) (Const. Art. XIX §13)	Contracts calling for more than lawful rate are void as to unpaid interest and debtor may recover twice amount of interest paid (Const. Art. XIX §13)	Judgments on contracts bear interest at rate in contract or 10%, whichever is greater, but never more than that allowed by Const. Art. XIX §13.	
CALIFORNIA	Loans made for individual, family, or household: not over 10%; for other loans, maximum rate is the higher of 10% or 5% plus Federal Reserve discount rate of San Francisco on certain statutorily set day (Const. Art. XV §1)	Forfeiture of all interest plus 3 times amount of usurious interest paid	Set by legislature at not over 10% rate (Const. Art. XV §1)	Incorporated insurer (Ins. §1100.1); licensed broker-deals (Corp. §25211.5); indebtedness issued pursuant to corporate securities law (Corp. §25116); licensed business and industrial development corporation (Fin. §31410); state and national banks acting as trustees (Fin. §1504); foreign banks (Fin. §1716); bank holding companies (Fin. §3707); state and federal savings and loans (Fin. §7675)

(Continued)

Table 4: Interest Rates—Continued

State	Legal Maximum Rate of Interest	Usury Penalty	Judgments	Exceptions
COLORADO	8% (§5-12-101); maximum rate that may be contracted for is 45% (§5-12-103); interest on consumer loan may not exceed 12% unless made by supervised lender (§§5-3-201, 508)	Criminal penalty for knowingly exceeding 45% (§18-15-104)	8% if none specified in contract; if contract rate is variable, then at rate on day of judgment (§5-12-102[4])	Savings and loans (§11-41-115); mortgages (§5-13-101); business and agricultural loans (§5-13-102); small business loans (§5-13-103); loans governed by certain federal acts (§5-13-104); all others generally (§5-13-105)
CONNECTICUT	12% (§37-4)	Loan is not enforceable (§36-243)	Absent agreement to contrary, 8% (§37-1)	Loans before September 12, 1911 (§37-9); bank; savings and loan; credit union; certain mortgages; loan for motor vehicle; boat; loan for higher education; loan under $5,000 (§36-233); pawnbroker and loan broker (§21-44)
DELAWARE	5% over Federal Reserve discount rate; same maximum rate even if agreed upon in writing (Tit. 6 §2301)	Debtor not required to pay excess over legal rate; if whole debt is paid with interest over legal rate, debtor may recover 3 times amount of excess interest or $500, whichever is greater, if action brought within 1 year (Tit. 6 §2304[b]	At legal rate (22 A.2d 865)	No limit where loan exceeds $100,000 and is not secured by mortgage on borrower's personal residence (Tit. 9 §6-2301[c])
DISTRICT OF COLUMBIA	In absence of agreement: 6%/yr. (§28-3302); by contract in writing: Up to 24% (§28-3301)	Small loans: Loss of interest and ¼ of principal: $300 fine and prison 30-90 days and restitution of property illegally obtained; in other cases: forfeiture of interest; usurious interest paid may be recovered (§26-705, 707; 28-3303; 3304)	4% allowed on judgments against the District of Columbia, its officers, employees acting within scope of employment (26 USC §6621; see also §28-3302)	Federally insured bank or savings and loan and on direct motor vehicle installment loans (§§28-3308; 28-3601 to 3602)

(Continued)

Table 4: Interest Rates—Continued

State	Legal Maximum Rate of Interest	Usury Penalty	Judgments	Exceptions
FLORIDA	12% without contract; parties may contract for a greater or lesser rate (§687.01)	All interest forfeited and repaid double (§687.04); criminal usury: credit at rate of 25-45% is misdemeanor with penalty of up to 60 days in prison and/or $500 fine; over 45% is 3rd degree felony; keeping the books/records for loan at 25% is 3rd degree misdemeanor, and if loan or forbearance is criminal, debt is not enforceable (§687.071)	12% per year; if contract, then contract is less (§§55.03[1]; 55.04)	If specifically licensed in business and making loan (§516.031); on sale of motor vehicles (§§520.01, *et seq.*)
GEORGIA	7% per year when rate not specified; higher than 7% must be in writing; maximum 16% where principal is $3000 or less; no limit on rate if loan is between $3000 and $250,000 and must be in simple interest in written contract (§7-4-2)	Forfeiture of entire interest (§7-4-10); criminal penalty (§7-4-18)	12% unless contract specifies rate (§7-4-12)	Small industrial loans (§7-3-14)
HAWAII	10% (§478-2)	Creditor may recover principal only; debtor recovers costs; creditor fined up to $250 and/or prison up to 1 year (§478-6)	10% on judgment for any civil suit (§478-3)	Small loans (§409-16); credit unions (§410-15); industrial loan company (§408-15)
IDAHO	12% unless express contract (§28-22-104; see also §28-42-201)		5% plus annual average yield on U.S. Treasury securities as determined by Idaho state treasurer (§28-22-104)	
ILLINOIS	5% unless contract (394 N.E.2d 380)	Recipient subject to suit for twice total of all interest, charges, and attorney's fees and court costs (815 ILCS 205/6)	9% or 6% when judgment debtor is unit of local government, school district, or community college (735 ILCS 5/2-1302; 735 ILCS 5/12-109)	Under Consumer Installment Loan Act (205 ILCS 670/1); short-term loans (815 ILCS 205/4.1a); installment loans (815 ILCS 205/4a; 205 ILCS 670/15); pawnbrokers (§205 ILCS 510/2); farm development loan (205 ILCS 3605/5 to 3605/12); reverse mortgage loan (205 ILCS 305/46)

(Continued)

Table 4: Interest Rates—Continued

State	Legal Maximum Rate of Interest	Usury Penalty	Judgments	Exceptions
INDIANA	21% for unsupervised consumer loan (24-4.5-3-201)	Most business loans not subject to limit; Class B misdemeanor for supervised lender to knowingly charge in excess of 24-4.5-3-508 for consumer loan (24-4.5-5-301); consumer has right to refund of amount paid in excess of statute and up to 3 times the amount in its discretion (24-4.5-5-202)	At contract rate up to 10% and 10% if no contract (24-4.6-1-101); government entities liable for 8% from date of judgment or settlement if not paid within 180 days (34-4-16.5-17)	
IOWA	5% unless agreed upon in writing then not to exceed amount specified in §535.2(3)	Plaintiff may have judgment only for principal debt without interest or costs; forfeiture of 8% by the year of principal remaining unpaid at time of judgment (§535.5)	10% unless rate (up to §535.2 amount) expressed in contract (§535.3)	Automobile installment contract; mobile/modular home sales contract; semi-tractor and travel trailer installment sales (§321)
KANSAS	10% (§16-201); maximum rate at which parties may contract: 15% (§16-207)	Forfeit all interest; lose a sum of money to pay borrower's attorney fees (§16-207)	4% above federal discount rate as of July 1 preceding judgment (§16-204); where judgment on contract, contract rate controls (§16-205)	Business and agricultural loans; note secured by real estate mortgage; qualified plan loans (§16-207)
KENTUCKY	8% absent agreement otherwise (KRS §360.010)	Borrower may recover twice amount paid (KRS §360.020)	12% unless contract, then contract rate (KRS §360.040)	Banks (§360.010(2)); credit union (§290.425); small loans (§288.530)
LOUISIANA	Maximum rate under contract: 12% (§9:3503); one point over average prime subject always to cap of 14% and floor of 7% (Civ. Code Ann. Art. 2924)	Entire interest forfeited (§9:3501)	Legal interest (§13:4203); state agencies: 6% (§13:5112)	Secured by mortgage (§9:3504); borrowing for commercial/business purposes (§9:3509); obligation secured by a mortgage (§9:3504)
MAINE	6% unless otherwise agreed (Tit. 9-B §432)		15% for damages not exceeding $30,000 (Tit. 14 §1602-A)	

(Continued)

Table 4: Interest Rates—Continued

State	Legal Maximum Rate of Interest	Usury Penalty	Judgments	Exceptions
MARYLAND	6% (Const. Art. III §57); up to 8% in written agreement (Com. Law §12-103)	Forfeit 3 times excess of interest and charges collected or $500, whichever is greater (Com. Law §12-114)	10%; money judgment may carry contract rate until originally scheduled maturity date (Cts. & Jud. Proc. §11-106, 107, 301)	Student loan (Com. Law §11-106); mortgage secured loans (Com. Law §12-103); unsecured loans secured by other than savings (Com. Law §12-103); installment loans not secured by real property (Com. Law §12-103); open-end retail accounts (Com. Law §12-506); installment sales contract for motor vehicles and other consumer goods (Com. Law §12-609, 610)
MASSACHUSETTS	6% unless contract (Ch. 107 §3)	Over 20%: criminal usury; usurious loan may be voided by Supreme Court (Ch. 271 §49)	12% (Ch. 231 §6B); at contract rate if contract up to 12% (Ch. 231 §6C); sanctions defenses/counterclaims for frivolous or not in good faith actions (Ch. 231 §6F)	Small loans (Ch. 140 §96); open-end credit transaction (Ch 140 §114B); life insurance policy loans (Ch. 175 §142)
MICHIGAN	5% (MCL 438.31, *et seq.*); maximum rate with written agreement: 7%	Loss of all interest (§438.32) and loss of entire loan under Small Loan Act (MCL 493.13, 493.19)	13% (MCL 600.6013, 600.6301)	Small loans (MCL 493.1); credit union loans (MCL 490.14)
MINNESOTA	6% legal rate (§334.01); written contract up to 8%	Contract for greater interest void (§§47.20; 48.196; 334.03); payor may recover full interest and premiums paid with costs (§334.02); usurious interest by banks, savings and loans and credit unions results in forfeitures of all interest and payor may recover twice interest paid (§48.196)	Determined on or before December 20 of prior year by state court, administrator based on secondary market yield (§549.09)	State banks/savings associations (§48.195); state credit union (§52.14); dealers under Securities Exchange Act (§334.19); mortgage loans (§47.204); business and agricultural loans (§334.011)

(Continued)

Table 4: Interest Rates—Continued

State	Legal Maximum Rate of Interest	Usury Penalty	Judgments	Exceptions
MISSISSIPPI	8% (§75-17-1[1]); contract rate not to exceed greater of 10% or 5% above discount rate (§75-17-1[2])	Forfeit all interest and finance charge; if rate exceeds maximum by 100%, any amount paid (principal or interest) may be recovered (§75-67-119); person willfully charging usurious rates guilty of misdemeanor and fine up to $1000 (§75-67-119)	Judgments at contract rate if contract exists; otherwise at per annum rate set by judge (§75-17-7)	Residential real property loan (§75-17-1); small loans (§75-67-101); mobile homes (§75-17-23)
MISSOURI	Absent agreement, 9% (§408.020); otherwise, 10% (§408.030)	If usury collected, excess over legal rate applied to principal or debtor may recover (§408.060)	9% or higher rate lawfully stipulated (§408.040)	Loans to corporations, business loans, some real estate loans, agricultural (§408.035); business loan over $5000 (§408.035)
MONTANA	10% (§31-1-106); maximum rate by written agreement, up to 6 percentage points above prime rate of major New York banks (§31-1-107)	Forfeiture of double interest received (§31-1-108)	10% or contract rate (§25-9-205)	Regulated lenders exempt (§§31-1-111, 112)
NEBRASKA	Up to 16% for contract (§45-101.03); otherwise legal rate, 6% (§45-102)	Only principal recoverable (§§45-105, 110)	1% above bond equivalent yield; or rate of contract (§45-103)	Loans by Department of Banking, loan to any corporation; principal over $25,000; loan guaranteed by state/federal government on securities, open credit accounts; savings and loans; business or agricultural purpose loans; installment contract for goods and services (§45-101.04)
NEVADA	No limit for what parties may contract; otherwise prime rate of Nevada's largest bank plus 2% (§§99.040, 050)	Parties may agree for any rate on any contract (§99.050)	Contract rate or prime rate at largest bank in Nevada (§17.130)	Licensee may lend at any interest rate (§677.730)
NEW HAMPSHIRE	10% unless differently stipulated in writing (§336:10)	No usury provisions	10% unless otherwise agreed upon in writing (§336:1)	Educational institutions (§195-F:15); public utility (§374-C:14); pawnbrokers (§399-A:3); small loans (§399-A:3); home mortgage loan (§398-A:2)

(Continued)

Table 4: Interest Rates—Continued

State	Legal Maximum Rate of Interest	Usury Penalty	Judgments	Exceptions
NEW JERSEY	6% or up to 16% for contract (§31:1-1); loans in excess of 30% or 50% to corporations are not permitted (§2C:21-19)	Only amount lent may be recovered (§31:1-3)		Loan for over $50,000; savings and loans; banks; Department of Housing and Urban Affairs and other organizations authorized by the Emergency Home Finance Act of 1970; state or federal government or quasi-governmental organizations (§31:1-1)
NEW MEXICO	15% in absence of contract fixed rate (§56-8-3)	Forfeiture of all interest and if paid, borrower may recover twice amount (§56-8-13)	Same as contract rate (§56-8-4) or 15% if no contract (§56-8-4)	
NEW YORK	6% (Gen. Oblig. §5-501(1); Banking §14-a)	Usurious notes void; borrower may recover any amount in excess over legal rate (Gen. Oblig. §5-513); if bank, savings and loan, or trust company, interest forfeited and recovery of twice interest paid (Gen. Oblig. §5-511(1))	9% (Civ. Prac. L. & R. §§5003, 5004)	See Gen. Oblig. §§5-501, *et seq.*
NORTH CAROLINA	8% (§24-1); may contract for higher rate (§24-1.1)	Forfeiture of all interest; party paying may recover double interest paid (§24-2)	8% (§24-1) or at contract rate (§24-5)	Home loans secured by mortgage or first deed of trust (§24-1.1A); installment (§24-1.2); savings and loans (§24-1.4)
NORTH DAKOTA	6% (§47-14-05); if contract in writing, up to 5.5% higher than average interest on treasury bills (§47-14-09)	Forfeit all interest and 25% of principal; Class B misdemeanor (§47-14-11); if interest paid, twice amount paid may be recovered (§47-14-10)	Contract rate, otherwise 12% (§28-20-34)	Loans to corporations; agency funded by state/federal government; amount over $35,000 (§47-14-09)
OHIO	8% (§1343.01)	Excess interest applied to principal (§1343.04)	In accordance with §1343.01, §1343.02	Amount exceeds $100,000; broker/dealer registered; secured by mortgage or deed of trust; business loan (§1343.01)
OKLAHOMA	6%, or by contract (Tit. 15 §266)	Forfeiture of entire interest; if amount over legal interest is paid, it may be recovered double (Const. Art. XIV §3)	At contract rate or 4 percentage points above average treasury bill rate for preceding year, not to exceed 10% in action against state/political subdivision (Tit. 12 §727)	Pawnshops (Tit. 59 §1501); small loans and retail installment (Uniform Consumer Credit Code) (Tit. 14A §3-201)

(Continued)

Table 4: Interest Rates—Continued

State	Legal Maximum Rate of Interest	Usury Penalty	Judgments	Exceptions
OREGON	Unless otherwise agreed, 9% (§82.010)	Forfeit interest on loan but borrower must repay the principal (§82.010)	9% unless contract, then contract rate (§82.010)	Business or agricultural loan; loan under $50,000 (§82.010)
PENNSYLVANIA	6% (Tit. 41 §§201, 202)	Borrower not required to pay amount over legal rate and may recover triple the amount in excess; attorney's fees may be awarded and an intentional violation is 3rd degree misdemeanor (Tit. 41 §§501, *et seq.*)	Interest at lawful rate (Tit. 42 §8101)	Federal Housing Administration, Veteran's Administration or other department/agency of U.S. government (Tit. 41 §§301, 302)
RHODE ISLAND	12% absent agreement otherwise (§6-26-1); otherwise, 21% (§6-26-2)	Contract shall be void; knowing violation is criminal usury with imprisonment up to 5 years (§6-26-3); borrower may recover twice amount of usurious interest paid (§6-26-4)	12% unless otherwise already agreed upon rate (§9-21-10)	Corporation; pawnbroker (§19-26-18); persons licensed (§6-26-2); revolving or open-end credit plan (§6-27-4); finance charge for retail sales (§6-27-4)
SOUTH CAROLINA	8 ¾ % (§34-31-20)	Usury penalty laws repealed June 25, 1982, but old law may apply to transactions before then (formerly §34-31-50)	14% (§34-31-20)	See South Carolina Consumer Protection Code (§37-1-10)
SOUTH DAKOTA	Absent agreement, 15% (§54-3-4)	Penalties repealed July 1982	12% (§54-3-5.1)	Real estate mortgages; Uniform Credit Code security agreements; revolving charge accounts (§54-11-5)
TENNESSEE	10% (§47-14-103)	Contract unenforceable; if found unconscionable, lender must refund charges, fees, and commission fees and successful plaintiff may recover reasonable attorney's fees (§47-14-117)	10% or at contract rate (§47-14-121)	Installment loans (§§45-2-1106, 1107); loans under $1000; some home loans (§47-14-104); savings and loans (§45-3-705)

(Continued)

Table 4: Interest Rates—Continued

State	Legal Maximum Rate of Interest	Usury Penalty	Judgments	Exceptions
TEXAS	When not specified, 6% (Tex. Rev. Civ. Stat. Ann. Art. 5069-1.03)	Forfeits 3 times amount of usurious interest contracted for and unreasonable attorney's fees (§5069-1.06[1]); contract for interest in excess of twice allowed interest shall forfeit all principal plus above penalties; any usury is a misdemeanor with fine of up to $1000 (§5069-1.06[1], [2])	If contract rate, then lesser of the contract rate or 18%	Loans over $250,000 (§5069-1.04(b)(2))
UTAH	10% absent contract (§15-1-1)		12% or as agreed in contract (§15-1-4)	Pawnbroker (§11-6-4)
VERMONT	12% (Tit. 9 §41(a)	Lender knowingly charging in excess of legal rate may forfeit all interest and half principal (§9-50); contract void; criminal penalties up to $500 fine and/or 2 years in prison (Tit. 8 §2233)	12% (Tit. 12 §2903)	Retail installment contract (Tit. 9 §41(a), 2405); municipal bonds (Tit. 24 §1761); loan secured for recreational vehicle, aircraft, water craft, and farm equipment (Tit. 9 §41(a))
VIRGINIA	8% unless contract specifies (§6.1-330.53)	Borrower may recover twice interest paid, court costs, and unreasonable attorney's fees (§6.1-330.56, 57)	9% (§6.1-330.54) or at contract rate, whichever is higher	Revolving credit accounts (§6.1-330.64); private college/university (§6.1-330.66); state or national banks; savings and loans; credit unions (§6.1-330.48); secured by mortgage or deed of trust (§6.1-330.71)
WASHINGTON	12% absent written contract rate (§19.52.010[1])	Debtor entitled to costs, attorney's fees, and amount paid in excess of what lender is entitled to (§19.52.030[1])	Contract rate as long as within statutory limit or maximum rate (§4.56.110)	Small loans (§31.08.160-repealed effective 1/1/93)

(Continued)

Table 4: Interest Rates—Continued

State	Legal Maximum Rate of Interest	Usury Penalty	Judgments	Exceptions
WEST VIRGINIA	6% absent written agreement otherwise (§47-6-5); 8% maximum contract rate (§47-6-5(b))	Void as to all interest and debtor may recover 4 times all interest agreed to be paid with $100 minimum (§47-6-6); if supervised lender willfully makes excess charge it is guilty of misdemeanor (§46A-5-103)	10% (§§56-6-31; 46A-3-111)	Revolving accounts for consumer loans (§46A-3-106); loans secured by mortgage, etc. (§47-6-57); life insurer (§33-13-8); consumer credit sales (§46a-3-101)
WISCONSIN	5% unless otherwise agreed in writing (§138.04)	Lender intentionally violating fined $25 to $500 and prison up to 6 months (§138.06(2))	12% (§815.05(8)7)	State-chartered banks, credit unions, savings and loans, etc. (§138.041); residential mortgage loans (§138.052(7));loans to corporations (§138.05(5)); installment contract on auto (§218.01)
WYOMING	7% absent agreement otherwise or provision of law (§40-14-106)		10% unless agreement (§1-16-102(a))	Uniform Credit Code adopted (§§40-14-101 to 702)

5. LEMON LAWS

Everyone has heard of someone who has bought a new car that was a "lemon." The car had either one major defect that could not be repaired or numerous minor defects that were always in need of repair.

Prior to the 1970s, when consumer advocacy hit its peak and numerous laws were enacted to protect the buyers of lemons, the only recourse the purchaser had was his or her warranty. As long as the manufacturer and dealer exercised their best efforts to fix the car while it was under warranty, the owner was stuck with the lemon. After the warranty period expired, the owner paid for the repairs.

"Lemon laws," or new car warranty laws, were enacted to place limits on what the consumer must endure should he or she purchase a lemon. Under the terms of the lemon laws, if the car cannot be fixed, the consumer must be compensated, either with a new car or with a cash refund. States are split among those that leave the decision of the specific remedy up to the consumer, manufacturer, or seller. As of this writing, the only states that do not have lemon laws are Arkansas and South Dakota. In all other states, the consumer has at least one year from the date of purchase to make a claim under the law. Most states allow the consumer two years or 24,000 miles, whichever comes first, to make a claim.

Table 5: Lemon Laws

State	Code Section	Title of Act	Definition of Defects	Time Limit for Manufacturer Repair	Remedies
ALABAMA	8-20A-2	Motor Vehicle Lemon Law Rights	Nonconformity to any applicable express warranties	24 months following delivery of vehicle or 24,000 miles, whichever comes first	Consumer's option: replace with comparable new car or accept return of car and refund consumer full contract price and nonrefundable portions of extended warranties and services, all collateral charges, all finance charges incurred after first reported nonconformity and incidental damages; all this minus allowance for consumer's use of nonconforming vehicle
ALASKA	45.45.300, *et seq.*		Nonconformity to applicable express warranties	Term of express warranty or within 1 year from date of delivery to original owner, whichever is first	Replacement of vehicle with new, comparable one or refund full purchase price less a reasonable allowance for use of motor vehicle
ARIZONA	44-1262, *et seq.*		Nonconformity to applicable express warranties of any defect/condition which substantially impairs use and value of motor vehicle	Time period of express warranty or during one year period following date of original delivery to consumer, whichever is earlier	Replacement with new motor vehicle or refund to consumer of full purchase price including all collateral charges, less a reasonable allowance for consumer's use of vehicle
ARKANSAS	No statutory provisions				
CALIFORNIA	Civ. §1793.2		Nonconformity to applicable express warranties which substantially impairs the use, value, or safety of motor vehicle	1 yr. from date of delivery to buyer or 12,000 miles, whichever occurs first	Replace the goods or reimburse buyer in an amount equal to the purchase price paid by the buyer, less the amount directly attributable to the use by the buyer prior to the discovery of the nonconformity
COLORADO	42-12-101, *et seq.*		Nonconformity to express warranties which substantially impairs use and market value of motor vehicle	Warranty period or within 1 year following date of original delivery of vehicle to consumer, whichever is the earlier date	Manufacturer's option: (1) replace with comparable vehicle or (2) accept return of vehicle from consumer and refund full purchase price, including sales tax, fees and similar governmental charges, less a reasonable allowance for consumer's use

(Continued)

Table 5: Lemon Laws—Continued

State	Code Section	Title of Act	Definition of Defects	Time Limit for Manufacturer Repair	Remedies
CONNECTICUT	42-179		Nonconformity to applicable express warranties which substantially impairs the use, safety, or value of motor vehicle	Repair defects covered by written warranties within 2 years following original delivery or first 18,000 miles, whichever is first	Replace vehicle with new vehicle acceptable to consumer or refund (upon accepting return of vehicle) the (1) full contract price including but not limited to charges for undercoating, dealer prep, transportation, and installed options; (2) all collateral charges, including but not limited to sales tax, license and regulation fees, and similar government charges; (3) all finance charges after he first reports conformity and during any subsequent period vehicle is out of service due to repair; (4) all incidental damages, less a reasonable allowance for consumer's use
DELAWARE	Tit. 6 §5001		Nonconformity to any applicable express warranty which substantially impairs the use, value, or safety of motor vehicle	Term of warranty or during period of 1 year following date of original delivery to consumer, whichever is earlier	Consumer's option: replace with comparable new automobile acceptable to consumer or repurchase and refund full purchase, including all credits and allowances for any trade-in vehicle
DISTRICT OF COLUMBIA	40-1301, *et seq.*		Nonconformity to all warranties which results in significant impairment of vehicle	First 18,000 miles of operation or during period of 2 years following date of delivery to original purchaser, whichever is earlier	Consumer's option: replace with comparable vehicle or accept return and refund full purchase price, including all sales tax, license fees, registration fees, and any similar governmental charges; less reasonable allowance for use
FLORIDA	681.102, *et seq.*		Nonconformity to warranties which significantly impair the use, value, or safety of motor vehicle	1 year after date of original delivery to consumer or 12,000 miles of operation, whichever is earlier	Consumer's unconditional option: Replace with vehicle acceptable to consumer or repurchase vehicle and refund to consumer full purchase price, including all reasonably incurred collateral and incidental charges, less reasonable offset for use

(Continued)

Table 5: Lemon Laws—Continued

State	Code Section	Title of Act	Definition of Defects	Time Limit for Manufacturer Repair	Remedies
GEORGIA	10-1-780, *et seq.*	Motor Vehicle Warranty Rights Act	Nonconformity to applicable express warranties which significantly impair the use, value, or safety of motor vehicle	Within 12 months following purchase of vehicle or 12,000 miles following purchase of vehicle, whichever occurs first	Consumer's option: replace with identical or reasonably equivalent vehicle including payment of all collateral charges which consumer/lessor will incur a second time, less reasonable offset for use or repurchase and refund purchase price plus all collateral charges and incidental costs, less reasonable offset for use
HAWAII	490:2-313.1		Nonconformity to all applicable express warranties that substantially impairs the use and market value of vehicle	Within express warranty term	Replace with comparable vehicle or accept return and refund the full purchase price including all collateral charges, excluding interest, and less a reasonable allowance for consumer's use of vehicle
IDAHO	48-901, *et seq.*		Nonconformity to applicable express warranties which significantly impairs use, value, or safety of vehicle	1 year period following date of original delivery of vehicle to buyer or first 12,000 miles, whichever is earlier	Consumer's option: replace with comparable new vehicle or accept return and refund full purchase price including all collateral charges, less a reasonable allowance for buyer's use of vehicle
ILLINOIS	815 ILCS 380/3	New Vehicle Buyer Protection Act	Nonconformity to applicable express warranties which significantly impair the use, value, or safety of motor vehicle	Within statutory warranty period	Replace with new vehicle of like model line, if available, or otherwise a comparable motor vehicle or accept return and refund consumer full purchase price of new vehicle, including all collateral charges, less a reasonable allowance for consumer use of vehicle
INDIANA	24-5-13-8, *et seq.*	Indiana Motor Vehicle Protection Act of 1988	Nonconformity to applicable express warranties which significantly impairs the use, market value or safety of motor vehicle or renders vehicle nonconforming to terms of applicable manufacturer's warranty	If reported within term of protection	Consumer's option: Replace with vehicle of comparable value, including reimbursement to buyer of any fees of transferring registration or sales tax incurred as result of replacement or refund full contract price of vehicle, including all credits and allowances for any trade-in vehicle and less reasonable allowance for use.

(Continued)

Table 5: Lemon Laws—Continued

State	Code Section	Title of Act	Definition of Defects	Time Limit for Manufacturer Repair	Remedies
IOWA	322G.1, *et seq.*		Nonconformity to all applicable express warranties	Term of manufacturer's written warranty or during period of 2 years following date of original delivery of a motor vehicle to consumer or first 24,000 miles, whichever is first	Replace with identical or reasonably equivalent vehicle, including collateral and incidental charges less reasonable offset for use, or refund full purchase or lease price including all collateral and reasonably incurred incidental charges, less a reasonable offset for consumer's use
KANSAS	50-645, *et seq.*	Lemon Law	Nonconformity to applicable warranties which significantly impairs the use or value of motor vehicle	1 year from date of original delivery of vehicle to consumer or term of any warranties, whichever is earlier	Replace with comparable vehicle under warranty or accept return and refund full purchase price including all collateral charges, less a reasonable allowance for consumer's use
KENTUCKY	367.840, *et seq.*		Nonconformity to applicable express warranties which significantly impairs the use, value, or safety of the motor vehicle	First 12 months following date of delivery or first 12,000 miles, whichever is first	Consumer's option: replace vehicle with comparable motor vehicle or accept return and refund full purchase price including amount paid for vehicle, finance charge, all sales tax, license fee, registration fee, any similar governmental charges, plus all collateral charges, less reasonable offset for use
LOUISIANA	51:1942, *et seq.*	Acts 1984	Nonconformity to applicable express warranties	Term of warranty or during period of 1 year following date of original delivery, whichever is earlier	Manufacturer's option: Replace with comparable new motor vehicle or accept return and refund full purchase price plus any amounts paid by the consumer at the timet of sale and all collateral costs, less a reasonable allowance for use
MAINE	10-1163		Nonconformity to all express warranties which significantly impairs use, safety, or value of vehicle	Term of express warranties within a period of 2 years following date of original delivery to consumer, or during first 18,000 miles, whichever is earlier date	Buyer's option: replace with comparable new vehicle or accept return of vehicle and refund full purchase price (or in case of lease, payments made so far) including any paid financing charges, all collateral charges, and incidentals, less reasonable allowance for use

(Continued)

Table 5: Lemon Laws—Continued

State	Code Section	Title of Act	Definition of Defects	Time Limit for Manufacturer Repair	Remedies
MARYLAND	Com. Law §§14-1501, *et seq.*	Automotive Warranty Enforcement Act	Nonconformity to all applicable express warranties which significantly affects use or market value of vehicle	Warranty period equal to or greater than first 15,000 miles or first 15 months following date of original delivery of vehicle to consumer	Consumer's option: replace with comparable motor vehicle acceptable to customer or accept return and refund full purchase price including all excise tax license fees, registration fees, and any similar governmental charges, less reasonable allowance for consumer's use (not to exceed 15% of purchase price) and for damage not attributable to normal wear
MASSACHUSETTS	Ch. 90-7N½		Nonconformity to applicable express warranties or implied warranty which significantly affects use, market value, or safety of vehicle	Term of protection	Manufacturer's option: replace with vehicle acceptable to consumer or accept return and refund full contract price including all credits and allowances for any trade-in vehicle, less a reasonable allowance for use
MICHIGAN	257.1401, *et. seq.*	Warranties on New Motor Vehicles Act	Nonconformity to manufacturer's express warranties that significantly affects use or value of vehicle	Term of manufacturer's express warranty or 1 year from date of delivery of new motor vehicle to original consumer, whichever is earlier	Manufacturer's option: replace with a comparable replacement vehicle currently in production and acceptable to consumer or accept return of vehicle and refund full purchase price including cost of any options or other modifications installed or made by or for the manufacturer, less a reasonable allowance for consumer's use of vehicle, not to exceed 10¢ per mile driven at time of initial report of same defect or conditions or 10% of purchase price, whichever is less, and less an amount equal to any appraised damage that is not attributable to normal wear and tear

(Continued)

Table 5: Lemon Laws—Continued

State	Code Section	Title of Act	Definition of Defects	Time Limit for Manufacturer Repair	Remedies
MINNESOTA	325F.665		Nonconformity to all applicable express warranties which significantly affects the use or market value of vehicle	During term of applicable express warranty or during period of 2 years following date of original delivery of vehicle to consumer, whichever is earlier	Buyer's option: Replace with comparable vehicle or accept return and refund to consumer full purchase price including cost of any options or other modifications made/installed/arranged by manufacturer (or agents or dealer) within 30 days of original delivery, and all other charges, less a reasonable allowance for consumer use of vehicle
MISSISSIPPI	63-17-157, *et seq.*	Motor Vehicle Warranty Enforcement Act	Nonconformity to all applicable express warranties which significantly affects the use, market value, or safety of vehicle	Term of express warranties or during period of 1 year following date of original delivery of motor vehicle to consumer, whichever period expires earlier	Consumer's option: replace with comparable vehicle acceptable to consumer or accept return and refund full purchase price, including all reasonably incurred collateral charges, less a reasonable allowance for consumer's use
MISSOURI	407.565, *et seq.*		Nonconformity to all applicable express warranties which significantly affects the use, market value, or safety of vehicle	Term of express warranties or during 1 year following date of original delivery to consumer, whichever expires earlier	Manufacturer's option: replace with comparable new vehicle acceptable to consumer or take title from consumer and refund full purchase price, including all reasonably incurred collateral charges, less reasonable allowance for use
MONTANA	61-4-501, *et seq.*		Nonconformity to all applicable express warranties which significantly affects the use, market value, or safety of vehicle	Warranty period within 2 years after date of original delivery to consumer or during first 18,000 miles of operation, whichever is earlier	Manufacturer's option: replace with new vehicle of same model and style and of equal value unless for reasons of lack of availability such replacement is impossible, in which case it shall be replaced with vehicle of comparable market value or accept return and refund full purchase price plus reasonable collateral and incidental damages, less a reasonable allowance for consumer's use of vehicle

(Continued)

Table 5: Lemon Laws—Continued

State	Code Section	Title of Act	Definition of Defects	Time Limit for Manufacturer Repair	Remedies
NEBRASKA	60-2702, *et seq.*		Nonconformity to all applicable express warranties which significantly affects the use or market value of vehicle	Term of such express warranties or during period of 1 year following date of original delivery of new vehicle to consumer, whichever is earlier	Replace with comparable vehicle or accept return and refund full purchase price including all sales tax, license fees, registration fees, and any similar government charges, less a reasonable allowance for consumer's use
NEVADA	598.756, 766		Nonconformity to all applicable express warranties which significantly affects the use or market value of vehicle	Before expiration of manufacturer's express warranties or no later than 1 year after date of delivery to original buyer, whichever is earlier	Replace with comparable vehicle of same model having same features; if vehicle cannot be delivered within reasonable time, then a comparable vehicle substantially similar to replaced vehicle or accept return and refund full purchase price including all sales tax, license fees, registration fees, and other similar governmental charges, less a reasonable allowance for consumer's use
NEW HAMPSHIRE	357-D:2, *et seq.*		Nonconformity to all applicable express warranties or implied warranties which significantly affects the use or market value of vehicle	Term of express/implied warranty or within 1 year following date of original delivery, whichever is earlier	Replace with new motor vehicle or accept return and refund full purchase price including all collateral charges, less a reasonable allowance for consumer's use of the vehicle
NEW JERSEY	56:12-20, *et seq.*		Nonconformity to express warranties which significantly affects the use, market value, or safety of vehicle	Term of warranty or during period of 1 year following date of original delivery to consumer, whichever is earlier	Replace with comparable new automobile and consumer shall pay manufacturer a reasonable allowance for his use of vehicle and shall not pay, on the new replacement, the taxes, prep fees, or any other fees/charges usually paid by consumer; or refund full purchase price, including all taxes, prep fees, and other charges/fees paid by consumer, less a reasonable allowance for consumer's use

(Continued)

Table 5: Lemon Laws—Continued

State	Code Section	Title of Act	Definition of Defects	Time Limit for Manufacturer Repair	Remedies
NEW MEXICO	57-16A-2, *et seq.*	Motor Vehicle Quality Assurance Act	Nonconformity to all applicable express warranties which significantly affects the use or market value of vehicle	Term of express warranties or 1 year following date of original delivery, whichever is earlier	Replace with comparable vehicle or accept return and refund full purchase price including all collateral charges, less a reasonable allowance for consumer's use of vehicle
NEW YORK	Gen. Bus. §§23; 198-1	Lemon Law	Nonconformity to all express warranties	First 18,000 miles or during period of 2 years following date of original delivery, whichever is earlier	Consumer's option: replace vehicle with comparable motor vehicle or accept return and refund full purchase price, or if applicable, the lease price and any trade-in allowance plus fees and charges less reasonable allowance for consumer's use in excess of first 12,000 miles pursuant to mileage deduction formula and a reasonable allowance for any damage not attributable to normal wear and improvements; vehicle must be sold and registered in New York
NORTH CAROLINA	20-351, *et seq.*	New Motor Vehicles Warranties Act	Nonconformity to all applicable express warranties which significantly affects the value of vehicle	For period of 1 year or term of express warranties, whichever is greater, following date of original delivery of vehicle to consumer; can occur no later than 24 months or 24,000 miles following original delivery	Consumer's option: replace with comparable new vehicle or accept return and refund full contract price, all collateral charges, all finance charges incurred since reporting nonconformity, and any incidental damages and monetary consequential damages, less reasonable allowance for consumer's use
NORTH DAKOTA	51-07-16, *et seq.*		Nonconformity to all applicable express warranties which significantly affects the use or market value of vehicle	Term of express warranties or during period of 1 year following date of original delivery to consumer, whichever is earlier	Replace with comparable vehicle or accept return and refund full purchase price, including all collateral charges, less reasonable allowance for consumer's use

(Continued)

Table 5: Lemon Laws—Continued

State	Code Section	Title of Act	Definition of Defects	Time Limit for Manufacturer Repair	Remedies
OHIO	1345.72		Nonconformity to applicable express warranties which significantly affects the use, safety, or market value of vehicle	1 year following date of original delivery or during first 18,000 miles, whichever is earlier	Consumer's option: replace with new vehicle acceptable to consumer or accept return of vehicle from consumer and refund full purchase price, all collateral charges, all finance charges, and all incidental damages
OKLAHOMA	15-901		Nonconformity to any applicable express warranties which significantly affects the use or market value of vehicle	Term of express warranties or during 1 year following date of original delivery to consumer, whichever is earlier	Replace with new vehicle or accept return and refund full purchase price including all taxes, license, registration fees, and all similar governmental fees, excluding interest, less a reasonable allowance for consumer's use
OREGON	646.325, 335		Nonconformity to applicable manufacturer's express warranties which significantly affects the use or market value of vehicle	During period of 1 year following date of original delivery of motor vehicle to consumer or during period ending on date on which mileage reaches 12,000 miles, whichever is earlier	Replace with new motor vehicle or accept return and refund full purchase/lease price paid, including taxes, license and registration fees, and any similar collateral charges, excluding interest, less a reasonable allowance for consumer's use of vehicle
PENNSYLVANIA	Tit. 73 §§1951, *et seq.*	Automobile Lemon Law	Nonconformity to warranties which significantly affects the use, market value, or safety of vehicle	1 year following date of actual delivery to consumer, within first 12,000 miles of use or during time of the warranty, whichever may first occur	Purchaser's option: replace with comparable vehicle of equal value or accept return and refund full purchase price, including all collateral charges, less a reasonable allowance for purchaser's use not exceeding 10¢ per mile or 10% of purchase price, whichever is less
RHODE ISLAND	31-5.2-1, *et seq.*		Nonconformity to applicable express warranties or implied warranties	Term of protection equals 1 year or 15,000 miles from date of original delivery, whichever comes first	Consumer's option: replace with comparable new vehicle in good working condition or accept return and refund full contract price of vehicle including all credits and allowances for any trade-in vehicle, less a reasonable allowance for use

(Continued)

Table 5: Lemon Laws—Continued

State	Code Section	Title of Act	Definition of Defects	Time Limit for Manufacturer Repair	Remedies
SOUTH CAROLINA	56-28-30, *et seq.*		Nonconformity to all applicable express warranties which significantly affects the use, safety, or market value of vehicle	Within 1 year of purchase or first 12,000 miles of operation, whichever occurs first and if it is reported during terms of express warranty	Manufacturer's option: replace with comparable vehicle or accept return and refund full purchase price as delivered including applicable finance charges, sales taxes, license fees, registration fees, and any other similar governmental charges, less a reasonable allowance for consumer's use of vehicle
SOUTH DAKOTA	No statutory provisions				
TENNESSEE	55-24-201, *et seq.*		Nonconformity to all applicable express warranties	Term of applicable warranties or 1 year following date of original delivery of vehicle to consumer, whichever comes first	Replace with comparable vehicle or accept return and refund full purchase price (cost paid by consumer including all collateral charges, less a reasonable allowance for use)
TEXAS	Tex. Rev. Civ. Stat. Ann. Art. 4413(36) §6.07	Texas Motor Vehicle Commission Code	Nonconformity to all applicable express warranties which significantly affects the use or market value of vehicle	Term of such express warranties	Replace with comparable motor vehicle or accept return and refund full purchase price less a reasonable allowance for owner's use and any other allowances or refunds payable to owner
UTAH	13-20-1, *et seq.*	New Motor Vehicles Warranties Act	Nonconformity to all applicable express warranties which significantly affects the use, safety, or market value of vehicle	Term of express warranties or 1 year following date of original delivery of vehicle to consumer, whichever is earlier	Replace with comparable new vehicle or accept return and refund full purchase price, including all collateral charges, less a reasonable allowance for consumer's use

(Continued)

Table 5: Lemon Laws—Continued

State	Code Section	Title of Act	Definition of Defects	Time Limit for Manufacturer Repair	Remedies
VERMONT	Tit. 9 §4172		Nonconformity to applicable manufacturer's express warranties which significantly affects the use, safety, or market value of vehicle	Term of warranty	Consumer's option: replace with new vehicle from same manufacturer of comparable worth to the same make and model with all the options and accessories and with appropriate adjustments being allowed for any model year differences or accept return and refund full purchase price as indicated in purchase contract and all credits and allowances for any trade-in or downpayment, licensing fees, finance charges, credit charges, registration fees and any similar charges, and incidental and consequential damages, less reasonable allowance for use
VIRGINIA	59.1-207.9, *et seq.*	Virginia Motor Vehicle Warranty Enforcement Act	Nonconformity to all warranties which significantly affects the use, safety, or market value of vehicle	Manufacturer's warranty period or lemon law rights period ending 18 months after date of original delivery to consumer of new motor vehicle	Replace with comparable vehicle acceptable to consumer or accept return and refund full purchase price, including all collateral charges, and incidental damages, less a reasonable allowance for consumer's use of vehicle up to first notice of nonconformity given
WASHINGTON	19.118.021, *et seq.*		Nonconformity to the Warranty which significantly affects the use, value, or safety of the vehicle	Term of the warranty period (period ending 2 years after date of original delivery or first 24,000 miles, whichever is first) or period of coverage of applicable manufacturer's written warranty, whichever is less	Consumer's option: replace with identical or reasonably equivalent vehicle; compensation for reasonable offset for use to be paid by consumer or repurchase and refund to consumer purchase price, all collateral charges an incidental costs, less a reasonable offset for use
WEST VIRGINIA	46A-6A-3	Consumer Credit and Protection Act	Nonconformity to all applicable express warranties which significantly affects the use or market value of vehicle	Term of express warranties or during 1 year following date of original delivery of vehicle to consumer, whichever is later date	Repair or replace with comparable new vehicle which does conform to the warranties

(Continued)

Table 5: Lemon Laws—Continued

State	Code Section	Title of Act	Definition of Defects	Time Limit for Manufacturer Repair	Remedies
WISCONSIN	218.015		Nonconformity to applicable express warranties which significantly affects the use, safety, or market value of vehicle	Term of warranty or 1 year after first delivery of motor vehicle to consumer, whichever is sooner	Consumer's option: accept return and replace with comparable new vehicle and refund any collateral costs or accept return and refund full purchase price plus any sales tax, finance charge, amount paid by the consumer at point of sale, and collateral costs, less a reasonable allowance for use
WYOMING	40-17-101		Nonconformity to applicable express warranties which significantly affects the use or market value of vehicle	1 year following original delivery of vehicle to consumer	Replace with new or comparable vehicle of same type and similarly equipped or accept return and refund full purchase price including all collateral charges less a reasonable allowance for consumer's use

II. CRIMINAL LAWS

6. CAPITAL PUNISHMENT

The acceptance of capital punishment, or the death penalty, as a sentence for heinous criminal acts has been hotly debated across the nation over the last few decades. On the books in most states, the death penalty has been challenged by many, originally on grounds that it violated the Constitutional prohibition against cruel and unusual punishment, and later on the procedural grounds that there were not enough due process protections for defendants accused of capital crimes. In general, it was held that since the sentence was so severe, the law must impose the strictest standards of proof to sentence a defendant to death. Consequently, many states have gone through periods in which the death penalty was held as legal, then illegal, then revised and held as legal, then illegal again, and then further revised and held as legal once more. This shifting status often brought unbalanced—unjust—sentencing. For instance, in many of these states one of two defendants accused of identical unrelated crimes committed within weeks of each other drew the death sentence while the other did not, merely because the statute under which they were sentenced was ruled unconstitutional in the intervening time.

The Supreme Court has since handed down explicit guidelines defining the legal imposition of the death penalty, allowing states a new opportunity to legislate a legal death penalty statute that is less likely to be ruled unconstitutional in the future. This does not mean that the process is not still open to attack. As of this writing, new cases on the death penalty are currently wending their way through the courts to the Supreme Court.

Thirty-six states currently have death penalty statutes on the books. In a few states the statute remains on the books though it has been declared unconstitutional. In some of these cases, the state legislature can either revise or rewrite the death penalty statute if it chooses to make it the law.

There are six states that authorize the death penalty for non-homicide crimes. Of note is California, often known for its radical politics, which lists treason as a capital crime. Other common non-homicide capital offenses are kidnapping, hijacking, and other serious crimes that involve hostage-taking or placing a victim in extreme danger.

Some states have very complicated criminal statutes; therefore, the following tables may contain less information on some states if nothing explicit can be determined from the state statute alone. Occasionally it is necessary to consult lists or sentencing guidelines that are not part of the code to determine these rules.

Table 6: Capital Punishment

State/Code Section	Allowed	Effect of Incapacity	Minimum Age	Non-homicidal	Homicide with Aggravating Circumstances	Method of Execution
ALABAMA 13A-5-39, *et seq.*	Yes	Mitigating circumstance if defendant under influence of extreme mental or emotional disturbance; forbid execution of "insane" person	No minimum age	None	Kidnapping; robbery; rape/sodomy; burglary; sexual abuse; arson; hijacking; murder of police officer or public official while on duty; murder for pecuniary or other valuable consideration; two or more persons murdered in same act/course of conduct; victim less than 14 years old	Electrocution
ALASKA 12.55.015 (1987), *et seq.*	Not authorized					
ARIZONA 13-703	Yes, for 1st degree murder with mitigating factors	If defendant found insane at any time prior to execution, the execution is suspended. Upon recovery, execution is rescheduled	15	None	Death penalty legal with one or more of following: Previous homicide convictions; previous felonies with use or threat of violence; knowingly created grave risk of death to persons in addition to victim; procured commission of offense by payment; especially heinous, cruel or depraved manner; adult person and victim under 15; victim on duty peace officer and defendant knew or should have known; in custody of state dept. of corrections, law enforcement agency or jail at time of homicide	Lethal gas
ARKANSAS 5-4-602, *et seq.*	Yes, capital offense cases	Committed while under extreme mental or emotional distress is mitigating factor; suspend sentence of insane	Chronological age does not necessarily control jury's determination (*Giles v. Statz* 549 S.W. 2d 479 (1977))		Previous felony conviction; committed by person unlawfully at liberty after being imprisoned for felony conviction; use of threat or violence in commission of felony; knowingly created grave risk of death to person other than victim; committed in order to prevent arrest or escape custody; committed for pecuniary gain; committed for purposes of disrupting/hindering lawful exercise of any government or political function; especially heinous, cruel, atrocious manner; committed by means of destructive explosive, bomb, similar device	Lethal injection or electrocution if lethal injection held unconstitutional

(Continued)

Table 6: Capital Punishment—Continued

State/Code Section	Allowed	Effect of Incapacity	Minimum Age	Non-homicidal	Homicide with Aggravating Circumstances	Method of Execution
CALIFORNIA Pen. Code §§37; 190, *et seq.;* 3700-3704.5; §3604	Yes, murder in first degree; other aggravating circumstances	Suspend sentence	18	Treason	Intentional, for financial gain; previously convicted of first/second degree murder; multiple murders in same proceeding; bomb, explosives, grave risk; for purposes of avoiding lawful arrest or attempt to escape lawful custody; victim was peace officer, federal law officer/agent, fireman in performance of duties intentionally killed an defendant should have known or knew; witness of crime intentionally killed to prevent retaliatory testimony at criminal proceeding; retaliation against judge, prosecutor, etc.; state officials; lying in wait; especially cruel, atrocious, heinous; racial; committed along with robbery, kidnapping, rape, sodomy, burglary, lewd act upon child, arson, train wrecking; intentionally poisoned	Lethal gas or lethal injection, defendant's choice
COLORADO 16-11-103; 16-8-110; 16-17-101; 16-11-401	Yes for Class 1 felonies	Mitigating factor; suspend sentence	Age is mitigating factor; no one under 18 (*Sullivan v. People,* 111 Colo. 205, 139 P.2d 876 (1943))		Committed by person imprisoned for Class 1, 2 or 3 felony; previous crime of violence; intentionally killed peace officer/former peace officer, judge, firefighter, elected official, federal officer he knew or should have known to be engaged in official duties or retaliation for past official duties; kidnapped person intentionally killed; agreement to kill; explosives or incendiary device; pecuniary gain	Lethal injection
CONNECTICUT 53a-46a; 54-100, *et seq.*	Yes	Suspend sentence	18		Committed in commission of felony; 2 or more prior felonies involving infliction of serious bodily injury; knowingly created grave risk of death to other persons; especially heinous, cruel, depraved manner; pecuniary gain	Electrocution

(Continued)

Table 6: Capital Punishment—Continued

State/Code Section	Allowed	Effect of Incapacity	Minimum Age	Non-homicidal	Homicide with Aggravating Circumstances	Method of Execution
DELAWARE Tit. 11, §§636, 4209; §406	Yes	Exempt from execution	No minimum age		Committed while escaped from custody/confinement; committed for purposes of avoiding arrest or for effecting escape from custody; committed against law enforcement officer, corrections employee, fireman engaged in duties; committed against judge, attorney general, other state officer (former or present) because of exercise of official duty; hostage/ransom; witness to crime to avoid testimony; paid for it/pecuniary gain; convicted of prior felony using or threat of violence; rape, sodomy, unlawful sexual intercourse, arson, kidnapping, burglary; multiple victims; outrageously or wantonly vile, horrible or inhumane; defendant serving life sentence; victim was pregnant, handicapped, severely disabled or 62 years of age or older	Lethal injection or hanging by the neck if lethal injection is held unconstitutional by court
DISTRICT OF COLUMBIA 22-2404 (1981)	No					
FLORIDA 775.082, 782.04(1); 921.141; 922.07; 922.10	Yes	Exempt from execution	No minimum age	Capital felony circumstances may apply	Capital felony committed by person serving sentence of imprisonment or under community control; previous capital felony or felony using or threat of violence; knowingly created great risk of death to many persons; in connection with robbery, sexual battery, arson, burglary, kidnapping, aircraft piracy or bombings; capital felony for purposes of avoiding lawful arrest or effecting escape from custody; capital felony for pecuniary gain; capital felony to hinder lawful exercise of governmental function or enforcement of laws; capital felony especially heinous, atrocious or cruel; premeditated homicide; victim of capital felony was public official or law enforcement officer engaged in official duties	Electrocution

(Continued)

Table 6: Capital Punishment—Continued

State/Code Section	Allowed	Effect of Incapacity	Minimum Age	Non-homicidal	Homicide with Aggravating Circumstances	Method of Execution
GEORGIA 17-9-3; 17-10-30, 61; 27-2512	Yes	Suspend sentence; shall not be executed	17	Aircraft hijacking or treason in any case	Murder, rape, armed robbery, kidnapping committed by person with prior record of conviction for capital felony; murder, rape, armed robbery, kidnapping committed while engaged in commission of other capital felony; knowingly created grave risk of death to multiple persons in public place by use of weapon/device; monetary value; judicial officer, district attorney or solicitor (or formers) because of exercise of duties; committed as agent of another; outrageously or wantonly vile, horrible or inhuman; against peace officer, corrections officer, fireman while performing duties; offender escaped from lawful custody/confinement; avoiding lawful arrest	Electrocution
HAWAII 706-656	No					
IDAHO 19-2515; 18-210; 18-4001, *et seq.*; 19-2716	Yes	If as result of mortal disease or defect a person lacks capacity to understand proceedings against him, he cannot be tried, convicted, sentenced or punished so long as incapacity endures	No minimum age	None	Court must find at least 1 statutory aggravating circumstance to impose death sentence. Previous conviction of another murder; knowingly created great risk of death; committed for remuneration; especially heinous, atrocious or cruel; circumstances show utter disregard for human life; murder of 1st degree with specific intent to cause death; propensity to commit murder, i.e., a continuing threat to society; murder of peace officer, etc.; murder of witness in criminal or civil proceeding;	Lethal injection; firing squad if lethal injection not possible
ILLINOIS 720 ILCS 5/9-1; 725 ILCS 5/119-5	Yes		18			Lethal injection or electrocution if lethal injection held illegal or unconstitutional

(Continued)

Table 6: Capital Punishment—Continued

State/Code Section	Allowed	Effect of Incapacity	Minimum Age	Non-homicidal	Homicide with Aggravating Circumstances	Method of Execution
INDIANA 35-50-2-9, *et seq.*; 35-38-6-1	Yes	Hearing to determine whether defendant has ability to understand proceedings. If ability lacking, court can delay or continue trial	16	None	At least one aggravating circumstance proved beyond a reasonable doubt. Intentional murder while committing/attempting to commit arson, burglary, child molesting, criminal deviate conduct, kidnapping, rape, robbery, dealing in cocaine or narcotic drug; unlawful detonation of explosive with intent to injure; lying in wait; hiring or hired to kill; victim was law enforcement officer, etc.; another conviction of murder; under sentence of life imprisonment and time; victim dismembered; victim less than 12 years old	Electrocution
IOWA 902.1 (1987)	No					
KANSAS 22-4001 to 22-4014; 21-3401, 21-4501(a)	Still on books but sentence for Class A felony currently does not include death penalty	Suspend sentence				
KENTUCKY 431.220; 431.240; 532.025; 640.040	Yes	Execution suspended if person is insane or pregnant with child until restored to sanity or delivered of child	16	Kidnapping by person with prior capital offense conviction; kidnapping while committing arson, robbery, burglary, rape, sodomy; kidnapping or armed robbery knowingly created great risk of death to more than 1 person in public place	Prior capital offense conviction; substantial history of serious assaultive criminal convictions while committing arson, robbery, burglary, rape, sodomy; knowingly created great risk of death to more than 1 person in a public place; for remuneration; intentional and resulted in multiple deaths; intentional and victim state or local official or police officer in performance of duties	Electrocution

(Continued)

Table 6: Capital Punishment—Continued

State/Code Section	Allowed	Effect of Incapacity	Minimum Age	Non-homicidal	Homicide with Aggravating Circumstances	Method of Execution
LOUISIANA Crim. Proc. §§905, *et seq.*; 14:30(c); 14:113; 641	Yes	Mental incapacity may be raised at any time by defense; no further steps in criminal prosecution until defendant is found to have mental capacity to proceed	No minimum age		At least 1 aggravating circumstance must be found. Aggravated rape, forcible rape; aggravated kidnapping; aggravated burglary; aggravated arson; aggravated escape; armed robbery or simple robbery or first degree robbery victim was fireman or police officer engaged in lawful duties; previous conviction of murder and other serious crimes; knowingly created a risk of death or great bodily harm to more than 1 person; for remuneration; especially heinous, atrocious or cruel; victim under age of 12 years; distribution, etc. of a controlled dangerous substance; victim was witness against defendant	Lethal injection
MAINE Tit. 17A §§1251, 1152	No					
MARYLAND Art. 27 §§71, 75, 412, 413, 627	Yes	Execution of incompetent prohibited	18	None	Victim was law enforcement officer on duty; kidnapping; child abduction; for remuneration; more than one murder in first degree arising from same incident; while committing/attempting to commit robbery, arson, rape, sexual offense; defendant was confined to correctional institution, escaped/attempted to escape, under death or life sentence	Lethal gas
MASSACHUSETTS Ch. 279 §§57-71	No; statutes still on books but *Commonwealth v. Colon-Cruz*, 393 Mass. 150, 470 N.E.2d 116 (1984) said state statute violates state constitution	Suspend sentence	No minimum age		Victim was police officer, fireman, corrections officer, etc. acting in official duty; while defendant incarcerated; victim was judge, prosecuting attorney, juror or witness in official duty; previous murder conviction; for hire; to avoid arrest, while escaping; involved torture or infliction of extreme pain; course of conduct-killing or serious injury to more than one person; explosive device; while rape, assault and battery, kidnapping, robbery, arson, etc.	Electrocution or at election of prisoner, lethal injection
MICHIGAN Const. Art. 4 §46; §750.316	No					

(Continued)

Table 6: Capital Punishment—Continued

State/Code Section	Allowed	Effect of Incapacity	Minimum Age	Non-homicidal	Homicide with Aggravating Circumstances	Method of Execution
MINNESOTA 609.10; 609.185; 1911 Minn. Laws Ch. 387	No					
MISSISSIPPI 97-3-21; 97-7-67; 97-25-55; 99-19-49, *et seq.*	Yes	Suspend sentence	No minimum age	Treason; aircraft piracy; certain non-homicidal capital offenses	Under sentence of imprisonment; previous conviction of another capital offense or felony involving violence; knowingly created great risk of death to many persons; while committing/attempting to commit robbery, rape, arson, burglary, kidnapping, aircraft piracy; sexual battery, unnatural intercourse with child under 12 years; nonconsensual unnatural intercourse with mankind, battery of child, unlawful detonation of explosives; for pecuniary gain	Lethal injection; lethal gas if lethal injection held unconstitutional
MISSOURI 546.720; 552.060; 565.020; 565.032.2	Yes	Exempt from execution until certified as free of mental disease or defect	16	None	Prior conviction for murder in 1st degree; while committing or attempting to commit another homicide; knowingly created great risk of death to more than 1 person; for monetary value; victim was judicial or peace officer during exercise of official duty; outrageously or wantonly vile, horrible or inhuman; engaged in rape, sodomy, burglary, robbery, kidnapping; victim was witness; victim was employee of correctional system in course of duty; hijacking; while escaping or awaiting arrest; to conceal or prevent prosecution of a felony offense	Lethal gas or lethal injection
MONTANA 45-5-102; 46-18-301, *et seq.*; 46-19-103, 46-19-201	Yes	Exempt from execution but if fitness regained, execution must be carried out unless has so much time has elapsed that it would be unjust	No minimum age, however, if defendant is less than 18 years old this is a mitigating circumstance	Aggravated assault or aggravated kidnapping while incarcerated at state prison by person previously convicted for murder or persistent felony offender	Currently serving sentence of imprisonment; previous murder conviction; committed by torture; lying in wait or ambush; part of scheme or operation which would result in death of more than 1 person; victim was peace officer performing duty; aggravated kidnapping; while incarcerated at state prison by person previously convicted of murder or persistent felony offender; while committing sexual assault, sexual intercourse without consent, deviate sexual conduct or incest and victim less than 18 years	Hanging by the neck or lethal injection, at election of defendant

(Continued)

66

Table 6: Capital Punishment—Continued

State/Code Section	Allowed	Effect of Incapacity	Minimum Age	Non-homicidal	Homicide with Aggravating Circumstances	Method of Execution
NEBRASKA 28-105.01; 29-2523, *et seq.*	Yes	Suspend sentence	18		Previous felony conviction involving of violence; multiple victims; for hire, pecuniary gain; law enforcement official or public servant; committed to hinder lawful exercise of governmental function or enforcement of laws; to conceal crime or identity of person committing crime; especially heinous, atrocious, cruel; great risk of death to several persons	Electrocution
NEVADA 176.025; 176.355; 176.425-455; 200.033	Yes	Suspend sentence	16		Multiple victims (random, no motive); involved torture; peace officer or fireman engaged in official duties; for remuneration; avoid lawful arrest or effect escape from custody; connection with robbery, sexual assault, arson, burglary, kidnapping; knowingly created great risk of death to more than one person other than the victim; previous murder/felony convictions involving use/threat of violence; offender serving sentence	Lethal injection
NEW HAMPSHIRE 630:1, 5; 4:24; 21-B:1	Yes	Exempt from execution	17		Purposely killed or inflicted serious bodily injury which led to death; knowingly created grave risk of death; prior convictions resulting in death of person for which now serving life imprisonment or death sentence; 2 or more prior felony convictions; 2 or more prior convictions involving distribution of controlled substances; premeditation and substantial planning; particularly vulnerable victim due to age, youth or infirmity; especially heinous, cruel or depraved manner; for pecuniary gain; for purpose of avoiding lawful arrest or escape from custody	Lethal injection, or hanging if lethal injection becomes impractical to carry out

(Continued)

Table 6: Capital Punishment—Continued

State/Code Section	Allowed	Effect of Incapacity	Minimum Age	Non-homicidal	Homicide with Aggravating Circumstances	Method of Execution
NEW JERSEY 30:4-82; Code of Crim. Justice §§2A: 4A-22; 2C:11-3; 2C:49-2	Yes	Exempt from execution	18		Previous murder conviction; knowingly created grave risk of death to another other than victim; outrageously or wantonly vile, horrible or inhuman; for pecuniary value; defendant paid for it; purpose was to escape detection, apprehension, trial, punishment or confinement for another offense committed by defendant or another; in connection with murder, robbery, sexual assault, arson, burglary, kidnapping; victim was public servant, relating to official duties	Lethal injection
NEW MEXICO 31-14-4, *et seq.*; 28-6-1; 31-18-14(A); 31-20A-5	Yes	Suspend sentence	18		Peace officer engaged in duties; connection with kidnapping, criminal sexual contact of a minor or criminal sexual penetration; attempt to escape penal institution of New Hampshire; incarcerated at time of offense; employee of corrections and criminal rehabilitation, while incarcerated; for hire; witness to a crime to prevent testimony, reporting of crime or in retaliation	Lethal injection
NEW YORK Penal §60.06; 125.27; Correc. §650, *et. seq.*	No; declared unconstitutional except murder in 1st degree	Suspend sentence	18 at time of crime		Victim was public officer in official duty; victim was employee of state correctional institution in official duty; defendant was under sentence	Current of electricity
NORTH CAROLINA 14-17; 15A-1001, *et seq.*; 15A-2000; 122C-313	Yes	Exempt from execution	17; no minimum age for first degree murder while serving prison sentence for prior murder or which work on escape from such sentence.		Capital felony committed by person lawfully incarcerated; previous capital felony convictions; previous felony conviction involving use/threat of violence; avoid lawful arrest or escape from custody; in connection with homicide, rape or sex offense, robbery, arson, burglary, kidnapping or aircraft piracy or bombing; for pecuniary gain; hinder lawful exercise of governmental function or enforcement of laws; victim was law enforcement officer, employee of Corrections Department; jailer, fireman, judge or justice, prosecutor, juror or witness while engaged in duties or former; especially heinous, atrocious, or cruel; great risk of death to more than one person; in connection with other crimes of violence against other person(s)	Lethal gas or at convict's request lethal injection

(Continued)

Table 6: Capital Punishment—Continued

State/Code Section	Allowed	Effect of Incapacity	Minimum Age	Non-homicidal	Homicide with Aggravating Circumstances	Method of Execution
NORTH DAKOTA Ch. 12-50 repealed by N.D. Laws Ch. 116 §41	No					
OHIO 2929.02, *et seq.*; 2949.22, *et seq.*	Yes	Suspend sentence	18		Assassination of public official; for hire; escape detection, apprehension, trial or punishment for another offense; committed while a prisoner in detention facility; prior murder convictions or multiple victims now; peace officer; rape, kidnapping, aggravated arson, aggravated robbery, aggravated burglary; witness of crime to prevent testimony or retaliation for testimony	Electrocution
OKLAHOMA Tit. 21 §§701.10, *et seq.*; Tit. 22 §§1005-1008	Yes	Suspend sentence	No minimum age		Previous felony conviction involving use/threat of violence; knowingly created great risk of death to more than one person; for remuneration or employed another for remuneration; especially heinous, atrocious or cruel; avoiding lawful arrest or prosecution; committed while serving imprisonment sentence for felony; probability of defendant being continuing threat to society; peace officer	Lethal injection or electrocution if lethal injection held to be unconstitutional or firing squad if both of above found to be unconstitutional
OREGON 137.080, *et seq.*; 137.473; 161.295, *et seq.*	Yes	Prohibits death penalty	18		In determining aggravating circumstances, court shall consider any evidence received during proceeding; presentence report; any other relevant evidence court deems trustworthy and reliable	Lethal injection

(Continued)

Table 6: Capital Punishment—Continued

State/Code Section	Allowed	Effect of Incapacity	Minimum Age	Non-homicidal	Homicide with Aggravating Circumstances	Method of Execution
PENNSYLVANIA Tit. 18 §1102(a); Tit. 42 §9711; Tit. 61 §2121.1	Yes		No minimum age		Fireman, peace officer, public servant killed in performance of duties; paid or was paid; hostage/ransom; hijacking aircraft; prosecution witness to prevent testimony; in perpetration of a felony; knowingly created grave risk of death to another in addition to victim; torture; significant history of felony convictions involving use/threat of violence; previous life sentence or death	Lethal injection
RHODE ISLAND 11-23-2	No					
SOUTH CAROLINA 16-3-10, *et seq.*; 24-3-530; 44-23-210, *et seq.*	Yes	Incapable of standing trial	No minimum age		Murder in connection with any criminal sexual conduct, kidnapping, burglary, armed robbery, larceny with use of deadly weapon, poison, physical torture; prior murder conviction; knowingly created great risk of death to multiple persons in public place; for money or monetary value; judicial officer, solicitor, or other officer of the court (or formers) because of exercise of duties; agent/employee of another; law enforcement officer, peace officer, correction employees, fireman (or formers) related to duty; family members of above-mentioned; multiple victims; child 11 or under	Electrocution
SOUTH DAKOTA 22-16-4; 23A-27A-1, *et seq.*;	Yes	Exempt from execution	No minimum age		Prior felony convictions/serious assaultive criminal convictions; knowingly created great risk of death to others; for remuneration or as agent/employee of another; members of criminal justice system (judge, attorneys) related to their exercise of duties; outrageously or wantonly vile, horrible or inhuman; law officer, corrections employee, fireman while engaged in performance of official duties; offender escaped from lawful custody/confinement; avoiding lawful arrest of himself or another; in connection with distributing, manufacturing or dispensing illegal substances; testimony regarding impact of crime on victim's family	Lethal injection

(Continued)

Table 6: Capital Punishment—Continued

State/Code Section	Allowed	Effect of Incapacity	Minimum Age	Non-homicidal	Homicide with Aggravating Circumstances	Method of Execution
TENNESSEE 39-13-201, *et seq.*; 37-1-102, *et seq.*; 40-23-114	Yes	Prohibited for mentally retarded	18		Offender over 18, victim under 12; previous felony convictions; great risk of death to multiple persons other than victim; done for employment or remuneration; especially heinous, atrocious or cruel; avoiding lawful arrest of defendant or another; in connection with any first degree murder, arson, rape, robbery, burglary, theft, kidnapping, aircraft piracy, bombing; committed while in lawful custody/confinement; committed against law enforcement officer, corrections person, firefighter engaged in duties, also judge, attorney general, district attorney, etc. (and formers) due to performance of duties; against elected official; "mass" murderer	Electrocution
TEXAS Crim. Proc. §§8.07; 12.31; 19.03; 43.14	Yes	Exempt from execution	17		Victim is peace officer or fireman in official duty; while committing/attempting to commit kidnapping, burglary, robbery, aggravated sexual assault or arson; for remuneration; while escaping or incarcerated; murder more than one person during same criminal transaction or scheme or course of conduct	Lethal injection

(Continued)

Table 6: Capital Punishment—Continued

State/Code Section	Allowed	Effect of Incapacity	Minimum Age	Non-homicidal	Homicide with Aggravating Circumstances	Method of Execution
UTAH 77-15-1; 77-19-13; 77-18-5.5; 76-3-206, *et seq.*; 76-5-202	Yes	Exempt from execution	No minimum age		Offender confined in jail or other correctional facility; multiple murders; knowingly creates great risk of death to person other than victim; in connection with aggravated robbery, robbery, rape, rape of child, object rape, object rape of child, forcible sodomy, sodomy upon child, sexual abuse of child, child abuse of child under 14, aggravated sex assault, aggravated arson, arson, burglary, kidnapping; avoiding lawful arrest; pecuniary or other personal gain; contracted; previously convicted of murder or felony involving use/threat of violence; purpose of preventing witness from testifying in criminal procedure or person from offering evidence or hindering lawful governmental function or enforcement of laws; official or candidate for public office, homicide based on/related to official position; firefighter, peace officer, law officer or anyone involved in criminal justice system; bombs; in connection with unlawful control of aircraft, train, other public conveyance; poison; hostage/ransom	Defendant at time of execution may select either firing squad or lethal injection. If s/he does not select, then lethal injection
VERMONT Tit. 13 §§7101, *et seq.*	No. Vermont has death penalty statute but it has never been amended to conform to Supreme Court's decision in *Furman v. Georgia,* 408 U.S. 238 (1972); hence constitutionally invalid.					Electrocution
VIRGINIA 18.2-17, 31; 19.2-167, *et seq.*; 53.1-233	Yes	Cannot stand trial for criminal offense	No minimum age		In connection with abduction for extortion of money or pecuniary benefit; for hire; committed while confined to state correctional facility; armed robbery; rape, sodomy; law officer for purposes of interfering with official duties; multiple murders; child under 12 in commission of abduction, intended to extort money or for pecuniary benefit; controlled substance; outrageously or wantonly vile, horrible or inhuman; continuing serious threat to society	Electrocution

(Continued)

Table 6: Capital Punishment—Continued

State/Code Section	Allowed	Effect of Incapacity	Minimum Age	Non-homicidal	Homicide with Aggravating Circumstances	Method of Execution
WASHINGTON 10.95.010, *et seq.*; 10.95.180	Yes	Mitigating factor	No minimum age		Aggravated first degree murder defined as follows: law enforcement officer, corrections officer or firefighter in performance of official duties; offender escaped from confinement; offender in custody as consequence of felony conviction; agreement for money or value; contracted; victim was member or former member of criminal justice system (judge, attorney, juror, parole officer, etc.) related to their official duties; committed to conceal crime or identity of person committing crime; multiple victims; in connection with robbery, rape, burglary, kidnapping, arson; victim was news reporter and committed to obstruct investigation, research or reporting activities. If there are not sufficient mitigating circumstances, sentence shall be death.	Hanging or lethal injection
WEST VIRGINIA 61-11-2 (1984)	No					
WISCONSIN 939.50(3)(a); 940.01	No					
WYOMING 6-2-101, *et seq.*; 7-13-901, *et seq.*	Yes	Suspend sentence	No minimum age; age of defendant is a mitigating circumstance		While under sentence; previous conviction for murder in first degree or felony using violence; knowingly created great risk of death to 2 or more persons; while committing/attempting to commit robbery, sexual assault, arson, burglary, kidnapping or aircraft piracy or unlawful discharge of bomb; while escaping or avoiding arrest; for pecuniary gain; was especially heinous, atrocious or cruel; court official in exercise of official duty	Lethal injection or lethal gas if injection ruled unconstitutional

7. CRIMINAL STATUTES OF LIMITATION

A statute of limitation is a law allowing criminals to go free if they are not apprehended by authorities within a prescribed number of years after the crime in question is committed.

Statutes of limitation generally require the criminal to remain in the state, gainfully employed and visible, seeming to necessitate that the criminal remain "catchable." If the authorities fail to discover a criminal living in the open within a specified amount of time, society has determined that at that point the criminal should be able to live free from the possibility of prosecution. It appears that this notion is born out of a sense of mercy more than pragmatics: if the criminal is a fugitive, out of the state in which the crime was committed or otherwise living in hiding, this tolls, or suspends, the statute. (Once the criminal reenters the state the statute resumes running.) However, if the criminal were living an open, public, so-called "reformed" life, after a reasonable period of time he is allowed to be free from capture.

Not all crimes are governed by statutes of limitation. Murder, for example, has none. Sex offenses with minors, crimes of violence, kidnapping, arson, and forgery have no statutes of limitation in a number of states. In Arizona, California, Oklahoma, and Utah crimes involving public money or public records have no statutes of limitation. While in Colorado treason has none.

Many states have adopted systems that classify felonies by category. Therefore, in order to effectively compare statutes of limitation provisions, it is necessary to determine which crimes in that state fit into particular classes. For example, Missouri lists murder or Class A felonies as crimes with no statutes of limitation. Each crime must then be looked up in that state's statutes to determine its classification.

Table 7: Criminal Statutes Of Limitation

State	Code Section	Felonies	Misdemeanors	Acts that Toll the Statute
ALABAMA	15-3-1, *et seq.*	Arson, forgery, counterfeiting, use or threat of violence, felony with serious physical injury/death, any sex offense with one under 16, drug trafficking: none; other felonies: 3 yrs.	12 mos.	Prosecution commences upon indictment, issuing warrant or binding over of defendant
ALASKA	12.10.010, 020, 040	Murder: none; other felonies: 5 yrs. unless fraud is element, then extended 1 yr. after discovery of fraud; official misconduct: extension up to 3 yrs.	5 yrs.	If outside the state hiding, maximum extension 3 yrs.
ARIZONA	13-107	Murder, misuse of public money, falsifying public records: none; other felonies: 7 yrs.	1 yr.; petty offenses: 6 mos.	Absent from state or no reasonably ascertainable residence in state
ARKANSAS	5-1-109	Murder: none; Class Y and A felonies: 6 yrs.; Class B, C, D, or unclassified felonies: 3 yrs.	1 yr.	Absent from state, nonresident, no reasonably ascertainable place of abode or work; if offense committed against a minor, statutory periods do not begin running until minor turns 18
CALIFORNIA	Pen. §§799, 802, 19(d)	Murder, other offenses punishable by death or life imprisonment, embezzlement of public funds: none; offenses punishable by 8 or more years in prison: 6 yrs.; offenses punishable by imprisonment: 3 yrs.	1 yr. violations: 1 yr.; misdemeanor violation committed on a minor under 14: 2 yrs.	Not in state; statutory periods do not begin until offense is or should have been discovered
COLORADO	16-5-401	Murder or any attempted murder, kidnap, treason, forgery: none; others: 3 yrs.; bribery and corrupt influencing: additional 3 yrs.; sexual assault of victim under 15, incest, child prostitution: additional 7 yrs.	18 mos.; Class I and II and traffic offenses: 1 yr.; petty offenses: 6 mos.; 3rd degree sexual assault: additional 3 1/2 yrs.	Absent from state: 5 yrs. maximum extension
CONNECTICUT	54-193	Murder: none; if imprisonment is more than 1 yr.: 5 yrs.; any other: 1 yr.	1 yr.	Fleeing or outside state
DELAWARE	Tit. 11 §205(a), (b), (g)	Murder: none; others: 5 yrs.	Class A: 3 yrs.; others: 2 yrs.	Fleeing or hiding
DISTRICT OF COLUMBIA	23-113	1st or 2nd degree murder: none; others: 6 yrs.	3 yrs.	Fleeing or action commenced
FLORIDA	775.15	Capital or life felony: none; 1st degree felony: 4 yrs.; others: 3 yrs.	1st degree: 2 yrs.; 2nd degree and violations: 1 yr.	Continually absent from state, no reasonably ascertainable work or abode in state: maximum extension 3 yrs.

(Continued)

Table 7: Criminal Statutes Of Limitation—Continued

State	Code Section	Felonies	Misdemeanors	Acts that Toll the Statute
GEORGIA	17-3-1,2	Murder: none; crimes punishable by death or life imprisonment: 7 yrs.; others: 4 yrs.; crimes against victims under 14: 7 yrs.	2 yrs.	Nonresident
HAWAII	701-108	1st or 2nd degree murder or 1st or 2nd degree attempted murder: none; robbery, kidnapping, rape, sodomy: 6 yrs.; others: 3 yrs.; if fraud or breach is element: 2-6 yrs. extension after discovery; If based on misconduct in public office: 2-3 yrs. extension upon discovery	Parking violation: 2 yrs.; petty misdemeanors: 1 yr.	Absent from state or no reasonably ascertainable residence: maximum extension 3 yrs.
IDAHO	19-401, *et seq.*	Murder: none; others: 3 yrs.; felony against child: 5 yrs.	1 yr.	Absent from state
ILLINOIS	720 ILCS 5/3-5; 5/3-7	Murder, manslaughter, treason, arson, forgery: none; others: 3 yrs.	18 mos.	Nonresident
INDIANA	35-41-4-2	Murder, Class A felony, kidnapping, rape, deviant sex conduct, child molesting, robbery, arson: none; others, Class B, C, D felony: 5 yrs.	2 yrs.	Absent state, conceals self or evidence of crime; prosecution is considered timely if defendant pleads guilty
IOWA	802.1, *et seq.*	1st and 2nd degree murder: none; others: 3 yrs.; sexual abuse of child under 10: 4 yrs.; sexual abuse of child under 12: no later than 6 mos. after child turns 18	Serious misdemeanor: 3 yrs.; simple misdemeanor or violation of ordinances: 1 yr.; fraud: extension up to 3 yrs.	Outside state
KANSAS	21-3106	Murder: none; victim under 6, indecent liberties with child, aggravated criminal sodomy, solicitation of child, incest or sexual exploitation of child: 5 yrs.; others: 2 yrs.	2 yrs.	Absent state or concealed within state; concealed crime
KENTUCKY	500.050	None	1 yr.	
LOUISIANA	Crim. Proc. Art. 571, 572, 575	Punishment death or life imprisonment: none; hard labor: 6 yrs.; not hard labor: 4 yrs.	Punishment of fine: 6 mos.; fine and/or prison: 2 yrs.	Avoiding detection, fleeing, outside state, absent residence in state
MAINE	Tit. 17-A §8	Murder, 1st or 2nd degree homicide: none; Class A, B, C offenses: 6 yrs.; Class D, E, and all non-classed defenses: 3 yrs.	Class A, B, C offenses: 6 yrs.; Class D, E, and all non-classed defenses: 3 yrs.	Absent state or prosecution pending in state: maximum 5 yrs. extension

(Continued)

Table 7: Criminal Statutes Of Limitation—Continued

State	Code Section	Felonies	Misdemeanors	Acts that Toll the Statute
MARYLAND	Cts. & Jud. Proc. §§5-106, 107	None	Misdemeanor punishable by confinement: none; misdemeanor not punishable by confinement: 1 yr.; fine, penalty, or forfeiture: 1 yr.	
MASSACHUSETTS	Ch. 277§63	Murder: none; assault, robbery: 10 yrs.; others: 6 yrs.; extension of time if victim is under 16	6 yrs.	Tolled when defendant is not usually and publicly resident
MICHIGAN	767.24	Murder: none; kidnapping, extortion, assault with intent to murder: 10 yrs.; others: 6 yrs.	6 yrs.	Not resident, did not usually and publicly reside
MINNESOTA	628.26	Murder: none; bribery, medical assistance fraud, theft: 6 yrs.; familial sexual abuse, criminal sexual conduct: 7 yrs.; all others: 3 yrs.; if value of property/services stolen is over $35,000: 5 yrs.	3 yrs.	Not resident
MISSISSIPPI	99-1-5	Murder, manslaughter, arson, burglary, forgery, counterfeiting, robbery, larceny, rape, embezzlement, obtaining money under false pretenses, felonious abuse or battery of child or sexual battery: none; all others: 2 yrs.	2 yrs.	Absent state, fleeing, hiding
MISSOURI	556.036	Murder or Class A felony: none; others: 3 yrs.	1 yr.; violations: 6 mos.	Absent state, hiding: maximum 3 yr. extension
MONTANA	45-1-205	Murder: none; others: 5 yrs.	1 yr.	Absent state
NEBRASKA	29-110	Murder, treason, arson, forgery: none; others: 3 yrs.	18 mos.; if fine less than $100 or jail time less than 3 mos.: 1 yr.	Fleeing justice
NEVADA	171.080, 085, 090, 100	Murder: none; theft, robbery, arson, burglary, forgery, sexual assault: 4 yrs.; others: 3 yrs.	Gross misdemeanor: 2 yrs.; others: 1 yr.	Prosecution commences when indictment is presented
NEW HAMPSHIRE	625:8	Murder: none; others: 6 yrs.	1 yr.; violations: 3 mos.	Absent state, no residence or work in state
NEW JERSEY	2C:1-6; 2C:11-3	Murder, manslaughter: none; official misconduct, bribery: 7 yrs.; others: 5 yrs.; if victim under 18, prosecution must begin within 5 yrs. after victim attains 18	Petty offense: 1 yr.	Fleeing justice
NEW MEXICO	30-1-8	Murder, 1st degree felony: 15 yrs.; 2nd degree: 6 yrs.; 3rd and 4th degree: 5 yrs.	2 yrs.; petty: 1 yr.	Fleeing justice; enumerated procedural defects
NEW YORK	Crim. Proc. §30.10	Murder, Class A felony: none; others: 5 yrs.	2 yrs.; petty offenses: 1 yr.	Absent state: up to 5 yrs.

(Continued)

Table 7: Criminal Statutes Of Limitation—Continued

State	Code Section	Felonies	Misdemeanors	Acts that Toll the Statute
NORTH CAROLINA	15-1	None	Malicious misdemeanor: none; others: 2 yrs.	
NORTH DAKOTA	29-04-01 to 04	Murder: none; sexual abuse of children: 7 yrs.; others: 3 yrs.	2 yrs.	Absent state
OHIO	2901.13	Murder: none; others: 6 yrs.	2 yrs.; minor misdemeanor: 6 mos.	Absent state or undiscovered corpus delicti
OKLAHOMA	Tit. 22 §151	Murder: none; bribery, embezzlement or misappropriation of public money or other assets, falsification of public records, conspiracy to defraud state or other subdivision, rape or forcible sodomy: 7 yrs.; lewd or indecent proposals or acts against children crimes involving minors in pornography, sodomy, criminal conspiracy embezzlement, criminal state income tax violations: 5 yrs.; all others: 3 yrs.	3 yrs.	Absent state
OREGON	131.125(1)	Murder, manslaughter: none; sexual felonies: 6 yrs.; others: 3 yrs.	Sexual misdemeanors: 4 yrs.; violations: 6 mos.; others: 2 yrs.	Absent state, fleeing
PENNSYLVANIA	Tit. 42 §5551	Murder, manslaughter, voluntary manslaughter, conspiracy to murder, soliciting to commit murder and murder results, felony connected with 1st or 2nd degree murder: none; major offenses: 5 yrs.; others: 2 yrs.	2 yrs.; vehicular offenses: 30 days	Absent from state; not resident
RHODE ISLAND	12-12-17	Murder, 1st, 2nd, 3rd degree arson, murder arson, burglary, counterfeiting, forgery, robbery, larceny, 1st or 2nd degree child molestation, sexual assault, bigamy, conspiracy to commit any of above: none; all others: 10 yrs.	3 yrs.	Stolen, lost, destroyed information: 1 yr. maximum
SOUTH CAROLINA	No statute of limitation for any criminal prosecution			
SOUTH DAKOTA	23A-42-1, *et seq.*	Murder, Class A, B, or 1 felony: none; all other public offenses: 7 yrs.	7 yrs.	Absent state
TENNESSEE	40-2-101, *et seq.*	Any crime punishable by death or life imprisonment: none; Class A felony: 15 yrs.; Class B felony: 8 yrs.; Class C or D felony: 4 yrs.; Class E felony: 2 yrs.	Gaming: 6 mos.; others: 12 mos.	Concealing fact of crime, absent state

(Continued)

Table 7: Criminal Statutes Of Limitation—Continued

State	Code Section	Felonies	Misdemeanors	Acts that Toll the Statute
TEXAS	Crim. Proc. §12.01	Murder, manslaughter: none; thefts involving fiduciaries: 10 yrs.; other theft, burglary, robbery, arson, rape and certain other sexual offenses: 5 yrs.; others: 3 yrs.	2 yrs.	Absent state
UTAH	76-1-301	1st and 2nd degree murder, manslaughter, embezzlement of public monies or falsification of public records: none; other felony or negligent homicide: 4 yrs.	2 yrs.; infractions: 1 yr.	Absent state
VERMONT	Tit. 13 §§4501, *et seq.*	Arson causing death, kidnapping: none; larceny, aggravated sexual assault, burglary, arson, embezzlement, forgery, bribery, fraud, sex crimes with child under 16: 6 yrs.; others: 3 yrs.	3 yrs.; crimes with penalty of forfeiture: 2 yrs.	Prosecution commences when arrest is made, citation issues, indictment or information presented
VIRGINIA	19.2.8	None	2 yrs. with certain exceptions	Fleeing, concealing
WASHINGTON	9A.04.080	Murder, arson causing death: none; public official misconduct, arson: 10 yrs.; others: 3 yrs.	Gross misdemeanors: 2 yrs.; other offenses: 1 yr.	Not publicly a resident
WEST VIRGINIA	61-11-9	None	Petty larceny, perjury or procuring perjury: 3 yrs.; others: 1 yr.	Stolen, lost, destroyed information/indictment
WISCONSIN	939.74	Murder: none; others: 6 yrs.	Misdemeanors and adultery: 3 yrs.	Not publicly resident; if victim is unable to seek issuance of a complaint, that time period excluded
WYOMING	No statute of limitation for any criminal prosecution			

8. DRUNK DRIVING

Penalties for drunk driving have become tougher over the years as the cost of this dangerous behavior rises. Reckless alcohol consumption among young people has also risen markedly, and it has been met with sharp intolerance.

Drunk driving, or driving while intoxicated (DWI) or driving under the influence (DUI), is typically determined by the alcohol content found in the driver's blood. Blood alcohol content (BAC) may be determined in two ways: through breath analysis or urinalysis. Most states have set the legal limit of blood alcohol content at 0.10 percent. Six states have no set amount of blood alcohol to presume intoxication. In these states it is still illegal to drive while drunk, but blood alcohol content is merely one piece of evidence of intoxication.

Penalties for drunk driving are severe in most states. Virtually every state suspends the driver's license on a first offense, and the length of suspension increases sharply with each successive offense. There is, however, a great deal of variation in the lengths of suspension of driving privileges among the states. A few only impose suspension for as little as one year for multiple offenses. Michigan, however, revokes the driver's license on the second offense. Several states include revocation on the third or fourth offense.

The newest development in the laws of drunk driving concern court-ordered attendance at an alcohol abuse rehabilitation program upon conviction for driving while intoxicated. Six states still do not have rehabilitation requirements for offenders, while the rest have some sort of rehabilitation requirement for problem drinkers and drivers.

Table 8: Drunk Driving

State	Code Section	BAC Legal Limit	Rehabilitation Required?	Driver's License Suspension?	Other Penalties
ALABAMA	32-5A-191	.10% BAC per se at time of driving	Yes on first offense; DUI court referral program approved by state	1st offense: 90 days; 2nd: 1 yr.; 3rd: 3 yrs.	1st offense: imprisonment up to 1 yr. and/or $250-1000; 2nd within 5 yrs.: up to 1 yr. and $500-2500; 3rd within 5 yrs.: up to 1 yr. and $1000-$5000
ALASKA	28.35.030; 28.15.181	.10% BAC as determined by test taken within 4 hours	Yes, program of alcohol education or rehabilitation that court finds appropriate for term specified by court	1st: 90 days min.; 2nd: 1 yr. min.; 3rd: 10 yrs. min.	1st: min. 72 hrs. and min. $250; 2nd within 10 yrs.: min. 20 days and min. $500; 3rd within 10 yrs.: min. 30 days and min. $1000
ARIZONA	28-692, *et seq.*	.10% BAC at time of offense	Yes, alcohol abuse screening session by screening or treatment facility approved by health services; alcohol abuse classes or treatment facility if necessary: habitual abuse	1st: 90 days; 2nd within 5 yrs.: revocation; 3rd within 5 yrs.: revocation min. 3 yrs.	1st: min. 24 hrs. and min. $250 and 8-24 hrs. community service; 2nd within 5 yrs.: min. 60 days and min. $500; 3rd within five yrs.: min. 6 mos.
ARKANSAS	5-65-103, *et seq.*	.10% BAC as determined by test	Alcohol Education Program prescribed and approved of by Arkansas Highway Safety Program or alcohol treatment program approved by Office on Alcohol and Drug Abuse Prevention	1st: 90-120 days; 2nd: 12-16 mos.; 3rd: 24-30 mos.; 4th: 3 yrs.	1st: 1 day to 1 yr. prison, court can order public service in lieu of jail and $150-1000; 2nd within 3 yrs.: 7 days to 1 yr. and $400-3000; 3rd within 3 yrs.: 90 days to 1 yr. and $900-5000; 4th within 3 yrs.: felony, 1-6 yrs.; fine only for 2nd and 3rd offenses within 5 yrs.
CALIFORNIA	Veh. §§23152, *et seq.*	0.10% BAC at time of driving (rebuttably presumed that percentage at time of driving was more than at time of test); if test is less than .05% BAC, BAC presumed not .10% when driving; if test is .05-.10%, not presumption but evidence of .10%; .10% at time of test equals .10% at time of driving	1st: if probation, must participate in alcohol or drug education program designated by court if programs approved of are available in that county; 2nd: if probation, 1 yr. in program acceptable to court	1st: 6 mos., or if probation granted, could be 90 days with exception of traveling to work and rehab program; 2nd: restricted to necessary travel (work and rehab) for 1 yr.; 3rd: 3 yrs.	1st: 96 hrs. to 6 mos. prison and $390-1000; 2nd within 5 yrs.: 90 days to 1 yr. and $390-1000; 3rd within 5 yrs.: 120 days to 1 yr. and $390-$1000

(Continued)

Table 8: Drunk Driving—Continued

State	Code Section	BAC Legal Limit	Rehabilitation Required?	Driver's License Suspension?	Other Penalties
COLORADO	42-2-122.1; 42-4-1202	.15 g. of alcohol per 100 mm. of blood while driving or .15 g. of alcohol per 200 mm. of blood at time of test	Court's discretion up to 2 yrs.; drug and alcohol driving safety program	1 yr.	1st: 5 days to 1 yr. and court may fine $300-1000 and 48-96 hrs. useful community service; 2nd within 5 yrs.: 90 days to 1 yr. and court may fine $500-1500 and 60-120 hrs. useful community service
CONNECTICUT	14-227a	.10% BAC at time of offense	Court may order participation in alcohol education and treatment program in addition to any fine or sentence	1st: 1 yr. (court's discretion); 2nd: 2 yrs.; 3rd: 3 yrs.; 4th: permanently	1st: $500-1000 and jail up to 6 mos. or 100 hrs. community service; 2nd within 5 yrs.: $500-2000 and jail up to 1 yr.; 3rd within 5 yrs.: $1000-4000 and jail up to 2 yrs.; 4th within 5 yrs.: $2000-8000 and jail up to 3 yrs.
DELAWARE	Tit. 21 §4177	.10% BAC as shown by test taken within 4 hours of offense	1st: required program of rehabilitation or course of instruction which may include inpatient up to 6 mos.; 2nd: program of education or rehabilitation which may include inpatient treatment up to 15 mos.	1st or 2nd: 1 yr.; 3rd or more: 18 mos.	1st: $200-1000 or jail 60 days-6 mos.; for each subsequent offense within 5 yrs. of former offense: $500-2000 and jail 2 –18 mos.
DISTRICT OF COLUMBIA	40-716	.10% BAC; .13% alcohol in urine	No	Yes for unspecified time	1st: up to $300 and/or 90 days; 2nd within 15 yrs.: up to $5000 and/or up to 1 yr.; 3rd within 15 yrs.: up to $10,000 and/or up to 1 yr.

(Continued)

Table 8: Drunk Driving—Continued

State	Code Section	BAC Legal Limit	Rehabilitation Required?	Driver's License Suspension?	Other Penalties
FLORIDA	316.193	.10% BAC	Substance abuse course specified by the court	Revocation/ suspension upon conviction	1st: $250-500 and jail up to 6 mos.; 2nd within 3 yrs.: $500-1000 and jail up to 9 mos.; 3rd within 3 yrs.: $1000-2500 and jail up to 12 mos.; 4th within 3 yrs.: 3rd degree felony, prison up to 5 yrs.; if first offense BAC exceeds .20%: 1st: $500-100 and jail up to 9 mos.; 2nd within 3 yrs.: $1000-2000 and jail up to 12 mos.; 3rd within 3 yrs.: $2000-5000 and jail up to 12 mos.; additional penalties: 1st: probation up to 1 yr. and community service of 50 hrs. minimum or $10 fine per hour not worked
GEORGIA	40-5-63; 40-6-391	.10% BAC at time of test		1st: 1 yr.; 2nd within 5 yrs.: 3 yrs.; 3rd within 5 yrs.: considered habitual offender, 5 yrs.	1st: $300-1000 and 10 days to 12 mos.; 2nd within 5 yrs.: $600-1000 and 90 days to 12 mos.; 3rd: $1000-5000 and 120 days to 12 mos. mandatory
HAWAII	291-4	.10% BAC	1st: 14 hr. minimum alcohol abuse rehab program including education and counseling or comparable program approved by court; subsequent: may be required pending evaluation by substance abuse counselor	1st: 90 days (court can make it 30 days total prohibition and 60 days only for work and rehab); 2nd: 1 yr. absolute prohibition; 3rd: 1-5 yrs.	1st: $150-1000 and/or min. 48 hrs. jail and/or 72 hrs. community service; 2nd within 5 yrs.: $500-1000 and min. 48 hrs. jail or min. 80 hrs. community service; 3rd within 5 yrs.: $500-1000 and 10-180 days jail
IDAHO	18-8004, *et seq.*	.10% BAC	Alcoholic evaluation (own expense) approved facility; if necessary, an alcoholic treatment program best suited for individual	1st: mandatory up to 180 days (defendant may request for necessary privilege-work and family health needs); 2nd: mandatory 6 mos. after getting out of jail and possibly an additional time up to 1 yr.; 3rd: 1-5 yrs. (no privileges at all)	1st: up to $1000 and/or up to 6 mos.; 2nd within 5 yrs.: mandatory fine up to $2000 and jail 10 days to 1 yr.; 3rd within 5 yrs.: felony, jail up to 5 yrs. and may be fined up to $5000

(Continued)

Table 8: Drunk Driving—Continued

State	Code Section	BAC Legal Limit	Rehabilitation Required?	Driver's License Suspension?	Other Penalties
ILLINOIS	625 ILCS 5/ 11-501, *et seq.*	.10% BAC; less than .05% at test: presumed not to have required BAC at time of driving; .05%-.10% at test: no presumption of guilt but take it with other evidence; .10% at test: guilty	Professional evaluation to determine if there is abuse problem and extent; defendant pays cost; program must be approved/ licensed by Dept. of Alcohol and Substance Abuse	Up to 1 yr.	1st: Class A misdemeanor: jail up to 1 yr.; 2nd within 5 yrs.: mandatory min. 48 hrs. jail or min. 10 days community service; 3rd: Class 4 felony, 1-3 yrs. prison
INDIANA	9-30-5-1, *et seq.*	.10% BAC	No	1st: 90 days to 2 yrs.; 2nd 10 or more yrs. ago: 90 days to 2 yrs.; 2nd 5-10 yrs. ago: 6 mos. to 2 yrs.; 2nd within 5 yrs.: 1-2 yrs.	1st: Class A misdemeanor; 2nd within 5 yrs.: min. 5 days jail or min. 80 hrs. community service in addition to Class D felony (min. 2 yrs.) and may be fined up to $10,000
IOWA	3213.1, *et seq.*	.10% BAC	2nd offense: must undergo substance abuse evaluation prior to sentencing; 3rd offense or if evaluation recommends treatment: may be required to commit to treatment	1st: 180 days; 2nd within 6 yrs.: 1 yr.	1st: serious misdemeanor, $500-1000 and min. 48 hrs. jail, may perform up to 200 hrs. community service in lieu of fine if court allows; 2nd: aggravated misdemeanor, min. $750 and min. 7 days jail; 3rd: Class D felony, min. $750 and 30 days to 1 yr. jail
KANSAS	8-1008, 1014, 1567	.10% BAC at time of test	Presentence alcohol and drug evaluation conducted by community-based alcohol and drug safety action program, supervision and monitoring of all convicted persons	1st: 30 days or upon completion of required treatment program (whichever is longer); subsequent: 1 yr. or upon completion of required treatment program (whichever is longer)	1st: $200-500 and 48 hrs. to 6 mos. jail or 100 hrs. community service; 2nd: $500-1000 and 90 days to 1 yr. jail; 3rd: $1000-2500 and 90 days to 1 yr. jail

(Continued)

Table 8: Drunk Driving—Continued

State	Code Section	BAC Legal Limit	Rehabilitation Required?	Driver's License Suspension?	Other Penalties
KENTUCKY	189A.010, *et seq.*	No limit per se, "while under the influence of alcohol"	1st offense: 90 day alcohol or substance abuse program can lessen driver suspension from 6 mos. to 30 days	1st: 6 mos.; 2nd: 1 yr.; 3rd: 2 yrs.	1st: $250-500 or 48 hrs. to 30 days jail or 2-30 days community labor; 2nd within 5 yrs.: $350-500 and 7 days to 6 mos. jail and may get 10 days to 6 mos. community labor in addition to jail term; 3rd within 5 yrs.: $500-1000 and 30 days to 12 mos. jail and may get 10 days to 1 yr. community labor in addition to jail term
LOUISIANA	14:98; 32:414	.10% BAC	Rehabilitation provided for 1st and 2nd offense, includes screening procedure to determine portion of program which may be applicable and appropriate for individual offender	1st: 60 days	1st: $125-500 and 10 days to 6 mos. jail; 2nd: $300-500 and 30 days to 6 mos. jail; 3rd: up to $1000 and 1-5 yrs. jail; 4th: hard labor 10-30 yrs.
MAINE	Tit. 29 §1312	.10% BAC	1st: Education program conducted by Dept. of Human Services; 2nd: education program conducted by Dept. of Human Services and where required by Dept. of Human Services, alcohol or rehab program	1st: 30 days or successful completion of educational program, whichever is longer; 2nd: 1 yr. (may be reduced to 6 mos. on successful completion of educational program)	1st: up to $1000 and up to 90 days jail; 2nd: $250-2000 and 24 hrs. to 6 mos. jail
MARYLAND	Transp. 16-205; 16-212; 21-902; 27-101	"While intoxicated or while under the influence of a controlled dangerous substance"	Driver Improvement Program and Alcohol Education Program required	1st: up to 60 days ; 2nd within 3 yrs.: up to 120 days	1st: up to $1000 and/or up to 1 yr. jail; 2nd within 3 yrs.: up to $1000 and/or 48 hrs. to 2 yrs. jail, may also receive min. 80 hrs. community service; 3rd within 3 yrs.: up to $2000 and/or up to 3 yrs. jail

(Continued)

Table 8: Drunk Driving—Continued

State	Code Section	BAC Legal Limit	Rehabilitation Required?	Driver's License Suspension?	Other Penalties
MASSACHUSETTS	Ch. 90 §24	No limit per se	1st offense: appropriate to defendant with his/her consent as a condition of probation upon written finding that appropriate and adequate treatment is available to defendant and defendant would benefit and safety of public would not be endangered; minimum 14 days in residential alcohol treatment program	1st: 1 yr.; 2nd: 2 yrs.; 3rd: 5 yrs.; after 2 yrs. can apply for new license on limited basis on grounds of hardship and present/past violation dealt with and under control	1st: $100-1000 and/or up to 2 yrs. jail; 2nd within 6 yrs.: $300-1000 and 7 days to 2 yrs. jail; 3rd within 6 yrs.: $500-1000 and 60 days to 2 yrs. jail
MICHIGAN	MCL 9.2325	.10% BAC	Screening and assessment to determine the likely benefit from rehabilitation. court may order person to participate and successfully complete one or more rehab programs	1st: 6 mos. to 2 yrs. (can get restricted license); 2nd: revoked; 3rd: revoked	1st: $100-500 and/or up to 90 days jail and costs of prosecution and community service up to 45 days; 2nd within 7 yrs.: $200-1000 and either 10-90 days community service and up to 1 yr. jail or up to 90 days community service and 48 hrs. to 1 yr. jail; 3rd within 10 yrs.: $500-5000 and/or 1-5 yrs. jail
MINNESOTA	169.121, *et seq.*	.10% BAC within 2 hrs. of time of driving	Alcohol problem assessment in counties of more than 10,000 population and report made to court including recommendation as to treatment or rehab program	1st: min. 30 days; 2nd within 5 yrs.: min. 90 days and until court has certified treatment/rehabilitation has been successfully completed; 3rd within 5 yrs.: min. 1 yr. and until rehab completed; 4th within 5 yrs.: min. 2 yrs. and until rehab completed	2nd within 5 yrs.: gross misdemeanor, min. 30 days jail or 8 hrs. community service for each jail day; 3rd within 10 yrs.: gross misdemeanor, min. 30 days jail or 8 hrs. community service for each jail day
MISSISSIPPI	63-11-30	.10% BAC	1st: required alcohol safety education program; subsequent: may participate	1st: 90 days or successful completion of program, whichever is longer; 2nd: 2 yrs. (can be reduced after successful completion of program); 3rd: 5 yrs. (eligible for reinstatement after 3 yrs.); 4th: 5 yrs.	1st: $250-1000 and/or up to 24 hrs. jail; 2nd within 5 yrs.: $600-1000 and 48 hrs. to 1 yr. jail or 10 days to 1 yr. community service; 3rd within 5 yrs.: $800-1000 and 30 days to 1 yr. jail; 4th within 5 yrs.: $2000-5000 and 90 days to 5 yrs. jail

(Continued)

Table 8: Drunk Driving—Continued

State	Code Section	BAC Legal Limit	Rehabilitation Required?	Driver's License Suspension?	Other Penalties
MISSOURI	577.012, 049	.10% BAC	1st: Court may order participation and successful completion of alcohol or drug-related traffic offender education or rehab program which meets standards established by Dept. of Public Safety and Dept. of Mental Health	Upon failure to submit to breath test	1st: Class C misdemeanor, $50 min. and/or up to 3 mos. jail; 2nd within 3 yrs.: Class A misdemeanor, 7 days to 6 mos. jail; 3rd within 3 yrs.: Class D felony, 45 days to 1 yr. jail
MONTANA	61-5-200, 205; 61-8-406, 722	.10% BAC	Defendant shall complete alcohol information course at alcohol treatment program approved by Dept. of Corrections & Human Services which may include alcohol or drug treatment or both if considered necessary by counselor conducting program	Up to 1 yr. per offense	1st: $100-500 and up to 10 days jail; 2nd: $300-500 and 48 hrs. to 30 days jail; 3rd: $500-1000 and 48 hrs. to 6 mos. jail
NEBRASKA	28-106; 39-669.07, *et seq.*	.10% BAC	None	1st: 6 mos (if judge orders suspension of sentence or probation, 60 days from time of order); 2nd within 10 yrs.: 1 yr. (if judge orders suspension of sentence or probation, 6 mos. from time of order); 3rd within 10 yrs.: 15 yrs. (if judge orders suspension of sentence or probation, 1 yr. from time of order)	1st: $200-500 and 7-30 days jail; 2nd: $500 and 30 days jail; 3rd: $500 and 3-6 mos. jail

(Continued)

Table 8: Drunk Driving—Continued

State	Code Section	BAC Legal Limit	Rehabilitation Required?	Driver's License Suspension?	Other Penalties
NEVADA	484.379, *et seq.*	.10% BAC	1st or 2nd within 7 yrs.: may apply to undergo program of treatment for alcoholism or drug abuse for at least one yr. if classified by physician/counselor as alcoholic or drug abuser; if defendant pays costs and has served jail sentence; 1st: must do educational course on alcohol and substance abuse		1st: $200-1000 and 2 days to 6 mos. jail or 48 hrs. community service (jail sentence can be lessened if defendant participates in rehab program); 2nd within 7 yrs.: $500-1000 and 10 days to 6 mos. jail; 3rd within 7 yrs.: $2000-5000 and 1-6 yrs. jail; in addition to any penalty, civil penalty of $35 paid to court
NEW HAMPSHIRE	263:65-a; 265.82	.10% BAC	Yes, Impaired Driver Intervention Program; must successfully complete to get license back; must be approved by director of Office of Alcohol and Drug Abuse Prevention and commissioner	1st: 60 days to 2 yrs.; 2nd: 3 yrs.; 3rd: Indefinite, min. 3 yrs.	1st: up to $1000; 2nd within 7 yrs.: up to $1000 and 7 days to 6 mos. jail; 3rd within 7 yrs.: up to $1000 and 7 days to 6 mos. jail
NEW JERSEY	39:4-50	.10% BAC	Screening evaluation referral program and fee requirements of Div. of Alcoholism's Intoxicated Driving Programs Unit and 12-48 hrs. in two consecutive days in Intoxicated Driver Resource Center and a program of alcohol education and highway safety as proscribed by director of Div. of Motot Vehicles	6 mos. to 1 yr.; 2nd: 2 yrs.; 3rd: 10 yrs.	1st: $250-400 and up to 30 days jail; 2nd within 10 yrs.: $500-1000, 30 days community service, and 48 hrs. to 90 days jail; 3rd within 10 yrs.: $1000 and min. 180 days jail; up to 90 days of jail can be exchanged for community service

(Continued)

Table 8: Drunk Driving—Continued

State	Code Section	BAC Legal Limit	Rehabilitation Required?	Driver's License Suspension?	Other Penalties
NEW MEXICO	66-5-29; 66-8-102	.10% BAC	May be required by court to enroll in screening program to determine level of abuse and recommendation of treatment, if necessary; must complete any recommended treatment program required by court; 1st offense: can attend driver rehab program as a deferred sentence	1 yr. (on 1st offense suspension can be avoided by attending driver rehab program)	1st: $300-500 and/or 30-90 days jail; 2nd within 5 yrs.: up to $1000 and/or 90 days to 1 yr. jail; 3rd or more within 5 yrs.: up to $1000 and min. 6 mos. jail
NEW YORK	VEH. & TRAF. 1192(2)	.10% BAC	Court may require attendance at single session of "victims impact program"	1st: 6 mos.; 2nd within 10 yrs.: 1 yr.	1st: $350-500 and/or up to 1 yr. jail; 2nd: $500-5000 and/or min. 1 yr. jail, Class E felony
NORTH CAROLINA	20-138.1, 179	.10% BAC at time of test	Assessment may be required for alcoholism and substance abuse and appropriate treatment if necessary	1st: 1 yr.; 2nd within 3 yrs.: 4 yrs. (conditionally restored after 2 yrs.); 3rd with most recent within 5 yrs.: permanent (conditionally restored after 3 yrs.)	1st: up to $1000 and 7 days to 12 mos. jail; subsequent within 7 yrs.: $2000 and 14 days to 24 mos. jail
NORTH DAKOTA	39-06-31; 39-08-01	.10% BAC at time of test given within 2 hrs. of driving	Order for addiction evaluation by appropriate licensed addiction treatment program with appropriate treatment if necessary	1 yr. or period as recommended by trial court	1st: Class B misdemeanor, min. $250; 2nd within 5 yrs.: Class B misdemeanor, min. $500 and min. 4 days jail or 10 days community service; 3rd within 5 yrs.: Class A misdemeanor, $1000 and min. 60 days jail; 4th within 7 yrs.: Class A misdemeanor, $1000 and 180 days jail
OHIO	3793.10; 4507.16; 4511.19	.10% BAC	1st: Driver's Intervention Program (in suspended jail sentence); rehab may be required in sentences	1st: 60 days to 3 yrs.; 2nd within 5 yrs.: 120 days to 5 yrs.; 3rd within 5 yrs.: 180 days to 10 yrs.	1st: $150-1000 and 3 days to 6 mos. jail; 2nd within 5 yrs.: $150-1000, 10 days to 6 mos. jail; 3rd within 5 yrs.: $150-1000 and 30 days to 1 yr. jail
OKLAHOMA	Tit. 47 §§6-205.1, 11-902	.10% BAC at time of test	Dept. of Mental Health Treatment Program may be required upon evaluation	1st: 90 days; 2nd within 5 yrs.: 1 yr.; 3rd within 5 yrs.: 3 yrs.	Up to $1000 and 10 days to 1 yr. jail; subsequent within 10 yrs.: up to $2500 and 1-5 yrs. jail

(Continued)

Table 8: Drunk Driving—Continued

State	Code Section	BAC Legal Limit	Rehabilitation Required?	Driver's License Suspension?	Other Penalties
OREGON	161.615, *et seq.*; 813.010, *et seq.*	.08% BAC	Mandatory complete exam by court approved agency/ organization to determine whether individual has a problem condition involving alcohol or controlled substances; complete a treatment program if exam shows it necessary; if none necessary, then complete alcohol and drug information program.	1st: 1 yr.; 2nd within 5 yrs.: 3 yrs.; 3rd within 5 yrs.: 3 yrs.	1st: Class A misdemeanor, up to $2500, up to 1 yr. jail, fees for programs; 2nd: impound vehicle in addition to above
PENNSYLVANIA	Tit. 75 1548; 1532; 3731	.10% BAC	2nd or subsequent offense within 5 yrs.: evaluation to determine if person needs or would benefit from treatment for alcohol or drug abuse; may order treatment if necessary	12 mos.	1st.: min. $300 and min. 48 hr. jail
RHODE ISLAND	27-21	.10% BAC	1st: attendance required at special course on DWI or under the influence of controlled substance and/or alcoholic or drug treatment for individual; 2nd: drug and alcohol treatment	1st: 3-6 mos.; 2nd: 1-2 yrs.	1st: $100-300 and 10-60 hrs. community service and/or up to 1 yr. jail; 2nd within 5 yrs.: $400 and 10 days to 1 yr. jail; 3rd: in addition to 2nd offense penalties, may have car seized and sold by State of Rhode Island and proceeds going to general fund; in addition anyone convicted under this section pays highway assessment fine of $500
SOUTH CAROLINA	56-5-2930, *et seq.*	"Under influence of intoxicating liquors"	Successful completion of Alcohol and Drug Safety Action Program certified by South Carolina Commission on Alcohol and Drug Abuse prior to reinstatement of license	1st: 6 mos.; 2nd within 10 yrs.: 1 yr.; 3rd within 10 yrs.: 2 yrs.; 4th within 10 yrs.: 3 yrs.; 5th within 10 yrs.: permanent	1st: $200 and 48 hrs. to 30 days jail or 48 hrs. public service; 2nd within 10 yrs.: $2000-5000 and 48 hrs. to 1 yr. jail or min. 10 days public service; 3rd within 10 yrs.: $3500-6000 and 60 days to 3 yrs. jail; 4th within 10 yrs.: 1-5 yrs. jail

(Continued)

Table 8: Drunk Driving—Continued

State	Code Section	BAC Legal Limit	Rehabilitation Required?	Driver's License Suspension?	Other Penalties
SOUTH DAKOTA	32-23-1, *et seq.*	.10% BAC	1st: required if .17% BAC; court-ordered evaluation	1st: min. 30 days to 1 yr.; 2nd: min. 1 yr.; 3rd: min. 1 yr. (unconditional); 4th: min. 2 yrs.	1st: $1000 and/or 1 yr. jail; 2nd within 5 yrs.: $1000 and/or 1 yr. jail; 3rd within 5 yrs.: $2000 and/or 2 yrs. jail; 4th: Class 5 felony, 5 yrs. jail and may impose fine of $5000
TENNESSEE	55-10-401, 403	"Under the influence"	2nd offense: may be required to participate in court-approved inpatient alcohol and drug treatment program	1st: 1 yr.; 2nd: 2 yrs.; 3rd: 3-10 yrs.	1st: $250-1000 and 48 hrs. to 11 mos. 29 days jail; 2nd within 10 yrs.: $500-2500 and 45 days to 11 mos. 29 days jail; 3rd: $1000-5000 and 120 days to 11 mos. 29 days jail
TEXAS	Tex. Rev. Civ. Stat. Art. 67011-1	.10% BAC	Evaluation	1st: 90-365 days; 2nd or 3rd: 180 days to 2 yrs.	1st: $100-2000 and 72 hrs. to 2 yrs. jail; 2nd: $300-2000 and 15 days to 2 yrs. jail; 3rd: $500-2000 and 30 days to 2 yrs. jail or 60 days to 5 yrs. state penitentiary
UTAH	41-6-44	.08% BAC	1st: assessment and educational series at a licensed alcohol rehab facility; 2nd: same as above and treatment at court's discretion; 3rd: same as above and treatment at alcohol rehab facility is mandatory; 4th: treatment required	1st: 90 days; subsequent within 6 yrs. of prior conviction: 1 yr.	1st: Class B misdemeanor, up to $1000 and 48-240 hrs. jail or 24-50 hrs. community service; 2nd within 6 yrs.: up to $1000 and 240-720 hrs. jail or 80-240 hrs. community service; 3rd within 6 yrs.: 720-2160 hrs. jail or 240-720 hrs. community service; if prior two convictions were both after 4/23/90, then: $1000-2500 and 240-2160 hrs. jail or 240-720 hrs. community service; 4th within 6 yrs.; if all after 4/23/90, $1000-5000 and 720-2160 hrs. jail or 240-720 hrs. community service
VERMONT	1201, *et seq.*	.08% BAC	1st: alcohol assessment screening-therapy program or driver rehab if necessary at court's discretion; 2nd completion of therapy program at court's discretion	1st: 90 days; 2nd: 18 months; 3rd: 3 yrs.; 4th: life	1st: max. $750 and/or up to 2 yrs. jail; 2nd: up to $1500 and/or 48 hrs. to 2 yrs. jail; 3rd: up to $2500 and/or up to 5 yrs. jail

(Continued)

Table 8: Drunk Driving—Continued

State	Code Section	BAC Legal Limit	Rehabilitation Required?	Driver's License Suspension?	Other Penalties
VIRGINIA	18.2-266(i), *et seq.*	.10% BAC	Alcohol Safety Action Program for 1st or 2nd offense at court's discretion	1st: 1 yr.; 2nd within 10 yrs.: 3 yrs.; 3rd within 10 yrs.: 3 yrs.	2nd within 10 yrs.: $200-2500 and 1 mo. to 1 yr. jail; 3rd: $500-2500 and 2 mos. to 1 yr. jail
WASHINGTON	46.61.502 (1), 515	.10% BAC	1st: alcohol information course or more intensive treatment program as determined by court; 2nd: diagnostic evaluation by alcoholism agency approved by Dept. of Social & Health Services	1st: 90 days; 2nd within 5 yrs.: 1 yr.; 3rd within 5 yrs.: 2 yrs.	1st: $250-1000 and 24 hrs. to 1 yr. jail; 2nd within 5 yrs.: $500-2000 and 7 days to 1 yr. jail
WEST VIRGINIA	17C-5-2	.10% BAC	Motor Vehicle Alcohol Test and lock program upon revocation of license	1st: min. 6 mos.; 2nd: 10 yrs.; 3rd: life	1st: $100-500 and 1 day to 6 mos. jail; 2nd: $1000-3000 and/or 6 mos. to 1 yr. jail; 3rd: $3000-5000 and/or 1-3 yrs. jail
WISCONSIN	343.30; 346.63	.10% BAC	Not mentioned	1st: 6-9 mos.; 2nd within 5 yrs.: 1 yr. to 18 mos.; 3rd or more within 5 yrs.: 2-3 yrs.	1st: $150-300; 2nd within 5 yrs.: $300-1000 and 5 days to 6 mos. jail; 3rd within 5 yrs.: $600-2000 and 30 days to 1 yr. jail; 4th within 5 yrs.: $600-2000 and 60 days to 1 yr. jail; 5th within 5 yrs.: $600-2000 and 6 mos. to 1 yr. jail
WYOMING	31-5-233; 31-7-127	.10% BAC	No	3rd conviction within 5 yrs.: 3 yrs.	1st: up to $750 and/or up to 6 mos. jail; 2nd within 5 yrs.: $200-750 and 7 days to 6 mos. jail

9. GUN CONTROL

The state laws controlling the purchase of firearms are varied and constantly changing. The laws reviewed here are current as of January 1, 1993, but there is a great amount of legislation pending before state governments designed primarily to make the legal purchase of guns more difficult. Each state has some form of restriction on the buying of guns, though rural states tend to be less restrictive in controlling guns than highly urban states due to the greater numbers of hunters and sportsmen in their populations. Nonetheless, in most states convicted felons and minors cannot purchase guns; in some, aliens and individuals with mental disabilities cannot. Machine guns, automatic weapons, sawed-off shotguns, and guns with silencers are banned in many.

One of the more controversial restrictions applied to the purchase of guns is a waiting period, in which a certain amount of time must pass between the time an individual applies for a gun license and purchases that gun. With the rise in gun-related crimes, a number of states already have instituted waiting periods to discourage rash actions.

Table 9: Gun Control

State	Code Section	Illegal Arms	Waiting Period	Who May Not Own
ALABAMA	13A-11-63, *et seq.*	Short-barreled rifle or shotgun	Delivery 48 hrs. from time of application	1. Convicted of committing or attempting to commit crime of violence; 2. Drug addicts or habitual drunkard; shall not deliver to: a minor or an unsound minor; 3. Reasonable belief applicant has been convicted of crime; 4. Drug addict/habitual drunkard
ALASKA	11.61.200	Firearm capable of shooting one or more shots automatically without manual reloading, by a single function of trigger; rifle with barrel less than 16 inches; shotgun with barrel less than 18 inches or firearm made from a rifle or shotgun which has an overall length of less than 26 inches; possession, sale, transfer, or manufacture of above firearms is illegal	None	Convicted felon
ARIZONA	13-3101, 3102	Automatic weapons, rifle with barrel less than 16 inches or shotgun barrel less than 18 inches, or any firearm made from rifle/shotgun which as modified has overall length of less than 26 inches	None	1. Anyone found to constitute a danger to himself or others pursuant to court order and whose court-ordered treatment has not been terminated by court order; 2. Convicted felon involving violence or possession and use of deadly weapon or dangerous instrument and whose civil rights have not been restored; 3. Imprisoned or in correctional/detention facility
ARKANSAS	5-73-103, 104	Machine gun, sawed-off shotgun, firearm specially made or adapted for silent discharge	None	1. Convicted felon; 2. Adjudicated a mental defective; 3. Committed involuntarily to any mental institution
CALIFORNIA	Penal §§12020, 12021, 12071, 12072	Cane gun; wallet gun; plastic firearm; any firearm not immediately recognized as such; short-barreled shotgun or rifle; zip gun	15 days generally	1. Concealed weapons; under 21 yrs.; other firearms, under 18 yrs.; 2. Convicted felon; 3. Addicted to use of any narcotic drug; 4. Anyone whose express condition of probation is not to own firearm; 5. Persons convicted of certain misdemeanors

(Continued)

Table 9: Gun Control—Continued

State	Code Section	Illegal Arms	Waiting Period	Who May Not Own
COLORADO	18-12-102, *et seq.*	"Dangerous weapons": firearm silencer, machine gun, short rifle/shotgun	None	Previous conviction of burglary, arson, felony involving use of force or violence or use of deadly weapon, or attempt or conspiracy to commit such offenses, within the 10 yrs. next preceding or within 10 yrs. of his release or escape from incarceration, whichever is greater
CONNECTICUT	29-33, 34; 53a-211, *et seq.*	Sawed-off shotgun with barrel less than 18 inches or overall length of less than 26 inches; silencer	2 weeks from mailing of written application	1. Minors (pistol/revolver); 2. Conviction of capital, Class A felony (Class B and C also but with exceptions)
DELAWARE	Title 11	Destructive weapons: firearm silencer, sawed-off shotgun, machine gun or any other firearm which is adaptable for use as a machine gun	None	1. Convicted of felony or crime involving bodily injury to another, or having in his possession any weapon during commission of such crime; 2. Anyone ever committed for mental disorder to hospital mental institution; 3. Convicted of unlawful use, possession, or sale of narcotic or dangerous drug
DISTRICT OF COLUMBIA	22-3203, 3214	Machine gun, sawed-off shotgun, or weapon/instrument of kind commonly known as a blackjack, slingshot, sand club; silencers	None	Pistols: 1. Drug addict; 2. Convicted felon; 3. Convicted of soliciting prostitution, keeping bawdy or disorderly house; 4. Vagrants
FLORIDA	790	Short-barreled rifle or shotgun, machine gun	3 days	1. Minors; 2. Convicted felon (doesn't apply if civil rights have been restored)
GEORGIA	16-11-121, *et seq.*	Sawed-off shotgun or rifle; machine gun; dangerous weapon ("rocket launcher," "bazooka" or "recoilless rifle," "mortar," "hand grenade") or silencer	None	Convicted felon

(Continued)

Table 9: Gun Control—Continued

State	Code Section	Illegal Arms	Waiting Period	Who May Not Own
HAWAII	134-2, 7, 8	Automatic firearms; rifles with barrel length less than 16 inches; shotguns with barrels less than 18 inches; cannons; mufflers/silencers; hand grenades	10 days generally	1. Fugitive from justice; 2. Under indictment or convicted of felony or crime of violence or illegal sale of drug; 3. Under treatment for addiction to dangerous, harmful, or detrimental drug; or intoxicating liquor; 4. Under treatment for significant behavioral, emotional, or mental disorder; 5. Anyone under 25 yrs. and has been adjudicated by family court to have committed a felony, two or more crimes of violence or illegal sale of drugs; 6. Minors who are under treatment for addiction to drugs/alcohol, fugitives from justice or determined not to be responsible for a criminal act or who has been committed to an institution on account of mental disease/defect/disorder
IDAHO	18-3316		None	Convicted felon
ILLINOIS	720 ILCS 5/24-1, 5/24-3, 5/24-3.1	Machine gun; rifle with barrel less than 16 inches; shotgun with barrel less than 18 inches or any weapon made from rifle or shotgun and as modified has overall length less than 26 inches	72 hrs.	1. Concealed weapon: under 18 yrs.; 2. Under 21 yrs. if convicted of misdemeanor other than traffic offense or adjudged delinquent; 3. Narcotic addict; 4. Patient in mental hospital within past 5 yrs.; 5. Mentally retarded
INDIANA	35-47-1-7; 35-47-2-7, 8; 35-47-5-4.1, 8	Machine gun; sawed-off shotgun	7 days	1. Convicted felon; 2. Drug abuser; 3. Alcohol abuser; 4. Unsound mind
IOWA	724.1, *et seq.*	Offensive weapons: machine guns, short-barreled rifle or shotgun; any weapon other than shotgun or muzzle-loading rifle, cannon, pistol, revolver, or musket, which fires or can be made to fire a projectile by the explosion of a propellant charge	None	Convicted felon
KANSAS	21-4201, *et seq.*	Shotgun with barrel less than 18 inches; automatic weapons; cartridges which can be fired by handgun and have plastic-coated bullets with core of less than 60% lead by weight	Certain cities and counties have waiting period but not state-wide	1. Both addicted to and an unlawful user of a controlled substance; 2. Firearm with barrel less than 12 inches by anyone convicted of felony within past 5 yrs.; 3. Any firearm if convicted of felony within past 10 yrs.
KENTUCKY	527.010, *et seq.*	None listed	None	Convicted felon not granted full pardon/relief
LOUISIANA	14:95.1; 40:1751, *et seq.*	Machine guns	None	Convicted of certain felonies (murder, manslaughter, aggravated battery, etc.)

(Continued)

Table 9: Gun Control—Continued

State	Code Section	Illegal Arms	Waiting Period	Who May Not Own
MAINE	Tit. 15§393; Tit. 17A §§1051, *et seq.*	Machine gun; metal piercing ammunition	None	Convicted felons
MARYLAND	Article 27 Md. Ann. Code Art. 27 §§36B, *et seq.*, 291A, *et seq.*, 442, *et seq.*, 481A, *et seq.* (1957)	Short-barreled rifle or shotgun	7 days	1. Fugitive from justice; 2. Convicted of crime of violence; 3. Habitual drunkard; 4. Addict/ habitual user of narcotics/ amphetamines/barbiturates; 5. If spent more than 30 consecutive days in mental institution for treatment; 6. Under 21 yrs.
MASSACHUSETTS	Ch. 269 §§10, *et seq.*; Ch. 140 §§131, *et seq.*	Machine guns, etc. legal in appropriate circumstances (i.e., place of business, home, etc.)	None	1. Alien; 2. Convicted felon; 3. Convicted of unlawful use, possession, or sale of drugs; 4. Under 18 yrs.
MICHIGAN	MCL 750.223, 28.422, 28.92	Machine gun; automatic weapons; silencers; short-barreled rifle/shotgun	None	1. Under 18 yrs.; 2. Committed felony within previous 8 years; 3. Insane and not restored to sanity by court order
MINNESOTA	609.66, 67; 624.713; 624.7132	Silencer; machine gun; short-barreled shotgun	7 days	1. Minor under 18: Pistol, except under supervision of parent/ guardian, military instruction, firing range, successful completion of training course; 2. Convicted of crime of violence unless 10 yrs. has elapsed or civil rights have been restored; 3. Mentally ill; 4. Convicted for unlawful use, possession, sale of controlled substance other than small amount of marijuana or person who's been hospitalized or committed for treatment for habitual use of controlled substance or marijuana unless proof that they haven't abused in 2 yrs.; 5. Chemically dependent; 6. Peace officer who is informally admitted to treatment facility for chemical dependency unless he receives certificate for discharge.
MISSISSIPPI	97-37-1, *et seq.*	Carrying machine gun, short-barreled rifle/shotgun is illegal; silencer	None	1. Students on campus or within 2 miles of it; 2. Minors under 16; 3. Convicted felons
MISSOURI	571.020, *et seq.*	Machine gun; short-barreled rifle/ shotgun; silencer; gas gun	None	Concealable weapon: 1. Convicted of dangerous felony; 2. Fugitive from justice, habitually intoxicated or drugged condition, or mentally incompetent

(Continued)

Table 9: Gun Control—Continued

State	Code Section	Illegal Arms	Waiting Period	Who May Not Own
MONTANA	45-8-303, *et seq.*	Sawed-off rifle or shotgun; machine guns except on own property	None	County/city/town has discretion to disallow following from owning firearms: 1. Convicted felon; 2. Adjudicated mental incompetents; 3. Illegal aliens; 4. Minors
NEBRASKA	28-1201, *et seq.*	Machine gun; short rifle or short shotgun	None	1. Under 18: revolver, pistol, or any short-barreled hand firearm; 2. Convicted felon/fugitive from justice: barrel less than 18 inches
NEVADA	202.273, *et seq.*	Metal penetrating bullets; short-barreled rifle or shotgun; machine gun or silencer	Certain cities and counties may impose waiting period	1. Minor under 14 unless supervised; 2. Ex-felon unless pardoned or civil rights restored
NEW HAMPSHIRE	159:1, *et seq.*	None listed	None	1. Career criminals; 2. Convicted felons
NEW JERSEY	2C:39-1, *et seq.*; 2C:58-1, *et seq.*	Sawed-off shotgun, silencer	7 days	1. Convicted of aggravated assault, arson, burglary, escape, extortion, homicide, kidnapping, robbery, aggravated sexual assault, or sexual assault; 2. Committed for mental disorder unless satisfactory proof he no longer suffers from a disorder which interferes or handicaps him in handling a firearm; 3. Convicted of unlawful use, possession, or sale of controlled dangerous substance
NEW MEXICO	30-7-16		None	Convicted felon
NEW YORK	Penal §§265, *et seq.*	Machine gun, silencer	None	1. Convicted felon; 2. Alien; 3. Minor under 16: possession of air gun, spring gun, weapon where loaded or blank cartridges can be used
NORTH CAROLINA	14-409, *et seq.*	Machine gun, submachine gun, or other like weapons	None	Convicted felon cannot own handgun or gun with barrel less than 18 inches or overall length less than 26 inches or any weapon of mass death and destruction within 5 yrs. of conviction or termination of sentence, whichever is later

(Continued)

Table 9: Gun Control—Continued

State	Code Section	Illegal Arms	Waiting Period	Who May Not Own
NORTH DAKOTA	62.1-02-01, *et seq.*	Machine gun; fully automatic rifle; silencer; federally licensed firearm or dangerous weapon; short-barreled rifle or shotgun	None	1. Convicted of felony involving violence or intimidation from date of conviction or release from incarceration for 10 yrs. (whichever is later); 2. Convicted of other felonies not mentioned above or Class A misdemeanors for 5 yrs.; 3. Diagnosed and confined/committed to hospital or other institution as mentally ill or mentally deficient person; does not apply if more than 3 yrs. have passed; 4. Under 18 unless supervised and for purposes of safety training, hunting, target shooting
OHIO	2923.11, *et seq.*	Sawed-off automatic firearm; zip gun; firearm manufactured and designed for military purposes; silencer	Certain cities and counties may impose waiting period	1. Fugitive from justice; 2. Under indictment or convicted of felony of violence or adjudged juvenile delinquent for commission of such felony; 3. Under indictment or convicted of illegal possession, use, sale of drugs; 4. Drug dependent or chronic alcoholic; 5. Mentally incompetent
OKLAHOMA	Tit. 21 §§1273, *et seq.*	Sawed-off shotgun or rifle	None	1. Cannot sell to minors; 2. Convicted felon; 3. Mentally incompetent or insane
OREGON	166.250, *et seq.*	Machine gun; short-barreled rifle/ shotgun; silencer	15 days	1. Under 18 yrs.; 2. Convicted felon; 3. Committed to Mental Health and Developmental Disability Services Division within 4 years prior to 1/1/90 or mentally ill
PENNSYLVANIA	Tit. 18 §§908, 6105, 6110, 6111	Machine gun; sawed-off shotgun; firearm specially made or adopted for concealment or silent discharge	48 hrs.	1. Former convict of crime of violence; 2. No delivery to persons under 18 yrs.; reason to believe convicted of crime of violence; drug addict; habitual drunkard; unsound mind
RHODE ISLAND	11-47-2, *et seq.*	Sawed-off shotgun or rifle; machine gun; silencer	7 days	1. Aliens (less than 10 yrs.); 2. Mentally incompetent under treatment/confinement; 3. Drug addict adjudicated or in treatment; 4. Habitual drunkard adjudicated or in treatment

(Continued)

Table 9: Gun Control—Continued

State	Code Section	Illegal Arms	Waiting Period	Who May Not Own
SOUTH CAROLINA	16-23-30, 230	Machine gun; sawed-off shotgun/rifle	None	1. Convicted of crime of violence; 2.: Member of subversive organization; 3. Under 21 with military exception; 4. Anyone court has adjudged to be unfit to possess pistol
SOUTH DAKOTA	22-1-2; 22-14-6, 16; 23-7-9	Controlled weapon silencer; machine gun; short shotgun	48 hrs.	Convicted of crime of violence
TENNESSEE	39-17-1301, *et seq.*	Machine gun; short-barreled rifle or shotgun; silencer	15 days	1. Convicted of crime of violence; 2. Fugitives from justice; 3. Unsound mind; 4. Minors; 5. Addicted to alcohol; 6. Drug addict; 7. Convicted of illegal sale of alcoholic beverages
TEXAS	Penal §§46.05, *et seq.*	Machine gun; short-barreled firearm; silencer	None	1. Convicted felon of crime involving violence or threatened violence; 2. Sale, rental, lease, or gift to minor under 18
UTAH	76-10-501, *et seq.*	None listed	None	1. Convicted of crime of violence; 2. Addicted to use of narcotic drugs; 3. Mentally incompetent
VERMONT	Tit. 13 §§4001, *et seq.*	Silencer; "zip" gun	None	
VIRGINIA	18.2-290, *et seq.*	Sawed-off shotgun/rifle; plastic firearms; machine gun	Certain cities/counties may impose waiting period	1. Convicted felons; 2. Minors: handguns
WASHINGTON	9.41.040, *et seq.*	Machine gun	5 days	1. Aliens; 2. Convicted of crime of violence or felony which firearm was used or displayed: short firearm/pistol; delivery not permitted to: minors under 21, drug addict, unsound mind, habitual drunkard
WEST VIRGINIA	61-7-7, 9	Machine gun; submachine gun or other fully automatic weapon	None	1. Convicted of felony; 2. Discharged from armed forces (U.S.) less than honorably; 3. Mentally incompetent; 4. Alien; 5. Addicted to drugs/alcohol or unlawful user
WISCONSIN	175.35; 941.26, *et seq.*	Machine gun or other fully-automatic weapon; short-barreled rifle/shotgun; silencer	48 hrs.	1. Convicted of felony in this state or what would have been a felony if committed in this state; 2. Mental disease or defect reason for not guilty

(Continued)

Table 9: Gun Control—Continued

State	Code Section	Illegal Arms	Waiting Period	Who May Not Own
WYOMING	6-8-102, *et seq.*	Not listed	None	Convicted of violent felony or attempt to commit violent felony

10. ILLEGAL DRUGS

Although the 1960s and 1970s seemed to hail a new level of legal tolerance toward recreational drug use, the movement became mired in reality in the 1980s when society as a whole grew intolerant of drug use of any kind, largely due to the destructive nature and violent criminal character of the drug trafficking and distribution business.

As a result, what little ground gained toward the legalization of recreational drugs was either lost or frozen, and drug traffickers and dealers now face increasingly stiffer penalties. Notwithstanding the religious use of peyote and the medicinal use of marijuana, virtually no state recognizes legal possession or use of any recreational drug. Alaska is apparently the most liberal state, with no prescribed penalty for the personal use or possession of marijuana. (Many states have made possession of small amounts of marijuana a misdemeanor. But even in most of these states, there are stiff penalties for possession near school grounds—even an offense called "reckless" possession near school grounds.)

Drug laws are among the most complex criminal laws on the books. Often certain offenses are given class designations whereby any number of specific criminal offenses are grouped into various classes. In some states, in order to determine the exact penalty for a particular class of violations, it is necessary to contact a state department or office to get information about the schedules. Punishments, it seems, vary often enough not to put them on the books. Additionally, by placing them under the authority of a state agency, legislators do not need to take the responsibility for setting exact penalties for various crimes. It should be noted, though, that these states are the exception to the rule.

In most cases in the following tables, reference to the code sections give a picture of the potential punishments for the violation of a specific crime. Since the class schedules among illegal drugs overlap and because the penalties are often extremely involved and difficult to summarize, reference is often made only to the class designation. In these cases, however, it is still possible to draw comparisons among states by studying the degrees assigned to the violation. In addition, quick reference to the individual state code listed should provide easy access to more detailed information.

Table 10a: Illegal Drugs: Cocaine

State	Code Section	Possession	Sale	Trafficking
ALABAMA	20-2-1.; 13A-12-210 to 215	Class C felony	28-500 g.: Mandatory 3 yrs. and $50,000; 500 g. to 1 kg.: Mandatory 5 yrs. and $100,000; 1-10 kg.: Mandatory 15 yrs. and $250,000; Over 10 kg.: Mandatory life without parole; Sale to minor: Class A felony; Subsequent offense: Offenses subject to the Habitual Felony Offender Act	Class A felony
ALASKA	11.71.010, *et seq.*; 17.30.010, *et seq.*	Possessing any amount with reckless disregard that possession was within 500 feet of a school or on a school bus: Class B felony; Possessing any amount: Class C felony	Delivering to one under 19 and at least 3 yrs. younger: Class B felony	
ARIZONA	13-3401, *et seq.*; 36-2501, *et seq.*	Class 4 felony, but for one not previously convicted of felony, court can make it Class 1 misdemeanor; Fine of not less than $2000 or 3 times the value of substance, whichever is greater	Class 2 felony; On school property: Class 2 felony; Fine of greater of 3 times value of drugs or $2000	
ARKANSAS	5-64-401, *et seq.*	Class C felony	Class V felony: Depending on amount, prison from 10 to 40 yrs. or life and fines between $25,000 and $250,000; Subsequent offense: Double penalties	1 g. of cocaine in possession creates a rebuttable presumption of intent to deliver
CALIFORNIA	Health & Safety §§11000, *et seq.*	State prison and fine up to $70; if probation granted, there are additional requirements	State prison 2-4 yrs.; Possession for sale of "cocaine base ": state prison 3-5 yrs.; Sale to minors: State prison 3, 5, or 7 yrs.; Sale to school children: 5, 7, or 9 yrs.; Anyone over 18 who sells to a minor or uses a minor in the sale process is punishable in state prison for 3, 6, or 9 yrs.; Sale on many public areas punishable by state prison for 5, 7, or 9 yrs. if seller 5 yrs. older than minor	
COLORADO	12-22-301, *et seq.*; 18-18-101, *et seq.*	Class 3 felony Subsequent Offense: Twice or more within 6 months and amount greater than 28.5 g.: Defendant shall be sentenced to the Dept. of Corrections for at least the minimum and fined no less than $1000 but not over $500,000 with no probation or suspension	Class 3 felony; Sale to minor on public property: Dept. of Corrections for minimum 5 yrs.; Subsequent offense: Class 2 felony	

(Continued)

Table 10a: Illegal Drugs: Cocaine—Continued

State	Code Section	Possession	Sale	Trafficking
CONNECTICUT	21a 240; 243, 278	7 yrs. and $50,000; Subsequent offense: 15 yrs. and $100,000; Third offense: 25 yrs. and $250,000	15 yrs. and $50,000; 1 oz. or more: 5-20 yrs. minimum; maximum by a non-drug dependent person; Subsequent offense: 30 yrs. and $100,000	
DELAWARE	Tit. 16 §4701, *et seq.*	Possession, use, consumption: Class A misdemeanor	Class C felony: $5000-$50,000; If not addicted: Felony, mandatory 6 yrs.; To a minor: Class C felony; if under 16: mandatory 1 yr. prison; On school property: Up to 15 yrs. and $250,000; Subsequent offense: If not addicted: Mandatory 12 yrs.	If on any single occasion one has: 5-50 g.: 3 yrs. minimum and $5000; 50-100 g.: 5 yrs. minimum and $100,000; More than 100 g.: 15 yrs. minimum and $400,000
DISTRICT OF COLUMBIA	33-501, *et seq.*; 33-541	Misdemeanor, 1 yr. and/or $1000	Not over 30 yrs. and/or $500,000, never less than 4 yrs. for first offense; Subsequent offense: 7 yrs.; 10 yrs. for further offenses, if it involves 50 g. or more	
FLORIDA	775.082 to .084; 893.01, *et seq.*	3rd degree felony; possession of 28 g. is trafficking	2nd degree felony	28-200 g.: 3 yrs. and $50,000; 200-400 g.: 5 yrs. and $100,000; Over 400 g.: 15 yrs. and $250,000
GEORGIA	16-13-20, *et seq.*	Over 28 g. is trafficking; possession of any amount is a felony punishable with minimum 2-15 yrs.; Subsequent offense: Minimum 5-30 yrs.	Felony: 10-30 yrs.; Subsequent offense: Mandatory life	28-200 g.: Mandatory 10 yrs. and $200,000; 200-400 g.: Mandatory 15 yrs. and $300,000; Over 400 g.: Mandatory 25 yrs. and $1,000,000
HAWAII	329-1, *et seq.*; 712-1240, *et seq.*	1/8- 1 oz.: Class B felony; 1 oz. or more: Class A felony; Subsequent offense: Class A or B felony based on quantity	Any amount: Class B felony; 1/8 oz. or more, or any amount to a minor: Class A felony	
IDAHO	37-2701, *et seq.*	Felony, up to 7 yrs. and/or $15,000; Subsequent offense: Double penalties; possession of 28 g. or more is trafficking	Felony, up to life and $25,000; Subsequent offense: Double penalties	28-200 g.: Mandatory 3 yrs. and minimum $10,000; 200-400 g.: Mandatory 5 yrs. and minimum $15,000; Over 400 g.: Mandatory 10 yrs. and minimum $25,000; Maximum sentence life; maximum fine $100,000

(Continued)

Table 10a: Illegal Drugs: Cocaine—Continued

State	Code Section	Possession	Sale	Trafficking
ILLINOIS	720 ILCS 570/ 100, *et seq.*; Uniform Controlled Substances Act; 720 ILCS 550/1, *et seq.*	15-100 g.: Class 1 felony, mandatory 4-15 yrs.; 100-400 g.: Mandatory 6-30 yrs.; 400-900 g.: Mandatory 8-40 yrs.; Over 900 g.: Mandatory 10-50 yrs.; Fines for any offense involving 100 g. or more: Greater of $200,000 or street value	Under 10 g.: Class 2 felony, $200,000; 15-100 g.: 6-30 yrs.; 100-400 g.: 9-40 yrs.; 400-900 g.: 12-50 yrs.; Over 900 g.: 15-60 yrs.; Sale to minors: Double penalties	
INDIANA	35-48-1-2; 35-48-4-1, *et seq.*	Possession of any amount: At least Class D felony Under 3 g. but within 1000 feet of school property: Class B felony; Over 3 g.: Class C felony Possession of 3 g. or more within 1000 feet of school property: Class A felony	Class B felony unless amount is over 3 grams or delivery to minor 3 yrs. younger or delivery on/in school property or within 1000 feet of property or on school bus, then Class A felony	
IOWA	204.101, 206, 401		500 g. or less: Class C felony, $1000 to $50,000 500g. to 5 kg.: Class B felony, $5000 to $100,000 Over 5 kg.: Class B felony, up to 50 yrs. and $1,000,000 Subsequent offense: Triple penalties	
KANSAS	65-4101, *et seq.*	Class C felony; Subsequent offense: Class B felony; Third offense: Class A felony and life in prison	Class C felony; Subsequent offense: Class B felony; Third offense: Class A felony and life in prison	
KENTUCKY	218A.010, *et seq.*	1-5 yrs. and $3000-5000; Subsequent offense: 5-10 yrs. or $5000 to $10,000 or both	5-10 yrs. and/or $5000 to $10,000; Subsequent offense: 10-20 yrs. and/or $10,000 to $20,000	First offense: 5-10 yrs. and $5000 to $10,000; Subsequent offense: 10-20 yrs. or $10,000 to $20,000 or both
LOUISIANA	§§40:961, *et seq.*	Under 28 g.: 5 yrs. with or without hard labor and $5,000; 28-200 g.: 5-30 yrs. hard labor and $50,000 to $150,000; 200-400 g.: 10-30 yrs. hard labor and $100,000 to $350,000; Over 400 g.: 15-30 yrs. hard labor and $250,000 to $600,000; Subsequent offense: Double penalties	5-30 yrs. hard labor and/or up to $15,000; Subsequent offense: Double penalties	

(Continued)

Table 10a: Illegal Drugs: Cocaine—Continued

State	Code Section	Possession	Sale	Trafficking
MAINE	Tit. 17A §§1101, *et seq.*	Class D crime; Over 14 g.: Class B crime and creates presumption of trafficking	Class C crime; 1 g. or more creates presumption of furnishing	Possession of 14 g. or more is trafficking
MARYLAND	Art. 27 §§276, *et seq.*	Misdemeanor with penalty of up to 4 yrs. and/or $25,000; Bringing 28 g. into state: Felony with penalty of up to $50,000 and/or 25 yrs.; Subsequent offense: Double penalties	Felony with penalty of 20 yrs. and/or $25,000; Sale of more than 448 g.: Mandatory 5 yrs. without suspension; Subsequent offense: Double penalties; 2 yrs. mandatory	Any conviction under §286
MASSACHUSETTS	Ch. 94c §§1, *et seq.*	1 yr. and/or $1,000 Subsequent offense: 2 yrs. and/or $2000	1-10 yrs. and/or $1000 to $10,000; Subsequent offense: 5-15 yrs. and/or $2500 to $25,000	14-28 g.: 3-15 yrs. and/or $2500 to $25,000; 28-100 g.: 5-20 yrs. and/or $5000 to $50,000; 100-200 g.: 10-20 yrs. and/or $10,000 to $100,000; Over 200 g.: 15-20 yrs. and/or $50,000 to $500,000
MICHIGAN	333.7401, *et seq.*	Under 25 g.: Up to 4 yrs. and/or $25,000; 25-50 g.: 1-4 yrs. and/or up to $25,000 or probation for life; 50-225 g.: 10-20 yrs.; 225-650 g.: 20-30 yrs.; Over 650 g.: Life imprisonment; Subsequent offense: Under 50 g.: Double penalties; Over 50 g.: Life imprisonment	Under 50 g.: 1-20 yrs. and/or $25,000 or probation for life; 50-225 g.: 10-20 yrs.; 225-650 g.: 20-30 yrs.; Over 650 g.: Life imprisonment; Subsequent offense: Under 50 g.: Double penalties; Over 50 g.: Life imprisonment	
MINNESOTA	152.01, *et seq.*	Any possession: 5 yrs. and/or $10,000; 50-500 g.: Up to 25 yrs. and/or $500,000; Over 500 g.: Up to 30 yrs. and/or $1,000,000; Subsequent offense: Depends on level of prior offenses, 4-40 yrs. and/or up to $1,000,000	Any amount: Up to 15 yrs. and/or $100,000; 10-50 g.: Up to 25 yrs. and/or $500,000; Over 50 g.: Up to 30 yrs. and $1,000,000; Subsequent offense: Depends on level of prior offense, 4-40 yrs. and/or up to $1,000,000	
MISSISSIPPI	41-29-101, *et seq.*	Felony: Up to 3 yrs. and/or $1000 to $30,000 Subsequent offense: Double penalty	No specified term up to 30 yrs. and/or $1000 to $1,000,000 Subsequent offense: Double penalty	

(Continued)

Table 10a: Illegal Drugs: Cocaine—Continued

State	Code Section	Possession	Sale	Trafficking
MISSOURI	195.010, *et seq.*	Class C felony Subsequent offense: State penitentiary 5 yrs. to life Third offense: State penitentiary 10 yrs. to life	Class B felony Subsequent offense: 10 yrs. to life	Delivery associated/attempt to deliver: 140-450 g.: Class A felony;More than 450 g.: Class A felony term without parole; Buying/Attempting to buy: 140-450 g.: Class B felony; More than 450 g.: Class A felony
MONTANA	45-9-101, *et seq.*; 50-32-101, *et seq.*	Up to 5 yrs. and/or $50,000; Criminal possession with intent to sell: Up to 20 yrs. and/or $50,000	Two yrs. to life and/or $50,000; Subsequent offense: 10 yrs. to life and/or $50,000; Third offense: Not less than 20 yrs. and/or $50,000	
NEBRASKA	28-401, *et seq.*	Class 4 felony	1-7 oz.: Class 1D felony; Over 7 oz.: Class 1C felony	
NEVADA	453.011; 453.510	1-6 yrs. and $5000; Subsequent offense: 1-10 yrs. and $10,000; Third offense: 1-20 yrs. and $20,000	1-20 yrs. and $20,000 Subsequent offense: 5-20 yrs. and $20,000; Third offense: Life or 15 yrs. mandatory and $20,000	28-200 g.: 3-20 yrs. and $50,000; 200-400 g.: 5-20 yrs. and $100,000
NEW HAMPSHIRE	318-B:1, *et seq.*	Class B felony with fine up to $25,000; Subsequent offense: Class A felony with fine up to $50,000	Class A felony; Under .5 oz.: Up to 7 yrs. and/or $100,000; .5 to 5 oz.: Up to 20 yrs. and/or $300,000; 5 oz. and over: Up to 30 yrs. and/or $500,000; Subsequent offense: Under .5 oz.: Up to 15 yrs. and/or $200,000; .5 to 5 oz.: Up to 40 yrs. and/or $500,000; 5 oz. and over: Maximum life and/or $500,000	
NEW JERSEY	24:21-1, *et seq.*; 2C:35-5, *et seq.*	Crime of 3rd degree, $25,000	.5 oz. or less: Crime of 3rd degree, $50,000; .5 oz. to 5 oz.: Crime of 2nd degree; Over 5 oz.: Crime of 1st degree, fixed prison term and $300,000; Selling within 1000 feet of school: Fixed prison term and up to $100,000; Selling to minor or pregnant female: Double penalties	

(Continued)

Table 10a: Illegal Drugs: Cocaine—Continued

State	Code Section	Possession	Sale	Trafficking
NEW MEXICO	30-31-1, *et seq.*	Misdemeanor, up to 1 yr. and $500 to $1000	Second degree felony; Subsequent offense: First degree felony	
NEW YORK	Penal §§220, *et seq.*;	Knowingly possessing: Any amount: Class A misdemeanor; Over 500 mg.: Class D felony; Over ⅛ oz.: Class C felony; Over ½ oz.: Class B felony; Over 2 oz.: Class A-II felony; Over 4 oz.: class A-I felony; Any amount with intent to sell: Class D felony; Any amount of narcotic drug with intent to sell: Class B felony	Class D felony in general, then Over 1/2 oz.: Class A-II felony; Over 2 oz.: Class A-I felony	
NORTH CAROLINA	90-86, *et seq.*	Class I felony	Class H felony	28-200 g.: Class G felony, 7 yrs. and $50,000; 200-400 g.: Class F felony, 14 yrs. and $100,000; 400 g. and over: Class D felony, 35 yrs. and $250,000
NORTH DAKOTA	19-03.1-01, *et seq.*	Class C felony	Class A felony	
OHIO	2925.01, *et seq.*; 3719.01, *et seq.*	4th degree felony; Subsequent offense: 3rd degree felony	Under 10 g.: 3rd degree felony; 10-30 g.: 2nd degree felony, 3 yrs. mandatory; Over 30 g.: 1st degree felony, 5 yrs. mandatory	Under 10 g.: 2nd degree felony; 10-30 g.: Felony, 5 yrs. mandatory; Over 30 g.: 7 yrs. mandatory
OKLAHOMA	Tit. 63 §§2-101, *et seq.*	Felony, 2-10 yrs.; Subsequent offense: Felony, 4-20 yrs.	Felony, 5-20 yrs.; Subsequent offense: Double penalties; 3rd offense: 10 yrs. before chance for parole	28-300 g.: $25,000 to $100,000; 300 g. and over: $100,000 to $500,000
OREGON	63§2-201/401, *et seq.*	2-10 yrs.; Subsequent offense: 4-20 yrs.	Over 28 g.: 10 yrs. and $25,000 to $100,000 ; Over 300 g.: 10 yrs. and $100,000 to $500,000; Subsequent offense: If in above amounts, triple prison term up to 30 yrs.; Third offense: Life without parole	
PENNSYLVANIA	Tit. 35 §§780-101, *et seq.*	Misdemeanor, 1 yr. and/or $5000; Subsequent offense: 3 yrs. and/or $25,000	Felony, 15 yrs. and/or $250,00 or higher fine if necessary to recover drug profit; Subsequent offense: Double penalties	

(Continued)

111

Table 10a: Illegal Drugs: Cocaine—Continued

State	Code Section	Possession	Sale	Trafficking
RHODE ISLAND	21-28-4.01, *et seq.*	3 yrs. and/or $500 to $5000; Over 1 kg.: 20 yrs. to life and $25,000 to $1,000,000; Subsequent offense: Double penalties; Third offense: Triple penalties	Person not drug dependent: Life and/or $10,000 to $500,000; Drug dependent: 30 yrs. and or $3000 to $100,000; 1 kg. or more: Minimum 10-50 yrs. and/or $10,000 to $500,000; Subsequent offense: Double penalties; Third offense: Triple penalties	
SOUTH CAROLINA	44-53-110	Misdemeanor, up to 2 yrs. and/or $5000; Possession of 10 g. of cocaine prima facie evidence of violation of intent to sell; Subsequent offense: Felony, 3 yrs. and/or $5000; Third offense: Felony, 4 yrs. and/or $10,000	Any amount: Felony, up to 15 yrs. and/or $25,000; 10-28 g.: 3-10 yrs. and/or $10,000; 28-200 g.: 7-25 yrs. and/or $50,000; 200-400 g.: 10-25 yrs. and/or $100,000; Over 400 g.: 15-30 yrs. and/or $200,000; Subsequent offense: Felony, 5-30 yrs. and/or $50,000; Third offense: 15-30 yrs. and/or $50,000	10-28 g.: 3-10 yrs. without probation and $25,000; 28-100 g.: 7-25 yrs. without probation and $50,000; 100-200 g.: Mandatory 25 yrs. without probation and $50,000; 200-400 g.: Mandatory 25 yrs. without probation and $100,000; 400 g. and over: Mandatory 25-30 yrs. without probation and $200,000
SOUTH DAKOTA	22-42-1, *et seq.*	Class 5 felony	Class 4 felony, mandatory 1 yr. without suspension; Sale to minor: Class 2 felony; Subsequent offense: Mandatory 10 yrs. without suspension; To minor: Mandatory 15 yrs. without suspension	
TENNESSEE	39-17-408, *et seq.*	Possession or casual exchange: Class A misdemeanor unless adult to minor and adult is 2 yrs. the minor's senior, then felony; Subsequent offense: If 2 or more prior convictions: Class E felony	Class B felony and up to $100,000; Over 26 g.: Class B felony and up to $200,000; Over 300 g.: Class A felony and up to $500,000; Sale to minor under 12: One class higher than amount required; Minimum penalty amounts: 1st drug felony: $2000; 2nd: $2500; 3rd: $3000	

(Continued)

Table 10a: Illegal Drugs: Cocaine—Continued

State	Code Section	Possession	Sale	Trafficking
TEXAS	Health & Safety §§481.032, *et seq.*	Under 28 g.: 2nd degree felony ; Over 28 g.: Aggravated felony; 28-400 g.: 5-99 yrs. or Dept. of Corrections for life and/or $50,000; 400 g. and over: 10-99 yrs. or Dept. of Corrections for life and/or $100,000	Under 28 g.: 1st degree felony , 5-99 yrs. or Dept. of Corrections for life and/or $20,000; Over 28 g.: Aggravated offense; 28-200 g.: Dept. of Corrections for life or 5-99 yrs. and/or $50,000; 200-400 g.: Dept. of Corrections for life or 10-99 yrs. and/or $100,000; 400 g. and over: Dept. of Corrections for life or 15-99 yrs. and/or $250,000	
UTAH	58-37-8	3rd degree felony; Subsequent offense: One degree greater penalty than provided	2nd degree felony; Subsequent offense: 1st degree felony	
VERMONT	Tit. 18 §4231	Up to 2.5 g.: 1 yr. and/or $2000; 2.5 g. to 1 oz.: Up to 5 yrs. and/or $100,000; 1 oz. to 1 lb: Up to 10 yrs. and/or $250,000; 1 lb. and over: Up to 20 yrs. and/or $1,000,000; Subsequent offense: Double penalties	Delivery: 3 yrs. and/or $75,000; Sale: 5 yrs. and/or $100,000; Sale or delivery of:; Over 2.5 g.: 10 yrs. and/or $250,000; Over 1 oz.: 20 yrs. and/or $1,000,000; Subsequent offense: Double penalties	
VIRGINIA	18.2-247; 54.1-3400, *et seq.*	Class 5 felony	5-40 yrs. and up to $500,000 If defendant proves he gave drug (1) not for remuneration; (2) not to an inmate, or (3) not for recipient to become addicted, then Class 5 felony; Subsequent offense: At court or jury's discretion, life or not less than 5 yrs. and up to $500,000	
WASHINGTON	69.50.101, *et seq.*	Up to 5 yrs. and/or $10,000; With intent to deliver: Less than 2 kg.: Up to 10 yrs. and/or $25,000; Over 2 kg.: Up to 10 yrs. and/or up to $100,000 for first 2 kg. and $50 for each gram in excess of 250; Subsequent offense: Double penalties	Up to 5 yrs.; Subsequent offense: Mandatory 5 yrs. without suspension	
WEST VIRGINIA	60A-1-101 to 60A-8-13	Misdemeanor, 90 days to 6 months and/or $1000; Subsequent offense: Double penalties	Felony, 1-15 yrs. and/or $25,000; Subsequent offense: Double penalties	

(Continued)

Table 10a: Illegal Drugs: Cocaine—Continued

State	Code Section	Possession	Sale	Trafficking
WISCONSIN	161.001 to 161.62	Possession or attempt to possess: 1 yr. and/or $250 to $5000; Subsequent offense: 2 yrs. and/or $10,000	Under 10 g.: Up to 5 yrs. and $1000 to $200,000; 10-25 g.: 6 months-5 yrs. and $1000 to $250,000; 25-100 g.: 1-15 yrs. and $1000 to $500,000; 100-400 g.: 3-15 yrs. and $1000 to $500,000; 400-800 g. 10-30 yrs. and $1000 to $500,000	
WYOMING	35-7-1001 to 1057	Misdemeanor, up to 6 months and/or $750; Subsequent offense: Up to 5 yrs. and/or $5000	Up to 20 yrs. and/or $25,000; Subsequent offense: Double penalties	

Table 10b: Illegal Drugs: Heroin

State	Code Section	Possession	Sale	Trafficking
ALABAMA	20-2-1; 20-2-23(2); 20-5-25(1)(A); 13A-12-210 to 215	Class C felony	4-14 g.: Mandatory 3 yrs. and $50,000; 14-28 g.: 10 yrs. and $100,000; 28-56 g.: 25 yrs. and $500,000; 56 g. or more: Life without parole; Sale to minor: Class A felony; Unlawful distribution of controlled substance: Class B felony; Subsequent offense: Subject to Habitual Felony Offender Act	
ALASKA	11.71.010, *et seq.*	Possession of any amount: Class C felony	Sale to anyone under 19 at least 3 yrs. younger than seller: "Misconduct involving a controlled substance in the first degree"; Unclassified felony; Sale of heroin in general: Class A felony	
ARIZONA	13-3401, *et seq.*; 36-2501, *et seq.*	Class 4 felony, but for one not previously convicted of felony, court can make it Class 1 misdemeanor; fine of not less than $2000 or 3 times the value of substance, whichever is greater	Class 2 felony; On school property: Class 2 felony; Fine of greater of 3 times value of drugs or $2000; Sale within 300 feet of school: Class 2 felony	
ARKANSAS	5-64-101, *et seq.*	Class C felony	Class V felony; Depending on amount, prison from 10-40 yrs. or life and fines between $25,000 and $250,000	Rebuttable presumption of intent to deliver if person has 100 mg. or more
CALIFORNIA	Health & Safety §§11000, *et seq.*	State prison and fine up to $70; if probation granted, there are additional requirements	State prison 2-4 yrs.; Possession/ purchasing for sale: State prison 3-5 yrs.; Sale to minors: State prison 3, 5, or 7 yrs.; Sale to school children: 5, 7, or 9 yrs.; Anyone over 18 who sells to a minor or uses a minor in the sale process is punishable in state prison for 3, 6, or 9 yrs.; Sale on many public areas punishable by state prison for 5, 7, or 9 yrs. if seller is 5 yrs. older than minor	
COLORADO	12-22-301, *et seq.*; 18-18-101, *et seq.*	Class 3 felony Subsequent Offense: Twice or more within 6 months and amount greater than 28.5 g.: Defendant shall be sentenced to the Dept. of Corrections for at least the minimum and fined no less than $1000 but not over $500,000 with no probation or suspension (§18-18-105)	Class 3 felony; Sale to minor on public property: Dept. of Corrections for minimum 5 yrs.; Subsequent offense: Class 2 felony	

(Continued)

Table 10b: Illegal Drugs: Heroin—Continued

State	Code Section	Possession	Sale	Trafficking
CONNECTICUT	21a-240, 243, 278	7 yrs., $50,000; Subsequent offense: 15 yrs. and $100,000; Third offense: 25 yrs. and $250,000	15 yrs. and $50,000; 1 oz. or more: 5-20 yrs. minimum; maximum by a non-drug dependent person; Subsequent offense: 30 yrs. and $100,000	
DELAWARE	Tit. 16 §4701, *et seq.*	Possession, use, consumption: Class A misdemeanor	Class C felony: $5000-$50,000; If not addicted: Felony, mandatory 6 yrs.; To a minor: Class C felony, if under 16, mandatory 1 yr. prison; On school property: Up to 15 yrs. and $250,000; Subsequent offense: If not addicted, mandatory 12 yrs.	If on any occasion, one knowingly sells, delivers, brings: 5-15 g.: Minimum 3 yrs. and $75,000; 15-50 g.: Minimum 10 yrs. and $150,000; 50 g. and over: Minimum 25 yrs. and $750,000;
DISTRICT OF COLUMBIA	33-541	Misdemeanor, 1 yr. and/or $1000	Sale, manufacture, distribution: Crime with up to 30 yrs. and/or $500,000; mandatory minimum of 5 yrs. without parole for first offense; Subsequent offense: Mandatory 10 yrs. minimum if 500 g. or more	
FLORIDA	775.082, *et seq.*; 893.01	3rd degree felony; possession of 4 g. is trafficking	2nd degree felony; Sales of over 10 g.: 1st degree felony	4-14 g.: 3 yrs. and $5000; 14-28 g.: 10 yrs. and $100,000; 28 g. or more: 25 yrs. and $500,000
GEORGIA	16-13-20, *et seq.*	4 g. or more is trafficking: possession of any amount is a felony punishable with minimum 2-15 yrs.; Subsequent offense: Minimum 5-30 yrs.	Felony: 5-25 yrs.	4-14 g.: Mandatory 5 yrs. and $50,000; 14-28 g.: Mandatory 10 yrs. and $100,000; Over 28 g.: Mandatory 25 yrs. and $500,000
HAWAII	329-1, *et seq.*; 712-1240, *et seq.*	1/8-1 oz.: Class B felony; 1 oz. or more: Class A felony; Subsequent offense: Class A or B felony based on quantity	Any amount: Class B felony; 1/8 oz. or more, or any amount to a minor: Class A felony	

(Continued)

Table 10b: Illegal Drugs: Heroin—Continued

State	Code Section	Possession	Sale	Trafficking
IDAHO	37-2701, *et seq.*	Felony, up to 7 yrs. and/or $15,000; Subsequent offense: Double penalties; Possession of 2 g. or more is trafficking	Felony, up to life and $25,000; Subsequent offense: Double penalties	2-7 g.: Mandatory 3 yrs. and minimum $10,000; 7-28 g.: Mandatory 10 yrs. and minimum $15,000; 28 g. and over: Mandatory 25 yrs. and minimum $100,000; Second trafficking conviction: Double penalties
ILLINOIS	720 ILCS 570/ 100, *et seq.*; Uniform Controlled Substances Act; 720 ILCS 550/1, *et seq.*	15-100 g.: Class 1 felony, mandatory 4-15 yrs.; 100-400 g.: Mandatory 6-30 yrs.; 400-900 g.: Mandatory 8-40 yrs.; Over 900 g.: Mandatory 10-50 yrs.; Fines for any offense involving 100 g. or more: greater of $200,000 or street value	15-100 g.: 6-30 yrs.; 100-400 g.: 9-40 yrs.; 400-900 g.: 12-50 yrs.; Over 900 g.: 15-60 yrs.	
INDIANA	35-48-1-2; 35-48-4-1, *et seq.*	Possession of any amount: At least Class D felony; Under 3 g. but within 1000 feet of school property: Class B felony; Over 3 g.: Class C felony; Possession of 3 g. or more within 1000 feet of school property: Class A felony; Subsequent offense: Triple penalties	Class B felony unless amount is over 3 g. or delivery to a minor 3 yrs. younger or delivery in/on school property or within 100 feet of property or on school bus, then Class A felony	
IOWA	204.101, 204, 401, 411		Less than 100 g.: Class C felony, $1000 to $50,000; 100g. to 1 kg.: Class B felony, $5000 to $100,000; Over 1 kg.: Class B felony, up to 50 yrs. and $1,000,000; Subsequent offense: Triple penalties	
KANSAS	65-4101, *et seq.*	Class C felony; Subsequent offense: Class B felony; Third offense: Class A felony and life in prison	Class C felony; Subsequent offense: Class B felony; Third offense: Class A felony and life in prison	
KENTUCKY	218A.010, *et seq.*	1-5 yrs. and $3000 to $5000; Subsequent offense: 5-10 yrs. or $5000 to $10,000 or both	5-10 yrs. and/or $5000 to $10,000; Subsequent offense: 10-20 yrs. and/or $10,000 to $20,000	First offense: 5-10 yrs. and $5000 to $10,000; Subsequent offense: 10-20 yrs. or $10,000 to $20,000 or both

(Continued)

Table 10b: Illegal Drugs: Heroin—Continued

State	Code Section	Possession	Sale	Trafficking
LOUISIANA	§§40:961, *et seq.*	Minimum of 4 yrs. at hard labor up to 10 yrs. without probation or suspension and/or fine to $5000; Subsequent offense: Double penalties	Life imprisonment at hard labor without probation or suspension and perhaps fine up to $15,000; Subsequent offense: Double penalties	
MAINE	Tit. 17A §§1101, *et seq.*	Class C crime; 4 g. creates presumption of trafficking	Class C crime; 2 g. or more creates presumption of furnishing	Possession of 4 g. or more is trafficking
MARYLAND	Art. 27 §§276, *et seq.*	Misdemeanor with penalty of up to 4 yrs. and/or $25,000; Bringing 4 g. into state: Felony with penalty of up to $50,000 and/or up to 25 yrs.; Subsequent offense: Double penalties	Felony with penalty of 20 yrs. and/or $25,000; Sale of more than 28 g.: Mandatory 5 yrs. without suspension; Subsequent offense: Double penalties, 2 yrs. mandatory	Any conviction under §286
MASSACHUSETTS	Ch. 94c §§1, *et seq.*	2 yrs. and/or $2000; Subsequent offense: 2.5-5 yrs. and/or $5000	1-10 yrs. and/or $1000 to $10,000; Subsequent offense: 5-15 yrs. and/or $2500 to $25,000	28-100 g.: 5-20 yrs. and/or $5000 to $50,000; 100-200 g.: 10-20 yrs. and/or $10,000 to $100,000; Over 200 g.: 15-20 yrs. and/or $50,000 to $500,000
MICHIGAN	333.7401, *et seq.*	Under 25 g.: Up to 4 yrs. and/or $25,000; 25-50 g.: 1-4 yrs. and/or up to $25,000 or probation for life; 50-225 g.: 10-20 yrs.; 225-650 g.: 20-30 yrs.; Over 650 g.: Life imprisonment; Subsequent offense: Under 50 g.: Double penalties; Over 50 g.: Life imprisonment	Under 50 g.: 1-20 yrs. and/or $25,000 or probation for life; 50-225 g.: 10-20 yrs.; 225-650 g.: 20-30 yrs.; Over 650 g.: Life imprisonment; Subsequent offense: Under 50 g.: Double penalties; Over 50 g.: Life imprisonment	
MINNESOTA	152.01, *et seq.*	Any possession: 5 yrs. and/or $10,000; 50-500 g.: Up to 25 yrs. and/or $500,000; Over 500 g.: Up to 30 yrs. and/or $1,000,000; Subsequent offense: Depends on level of prior offenses; 4-40 yrs. and/or up to $1,000,000	Any amount: Up to 15 yrs. and/or $100,000; 10-50 g.: Up to 25 yrs. and/or $500,000; Over 50 g.: Up to 30 yrs. and $1,000,000; Subsequent offense: Depends on level of prior offense; 4-40 yrs. and/or up to $1,000,000	
MISSISSIPPI	41-29-101, *et seq.*	Felony: Up to 3 yrs. and/or $1000 to $30,000; Subsequent offense: Double penalty	No specified term up to 30 yrs. and/or $1000 to $1,000,000; Subsequent offense: Double penalty	

(Continued)

Table 10b: Illegal Drugs: Heroin—Continued

State	Code Section	Possession	Sale	Trafficking
MISSOURI	195.010, *et seq.*	Class C felony; Subsequent offense: State penitentiary 5 yrs. to life; Third offense: State penitentiary 10 yrs. to life	Class B felony; Subsequent offense: 10 yrs. to life	Delivering, attempting to distribute or produce: 30-90 g.: Class A felony; Over 90 g.: Class A felony, term without parole; Possessing, buying, attempting to buy: 30-90 g.: Class B felony; Over 90 g.: Class A felony
MONTANA	45-9-101, *et seq.*; 50-32-101, *et seq.*	Up to 5 yrs. and/or $50,000; Criminal possession with intent to sell: Up to 20 yrs. and/or $50,000	2 yrs. to life and/or $50,000; Subsequent offense: 10 yrs. to life and/or $50,000; Third offense: Not less than 20 yrs. and/or $50,000	
NEBRASKA	28-401, *et seq.*	Class 2 felony	1-7 oz.: Class 1D felony; Over 7 oz.: Class 1C felony	
NEVADA	453.011, 510	1-6 yrs. and $5000; Subsequent offense: 1-10 yrs. and $10,000; Third offense: 1-20 yrs. and $20,000	1-20 yrs., and $20,000; Subsequent offense: 5-20 yrs. and $20,000; Third offense: Life or 15 yrs. mandatory and $20,000	28-200 g.: 3-20 yrs. and $50,000; 200-400 g.: 5-20 yrs. and $100,000
NEW HAMPSHIRE	318-B:1, *et seq.*	Class B felony with fine up to $25,000; Subsequent offense: Class A felony with fine up to $50,000	Class A felony; Under 1 g.: Up to 7 yrs. and/or $200,000; 1-5 g.: Up to 20 yrs. and/or $300,000; 5 g. and over: Up to 30 yrs. and/or $500,000; Subsequent offense: Under 1 g.: Up to 15 yrs. and/or $200,000; 1-5 g.: Up to 40 yrs. and/or $500,000; 5 g. and over: Maximum life and/or $500,000	
NEW JERSEY	24:21-1, *et seq.*; 2C:35-5, *et seq.*	Crime of 3rd degree, $25,000	.5 oz. or less: Crime of 3rd degree, $50,000; .5 oz. to 5 oz.: Crime of 2nd degree; Over 5 oz.: Crime of 1st degree, fixed prison term and $300,000; Selling within 1000 feet of school: Fixed prison term and up to $100,000; Selling to minor or pregnant female: Double penalties	
NEW MEXICO	30-31-1, *et seq.*	Misdemeanor, up to 1 yr. and $500 to $1000	Second degree felony; Subsequent offense: First degree felony	

(Continued)

Table 10b: Illegal Drugs: Heroin—Continued

State	Code Section	Possession	Sale	Trafficking
NEW YORK	Penal §§220, *et seq.*;	Knowingly possessing: Over 500 mg.: Class D felony; Over ⅛ oz.: Class C felony; Over ½ oz.: Class B felony; Over 2 oz.: Class A-II felony; Over 4 oz.: Class A-I felony; Any amount with intent to sell: Class D felony; Any amount of narcotic drug with intent to sell: Class B felony	Class D felony in general, then Over 1/2 oz.: Class A-II felony; Over 2 oz.: Class A-I felony	
NORTH CAROLINA	90-86, *et seq.*	Class I felony	Class H felony	4-14 g.: Class F felony, 14 yrs. and $50,000; 14-28 g.: Class E felony, 18 yrs. and $100,000; 28 g. and over: Class C felony, 45 yrs. and $500,000
NORTH DAKOTA	19-03.1-01, *et seq.*	Class C felony	Class A felony	
OHIO	2925.01, *et seq.*; 3719.01, *et seq.*	4th degree felony; Subsequent offense: 3rd degree felony	Under 10 g.: 3rd degree felony; 10-30 g.: 2nd degree felony, 3 yrs. mandatory; Over 30 g.: 1st degree felony, 5 yrs. mandatory	Under 10 g.: 2nd degree felony; 10-30 g.: Felony, 5 yrs. mandatory; Over 30 g.: 7 yrs. mandatory
OKLAHOMA	Tit. 63 §§2-101, *et seq.*	Felony, 2-10 yrs.; Subsequent offense: Felony, 4-20 yrs.	Felony, 5-20 yrs. and up to $20,000; Adult sale to minor: Double penalties; Subsequent offense: Double penalties	10-28 g.: $25,000 to $50,000; 28 g. and over: $50,000 to $500,000
OREGON	63 §2-201/401, *et seq.*	2-10 yrs.; Subsequent offense: 4-20 yrs.	Over 10 g.: 10 yrs. and $25,000 to $50,000; Over 28 g.: 10 yrs. and $50,000 to $500,000; Subsequent offense: If in above amounts, triple prison term up to 30 yrs.; Third offense: Life without parole	
PENNSYLVANIA	Tit. 35 §§780-101, *et seq.*	Misdemeanor, 1 yr. and/or $5000; Subsequent offense: 3 yrs. and/or $25,000	Felony, 15 yrs. and/or $250,00 or higher fine if necessary to recover drug profit; Subsequent offense: Double penalties	
RHODE ISLAND	21-28-4.01, *et seq.*	3 yrs. and/or $500 to $5000; Over 1 kg.: 20 yrs. to life and $25,000 to $1,000,000; Subsequent offense: Double penalties; Third offense: Triple penalties	Person not drug dependent: Life and/or $10,000 to $500,000; Drug dependent: 30 yrs. and/or $3000 to $100,000; Over 1 oz.: Minimum 10-50 yrs. and/or $10,000 to $500,000; Subsequent offense: Double penalties; Third offense: Triple penalties	

(Continued)

Table 10b: Illegal Drugs: Heroin—Continued

State	Code Section	Possession	Sale	Trafficking
SOUTH CAROLINA	44-53-110, 370	Misdemeanor, up to 2 yrs. and/or $5000; Subsequent offense: Felony, 3 yrs. and/or $5000; Third offense: Felony, 4 yrs. and/or $10,000	Any amount: Felony, 15 yrs. and/or $25,000; Subsequent offense: Felony, 5-30 yrs. and $15,000; Third offense: 15-30 yrs. and $50,000	Trafficking in illegal drugs: 4-14 g.: 7-25 yrs. without parole or suspension and $50,000; 14-28 g.: Mandatory 25 yrs. without parole or suspension and $200,000; Over 28 g.: Mandatory 25-40 yrs. without parole or suspension and $200,000; Sale to minor: 20 without parole or suspension yrs. and $30,000
SOUTH DAKOTA	22-42-1, *et seq.*	Class 5 felony	Class 4 felony, mandatory 1 yr. without suspension; Sale to minor: Class 2 felony; Subsequent offense: Mandatory 10 yrs. without suspension; To minor: Mandatory 15 yrs. without suspension	
TENNESSEE	39-17-408, *et seq.*	Possession or casual exchange: Class A misdemeanor unless adult to minor and adult is 2 yrs. the minor's senior, then felony; Subsequent offense: If two or more prior convictions: Class E felony	Class B felony and/or $100,000; Over 15 g.: Class B felony and/or $200,000; Over 150 g.: Class A felony and/or $500,000; Sale to minor under 12: One class higher than amount required	
TEXAS	Health & Safety §§481.032, *et seq.*	Under 28 g.: 2nd degree felony; Over 28 g.: Aggravated felony; 28-400 g.: 5-99 yrs. or Dept. of Corrections for life and/or $50,000; 400 g. and over: 10-99 yrs. or Department of Corrections for life and/or $100,000	Under 28 g.: 1st degree felony in, 5-99 yrs. or Dept. of Corrections for life and/or $20,000; Over 28 g.: Aggravated offense; 28-200 g.: Dept. of Corrections for life or 5-99 yrs. and/or $50,000; 200-400 g.: Dept. of Corrections for life or 10-99 yrs. and/or $100,000; 400 g. and over: Dept. of Corrections for life or 15-99 yrs. and/or $250,000	
UTAH	58-37-8	3rd degree felony; Subsequent offense: One degree greater penalty than provided	2nd degree felony; Subsequent offense: 1st degree felony	

(Continued)

Table 10b: Illegal Drugs: Heroin—Continued

State	Code Section	Possession	Sale	Trafficking
VERMONT	Tit. 18 §4233	Up to 200 mg.: Up to 1 yr. and/or $2000; 200 mg.-1 g.: Up to 5 yrs. and/or $100,000; 1-10 g.: Up to 10 yrs. and/or $250,000; 2 g. and over: Up to 20 yrs. and/or $1,000,000; Subsequent offense: Double penalties	Delivery: Up to 3 yrs. and/or $75,000; Sale: Up to 5 yrs. and/or $100,000; Sale or delivery of: Over 200 mg.: 10 yrs. and/or $250,000; Over 1 g.: 20 yrs. and/or $1,000,000; Subsequent offense: Double penalties	
VIRGINIA	54.1-3400, *et seq.*; 18.2-250	Class 5 felony	5-40 yrs. and up to $500,000; If defendant proves he gave drug (1) not for remuneration, (2) not to an inmate, or (3) not for recipient to become addicted, then Class 5 felony; Subsequent offense: At court or jury's discretion, subsequent offense involving an opiate carries 5 yrs. to life and/or $100,000	
WASHINGTON	69.50.401, *et seq.*	Up to 5 yrs. and/or $10,000; With intent to deliver: Up to 10 yrs. and/or $25,000; Subsequent offense: Double penalties	Mandatory 2 yrs. without suspension and fine in amount to eliminate all profits gained up to $500,000 for each count; Subsequent offense: Mandatory 10 yrs. without suspension and fine in amount to eliminate all profits gained up to $500,000 for each count	
WEST VIRGINIA	60A-1-101 to 60A-8-13	Misdemeanor, 90 days-6 months and/or $1000; Subsequent offense: Double penalties	Felony, 1-15 yrs. and/or $25,000; Subsequent offense: Double penalties	
WISCONSIN	161.001 to 161.62	1 yr. and/or $5000; Subsequent offense: Double penalties	Under 3 g.: Up to 15 yrs. and/or $1000 to $200,000; 3-10 g.: 6 months-15 yrs. and/or $1000 to $250,000; 10-50 g.: 1-15 yrs. and/or $1000 to $500,000; 50-200 g.: 3-15 yrs. and/or $1000 to $500,000; 200-400 g.: 5-15 yrs. and/or $1000 to $500,000; Over 400 g.: 10-30 yrs. and $1000 to $1,000,000	
WYOMING	35-7-1001 to 1057	Misdemeanor, up to 6 months and/or $750; Subsequent offense: Up to 5 yrs. and/or $5000	Up to 10 yrs. and/or $25,000; Subsequent offense: Double penalties	

Table 10c: Illegal Drugs: Marijuana

State	Code Section	Possession	Sale	Trafficking
ALABAMA	20-1-1, *et seq.*; 13A-12-210 to 215	Personal use Class A misdemeanor; $1000 additional penalty; Subsequent offense: Class C misdemeanor; $2000 additional penalty	Class B felony; Class A for sale to minor; 5 yr. prison for sale on school campus or within 3 mile radius	1 kilo-100 lbs: 3 yrs. and mandatory $25,000; 100-500 lbs.: 5 yrs. and mandatory $50,000; 500-1000 lbs.: 15 yrs. and mandatory $200,000; Over 1000 lbs.: Life without parole
ALASKA	11.71.010, *et seq.*; 17.30.010, *et seq.*	Class C felony to possess marijuana with reckless disregard that possession is occurring within 800 feet of a school or on a school bus or knowingly maintaining storage or transportation facilities for keeping/ distributing or rendering a drug counterfeit		
ARIZONA	13-3401, *et seq.*; 36-2501, *et seq.*	Under 1 lb.: Class 6 felony; 1-8 lbs.: Class 5 felony; 8 lbs. and over: Class 4 felony; Fine of not less than $750 or 3 times the value of the controlled substance, whichever is greater	Under 1 lb.: Class 4 felony; 1 lb. or more: Class 3 felony; Fine of the greater of $750 or 3 times value of substance; Sale within 300 feet of school: Class 3 felony	Class 2 felony
ARKANSAS	5-64-101, *et seq.*	1st offense: Class A misdemeanor; 2nd offense: Class D felony; 3rd offense: Class C felony	Delivery or intent to deliver marijuana is a Class C felony, 4-30 yrs., depending on the amount sold, and/or fine of $25,000 to $100,000	1 oz. possession of marijuana creates rebuttable presumption or intent to deliver
CALIFORNIA	Health & Safety §§11000, *et seq.*	Possession of any concentrated cannabis: Prison in county jail up to 1 yr. or fine up to $500 or both; Up to 28.5 grams: Misdemeanor and fine of up to $100; Over 28.5 grams: Prison up to 6 months or fine up to $500 or both; If over 18 and possession under 28.5 grams on grounds of school: Misdemeanor and fine up to $500; Under 18 and possession under 28.5 grams on grounds of school: Misdemeanor and fine up to $250; Subsequent offense: Subject to treatment or rehabilitation program	Possession for sale: Imprisonment in state prison 2, 3, or 4 yrs. for transporting, selling, etc. If under 28.5 grams: Misdemeanor and fine up to $100	

(Continued)

Table 10c: Illegal Drugs: Marijuana—Continued

State	Code Section	Possession	Sale	Trafficking
COLORADO	12-22-301, *et seq.*; 18-18-101, *et seq.*	Under 1 oz.: Class 2 petty offense, $100 fine; 1-8 oz.: Class 1 misdemeanor Over 8 oz.: Class 5 felony; Public use: Class 2 petty offense, $100 fine and 15 days; Subsequent offense: 1-8 oz.: Class 5 felony; Over 8 oz.: Class 4 felony	Class 4 felony (transferring under 1 oz. for no consideration is possession, not a dispensing offense); Over 18 yrs. old selling to minor at least 15: Class 4 felony, fine up to $5,000; Subsequent offense: Class 3 felony	
CONNECTICUT	21a-240	Under 4 oz.: 1 yr. and $1000; Over 4 oz.: 5 yrs. and $2000; Subsequent offense: Under 4 oz.: 5 yrs. and $3000; Over 4 oz.: 10 yrs. and $5000	7 yrs. and $1000; Subsequent Offense: 15 yrs. and $5000	
DELAWARE	Tit. 16 §§4701, *et seq.*	2 yrs. and $500; Subsequent offense: 7 yrs.	Felony: 10 yrs. and $1000 to $10,000	5-100 lbs.: $25,000 and minimum 3 yrs.; 100-500 lbs.: $50,000 and minimum 5 yrs.; Over 500 lbs.: $100,000 and minimum 15 yrs.
DISTRICT OF COLUMBIA	33-501, *et seq.*	Misdemeanor up to 1 yr. and/or $1000; Subsequent offense: Double penalties	Crime with penalty of 1 yr. and/or $10,000; if quantity worth over $15,000 retail value, mandatory 1 yr. without parole; Subsequent offense: Double penalties	
FLORIDA	893.13, *et seq.*	Third degree felony; under 20 g.: 1st degree misdemeanor	Third degree felony, unless less than 20 g. for no consideration: 1st degree misdemeanor; penalty as in §§775.082, 083, 084; Subsequent offense: 10 yrs.	100-2000 lbs.: 3 yrs. and mandatory $25,000; 2000-10,000 lbs.: 5 yrs. and mandatory $50,000; Over 10,000 lbs.: 15 yrs. and mandatory $200,000
GEORGIA	16-13-20, *et seq.*	Over 50 lbs. is trafficking; possession at all is a felony with penalty of 1-10 yrs.	Felony: 5-15 yrs.	50-2000 lbs.: 5 yrs. and mandatory $100,000; 2000-10,000 lbs.: 7 yrs. and mandatory $250,000; Over 10,000 lbs.: 15 yrs. and mandatory $1,000,000

(Continued)

Table 10c: Illegal Drugs: Marijuana—Continued

State	Code Section	Possession	Sale	Trafficking
HAWAII	329-1, *et seq.*; 712-1240, *et seq.*	Possession of 25 or more marijuana plants or possession of 1 lb. or more of anything containing marijuana: Class C felony; 2 lbs. or more: Class B felony; 25 lbs. or more: Class A felony; Possessing over 100 plants: Class A felony	Sale of any amount: Class C felony; 1 lb. or more: Class B felony; 5 lbs. or more: Class A felony	
IDAHO	37-2701, *et seq.*	Under 3 oz.: Misdemeanor with penalty of up to 1 yr. or $1,000 or both; Over 3 oz.: Felony, 5 yrs. and $10,000; Subsequent offense: Double penalty	Felony: 5 yrs. and $15,000; Subsequent offense: Double penalty	1 lb. or more or 25 plants or more: Felony; 1-5 lbs. or 25-50 plants: Mandatory 1 yr. and $5,000; 5-25 lbs. or 50-100 plants: Mandatory 3 yrs. and $10,000; 25-100 lbs. or over 100 plants: Mandatory 5 yrs. and $15,000; Maximum number of yrs. 15 and maximum fine $50,000
ILLINOIS	720 ILCS 550/ 100, *et seq.*, Uniform Controlled Substances Act; 720 ILCS 550/1, *et seq.*	Under 2.5 g.: Class C misdemeanor; 2.5-10 g.: Class B misdemeanor; 10-30 g.: Class A misdemeanor; 30-500 g: Class 4 felony; Over 500 g.: Class 3 felony; Subsequent offense: 10-30 g.: Class 4 felony; 30-500 g.: Class 3 felony; Unlawful to possess plants: Under 5 plants is misdemeanor; 5-50 plants is felony; over 50 plants fine of $100,000 may be imposed; Producing plants: 1-5: Class A misdemeanor; 5-20: Class 4 felony; 20-50: Class 3 felony; Over 50: Class 2 felony with fine up to $100,000	Under 2.5 g.: Class B misdemeanor; 2.5-10 g.: Class A misdemeanor; 10-30 g.: Class 4 felony; 30-500 g.: Class 3 felony; Over 500 g.: Class 2 felony for which a fine not to exceed $100,000 may be imposed	

(Continued)

Table 10c: Illegal Drugs: Marijuana—Continued

State	Code Section	Possession	Sale	Trafficking
INDIANA	35-48-1-2, *et seq.*	Under 30 g.: Class A misdemeanor; Over 30 g.: Class D felony; Subsequent offense: Class D felony	Class C felony if 10 lbs. or more or delivered on school property or bus or within 1000 feet of either; Class D felony if 30 g. to 10 lbs. and recipient a minor	
IOWA	204.101, *et seq.*		Under 50 kg.: Class D felony, fine $1000 to $5000; 50 to 100 kg.: Class C felony, fine $1000 to $50,000; 100 to 1000 kg.: Class B felony, $5000 to $100,000; Over 1000 kg.: Class B felony with penalty of up to 50 yrs. and $1,000,000; Subsequent offense: Triple penalties	
KANSAS	65-4101, *et seq.*	Class A misdemeanor; Subsequent offense: Class D felony	Class C felony	
KENTUCKY	218A.010, *et seq.*	Under 8 oz.: 90 days and fine up to $250 and may be ordered to Cabinet for Human Resources for rehabilitation; Possession of 5 or more plants creates presumption they were for purpose of sale; penalty of 1-5 yrs. and $3000 to $5000 or both	Under 8 oz.: 1 yr. or $500 or both; 8 oz. to 5 lbs.: Class D felony; Over 5 lbs.: 5-10 yrs. and $5000 to $10,000; Subsequent offense: Each offense penitentiary for minimum of 1-5 yrs. and/or fine of $3000 to $5000	
LOUISIANA	§§40:961, *et seq.*	Up to 6 mos. in parish jail and/or up to $500; 60-2000 lbs.: 5-15 yrs. hard labor and $25,000 to $50,000; 2000-10,000 lbs.: 10-40 yrs. hard labor and $50,000 to $200,000; Over 10,000 lbs.: 25-40 yrs. hard labor and $200,000 to $500,000	Imprisoned at hard labor for 5 yrs. minimum to 30 yrs. and fine up to $15,000	
MAINE	Tit. 22 §2383-A, B; Tit. 174A §§1101, *et seq.*	Over 2 lbs.: Class E crime, presumed trafficking ; Subsequent offense: Class D crime	Over 1.25 oz. creates presumption of furnishing	Possession of over 2 lbs. or over 100 plants: Class C crime; Over 20 lbs. or over 500 plants: Class C crime
MARYLAND	Art. 27 §§276, *et seq.*	1 yr. and/or $1,000; Bringing 100 or more lbs. into state is felony with penalty of up to 25 yrs. and/or fine up to $50,000; Subsequent offense: Double penalties	Felony with penalty of 5 yrs. and/ or fine of $15,000; 50 lbs. or more: Felony with mandatory 5 yrs. with no suspension; Subsequent offense: Double penalties, mandatory 2 yrs.	Any conviction under §286

(Continued)

Table 10c: Illegal Drugs: Marijuana—Continued

State	Code Section	Possession	Sale	Trafficking
MASSACHUSETTS	Ch. 94c §§1, *et seq.*	6 months and/or $500; Subsequent offense: 2 yrs. and/or $2000	1-2 yrs. and/or $500 to $5000; Subsequent offense: 1-2.5 yrs. and/or $1000 to $10,000	50-100 lbs.: 2.5-15 yrs and $500 to $10,000; 100-2000 lbs.: 3-15 yrs. and $2500 to $25,000; 2000-10,000 lbs.: 5-15 yrs. and $5000 to $50,000; Over 10,000 lbs.: 10-15 yrs. and $20,000 to $200,000
MICHIGAN	333.7401, *et seq.*	Misdemeanor with penalty of 1 yr. and/or $1000; Subsequent offense: Double penalties	Felony with penalty of 4 yrs. and/or $2000; Subsequent offense: Double penalties	
MINNESOTA	152.01, *et seq.*	Small amount: Petty misdemeanor $200 and maybe drug education program; 10+ kg.: Up to 20 yrs. and/or $250,000; 50+ kg.: Up to 25 yrs. and/or $500,000; 100+ kg.: Up to 30 yrs. and/or $1,000,000; Subsequent offense: Depends on level of prior offense; if misdemeanor, may be required to participate in chemical dependency evaluation and treatment	Any small amount for sale: Up to 5 yrs. and/or $10,000; Small amount without remuneration: Petty misdemeanor with fine of up to $200 and maybe drug education program; 5+ kg.: Up to 20 yrs. and/or $250,000; 25+ kg.: Up to 25 yrs. and/or $500,000; 50+ kg.: Up to 30 yrs. and/or $1,000,000; Any amount in school or park or public housing zone: Up to 15 yrs. and/or $100,000; Subsequent offense: Depends on level of prior offense	
MISSISSIPPI	41-29-101, *et seq.*	Under 1 oz.: $100 to $250; 1 oz. to 1 kg.: $1000 and county jail or $3000 and 3 yrs. penitentiary; Over 1 kg.: 20 yrs. and/or $1,000,000; Subsequent offense: Misdemeanor 5-60 days and $250 and mandatory participation in drug education program; Third offense: Misdemeanor 5 days-6 months and $250 to $500	Under 1 oz.: Up to 3 yrs. and/or $3000; First-time offender with over 1 oz. but less than 1 kg.: Up to 20 yrs. and/or $30,000; Over 1 oz.: Up to 30 yrs. and/or $1,000 to $1,000,000; Subsequent offense: Double penalties	Anyone over 21 selling 10 lbs. or more of marijuana during any 12 month period shall have life in prison without suspension/parole

(Continued)

Table 10c: Illegal Drugs: Marijuana—Continued

State	Code Section	Possession	Sale	Trafficking
MISSOURI	195.010, *et seq.*	Under 35 g.: Class A misdemeanor; Subsequent offense: 5 yrs. state penitentiary or 1 yr. county jail or $1000	Less than 5 g.: Class C felony; More than 5 g.: Class B felony; Subsequent offense: 10 yrs. to life in state penitentiary	Distribution associated: 30-100 kg.: Class A felony; 100+ kg.: Term of prison for Class A felony without parole; Buying associated: 300-100 kg.: Class B felony; 100+ kg.: Class A felony
MONTANA	45-9-101, *et seq.*; 50-32-101, *et seq.*	Under 60 g.: Misdemeanor with penalty of 6 months in county jail and fine of $100 to $500; Subsequent offense: $1000 fine and 1 yr. in county jail or up to 3 yrs. in state penitentiary	1 yr. to life and $50,000; Subsequent offense: 20 yrs. and $50,000	
NEBRASKA	28-401, *et seq.*	Under 1 oz.: $100 and attend a course; Over 1 oz.: Class 3A misdemeanor; Over 1 lb.: Class 4 felony; Subsequent offense: Under 1 oz.: Class 4 misdemeanor, 5 days and $200; Third offense under 1 oz.: Class 3A misdemeanor, 7 days and $300	Class 4 felony	
NEVADA	453.011, *et seq.*	For someone under 21: 1-6 yrs.	1-15 yrs. and/or $5000; Subsequent offense: 1-15 yrs. and/or $5000; 3rd offense: 15 yrs. to life and mandatory $20,000	1000-2000 lbs.: 3-20 yrs. and min. $25,000; 2000-10,000 lbs.: 5-20 yrs. and min. $50,000; Over 10,000 lbs.: 15 yrs. to life and min. $200,000
NEW HAMPSHIRE	318-B:1, *et seq.*	Misdemeanor	Under 1 oz: Up to 3 yrs. and/or $25,000; 1 oz. to 5 lbs.: Up to 7 yrs. and/or $200,000; Over 5 lbs.: Up to 20 yrs. and/or $300,000; Subsequent offense: Under 1 oz.: Up to 6 yrs. and/or $50,000; 1 oz. to 5 lbs.: Up to 15 yrs. and/or $200,000; Over 5 lbs.: Up to 40 yrs. and/or $500,000	

(Continued)

Table 10c: Illegal Drugs: Marijuana—Continued

State	Code Section	Possession	Sale	Trafficking
NEW JERSEY	24:21-1, *et seq.*; 2C:35-5, *et seq.*	Under 50 g.: Disorderly person; Over 50g.: 4th degree crime , $15,000	Less than 1 oz.: 4th degree crime; 1 oz. to 5 lbs.: 3rd degree crime, up to $15,000; Over 5 lbs.: 2nd degree crime	
NEW MEXICO	30-31-1, *et seq.*	Under 1 oz.: Petty misdemeanor, 15 days and $50-100; 1-8 oz.: Misdemeanor, 1 yr. and $100-1000; Over 8 oz.: 4th degree felony; Subsequent offense: Under 1 oz.: Misdemeanor, 1 yr., $100-1000	4th degree felony; Subsequent offense: Over 100 lbs.: 3rd degree felony	
NEW YORK	Penal §§220, *et seq.*; Pub. Health §§3300, *et seq.*	Under 25g: $100; Over 25 g. or public use: Class B misdemeanor; Over 2 oz.: Class A misdemeanor; Over 8 oz.: Class E felony; Over 16 oz.: Class D felony; Over 10 lbs.: Class C felony; Subsequent offense: Under 25 g.: $200; Third offense: $250 and 15 days	Under 2 g.: Class B misdemeanor; Under 25 g.: Class A misdemeanor; Over 25 g.: Class E felony; Over 4 oz. or sale to a minor: Class D felony; Over 16 oz.: Class C felony	
NORTH CAROLINA	90-86, *et seq.*	Under .5 oz.: Up to 30 days and/or $100; Over .5 oz.: Misdemeanor $100 fine; Over 1.5 oz.: Class I felony; Subsequent offense: If prior offense included punishment for under 6 months, next offense carries penalty of up to 2 yrs. and/or $2000	Class I felony but not when under 5 g. for no consideration	50-100 lbs.: Class H felony, 5 yrs. and/or $5000; 100-2000 lbs.: Class G felony, 7 yrs. and/or $25,000; 2000-10,000 lbs.: Class F felony, 14 yrs. and/or $50,000; Over 10,000 lbs.: Class D felony, 35 yrs. and/or $200,000
NORTH DAKOTA	19-03.1-01, *et seq.*	Under .5 oz.: Class B misdemeanor; Under 1 oz.: Class A misdemeanor; Under .5 oz. while operating a motor vehicle: Class A misdemeanor	Class B felony; 100 lbs. or more: Class A felony	

(Continued)

Table 10c: Illegal Drugs: Marijuana—Continued

State	Code Section	Possession	Sale	Trafficking
OHIO	2925.01, *et seq.*; 3719.01, *et seq.*	Under 100 g.: Minor misdemeanor; 100-200 g.: 4th degree misdemeanor; 200-600 g.: 4th degree felony; Over 600 g.: 3rd degree felony; Subsequent offense: 200-600 g.: 3rd degree felony; Over 600 g.: 2nd degree felony	Under 200 g.: 4th degree felony; 200-600 g.: 3rd degree felony; Over 600 g.: 2nd degree felony, 6 mos. mandatory; Subsequent offense: Under 200 g.: 3rd degree felony; 200-600 g.: 2nd degree felony; Over 600 g.: 1 yr. mandatory	2nd degree felony, 2 yrs.
OKLAHOMA	Tit. 63 §2-101, *et seq.*	Misdemeanor with penalty of up to 1 yr.; Subsequent offense: Felony, 2-10 yrs.	Felony, 2-10 yrs. and/or up to $5000; Subsequent offense: Double penalties	Between 25-1000 lbs.: $25,000 to $100,000; Over 1000 lbs.: $100,000 to $500,000
OREGON	63 §2-201/401, *et seq.*	Misdemeanor, up to 1 yr.; Subsequent offense: Felony, 2-10 yrs.	Over 25 lbs.: 4 yrs. and $25,000 to $100,000; Over 1000 lbs.: 4 yrs. and $100,000 to $500,000; Subsequent offense: 6 yrs.; Third offense: Life without parole	
PENNSYLVANIA	Tit. 35 §§780-101, *et seq.*	Under 30 g.: Misdemeanor, 30 days and/or $500 also, driver's license suspended for 90 days; Subsequent offense: 3 yrs. and/or $25,000, also driver's license suspended for 1 yr. (2nd offense) or 2 yrs. (3rd offense)	Over 1000 lbs.: Felony, up to 10 yrs. and/or $100,000 or enough to recoup drug profit and driver's license suspended for 90 days; Subsequent offense: Double penalties and driver's license suspended for 1 yr. (2nd offense) or 2 yrs (3rd offense)	
RHODE ISLAND	21-28-1.01, *et seq.*	Misdemeanor, up to 1 yr. and/or $200 to $500; Over 5 kg.: 20 yrs. to life and $25,000 to $1,000,000; Subsequent offense: Double penalties; Third offense: Triple penalties	30 yrs. and $100,000; Subsequent offense: Double penalties; Third offense: Triple penalties	
SOUTH CAROLINA	44-53-110	Misdemeanor: Up to 1 yr. and/or $2000; Under 1 oz.: 30 days and/or $100 to $200; Over 1 oz.: Prima facie guilty of sale; Subsequent offense: Under 1 oz., 1 yr. and/or $200 to $1000	Misdemeanor: Up to 5 yrs. and/or $5,000; Subsequent offense: Felony, up to 10 yrs. and/or $10,000; Third offense: Felony, 5-20 yrs. and/or $20,000	10-100 lbs.: 1-10 yrs. and $10,000; 100-2000 lbs.: Mandatory 25 yrs. and $25,000; 2000-10,000 lbs.: Mandatory 25 yrs. and $50,000; Over 10,000 lbs.: 25-30 yrs. and $200,000

(Continued)

Table 10c: Illegal Drugs: Marijuana—Continued

State	Code Section	Possession	Sale	Trafficking
SOUTH DAKOTA	22-42-6, *et seq.*; 34-20B-1 to 114	Under .5 lb.: Class 1 misdemeanor; .5 to 1 lb.: Class 6 felony; 1-10 lbs.: Class 5 felony; Over 10 lbs.: Class 4 felony; May be civil penalty for violation up to $10,000 in any of the above cases	Under .5 oz. or without consideration: Class 2 misdemeanor; Under 1 oz.: Class 1 misdemeanor, mandatory 15 days without suspension; 1 oz.-.5 lb.: Class 5 felony; Over 1 lb.: Class 4 felony; Sale to a minor: Class 5 felony; Also may be civil penalty up to $10,000 in any of above cases; Subsequent offense: Mandatory 30 days without suspension; Next: Mandatory 1 yr.	
TENNESSEE	39-17-408, *et seq.*	Possession or casual exchange of: Less than .5 oz.: Class A misdemeanor and attendance at drug offender school and minimum $250 fine; Casual exchange to a minor from an adult 2 yrs. his senior and adult knows minor is a minor: Felony; Subsequent offense: $500 minimum; Third: $750 minimum; Two or more prior convictions, then Class E felony	.5 oz. to 10 lbs.: Class E felony and/or $5000; 10 lbs. + 1 g. to 70 lbs.: Class D felony and/or $50,000; 70 lbs. + 1 g.: Class B felony and/or $200,000; Over 700 lbs.: Class A felony and/or $500,000; Sale to minor under 12: One class higher than amount required; Minimum penalty amounts: 1st drug felony offense: $2000; 2nd: $2500; 3rd: $3000	
TEXAS	Health & Safety §§481.032, *et seq.*; 481.119	Under 2 oz.: Class B misdemeanor; 2-4 oz.: Class A misdemeanor; 4 oz. to 5 lbs.: 3rd degree felony; 5-50 lbs.: 2nd degree felony; 50-200 lbs.: Department of Corrections for life or 5-99 yrs. and $50,000; 200-2000 lbs.: Dept. of Corrections for life or 10-99 yrs. and $100,000; Over 2000 lbs.: Dept. of Corrections for life or 15-99 yrs. and $250,000	.25 oz. or less: Class B misdemeanor (if no remuneration); .25oz. or less: Class A misdemeanor (with remuneration); .25 oz. to 4 oz.: 3rd degree felony; 4 oz. to 5 lbs.: 2nd degree felony; 5-50 lbs.: 1st degree felony	Over 50 lbs. Aggravated offense; 50-200 lbs.: Dept. of Corrections for life or 5-99 yrs. and $50,000; 200-2000 lbs.: Dept. of Corrections for life or 10-99 yrs. and $100,000; Over 2000 lbs.: Dept. of Corrections for life or 15-99 yrs. and $250,000

(Continued)

Table 10c: Illegal Drugs: Marijuana—Continued

State	Code Section	Possession	Sale	Trafficking
UTAH	58-37-1, *et seq.*	Under 1 oz.: Class B misdemeanor; 1-16 oz. not yet extracted from plant: Class A misdemeanor; Over 1 lb.-100 lbs.: 3rd degree felony; Over 100 lbs.: 2nd degree felony; Subsequent offense: One degree greater penalty than provided for	3rd degree felony; Subsequent offense: 2nd degree felony	
VERMONT	Tit. 18 §§4205; 4230, *et seq.*	Under 2 oz. and/or less than 3 plants: Up to 6 months and/or $500; More than 2 oz. and/or more than 3 plants: Up to 3 yrs. and/or $10,000; More than 1 lb. or more than 10 plants: Up to 5 yrs. and/or $100,000; More than 10 lbs. or more than 25 plants: Up to 15 yrs. and/or $500,000; Subsequent offense: Under 2 oz.: Up to 2 yrs. and/or $2000	Under .5 oz.: 2 yrs. and/or $10,000; .5 oz.-1 lb.: Up to 5 yrs. and/or $100,000; More than 1 lb.: Up to 15 yrs. and/or $500,000; Subsequent offense: Double penalties	
VIRGINIA	54.1-3400, *et seq.*; 18.2-247	Misdemeanor, jail up to 30 days and/or $500; Subsequent offense: Class 1 misdemeanor	Up to .5 oz.: Class 1 misdemeanor; .5 oz.-5 lbs.: Class 5 felony; Over 5 lbs.: 5-30 yrs.; Proof that person gave drug only as an accommodation not for remuneration or to induce him to become addicted shall be guilty of Class 1 misdemeanor	
WASHINGTON	69.50.101, *et seq.*	Up to 5 yrs. and/or $10,000; With intent to deliver: Up to 5 yrs. and/or $10,000; 40 g. or less is misdemeanor; Subsequent offense: Double penalties	Up to 5 yrs. in correctional facility; Subsequent offense: Mandatory 5 yrs. without suspension; Unlawful delivery of controlled substance used by person delivered to and resulting in user's death: Deliverer guilty of controlled substance homicide: Class B felony	
WEST VIRGINIA	60A-1-101 to 8-13	Misdemeanor, 90 days-6 mos. and/or $1000; Court may mitigate first offense of under 15 g.; Subsequent offense: Double penalties	Felony, 1-3 yrs. and/or $10,000; Subsequent offense: Double penalties	

(Continued)

Table 10c: Illegal Drugs: Marijuana—Continued

State	Code Section	Possession	Sale	Trafficking
WISCONSIN	161.001 to 161.62	Misdemeanor, up to 6 mos. and/or fine up to $1000; Subsequent offense: Double penalties	500 g. or less: Up to 3 yrs. and $500 to $25,000; 500 to 2500 g.: 3 mos. to 5 yrs. and $1000 to $50,000; Over 2500 g.: 1 to 10 yrs. and $1000 to $100,000; Subsequent offense: Double penalties	
WYOMING	35-7-1001 to 1057	Misdemeanor, up to 6 mos. and/or $750; Subsequent offense: Up to 5 yrs. and/or $5000	Up to 10 yrs. and/or $10,000; Subsequent offense: Double penalties	

III.   EDUCATION LAWS

11. COMPULSORY EDUCATION

Public schools are a relatively new concept in Western culture. Not until the nineteenth century did states officially begin to take responsibility for educating children. Before that time education was a private matter, either handled by parents, churches, or communities that joined together and paid a teacher to educate their children. Some early state constitutions and territory charters specifically stated that the government was responsible for the training of children in morals and the overall knowledge necessary for them to become responsible citizens. Often this responsibility was acted upon merely by subsidizing the building of schools; minimum requirements for the type of education or the number of years of education that were required of students were not set.

Today education is a responsibility that local, state, and federal governments take seriously. The teaching of morality has given way to standard academic focuses, and compulsory education laws, requiring public school attendance of all children generally between the ages of seven and sixteen, have been enacted. However, these rules frequently exempt children with permanent or temporary mental or physical disabilities, and a few states exempt student who live more than two miles from a public transportation route. Alternatives to state-run schools, including private and parochial schools and home schools, are also available.

Table 11: Compulsory Education

State	Code Section	Age Requirements	Exceptions	Home School Provisions	Penalties on Parents for Noncompliance
ALABAMA	16-28-1, *et seq.*	Between 7 and 16	Church school students; child privately tutored by certified instructor; child whose physical/ mental condition prevents attendance; child would be compelled to walk over 2 miles to attend public school; child legally and regularly employed	Exempted from Chapter 46 regulating certain schools and courses of instruction (§§16-46-1, *et seq.*)	Misdemeanor: Fine up to $100 and possibly up to 90 days hard labor for the county
ALASKA	14.30.010, *et seq.*	Between 7 and 16	Comparable education provided through private school or tutoring; attends school operated by federal government; child has physical/mental condition making attendance impractical; child is in custody of court or law enforcement officer; child is temporarily ill or injured, resides over 2 miles from a route for public transportation, or has completed the 12th grade; child is enrolled in an approved correspondence study or is well-served by an educational experience of another kind that is approved	Tutoring by personnel certified according to §14.20.020 who holds bachelor's degree from accredited institution among other requirements	Knowing noncompliance is violation with fine up to $300; every 5 days of noncompliance is separate violation
ARIZONA	15-802	Between 6 and 16	Child receives home instruction and takes a standardized achievement test; child attends a private school; physical/mental condition makes attendance impractical; child has completed 10th grade; child is over 14 and employed at a lawful wage-earning occupation; child enrolled in vocational education; child enrolled in another state-provided education program; waiver may be granted for good cause	Instruction must be in reading, grammar, mathematics, social studies, and science by a person passing a reading, grammar, and mathematics proficiency exam	Class 3 misdemeanor

(Continued)

Table 11: Compulsory Education—Continued

State	Code Section	Age Requirements	Exceptions	Home School Provisions	Penalties on Parents for Noncompliance
ARKANSAS	6-18-201	Between 5 and 17	Child has received a high school diploma; parent may elect to withhold child from kindergarten; any child enrolled in post-secondary vocational institution or college	Parents must give notice of intent to home school; with curriculum, schedules, and qualifications of teacher presented to superintendent for each semester; child must submit to standardized achievement tests and at 8, if test results are unsatisfactory, child shall be enrolled in a public, private, or parochial school (§6-15-501)	Misdemeanor; each day is separate offense and fine of $10 to $50
CALIFORNIA	Educ. §§48200, *et seq.*; 48400; 48293	Between 6 and 18; unless otherwise exempted must attend special continuation education classes	Children attending private schools; child being tutored by person with state credential for grade being taught; children holding work permits; child of 15 may take a leave of absence for supervised travel, study, training, or work not available to the student under another education option if certain conditions are met		Guilty of an infraction; 1st conviction: fine up to $100; 2nd conviction: fine up to $250; 3rd or subsequent convictions: fine up to $500; in lieu of any fines, court may order person placed in parent education and counseling program
COLORADO	22-33-104	Between 7 and 16	Child ill or injured temporarily; child attends a parochial school that provides a "basic academic education"; child absent due to a physical/mental/emotional disability; child is lawfully employed; child is in custody of court or law enforcement authority; child graduated 12th grade; child is instructed at home	Parents not subject to "Teacher Certification Act of 1975"; must provide 4 hours of instruction on average a day; must include reading, writing, speaking, math, history, civics, literature, science, and the Constitution; parents must give notice every year and children shall be evaluated at grades 3, 5, 7, 9 and 11	Attendance officer designated for enforcement of compulsory education; courts may compel compliance with a fine up to $25 per day or confine the parent in the county jail until compliance

(Continued)

Table 11: Compulsory Education—Continued

State	Code Section	Age Requirements	Exceptions	Home School Provisions	Penalties on Parents for Noncompliance
CONNECTICUT	10-184	Between 7 and 16	Child receiving equivalent instruction elsewhere	Must include: reading, writing, spelling, English grammar, geography, arithmetic, U.S. history and citizenship; child must be receiving an equivalent instruction	Fine maximum $25 per day
DELAWARE	Tit. 14 §§2702, *et seq.*	Between 5 and 16	Private school attendance; mentally or physically handicapped		1st offense: $5 minimum; subsequent offenses: fine of $25 to $50
DISTRICT OF COLUMBIA	31-401, *et seq.*	Between 5 and 18	Child obtained diploma; if 17 and lawfully employed, school hours may be flexible	Regular attendance in an independent school; private instruction	Misdemeanor; at least $100 fine or prison up to 5 days or both per offense; One offense is the equivalent of missing 2 full-day sessions or 4 half-day sessions in one month; failure to enroll child is also offense
FLORIDA	232.01, *et seq.*	Between 6 and 16	Enrolled in parochial school or home education program; child whose physical, mental, or emotional condition prevents successful participation; child 14 or over who is employed under child labor laws; certificate of exemption has been granted from a circuit judge; parent does not have access to childcare	Parent must either hold a valid Florida certificate or notify superintendent of schools, maintain a portfolio of records and materials, and evaluate education annually, including a national student achievement test	Non-enrollment: superintendent shall begin criminal prosecution; refusing to have child attend regularly is second degree misdemeanor
GEORGIA	20-2-690.1	Between 7 and 16	Private school or home study	Must teach at least reading, language arts, math, social studies, and science; parents must give notice; parent must have at least a high school diploma or may employ a tutor with a baccalaureate college degree; subject to standardized testing	Misdemeanor; fine up to $100 and/or prison up to 30 days

(Continued)

Table 11: Compulsory Education—Continued

State	Code Section	Age Requirements	Exceptions	Home School Provisions	Penalties on Parents for Noncompliance
HAWAII	298-9	Between 6 and 18	Child is physically or mentally unable to attend; child is at least 15 and suitably employed; permission after investigation by the family court; child has graduated high school; child is enrolled in an appropriate alternative educational program		Petty misdemeanor
IDAHO	33-202, *et seq.*	Between 7 and 16	Child is otherwise comparably instructed; child's physical/mental/emotional condition does not permit attendance	Comparably instructed	Proceedings brought under provisions of the Youth Rehabilitation Act
ILLINOIS	105 ILCS 5/26-1	Between 7 and 16	Child attending private or parochial school; child is physically/mentally unable to attend school; child is excused by county superintendent; child 12 to 14 attending confirmation classes; pregnant female with complications to pregnancy; child is necessarily and lawfully employed	*People v. Levisen,* 90 N.E.2d 213 (1950). Home instruction may constitute a private school.	Conviction is Class C misdemeanor subject to up to 30 days imprisonment and/or fine up to $500
INDIANA	20-8.1-3-17, *et seq.*	Between 7 and 16 if an exit interview requirement is met; otherwise 18	Child attends another school taught in the English language; child provided with instruction equivalent to public education; child is physically/mentally unfit for attendance	Notice to superintendent of school and must provide an "equivalent education" (*See Mazanec v. North Judgson-San Pierre Sch. Corp.,* 614 F. Supp. 1152 (N.D.Ind. 1875), affirmed. 798 F. 2d 230 (7th Cir. 1986))	Class B misdemeanor

(Continued)

Table 11: Compulsory Education—Continued

State	Code Section	Age Requirements	Exceptions	Home School Provisions	Penalties on Parents for Noncompliance
IOWA	299.1, *et seq.*	Between 6 and 16	Accredited nonpublic school or competent private instruction; completed requirements for graduation from accredited school or GED; sufficient reason by court of record or judge; while attending religious services or receiving religious instruction; physical/mental conditions do not permit attendance	Competent private instruction; basic arithmetic, reading, writing, grammar, spelling, U.S. history, history of Iowa, American government of acceptable levels; minimum 140 days	School officers will use means available to school; if persists, referred to county attorney for mediation or prosecution; violations of agreement (mediation): 1st offense: up to 10 days jail or up to $100 fine; 2nd offense: up to 20 days jail and/or up to $500 fine; 3rd or more: up to 30 days jail and/or up to $1000 fine
KANSAS	72-1111, *et seq.*	Between 7 and 16	Private, denominational, or parochial school taught by competent instructor	Home school held not to be equivalent of "private, denominational or parochial school," *State v. Lowry,* 191 K. 701-704; 383 P. 2d 962. Home school does not meet requirements of compulsory school attendance law. *State v. Garber,* 197 K. 567-569, 419 P.2d 896.	Secretary of Social & Rehabilitative Services investigates matter; determination made as to criminal prosecution or county attorney can make petition alleging child in need of care
KENTUCKY	159.010, *et seq.*	Between 6 and 16	Graduate from approved 4 year high school; enrolled in private, parochial, or church school; child less than 7 years old and in regular attendance in a private kindergarten-nursery school; physical/mental condition prevents it; enrolled in state supported school for exceptional children		1st offense: $100 fine; 2nd offense: $250 fine; subsequent: Class B misdemeanor

(Continued)

Table 11: Compulsory Education—Continued

State	Code Section	Age Requirements	Exceptions	Home School Provisions	Penalties on Parents for Noncompliance
LOUISIANA	17:221, *et seq.*; 17:236.1, *et seq.*	Between 7 and 17	Graduates early; private school; married/pregnant persons; mentally/physically/emotionally incapacitated to perform school duties; students unable to profit from further school experience; children living outside boundaries of city, town, or municipality; children temporarily excused from school (personal or relative's illness, death, religion)	Sustained curriculum of quality at least equal to that offered by public schools; competency-based education exams may be administered by local school board upon parental request	Fine up to $15 for each offense; each day violated is separate offense
MAINE	Tit. 20-A §5001A	Between 7 and 17	Graduates early; 15 years old or finished 9th grade; permission from parent; approved by principal for suitable program of work and study; permission from school board and written agreement that parent and board will annually meet until 17th birthday to review educational needs; habitual truant; matriculated and attending post-secondary, degree-granting institution full-time; equivalent instruction from private school or other approved manner	"Equivalent instruction" approved by commissioner; local boards not required to play any role in application, review and approval, or oversight of program	Meeting with superintendent; hearing with school board; District court may order injunctive relief or counseling
MARYLAND	Educ. 7-301	Between 5 and 16	Receiving other regular, thorough instruction in studies usually taught in public schools to children of same age group; mental/emotional/physical condition which makes his instruction detrimental to his progress or whose presence presents danger of serious physical harm to others	Receiving otherwise regular, thorough instruction in studies usually taught in public schools to children of same age group	Guilty of misdemeanor; subject to fine up to $50 and/or up to 10 days jail
MASSACHUSETTS	76 §1, *et seq.*	Established by Board of Education; no statutory fixed age; 7 minimum (*Alvord v. Chester*, 180 Mass. 20, 61 N.E. 263 (1901); *Needham v. Wellesley*, 139 Mass. 372, 31 N.E. 732 (1985))	14 to 16 years old, completed 6th grade, holds permit for employment in domestic service or farm, and is regularly employed there 6 hours per day minimum; 14 to 16 years old, meets requirements and has written permission of superintendent to engage in non-wage earning employment at home; physical/mental condition does not permit	Approval falls within standards for approval of private school (*Commonwealth v. Renfew*, 332 Mass. 492, 126 N.E.2d 109 (1955))	Up to $20 fine

(Continued)

Table 11: Compulsory Education—Continued

State	Code Section	Age Requirements	Exceptions	Home School Provisions	Penalties on Parents for Noncompliance
MICHIGAN	MCL 380.1561	Between 6 and 16	Enrolled in approved non-public school which teaches subjects comparable to those in public schools to children of same age including reading, mathematics, and writing; child regularly employed as page or messenger; under 9 years old and doesn't reside within 2.5 miles of nearest traveled road of public school and transportation not provided; age 12 to 14 while in attendance of confirmation classes not to exceed 5 months	Parent's right to educate their children through home study program free from requirement of compliance with state education laws involving teacher certification does not rise above personal or philosophical choice and therefore is not within bounds of constitutional protection (*Hanson v. Cushman*, 490 F. Supp. 109). Parent may not provide for education of his child in the home unless a certified teacher is present to provide instruction comparable to that in the public school district (Op. Atty. Gen., 9/27/79, No. 5579)	Warrant issued, hearing and determination made; misdemeanor: fine of $5 to $50 and/or 2 to 90 days jail
MINNESOTA	120.101, *et seq.*	Between 7 and 16	"Good cause" determined by school board including: developmental immaturity of child; significant family stress; physical/mental condition prevents it; complete graduation requirements	Writing, reading, literature and fine arts, math, science, social studies including history, geography, and government, and health and physical education; instruction, textbooks, and materials must be in English; superintendent can make on-site visits to evaluate	Misdemeanor
MISSISSIPPI	37-13-91	Between 6 and 17	Child is physically/mentally/emotionally incapable of attendance; child enrolled in special or remedial type education; educated in legitimate home instruction program	Parent must file a "certificate of enrollment" and education must be a "legitimate home instruction program."	Guilty of "contributing to the neglect of a child" and punished according to §97-5-39: misdemeanor with fine up to $1000 and/or up to 1 year in jail

(Continued)

144

Table 11: Compulsory Education—Continued

State	Code Section	Age Requirements	Exceptions	Home School Provisions	Penalties on Parents for Noncompliance
MISSOURI	167.031, *et seq.*	Between 7 and 16	Determined mentally/physically incapable of attendance; child is 14 to 16 and legally and desirably employed	No more than 4 pupils may be unrelated by consanguinity to the 3rd degree; no tuition charged; parents must keep written records, samples of child's work, evaluation of progress; instruction in reading, language arts, math, social studies, science; enroll child with recorder of deeds	Class C misdemeanor; upon conviction each successive school day is separate violation
MONTANA	20-5-102, *et seq.*	Between 7 and the later of attaining 16 or finishing 8th grade	Enrolled in another district or state; supervised correspondence or home study; excused by district judge or board of trustees; enrolled in nonpublic or home school	Give notice to county superintendent; maintain records; give 180 days of instruction; building complies with health and safety regulations	Fine of $5 to $20; if parent refuses to pay he shall be imprisoned in county jail 10 to 30 days
NEBRASKA	79-201, *et seq.*; 43-2007	Between 7 and 16	Child has graduated high school; child 14 is employed and earnings are necessary for his support or dependents; child is physically/mentally incapacitated	Home school valid if complies with §§79-1701 through 79-1707; subject to and governed by the provisions of the general school laws of the state so far as the same apply to grades, qualifications, and certification of teachers and promotion of pupils; adequate supplies and equipment, course of study substantially same as given in the public schools where children would have attended	Attendance officer gives warning and subsequently files a complaint with judge in county court; another violation and no notice is given parent and complaint may be filed immediately
NEVADA	392.040, *et seq.*	Between 7 and 17	Private school; physical/mental condition preventing attendance; completion of 12 grades; receiving equivalent, approved instruction; residence too far from nearest school	Equivalent instruction of the kind and amount approved by the state board of education	Misdemeanor

(Continued)

Table 11: Compulsory Education—Continued

State	Code Section	Age Requirements	Exceptions	Home School Provisions	Penalties on Parents for Noncompliance
NEW HAMPSHIRE	193.1, *et seq.*	Between 6 and 16	If in the best welfare of the child; regular and lawful occupation; approved private school; physical/mental condition prevents or makes attendance undesirable	Planned and supervised instructional and related educational activities including curriculum and instruction in science, math, language, government, history, health, reading, writing and spelling, history of U.S. and New Hampshire constitution and exposure to and appreciation of art and music	Guilty of violation and fines levied
NEW JERSEY	18A:38-25, *et seq.*	Between 6 and 16	Mental condition such that student cannot benefit; physical condition prevents attendance; day school where instruction is equivalent to that provided in public schools for children of similar grades and attainments	Academically equivalent instruction other than at school (*State v. Massa*, 95 N.J. Super. 382, 231 A.2d 252 (Co. 1967); *Everson v. Board of Education of Ewing Twp.*, 133 N.J.L. 350, 44 A.2d 333 (1945))	Convicted as disorderly persons; 1st offense: up to $25 fine; subsequent: up to $100 fine
NEW MEXICO	22-12-1, *et seq.*	5 years to age of majority	Private school, home school, or state institution; graduated from high school; 16 years old and employed in gainful trade or occupation or engaged in alternative form of education sufficient for the person's educational needs and the parent/guardian consents; consent of parent/guardian if resident and under 8 years old; unable to benefit because of learning disabilities, mental/physical/emotional condition	Means of meeting requirement of compulsory education	1st offense: $25 to $100 fine or community service; 2nd and subsequent: petty misdemeanor, up to $500 fine or up to 6 months jail

(Continued)

Table 11: Compulsory Education—Continued

State	Code Section	Age Requirements	Exceptions	Home School Provisions	Penalties on Parents for Noncompliance
NEW YORK	Educ. §§3201, *et seq.*	Between 6 and 16 (through end of school year in which child turns 16)	Non-public or home instruction; mental/physical condition endangers him or others; completed 4 year high school program; full-time employment certificate	Must be evaluated by school superintendent to determine if education is substantially equivalent to that provided in local public schools; parent does not have to be certified to be considered competent (*In Re Blackwelder,* 139 Misc. 2d 776, 528 N.Y.S.2d 759 (1988); *In Re Franz,* 55 A.D.2d 424, 390 N.Y.S.2d 940 (1977))	
NORTH CAROLINA	115C-378	Between 7 and 16	Approved	Maintain such minimum curriculum standards as are required of public schools; course of instruction must run concurrently with public school and be at least as long; must be recognized by Office of Non-Public Schools and meet requirements of Article 39 of Chapter 115C (standardized testing, high school competency, health and safety standards)	Misdemeanor: up to $50 fine and/or up to 30 days jail
NORTH DAKOTA	15-34.1-01	Between 7 and 16	Enrolled in approved private/ parochial school; has completed high school; child needed to support family; child has handicap rendering participation impracticable	Home instructors must be certified. (*See State v. Melin,* 428 N.W.2d 227 (N.D. 1988), also *State v. Sharer,* 294 N.W.2d 883 (1980))	Guilty of infraction

(Continued)

Table 11: Compulsory Education—Continued

State	Code Section	Age Requirements	Exceptions	Home School Provisions	Penalties on Parents for Noncompliance
OHIO	3321.01, *et seq.*	Between 6 and 18	Child received high school diploma; lawfully employed; physical/mental condition does not permit attendance	Instructed by person qualified to teach in required branches; approval necessary by district superintendent; if challenged, a religious-based exemption must pass 3-pronged test: (1) Are religious beliefs sincere? (2) Will application of compulsory education law infringe on right to free exercise of religion? (3) Does the state have an overriding interest? *Wisconsin v. Yoder*, 406 U.S. 205 (1972)	$5 to $20 fine; upon refusal to pay fine, imprisonment 10 to 30 days
OKLAHOMA	Tit. 70 §1744; 10-105	Between 5 and 18; deaf children between 7 and 21	Mental/physical disability prevents attendance; child is 16 and has permission of school and parents; emergency	Instruction must be in good faith and equivalent to that given by the state; *see Wright v. State*, 209 P. 179 (1922)	Misdemeanor; 1st offense: $5 to $25; 2nd offense: $10 to $50; subsequent: $25 to $100
OREGON	339.005, *et seq.*	Between 7 and 18	Child has completed 12th grade; attending private school; proof of equivalent knowledge of subjects through 12th grade; children taught by parent or private teacher; over 16 and lawfully employed	Give notice to superintendent and notice must be acknowledged by him; annual examination given and results submitted to superintendent; if insufficient score, student may be ordered to attend public school	Notice to parent given; upon noncompliance, complaint made to court which shall issue a warrant and conduct a hearing
PENNSYLVANIA	Tit. 24 §§13-1326, *et seq.*	Between 8 and 17	Graduated high school; 15 and with approval, child may enroll in private trade school; enrolled in home education program pursuant to Tit. 24 §13-1327.1 or private school; physical/mental defects rendering education impracticable; 16 and lawfully employed; 15 and engaged in farming or domestic service or 14 if engaged in same having achieved highest elementary grade; resides over 2 miles from nearest public highway, school or free public transportation is not furnished	File notice with a notarized affidavit of various information including proposed education objectives and immunization record; evaluation by teacher or administrator, etc.	$2 for first offense and up to $5 for each subsequent offense together with costs and upon default of payment subjected to county jail up to 5 days

(Continued)

Table 11: Compulsory Education—Continued

State	Code Section	Age Requirements	Exceptions	Home School Provisions	Penalties on Parents for Noncompliance
RHODE ISLAND	16-19-1, *et seq.*	Between 6 and 16	Child attends private school or is home instructed by approval of school committee; physical/mental condition of child renders attendance impracticable	Register kept and reading, writing, geography, arithmetic, history of Rhode Island and U.S., and principles of American government are taught	$50 for each absent day and if days exceed 30 during a school year parent shall be imprisoned up to 6 months and/or fined up to $500
SOUTH CAROLINA	59-65-10, *et seq.*	Between 5 and 17	Enrolled in private, parochial, or other approved program; child graduated; physical/mental disability; 8th grade completed and gainfully and lawfully employed; child is married or unmarried but pregnant; child is age 10 and has been out of school for over 3 years; 16 and attending vocational school	Instruction must be approved; parent has at least a high school diploma and a passing score on a basic skills exam; evidence of student's progress given; access to library facilities; participate in Basic Skills Assessment, etc. or instruction given under South Carolina Association of Independent Home Schools and its requirements	$50 fine or prison up to 30 days; each absence is separate offense
SOUTH DAKOTA	13-27-1, *et seq.*	Between 6 and 16	Child achieved 8th grade and fits into a religious exemption; competent instruction received from another source	Parent need not be certified but Department of Education may ensure teaching is done by a competent person; may not instruct over 22 children; must take national standardized test	Class 2 misdemeanor; each subsequent offense is Class 1 misdemeanor
TENNESSEE	49-6-3001, *et seq.*	Between 7 and 17 inclusive	Child has graduated high school or has GED; physical/mental incapacity; child is 17 and conduct is detrimental to good order and benefit of other children; homebound instruction	Approved by local education agency; teacher/parent must have at least GED for teaching K-8, baccalaureate degree for 9-12; give notice; maintain records; standardized tests taken	Class C misdemeanor; each day absent is separate offense

(Continued)

Table 11: Compulsory Education—Continued

State	Code Section	Age Requirements	Exceptions	Home School Provisions	Penalties on Parents for Noncompliance
TEXAS	Educ. §§4.25; 21-032, *et seq.*	Between 6 and 17	Child is 17 and has a high school certificate; enrolled in private or parochial school which includes a course in good citizenship; handicapped child or child with mental condition; child enrolled in Texas Academy or Leadership in Humanities	Allowed	Criminal action against parents not precluded (Op. Atty. Gen. 1960, No. WW-862)
UTAH	53A-11-101, *et seq.*	Between 6 and 18	Child 16 may be partially released; completed work for graduation; home-schooled; physical/mental condition making attendance impracticable; employment provides proper influences and adequate educational opportunities; child is 16 and determined unable to profit from school because of inability or negative attitude toward discipline	Allowed	Misdemeanor
VERMONT	Tit. 16 §§1121, *et seq.*	Between 7 and 16	Child physically/mentally unable to attend; child has completed 10th grade; child is excused by superintendent	Allowed	Truant officer gives notice and upon noncompliance without a legal excuse fine of up to $1000; also complaint entered to town grand juror
VIRGINIA	22.1-254, *et seq.*	Between 5 and 18	Enrolled in private, parochial, or home instruction or taught by qualified tutor; children suffering infectious diseases; children under 10 living over 2.5 miles from school unless transportation provided within 1 mile; children 10 to 17 living over 2.5 miles from school unless transportation within 1.5 miles	Parent must hold baccalaureate degree or be certified teacher or use approved correspondence course or other approved program; parent must give notice; approved achievement tests required	Class 4 misdemeanor

(Continued)

Table 11: Compulsory Education—Continued

State	Code Section	Age Requirements	Exceptions	Home School Provisions	Penalties on Parents for Noncompliance
WASHINGTON	28A.225.010	Between 8 and 18	Enrolled in private school; home-based instruction; physically/mentally incapable of attending; child otherwise excused by reasons parents and school authorities agree on; child is 15 or older and legally employed or proficient through 9th grade or has met graduation requirements or has received certificate of educational competence	Instruction in occupational education, science, math, language, social studies, history, health, writing, reading, spelling, and appreciation for art and music; must be supervised by certified person or by a parent with 45 college level credit hours	$25 for each day of unexcused absence and/or attendance officer may, through school district's attorney, petition juvenile court to assume jurisdiction
WEST VIRGINIA	18-8-1	Between 6 and 16	Enrolled in private, parochial, or other approved school; instruction in home; physical/mental incapacity; residence over 2 miles from school or school bus route; conditions rendering attendance impossible or hazardous; child has graduated; work permit granted; serious illness or death in family; destitution in the home	Records kept; if child's education is suffering or for another compelling reason, superintendent may seek court order denying home instruction; instructor must have graduated high school or had formal education 4 hours higher than the most advanced student; child must take standardized test	$50 to $100 and cost of prosecution or 5 to 20 days jail; each absent day is separate offense
WISCONSIN	118.15	Between 6 and 18	Child has graduated; physical/mental condition renders incapable; child is home-schooled or attends private school; at 16 child may attend vocational or technical school	Must meet requirements for a private school such as at least 875 hours of instruction each year; instruction in reading, language arts, math, social studies, science, and health	Fine up to $500 and/or prison up to 30 days
WYOMING	21-4-101, *et seq.*	Between 7 and 16 or completion of 8th grade	Board believes attendance detrimental to mental/physical health of child or other children; attendance would be undue hardship; home-schooled or private school	Meets requirements of basic, academic educational program; parent must submit curriculum to local board	Misdemeanor: at least $5 to $25 fine and/or prison up to 10 days

12. CORPORAL PUNISHMENT IN PUBLIC SCHOOLS

In 1977 the U.S. Supreme Court ruled in *Ingraham* v. *Wright,* that schools may use corporal punishment despite parental objection. Prior to that ruling, there were few, if any, state statutes regulating the use of physical means of discipline in schools. After the decision, states began to address the issue. At present, twenty-five states have statutes covering corporal punishment.

The following chart covers only state statutes regarding corporal punishment. It should be noted that there are also local rules that authorize the use of corporal punishment or that require parental consent before corporal punishment can be imposed upon a child. Local school districts, and even individual schools, often have their own policies and procedures for handling disciplinary problems.

This issue has become very controversial lately. With heightened public awareness of child abuse and increased sensitivity to the emotional well-being of children, many schools and teachers, unfortunately, are loath to impose any discipline whatsoever upon students for fear of emotionally scarring them or being accused of child abuse themselves.

Table 12: Corporal Punishment In Public Schools

State	Code Section	Punishment Allowed	Circumstances Allowable
ALABAMA	No statutory provisions		
ALASKA	No statutory provisions		
ARIZONA	15-843	Procedures for disciplining pupils, including the use of corporal punishment, are to be prescribed; use of corporal punishment is to be consistent with state guidelines.	
ARKANSAS	6-18-505	Corporal punishment in a reasonable manner specifically authorized.	"For good cause."
CALIFORNIA	Educ. §§49000, *et seq.*	Corporal punishment prohibited.	
COLORADO	No statutory provisions		
CONNECTICUT	No statutory provisions		
DELAWARE	Tit. 14, §701	Teachers may exercise same authority as parents, including the administration of corporal punishment.	
DISTRICT OF COLUMBIA	No statutory provisions		
FLORIDA	232.27	Corporal punishment allowed, subject to prescribed procedures, including approval in principle by the principal before it is used; presence of another adult; and that an explanation is provided to parents; certain exceptions provided for.	
GEORGIA	20-2-730, *et seq.*	Corporal punishment allowed, subject to various restrictions, including: it may not be excessive or unduly severe or be used as a first line of punishment; it must be administered in the presence of a school official; a written explanation must be provided on request; and it may not be administered if a physician certifies that the child's mental or emotional stability could be affected.	
HAWAII	298-16	Physical punishment may not be used, but a teacher may use reasonable force to restrain a student in attendance from hurting himself or any other person or property.	
IDAHO	No statutory provisions		
ILLINOIS	No statutory provisions		
INDIANA	No statutory provisions		
IOWA	No statutory provisions		
KANSAS	No statutory provisions		
KENTUCKY	No statutory provisions		

(Continued)

Table 12: Corporal Punishment In Public Schools—Continued

State	Code Section	Punishment Allowed	Circumstances Allowable
LOUISIANA	17:223, 17:416.1	Board to issue rules regarding corporal punishment; corporal punishment allowed in a reasonable manner; corporal punishment discretionary, but rules to implement and control any form of corporal punishment to be adopted by board.	"Good cause."
MAINE	No statutory provisions		
MARYLAND	Educ. 7-305	Corporal punishment may not be administered in state except in 12 counties listed in Educ. §7-305(a)	
MASSACHUSETTS	Ch. 71 §37G	Prohibits corporal punishment, but any member of school committee, teacher, or agent of school may use reasonable force to protect themselves, pupils, or other persons from an assault by a pupil.	
MICHIGAN	380.1312	Corporal punishment or threats of corporal punishment prohibited, but "reasonable physical force" may be used in self-defense or in defense of others, to obtain possession of weapon or other dangerous object or to protect property.	
MINNESOTA	No statutory provisions		
MISSISSIPPI	No statutory provisions		
MISSOURI	160.261	"Spanking" approved when administered in reasonable manner and in accordance with board rules approved; where unreasonableness is alleged, initial investigation to be by school and not division of family services.	
MONTANA	20-4-30	Corporal punishment permitted by principal if he or she deems it necessary and requires it to be administered in the presence of a witness, without undue anger, and not administered as an undue or severe punishment; advance notice to parents required except in cases of open and flagrant defiance of authority, in which case either teacher or principal may administer without notice to parents; undue or severe punishment by teacher or principal is a misdemeanor.	
NEBRASKA	No statutory provisions		
NEVADA	392.465	Corporal punishment allowed, but discouraged; board to adopt rules regulating use; parents to be notified; punishment shall not be administered about head or face.	After all other methods of discipline have proven ineffective.
NEW HAMPSHIRE	No statutory provisions		
NEW JERSEY	18A:6-1	Corporal punishment prohibited, but reasonable force may be used to quell a disturbance, obtain possession of weapons, etc., for self-defense or for protection of person or property.	

(Continued)

Table 12: Corporal Punishment In Public Schools—Continued

State	Code Section	Punishment Allowed	Circumstances Allowable
NEW MEXICO	No statutory provisions		
NEW YORK	No statutory provisions		
NORTH CAROLINA	115C-288; 115C-390, 391	Principals, teachers, and others may use reasonable force in the exercise of lawful authority to restrain or correct pupils and maintain order; local boards may not prohibit use of such force but are to adopt policies governing administration.	
NORTH DAKOTA	12.1-05-05	Use of force in disciplining students permitted provided it does not create substantial risk of death, serious bodily injury, disfigurement, or gross degradation.	
OHIO	3313.20; 3319.41	Corporal punishment allowed if reasonable and necessary to preserve discipline unless prohibited by board; board may not prohibit use of force to quell a disturbance threatening physical injury.	
OKLAHOMA	Tit. 70, §6-114	Boards to adopt policy for the control and discipline of students.	
OREGON	No statutory provisions		
PENNSYLVANIA	No statutory provisions		
RHODE ISLAND	No statutory provisions		
SOUTH CAROLINA	59-63-260	Boards may provide corporal punishment for any pupil that it deems just and proper.	
SOUTH DAKOTA	No statutory provisions		
TENNESSEE	49-6-4103	Corporal punishment allowed if imposed in reasonable manner; corporal punishment allowed in reformatory schools; Dept. of Corrections to establish procedures; punished pupil has right to physical exam to determine if punishment was excessive.	"Good cause."
TEXAS	No statutory provisions		
UTAH	No statutory provisions		
VERMONT	Tit. 16, §1161a	Corporal punishment prohibited, but reasonable and necessary force may be used to quell a disturbance, obtain possession of weapon, in self-defense, or protection of persons or property.	
VIRGINIA	22.1-279.1	Corporal punishment prohibited, but "incidental, minor or reasonable physical contact or other actions" permitted to maintain order and control; reasonable and necessary force permitted to quell a disturbance or remove a child to prevent harm, in self-defense, to obtain possession of weapon, etc.	
WASHINGTON	No statutory provisions		

(Continued)

Table 12: Corporal Punishment In Public Schools—Continued

State	Code Section	Punishment Allowed	Circumstances Allowable
WEST VIRGINIA	18A-5-1	Principal may administer corporal punishment subject to numerous requirements, including that it is administered in the presence of an adult witness and it may not be excessive or unduly severe or be used as a first line of punishment.	Last resort.
WISCONSIN	118.31	Corporal punishment generally prohibited; reasonable and necessary force allowed in self-defense, to protect others, etc.	
WYOMING	21-4-308	Boards may adopt rules for reasonable forms of punishment and disciplinary measures; teachers, etc., are authorized to impose reasonable forms of punishment and disciplinary measures.	

13. PRAYER IN PUBLIC SCHOOLS

Although the United States Supreme Court ruled prayer in public schools unconstitutional in 1962, many individual states have not taken action to repeal the original acts authorizing the opening of the school day with prayer. Until the early 1960s there were no laws on the subject of prayer in schools. After the Supreme Court struck down the practice—without reference to any legal precedent or established legal theory—states responded by drafting laws authorizing prayers and moments of silence designed to avoid the Supreme Court's definition of impermissible activity. Thirty states have enacted such laws. For example, Delaware authorizes two to three minutes of prayer to "voluntarily participate in moral, philosophical, patriotic or religious activity," and other states' statutes authorize "brief times" or one, two, or three minutes of "silent prayer," "silent reflection," or "silent meditation."

The law in this area, though settled, is still controversial. There are strong efforts afoot to reintroduce prayer in public schools, particularly by individuals who maintain that the current crisis in public education (low test scores, violence in the classrooms, drug and alcohol abuse) began when prayer was made illegal, and, conversely, strong efforts to fight the reintroduction, particularly by proponents of the theory of the separation of church and state.

The prevailing theme in the proposals to reintroduce prayer in public schools is one of voluntariness. Such efforts, however, are doomed as long as peer pressure in the classroom is equated with state action; that is, as states cannot encourage a particular religious practice, peer pressure exerted upon nonparticipants in a "voluntary" program is considered coercive.

Table 13: Prayer In Public Schools

State	Code Section	Provisions
ALABAMA	16-1-20.1, *et seq.*	Period of silence not to exceed one minute in duration, shall be observed for meditation or voluntary prayer, and during any such period no other activities shall be engaged in
ALASKA	No statutory provisions	
ARIZONA	15-522	One minute period of silence for meditation
ARKANSAS	6-16-119	Brief period of silent meditation and reflection
CALIFORNIA	No statutory provisions	
COLORADO	No statutory provisions	
CONNECTICUT	10-16a	Silent meditation
DELAWARE	Tit. 14 §4101	Two to three minutes to voluntarily participate in moral, philosophical, patriotic, or religious activity
DISTRICT OF COLUMBIA	No statutory provisions	
FLORIDA	233.062	Brief period not to exceed two minutes, for the purpose of silent prayer or meditation
GEORGIA	20-2-1050	Brief period of silent prayer or meditation
HAWAII	No statutory provisions	
IDAHO	No statutory provisions	
ILLINOIS	105 ILCS 20/1	Brief period of silence which shall not be conducted as a religious exercise but shall be an opportunity for silent prayer or for silent reflection
INDIANA	20-10.1-7-11	Brief period of silent prayer or meditation
IOWA	No statutory provisions	
KANSAS	72-5308a	Brief period of silence to be used as opportunity for silent prayer or for silent reflection
KENTUCKY	158.175	Recitation of Lord's prayer to teach our country's history and as an affirmation of the freedom of religion in this country
LOUISIANA	17:2115(A)	Brief time of silent meditation
MAINE	Tit. 20-A, §4805	Period of silence shall be observed for reflection or meditation
MARYLAND	Educ. §7-104	Meditate silently for approximately one minute; student or teacher may read the holy scriptures or pray
MASSACHUSETTS	Ch. 71 §1A	Period of silence not to exceed one minute in duration shall be observed for personal thoughts
MICHIGAN	§380.1565	Opportunity to observe time in silent meditation
MINNESOTA	No statutory provisions	
MISSISSIPPI	37-13-4	Teacher may permit the voluntary participation by students or others in prayer
MISSOURI	No statutory provisions	
MONTANA	20-7-112	Any teacher, principal, or superintendent may open the school day with a prayer

(Continued)

Table 13: Prayer In Public Schools—Continued

State	Code Section	Provisions
NEBRASKA	No statutory provisions	
NEVADA	No statutory provisions	
NEW HAMPSHIRE	189:1-b	Period of not more than five minutes shall be available to those who wish to exercise their right to freedom of assembly and participate voluntarily in the free exercise of religion
NEW JERSEY	18A:36-4	Observe a one minute period of silence to be used solely at the discretion of the individual student for quiet and private contemplation or introspection
NEW MEXICO	22-5-4.1	Period of silence not to exceed one minute to be used for contemplation, meditation, or prayer; held to be unconstitutional: *Duffy* v. *Las Cruces Public Schools*, 557 F. Supp 1013
NEW YORK	Educ. §3029-a	Brief period of silent meditation which may be opportunity for silent meditation on a religious theme or silent reflection
NORTH CAROLINA	No statutory provisions	
NORTH DAKOTA	15-47-30.1	Period of silence not to exceed one minute for meditation or prayer
OHIO	3313.601	Reasonable periods of time for programs or meditation upon a moral, philosophical, or patriotic theme
OKLAHOMA	11-101.1	Shall permit those students and teachers who wish to do so to participate in voluntary prayer
OREGON	No statutory provisions	
PENNSYLVANIA	Tit. 24 §15-1516.1	Brief period of silent prayer or meditation which is not a religious exercise but an opportunity for prayer or reflection as child is disposed
RHODE ISLAND	16-12-3.1	Period of silence not to exceed one minute in duration shall be observed for meditation
SOUTH CAROLINA	No statutory provisions	
SOUTH DAKOTA	No statutory provisions	
TENNESSEE	49-6-1004(a)	Mandatory period of silence of approximately one minute
TEXAS	No statutory provisions	
UTAH	No statutory provisions	
VERMONT	No statutory provisions	
VIRGINIA	22.1-203	School may establish the daily observance of one minute of silence
WASHINGTON	No statutory provisions	
WEST VIRGINIA	Const. Art. III, §15A	Designated brief time for students to exercise their right to personal and private contemplation, meditation, etc.
WISCONSIN	No statutory provisions	
WYOMING	No statutory provisions	

14. PRIVACY OF SCHOOL RECORDS

The question of the right of privacy and, specifically, who should have access to student records has divided parents and students from school teachers and administrators. There are strong arguments on both sides. School teachers and administrators believe, traditionally, that they should be able to deal with the children they teach in utter confidence—especially when it comes to evaluation of ability, behavior, and psychological factors. School administrators may have critical opinions and evaluations to make and pass on to colleagues in order to effectively deal with a particular student's potential for success or failure in school. Release of these opinions to the family or the student may actually have a detrimental effect on the student and/or the teacher or the school's ability to help the student.

On the other hand, students and parents have a deep interest in knowing how they or their child is evaluated—to know what school administrators are saying about the child and what impact those opinions are having on his or her progress in school. Parents may worry that negative evaluations or assessments may be off-base, inaccurate, or the result of an objective evaluation that misses personal situations and emotions. In addition, negative evaluations may be the result of physical or psychological handicaps or deficiencies in ability that need special attention and may be helped if parents or students are made aware of them. Parents have a responsibility for the quality of education that their children receive as well as a right to participate in decisions that affect class placement and particular courses and subjects taught.

This dynamic between the parents' right to have input into their child's education and the school's responsibility to professionally teach and discipline their students is what has driven the development of certain privacy rules. But there is also a new dynamic that is becoming a factor in education and, specifically, access to records: over the last thirty years the growing disillusionment with our traditional education system, which insisted on certain standards of performance for all students, has given way to the belief that each child has different learning curves and behavioral norms that need to be respected. As a result, standards of education and behavior are no longer standard and regular but adjust to the needs, wants, and potential of each student and his or her family. In order to monitor the attention that individual children are getting, laws have guaranteed parents access to student records.

Another area concerning school records that is becoming an issue encompasses child abuse, neglect, and personal health. With today's broader definition of abuse, a family's religious convictions or practices, cultural heritage, social orientation, or lack of awareness may qualify. In an extreme example, state authorities took custody of minor children because their parents failed to keep their children's dental appointments! There may be a need for parents to monitor school records in order to see that educators are not misinterpreting and misconstruing various family customs, practices, and behavior or undermining certain training being done at home.

FERPA

The Family Educational Records Protection Act (FERPA) was originally passed in 1976 and has been amended many times since. Its purpose is to guarantee parents free access to student school records. Under provisions of the Act, the Secretary of Education has the authority to withhold all federal funding to institutions that do not make school records available to a student's parents. There are exceptions to this rule, such as authorizing the transfer of transcripts when a student changes schools or applies for admission elsewhere, for researchers doing studies of educational techniques and practices when such research can be conducted confidentially and anonymously, for state or federal officials conducting audits of public assistance programs, or in the course of normal business. Many states now rely on FERPA to protect student privacy and insure parental access. A few states have gone beyond the protections of the federal act.

Table 14: Privacy of School Records

State	Code Section	Who Has Access	Penalties
FEDERAL	20 U.S.C. §1232g Family Educational Records Protection Act	Parents, specifically authorized state or federal officials for purposes of auditing public assistance programs, researchers for purposes of gathering data to improve educational testing or educational curriculum, authorized school administrators or other educational institutions as authorized by student or parents for purposes of application for admission to an educational institution or for employment	Withdrawal of all federal funding
ALABAMA	36-12-40	Parent of minor child may inspect regulation and circulation records of any school that pertain to his child	
ALASKA	25.20.130	Both custodial and non-custodial parent	
ARIZONA	15-141, *et seq.*	Governed by FERPA; if school district permits release of directory information, it must provide it also for recruiting representatives of militia. Department of Youth Treatment and Rehabilitation has access to any pupil referred.	Injunctive or special relief by Superior Court
ARKANSAS	6-20-510	Records regarding handicapped students are to be kept confidential	
CALIFORNIA	Educ. §§49060, *et seq.*	Implements FERPA and eliminates conflicts with it.	
COLORADO	22-2-111; 24-72-204	Unless contrary to federal law, employers or law enforcement officers have access without parental consent. Student records are confidential except when requested by the governor or a committee of the general assembly.	
CONNECTICUT	10-154a	Parents generally assured access. Communication relating to alcohol or drugs between the nurse and student need not be disclosed to parent.	
DELAWARE	Tit. 14 §4111	Confidential with stated exceptions: authorized school personnel by request of pupil aged 14 or older; parent/guardian. Immunity granted by reason of contents.	Unless malice can be proven, no cause of action for participation in formulation or disclosure of records
DISTRICT OF COLUMBIA	No known provisions		
FLORIDA	228-093, *et seq.*	FERPA mostly implemented. Parents and pupils have access; after pupil is 18 or attending post-secondary educational institution, the right belongs to the student only.	Injunctive relief and attorney's fees available
GEORGIA	No known provisions		
HAWAII	298-19	§298-19 provides for the keeping of records but mentions nothing about access	
IDAHO	32-717A	Custodial and non-custodial parent	

(Continued)

Table 14: Privacy of School Records—Continued

State	Code Section	Who Has Access	Penalties
ILLINOIS	105 ILCS 10/1, *et seq.*	Inspection allowed by students and parents but restricted to third parties. Information communicated in confidence by a student or parents to school personnel is not available.	Damages and other remedies available
INDIANA	No known provisions		
IOWA	22.7	Student's personal information in records is confidential	
KANSAS	72-6214	Governed by FERPA	
KENTUCKY	164.283; 421.216	Counselor-student communications are privileged. Post-secondary school records are confidential.	
LOUISIANA	AG Opinions #89-500; 91-73	Public school student's names and addresses are public information. Custodial and non-custodial parent has right to inspect child's records	
MAINE	Tit. 20-1 §6001	Governed by FERPA	
MARYLAND	Educ. 7-410; 10-616	Teacher's, principal's, or counselor's observations during consultations are not admissible as evidence against student. Only "persons in interest" may inspect student's records.	
MASSACHUSETTS	Ch. 71 §34A, *et seq.*	Student (transcript), parent, guardian, student over 18 may inspect	
MICHIGAN	600.2165	Test results open only to qualified education personnel. In legal proceedings, counselors, teachers, and school employees may not disclose information received in confidence.	
MINNESOTA	13.02, *et seq.*	Records are confidential except for directory information and shall be released only pursuant to valid court order. Statute specifically authorizes access to or disclosure of information in health and safety emergencies. Minor may request information to be witheld from parent or guardian.	
MISSISSIPPI	37-15-3	Governed by FERPA; records not available to the general public	
MISSOURI	No known provisions		
MONTANA	123.35	Parent and non-custodial parent	
NEBRASKA	79-4; 79-157, *et seq.*	Administrator, auditors, teachers, parents, pupil; academic and disciplinary records segregated; disciplinary records destroyed at graduation if authorized by state records board.	
NEVADA	49.290, 291; 125.520	Both custodial and non-custodial parent; privilege for counselor-pupil and teacher-pupil communication	
NEW HAMPSHIRE	91-A:5	Guardian ad litem (Guidelines for Guardians ad litem Guideline 4); no public access	

(Continued)

National Survey of State Laws

Table 14: Privacy of School Records—Continued

State	Code Section	Who Has Access	Penalties
NEW JERSEY	18A:36-19	State board establishes rules. Outside access permitted, although regulations may limit it somewhat. Personnel protected from legal action based on statements in records.	
NEW MEXICO	40-4-9.1	Both custodial and non-custodial parent	
NEW YORK	Comm. Educ. Dec. 9/20/60	Parental access in conference with school officials; records of telephone number available in emergency circumstances	
NORTH CAROLINA	8-53.4; 115C-3; 115C-174.13; 115C-402	Not subject to public inspection; minimum competency test scores of students available consistent with FERPA; counselor communication privileged	
NORTH DAKOTA	15-21.1-06; 31-06.1	Student's educational record is confidential and may not be released without written consent of student. If student is under 14, written consent of student's parent/guardian is required.	
OHIO	149.41; 3319.321	No release without student's consent if over 18; if 18 or under, consent of parent or guardian is necessary. Directory information may be released. Rights of school district to renew or select student records are restricted.	
OKLAHOMA	Tit. 51§24A.16; Tit. 70 §6-115	Confidential except for directory information; teacher may not reveal student-obtained information unless required by contract or released to a parent.	Misdemeanor for teacher to reveal information regarding any child except as required in performance of contractual duties or requested by parents.
OREGON	336.195	Parents, but they may see behavioral records only in conference with professional. Records are confidential with certain parent/guardian exceptions (§§336-185, *et seq.*). Elementary and secondary school teachers' communications are privileged.	
PENNSYLVANIA	Tit. 43 §68	Parents	
RHODE ISLAND	16-38-5		Misdemeanor to circulate a questionnaire "so framed as to ask intimate questions about themselves or families, thus trespassing upon the pupils' constitutional rights and invading the privacy of the home" without approval of local school commissioner and department of education
SOUTH CAROLINA	No known provisions		

(Continued)

Table 14: Privacy of School Records—Continued

State	Code Section	Who Has Access	Penalties
SOUTH DAKOTA	19-13-21.1; 25-5-7.3; 27B-6-2	Access may not be denied parent who is not child's primary residential parent. County board of mental retardation has access to the school records of any case under investigation. Elementary and secondary school counselors' communications are privileged except in cases of child abuse. College and university counselor-student communications are privileged.	
TENNESSEE	10-7-504	School records are confidential except when compelled under legal process or released for safety of person or property. Outsiders are authorized access to pupil records for research and pupil may give consent for others to have access.	
TEXAS	Tex. Rev. Civ. Stat. Ann. Art. 6:52-17a§3(a)(14)	Records are confidential and to be released only on request of education personnel, student, parent or spouse, or person conducting a child abuse investigation.	
UTAH	30-3-29	Both custodial and non-custodial parent	
VERMONT	Tit. 1 §317(11)	Confidential; limits on release of school records except as required by FERPA	
VIRGINIA	12.1-287; 22.1-380.1	Limits on access; equal access to student directory information must be given to representatives of armed forces.	
WASHINGTON	42.17.310	School records exempt from state public records act	
WEST VIRGINIA	No known provisions		
WISCONSIN	118.125, 126	Pupil, parents, courts, school officials, and persons designated by parents or pupil. Behavioral records must be destroyed one year after graduation unless graduate requests otherwise. Records created before September 1974 are not affected. School psychologist, counselor, social worker and nurse, teacher, or administrator working in alcohol or drug abuse program activities shall keep student communications regarding such confidential unless pupil consents to disclosure, if there is serious and imminent danger to anyone's health or safety or if required to be disclosed by law.	
WYOMING	No known provisions		

IV.   EMPLOYMENT LAWS

15. LEGAL HOLIDAYS

The diversity of our country is reflected in the various holidays recognized by the individual states. While many holidays, including New Year's Day, Memorial Day, and Labor Day, are considered legal holidays in all states, others, such as Good Friday and Robert E. Lee's Birthday, are recognized in only a handful, while a few are particular to only one state, for example Alaska Day and Pioneer Day.

The recognition of civil rights leader Martin Luther King, Jr.'s birthday has sparked a great deal of controversy. It is not recognized in every state, and in some of the states where it is recognized, it is not a paid holiday for state employees. And in a few states, though it is an official day of recognition, it is not a legal holiday. The most interesting variation on the celebration of Martin Luther King, Jr. Day is in Louisiana, where it is one of six other days that are interchangeably recognized. Each year the governor is authorized to declare any two of these days as an official state holiday, except that every two years Martin Luther King, Jr.'s birthday must be one of the two days selected.

Due to the myriad local holidays in the states, only the major holidays are featured below for comparison.

Table 15: Legal Holidays

State	Code Section	Holidays
ALABAMA	1-3-8	New Year's Day; Martin Luther King, Jr.'s Birthday; Mardi Gras (Mobile & Baldwin Counties only); Washington's and Jefferson's Birthday; Memorial Day; Independence Day; Labor Day; Columbus Day; Veterans Day; Thanksgiving; Christmas; Jefferson Davis Birthday; Confederate Memorial Day; Robert E. Lee's Birthday
ALASKA	44.12.010	New Year's Day; Martin Luther King, Jr.'s Birthday; President's Day; Memorial Day; Independence Day; Labor Day; Veterans Day; Thanksgiving; Christmas; Alaska Day
ARIZONA	1-301	New Year's Day; Washington's Birthday; Lincoln's Birthday; Memorial Day; Independence Day; Labor Day; Columbus Day; Veterans Day; Thanksgiving; Christmas
ARKANSAS	1-5-101; 69-101	New Year's Day; Martin Luther King, Jr.'s and Robert E. Lee's Birthday; Washington's Birthday; Memorial Day; Independence Day; Labor Day; Veterans Day; Thanksgiving; Christmas Eve; Christmas
CALIFORNIA	Gov. Code §6700	New Year's Day; Martin Luther King, Jr.'s Birthday; Washington's Birthday; Lincoln's Birthday; Good Friday; Admission Day; Memorial Day; Independence Day; Labor Day; Columbus Day; Veterans Day; Thanksgiving; Christmas
COLORADO	24-11-101	New Year's Day; Martin Luther King, Jr.'s Birthday; Washington's Birthday; Memorial Day; Independence Day; Columbus Day; Veterans Day; Thanksgiving; Christmas
CONNECTICUT	§1-4	New Year's Day; Martin Luther King, Jr.'s Birthday; Washington's Birthday; Good Friday; Memorial Day; Independence Day; Labor Day; Columbus Day; Veterans Day; Thanksgiving; Christmas;
DELAWARE	Tit. 1 §501	New Year's Day; Martin Luther King, Jr.'s Birthday; Washington's Birthday; Good Friday; Memorial Day; Independence Day; Labor Day; Columbus Day; Veterans Day; Thanksgiving; Christmas; Day of biennial general elections
DISTRICT OF COLUMBIA	§28-2701	New Year's Day; Martin Luther King, Jr.'s Birthday; Washington's Birthday; Memorial Day; Independence Day; Labor Day; Columbus Day; Veterans Day; Thanksgiving; Christmas
FLORIDA	110.117; 683.01; Fla. Admin. Code, 60k-5.009	New Year's Day; Martin Luther King, Jr.'s Birthday; Memorial Day; Independence Day; Labor Day; Veterans Day; Thanksgiving; friday after Thanksgiving; Christmas. Following are not official holidays but paid days off for state employees: Robert E. Lee's Birthday; Lincoln's Birthday; Susan B. Anthony's Birthday; Washington's Birthday; Shrove Tuesday; Good Friday; Pascua Florida Day; Confederate Memorial Day; Jefferson Davis's Birthday; Columbus Day
GEORGIA	1-4-1; Ga. Gov. Memos dated 10/18/90 and 10/16/91	New Year's Day; Martin Luther King, Jr.'s Birthday; Memorial Day; Independence Day; Labor Day; Columbus Day; Veterans Day; Thanksgiving; Friday after Thanksgiving; Christmas Eve; Christmas; Confederate Memorial Day; Washington's Birthday is holiday but paid day off is taken by state employees at Christmastime; Friday after Thanksgiving is designated as paid day off in honor of Robert E. Lee's Birthday
HAWAII	8-1	New Year's Day; Martin Luther King, Jr.'s Birthday; President's Day; Good Friday; Memorial Day; Independence Day; Labor Day; Veterans Day; Thanksgiving; Christmas; Prince Jonah Kuhio Kalanianaole Day; King Kamehameha Day; Admission Day; Election Day except primary election

(Continued)

172

Table 15: Legal Holidays—Continued

State	Code Section	Holidays
IDAHO	73-108	New Year's Day; Martin Luther King, Jr.'s Birthday and Idaho Human Rights Day; Washington's Birthday; Memorial Day; Independence Day; Labor Day; Columbus Day; Veterans Day; Thanksgiving; Christmas
ILLINOIS	205 ILCS 630/17	New Year's Day; Martin Luther King, Jr.'s Birthday; President's Day; Lincoln's Birthday; Casimir Pulaski's Birthday; Good Friday; Memorial Day; Independence Day; Labor Day; Columbus Day; Veterans Day; Thanksgiving; Christmas
INDIANA	1-1-9-1, 2	New Year's Day; Martin Luther King, Jr.'s Birthday; Washington's Birthday (celebrated day after Christmas); Lincoln's Birthday (celebrated Friday after Thanksgiving); Good Friday; Independence Day; Labor Day; Columbus Day; Veterans Day; Thanksgiving; Christmas; day of any primary or general election for national, state, or city officials
IOWA	33.1, 2	New Year's Day; Martin Luther King, Jr.'s Birthday; Washington's Birthday (public holiday but not paid day off for state employees); Memorial Day; Independence Day; Labor Day; Columbus Day; Veterans Day; Thanksgiving; Friday after Thanksgiving; Christmas Eve; Christmas
KANSAS	SA §35-107	New Year's Day; Martin Luther King, Jr.'s Birthday; Washington's Birthday; Lincoln's Birthday; Memorial Day; Independence Day; Labor Day; Columbus Day; Veterans Day; Thanksgiving; Friday after Thanksgiving; Christmas
KENTUCKY	2.110	New Year's Day; Martin Luther King, Jr.'s Birthday; Washington's Birthday; Lincoln's Birthday; Memorial Day; Independence Day; Labor Day; Columbus Day; Veterans Day; Thanksgiving; Christmas; Jefferson Davis's Birthday; Robert E. Lee's Birthday; Confederate Memorial Day; Franklin D. Roosevelt's Birthday
LOUISIANA	1:55	New Year's Day; Mardi Gras; Memorial Day; Independence Day; Labor Day; Veterans Day; Thanksgiving; Christmas; Good Friday; general election day in even numbered years; Also, governor has authority to declare following paid holidays: Martin Luther King, Jr.'s Birthday; Robert E. Lee's Birthday; Washington's Birthday; Memorial Day; Confederate Memorial Day; Acadian Day; s/he must declare 2, including national Memorial Day every year and Martin Luther King, Jr.'s Birthday every other year
MAINE	Tit. 4, §1051; 20-A, §4802	New Year's Day; Martin Luther King, Jr.'s Birthday; Washington's Birthday; Memorial Day; Independence Day; Labor Day; Columbus Day; Veterans Day; Thanksgiving; Christmas; Patriot's Day
MARYLAND	Art. 1 §27	New Year's Day; Martin Luther King, Jr.'s Birthday; Washington's Birthday; Lincoln's Birthday; Good Friday; Memorial Day; Independence Day; Labor Day; Columbus Day; Veterans Day; Thanksgiving; Christmas; Maryland Day; Defender's Day; any day of general or congressional election
MASSACHUSETTS	Ch. 4 §7, cl. Eighteenth Eighteenth A	New Year's Day; Martin Luther King, Jr.'s Birthday; Washington's Birthday; Memorial Day; Independence Day; Labor Day; Columbus Day; Veterans Day; Thanksgiving; Christmas; Patriot's Day

(Continued)

Table 15: Legal Holidays—Continued

State	Code Section	Holidays
MICHIGAN	435.101	New Year's Day; Martin Luther King, Jr.'s Birthday; President's Day; Washington's Birthday (not paid day off for state employees); Lincoln's Birthday (not paid day off for state employees); Memorial Day; Independence Day; Labor Day; Veterans Day; Thanksgiving; Friday after Thanksgiving; Christmas Eve; Christmas; New Year's Eve
MINNESOTA	645.44 subd. 5	New Year's Day; Martin Luther King, Jr.'s Birthday; Washington's and Lincoln's Birthday; Memorial Day; Independence Day; Labor Day; Columbus Day; Veterans Day; Thanksgiving; Friday after Thanksgiving; Christmas
MISSISSIPPI	3-3-7	New Year's Day; Martin Luther King, Jr.'s and Robert E. Lee's Birthday; Washington's Birthday; Memorial Day and Jefferson Davis's Birthday; Independence Day; Labor Day; Veterans Day; Thanksgiving; Christmas; Confederate Memorial Day
MISSOURI	9.010	New Year's Day; Martin Luther King, Jr.'s Birthday; Washington's Birthday; Lincoln's Birthday; 8th day of May; Memorial Day; Independence Day; Labor Day; Columbus Day; Veterans Day; Thanksgiving; Christmas
MONTANA	1-1-216	New Year's Day; Martin Luther King, Jr.'s Birthday; Lincoln's and Washington's Birthday;
NEBRASKA	25-2221	New Year's Day; Martin Luther King, Jr.'s Birthday; President's Day; Arbor Day; Memorial Day; Independence Day; Labor Day; Columbus Day; Veterans Day; Thanksgiving; Christmas Eve; Christmas
NEVADA	236.015	New Year's Day; Martin Luther King, Jr.'s Birthday; Washington's Birthday; Memorial Day; Independence Day; Labor Day; Veterans Day; Thanksgiving; Friday after Thanksgiving; Christmas
NEW HAMPSHIRE	288:1, 2	New Year's Day; Washington's Birthday; Memorial Day; Independence Day; Labor Day; Columbus Day (not paid day off for state employees); Veterans Day; Thanksgiving; Friday after Thanksgiving; Civil Rights Day (not paid day off for state employees); biennial election days (not paid day off for state employees)
NEW JERSEY	36:1-1, 1.2	New Year's Day; Martin Luther King, Jr.'s Birthday; Washington's Birthday; Lincoln's Birthday; Good Friday; Memorial Day; Independence Day; Labor Day; Columbus Day; Veterans Day; Thanksgiving; Christmas; any general election day
NEW MEXICO	12-5-2	New Year's Day; Martin Luther King, Jr.'s Birthday; President's Day; Washington's and Lincoln's Birthday; Memorial Day; Independence Day; Labor Day; Columbus Day; Veterans Day; Thanksgiving; Christmas
NEW YORK	Gen. Constr. Law §24, 25	New Year's Day; Martin Luther King, Jr.'s Birthday; Washington's Birthday; Lincoln's Birthday; Memorial Day; Independence Day; Labor Day; Columbus Day; Veterans Day; Thanksgiving; Christmas Flag Day; any general election day

(Continued)

Table 15: Legal Holidays—Continued

State	Code Section	Holidays
NORTH CAROLINA	103-4; Office of State Personnel Memo dated 1/25/91	New Year's Day; Martin Luther King, Jr.'s Birthday; Good Friday; Independence Day; Labor Day; Columbus Day; Veterans Day; Thanksgiving; Friday after Thanksgiving; Christmas Eve; Christmas; in addition, Easter Monday and Memorial Day are bank holidays only and Robert E. Lee's Birthday, Washington's Birthday, Greek Independence Day, Anniversary of signing of Halifax Resolves, Confederate Memorial Day, Anniversary of Mecklenburg Declaration of Independence, Yom Kippur, and Columbus Day are public holidays but not paid days off for state employees
NORTH DAKOTA	1-03-01, 2 and 2.1	New Year's Day; Martin Luther King, Jr.'s Birthday; Washington's Birthday; Good Friday; Memorial Day; Independence Day; Labor Day; Veterans Day; Thanksgiving; Christmas; state offices close at noon on Christmas Eve
OHIO	1.14	New Year's Day; Martin Luther King, Jr.'s Birthday; Washington's and Lincoln's Birthday; Memorial Day; Independence Day; Labor Day; Columbus Day; Veterans Day; Thanksgiving; Christmas
OKLAHOMA	Tit. 25 §§82.1, 82.2	New Year's Day; Martin Luther King, Jr.'s Birthday; President's Day; Memorial Day; Independence Day; Labor Day; Veterans Day; Thanksgiving; Friday after Thanksgiving; Christmas; Senior Citizen's Day
OREGON	187.010, 020	New Year's Day; Martin Luther King, Jr.'s Birthday; President's Day; Memorial Day; Independence Day; Labor Day; Columbus Day; Veterans Day; Thanksgiving; Christmas
PENNSYLVANIA	Tit. 44, §11	New Year's Day; Martin Luther King, Jr.'s Birthday; President's Day; Good Friday; Memorial Day; Independence Day; Labor Day; Columbus Day; Veterans Day; Thanksgiving; Christmas; Flag Day (not paid day off for state employees)
RHODE ISLAND	25-1-1	New Year's Day; Martin Luther King, Jr.'s Birthday; Washington's Birthday (legal holiday but not paid day off for state employees); Lincoln's Birthday; Good Friday; Memorial Day; Independence Day; Labor Day; Columbus Day; Veterans Day; Thanksgiving; Christmas; Rhode Island Independence Day (legal holiday but not paid day off for state employees)
SOUTH CAROLINA	53-5-10	New Year's Day; Washington's Birthday; Memorial Day; Independence Day; Labor Day; Veterans Day; Thanksgiving; Friday after Thanksgiving; Christmas; Day after Christmas; general election days in even numbered years
SOUTH DAKOTA	1-5-1	New Year's Day; Martin Luther King, Jr.'s Birthday; Washington's Birthday; Memorial Day; Independence Day; Labor Day; Veterans Day; Thanksgiving; Christmas; Native American Day
TENNESSEE	15-1-101	New Year's Day; Martin Luther King, Jr.'s Birthday; Washington's Birthday; Good Friday; Memorial Day; Independence Day; Labor Day; Columbus Day; Veterans Day; Thanksgiving; Christmas; any day set apart for county, state, or national elections throughout the state
TEXAS	Art. 4591; 4591.2	New Year's Day; Martin Luther King, Jr.'s Birthday; Washington's Birthday; Memorial Day; Independence Day; Labor Day; Veterans Day; Thanksgiving; Friday after Thanksgiving; Christmas Eve; Christmas; day after Christmas

(Continued)

Table 15: Legal Holidays—Continued

State	Code Section	Holidays
UTAH	63-13-2	New Year's Day; Martin Luther King, Jr.'s Birthday; President's Day; Memorial Day; Independence Day; Labor Day; Columbus Day; Veterans Day; Thanksgiving; Christmas; Pioneer Day
VERMONT	Tit. 1 §371	New Year's Day; Martin Luther King, Jr.'s Birthday (legal holiday but not paid day off for state employees); Washington's Birthday; Lincoln's Birthday (legal holiday but not paid day off for state employees); Memorial Day; Independence Day; Labor Day; Columbus Day; Veterans Day; Thanksgiving; Christmas; Town Meeting Day; Bennington Battle Day
VIRGINIA	2.1-21	New Year's Day; Lee-Jackson-King Day; Washington's Birthday; Memorial Day; Independence Day; Labor Day; Columbus and Yorktown Day; Election Day; Veterans Day; Thanksgiving; Friday after Thanksgiving; Christmas
WASHINGTON	1.16.050	New Year's Day; Martin Luther King, Jr.'s Birthday; Washington's Birthday; Lincoln's Birthday; Memorial Day; Independence Day; Labor Day; Veterans Day; Thanksgiving; Friday after Thanksgiving; Christmas
WEST VIRGINIA	2-2-1	New Year's Day; Martin Luther King, Jr.'s Birthday; Washington's Birthday; Lincoln's Birthday; Memorial Day; Independence Day; Labor Day; Columbus Day; Veterans Day; Thanksgiving; Christmas; West Virginia Day; any national, state, or other election day throughout any district or municipality
WISCONSIN	895.20	New Year's Day; Martin Luther King, Jr.'s Birthday; Washington's Birthday (official holiday but not paid day off for state employees); Good Friday; Memorial Day; Independence Day; Labor Day; any primary election day in September; Columbus Day (official holiday but not paid day off for state employees); any general election day in November; Veterans Day (official holiday but not paid day off for state employees); Thanksgiving; Christmas Eve; Christmas
WYOMING	8-4-101	New Year's Day; Martin Luther King, Jr.'s Birthday; Washington's and Lincoln's Birthday; Memorial Day; Independence Day; Labor Day; Veterans Day; Thanksgiving; Christmas; Wyoming Equality Day

16. MINIMUM WAGE

The federal government has established a minimum wage, or the least dollar amount that may be paid hourly workers, that applies to all workers in all fifty states who are engaged in interstate commerce or the production of goods for interstate commerce (and closely allied enterprises) or are employed by an enterprise engaged in interstate commerce or the production of goods for commerce. Businesses engaged in "interstate commerce" are defined as those with potential to come in contact with interstate travelers or consumers in other states.

Thus the federal minimum wage does not apply to all occupations. Domestic workers are not covered in many situations; fishermen, employees of certain small newspapers, babysitters, and agricultural seasonal workers in small family farms are some of the common exemptions from the federal minimum wage law. Others who are exempt include those in seasonal employment, such as at amusement parks or seasonal recreation centers, and in "exempt" occupations, such as managers, salesmen, or administrators who are not paid on an hourly basis. Further, if a local business does not qualify as participating in interstate commerce, it, too, would be exempt. These exempt occupations are covered by state minimum wage laws that can be higher or lower than the federal minimum wage (set on April 1, 1991 at $4.25 per hour).

However, if the state minimum wage is higher than the federal minimum wage and the employee is subject to both state and federal law, the higher rate will apply.

Subminimum wages are hourly rates below the established minimum wage that may be paid for a limited time to learners, apprentices, messengers, student workers, and those employed in occupations not ordinarily given to full-time workers. The subminimum wage permits businesses to be able to continue to hire certain types of workers in certain nontraditional, "convenience" occupations.

Overall, there is little variation among states in regard to the minimum wage. Since the federal government has established a national minimum wage covering virtually all occupations, most states have simply adopted that wage as their standard, though a few have established higher rates and a few lower. The only surprise is in the number of states that have simply taken no action at all, perhaps determining that the market is the best regulator of wages. That is, if the wage is too low, the employer will either get no applicants or ones with no experience and no skills. Generally, the higher the wage, the better the applicant pool. However, there are circumstances in which workers may be taken advantage of either out of desperation or ignorance. This is precisely why the minimum wage exists.

Table 16: Minimum Wage

State	Code Section	Minimum Wage Per Hour	Subminimum Wage Per Hour
FEDERAL	Federal Labor Standards Act	$4.25 (eff. 4/1/91); applies to all employees covered by FLSA in 50 states, territories, and possessions except for American Samoa; standard applies to employees, not specifically exempt, who are: (1) engaged in interstate commerce; (2) engaged in production of goods for commerce; or (3) employed in an enterprise engaged in commerce or production of goods for commerce	At least 85% of federal minimum wage ($3.61 as of 4/1/91) for up to 90 days of training for individuals under 20 years of age
ALABAMA	No statutory provisions		
ALASKA	23.10.065; 23.10.070; Rules & Regs 8AAL 15.125, eff. 12/9/78	$4.75	75%; percentage rate of statutory minimum for learners and/or apprentices
ARIZONA	No provision	None	None
ARKANSAS	11-4-201 to11-4-219	$4.00	None
CALIFORNIA	Labor Code §1182	$4.25	85%; percentage rate for first 160 hours of employment, by state wage board order
COLORADO	8-6-109, *et seq.*	$3.00 by state wage board order	None
CONNECTICUT	31-58j	$4.27	85%; percentage rate for first 200 hours of employment
DELAWARE	Tit. 19 §902(a)	$4.25	None
DISTRICT OF COLUMBIA	36-220.1(10), .220.2(a) and (b), effective 10/93	$1.00 over federal minimum wage	Specific rates established by wage orders for various categories of employees
FLORIDA	No statutory provisions		
GEORGIA	34-4-3, -4	$3.25	Rate set by Commissioner
HAWAII	387-2	$4.75	None
IDAHO	44-1502	$4.25	None
ILLINOIS	820 §105/4, 105/6	$4.25	70%; percentage rate for up to six months
INDIANA	22-2-2-4	$3.35	None
IOWA	91D.1(1)(a)	$4.65	None
KANSAS	44-1203(a) and (b); 49-31-5(c)	$2.65	80%; percentage rate for up to two months
KENTUCKY	337.275(1)	$4.25	None
LOUISIANA	No statutory provisions		
MAINE	Tit. 26 §664	$4.25	None
MARYLAND	Labor & Employment 3-413	$4.25	Not less than 80% of the minimum wage for most employees
MASSACHUSETTS	Ch. 151 §§1, *et seq.*	$4.25	Scale of rates for specified occupations

(Continued)

Table 16: Minimum Wage—Continued

State	Code Section	Minimum Wage Per Hour	Subminimum Wage Per Hour
MICHIGAN	408.384	$3.35	None
MINNESOTA	177.21-35	$4.25; $4.00 for employer whose annual gross income is less than $362,500	At minor's rate set by Dept. of Labor & Industry for first 300 hours of employment
MISSISSIPPI	No statutory provisions		
MISSOURI	290.502	$4.25	85% of federal minimum wage
MONTANA	39-3-404(1), 39-3-409	Must be equal to federal minimum wage, except if gross sales of employer are $110,000 or less, the minimum wage is $4.00	None
NEBRASKA	48-1203(1), (3)	$4.25	75%; percentage rate of the statutory minimum for learners and apprentices
NEVADA	Notice of Labor Commission dated 4/1/91 and §608.250(1)	$4.25; $3.61 for employees below age 18	85% for minors
NEW HAMPSHIRE	279:21	$3.95	75%; percentage rate of the statutory minimum for learners and apprentices
NEW JERSEY	34:11-56a4; 34:11-56a17	$5.05	85% for up to 90 days
NEW MEXICO	50-4-22(A)	$3.35	None
NEW YORK	Labor Law §652(1)	$4.25	None
NORTH CAROLINA	95-25.3(a) and (b)	$4.25	90%; percentage rate of the statutory minimum for learners and apprentices
NORTH DAKOTA	34-06-03, *et seq.*, General Wage Order dated 8/1/91	$4.25	85% for up to 240 hours or 60 days, whichever comes first
OHIO	4111.02	$4.25	80% for learners for period not exceeding 180 days and 85% for apprentices for period of up to 90 days
OKLAHOMA	Tit. 40 §197.2	$4.25	Wage and Hour Commission shall set amount if determined that learner's opportunities are limited
OREGON	653.025	$4.75	None
PENNSYLVANIA	Tit. 43 §333.104	$4.25	85%; percentage rate of the statutory minimum for learners and/or apprentices
RHODE ISLAND	28-12-3, 10	$4.45	At rate determined by director of labor, for up to 90 days; certain minors at 75%
SOUTH CAROLINA	No statutory provisions		
SOUTH DAKOTA	60-11-3; 60-12-3	$4.25	$3.61 for employees age 18 or 19 for up to 90 days; 75% for minor under 18

(Continued)

Table 16: Minimum Wage—Continued

State	Code Section	Minimum Wage Per Hour	Subminimum Wage Per Hour
TENNESSEE	No statutory provisions		
TEXAS	Tex. Civ. Stat. Ann. Art. 5159d§5(a)	$3.35	None
UTAH	4487-1-3(A)	$4.25	$4.00 for first 160 hours of employment; 85% for minors
VERMONT	Tit. 21 §384(a)	$4.25	85%; percentage rate for retail, wholesale, and service establishments by wage order for up to 240 hours or 30 days for learners
VIRGINIA	40.1-28.10	$4.25	$3.61
WASHINGTON	49.46.020	$4.25	85%; percentage rate of the statutory minimum for learners and/or apprentices, by state wage board order
WEST VIRGINIA	21-5C-2(a)	$4.25	85% or $3.35, whichever is greater, for first 90 days if under age 19
WISCONSIN	Ind. 72.03(1)	$3.90 (probationary); $4.25 (non-probationary)	$3.60 (probationary); $3.90 (non-probationary) if under 18
WYOMING	27-4-202	$1.60	None

17. RIGHT TO WORK

As labor unions began to organize and to bargain with employers on behalf of its members, many troublesome issues began to arise. For instance, if a union negotiated a contract with a company, did the contract cover only union members or those employees who refused to join the union too? Could the union insist that the employer refuse to hire nonunion members? If a member violated some union policy, could the union insist that the employer fire the employee?

To say that the union had the power to decide who worked and who did not meant that the employer was deprived of a fundamental right in running his business. Conversely, to an employer who hired and fired whom he pleased meant that potentially the union contract could be undermined simply by hiring only nonunion employees.

Over the years an intricate system of rules, regulations, and laws has evolved to manage the many thorny issues that have arisen in the context of union contracts, including the protection of the rights of nonunion employees to work for unionized employers. These "right to work" laws generally forbid both unions and employers from denying a nonunion employee a job solely on account of his union status. Twenty-one states are currently "right to work" states. Twenty-nine and the District of Columbia have no statutory provision, apparently allowing the union to bargain with the employer for the right to insist upon union membership as a condition for employment.

Table 17: Right to Work

State	Code Section	Policy	Prohibited Activity
ALABAMA	25-7-30, *et seq.*	The right of persons to work shall not be denied or abridged on account of membership or nonmembership in any labor union or labor organization.	Any agreement/combination between employer and labor union or organization denying nonmembers right to work is prohibited; labor organizations cannot require membership, abstention, or payment of union dues.
ALASKA	No statutory provisions		
ARIZONA	23-1302, *et seq.*; Ariz. Const. Art. XXV	No person shall be denied opportunity to work because of nonmembership in a union.	Threatened or actual interference with person, his family, or property to force him to join union, strike against his will, or leave job; conspiracy to induce persons to refuse to work with nonmembers; agreements which exclude person from employment because of nonmembership in union.
ARKANSAS	13-3-301, *et seq.*; Ark. Const. Amend. XXXIV	Freedom of organized labor to bargain collectively and unorganized labor to bargain individually.	Union affiliation or non-affiliation not to be condition of employment; contracts to exclude persons from employment.
CALIFORNIA	No statutory provisions		
COLORADO	No statutory provisions		
CONNECTICUT	No statutory provisions		
DELAWARE	No statutory provisions		
DISTRICT OF COLUMBIA	No statutory provisions		
FLORIDA	Fla. Const. Art. I §6	The right of persons to work shall not be denied or abridged by membership or nonmembership in any labor union or organization.	Public employees do not have right to strike; right of employees to bargain collectively through a labor union shall not be denied or abridged.
GEORGIA	34-6-21, *et seq.*		Membership in or payment to labor organization as condition of employment; contracts requiring membership in or payment to labor organization as contrary to public policy; deduction from wages of fees for labor organization without individual's order or request.
HAWAII	No statutory provisions		
IDAHO	44-2001, *et seq.*	The right to work shall not be subject to undue restraint or coercion, infringed upon or restrained in any way based on membership, affiliation, or financial support of a labor organization.	Freedom of choice guaranteed, discrimination prohibited; deductions from wages unless signed written authorization by employee; coercion and intimidation of employee, his family, or property.
ILLINOIS	No statutory provisions		
INDIANA	No statutory provisions		

(Continued)

Table 17: Right to Work—Continued

State	Code Section	Policy	Prohibited Activity
IOWA	731.1, *et seq.*		Refusal to employ because of membership in a labor organization; contracts to exclude; union dues as prerequisite to employment; deducting dues from pay unless signed written authorization from employee.
KANSAS	44-831; Kan. Const. Art. XV §12	There is a cause of action if there is a constitutional violation. No person shall be denied opportunity to obtain or retain employment because of membership or nonmembership in any labor organization.	Agreements to exclude persons from employment or continuance of employment based on membership or nonmembership in any labor organization.
KENTUCKY	No statutory provisions		
LOUISIANA	23:981 to 23:987	All persons shall have the right to form, join, and assist labor organizations or to refrain from such activities without fear of penalty or reprisals.	Cannot be required to become or remain member of labor organization or pay dues or fees as condition of employment; agreements between labor organization and employer.
MAINE	No statutory provisions		
MARYLAND	No statutory provisions		
MASSACHUSETTS	No statutory provisions		
MICHIGAN	No statutory provisions		
MINNESOTA	No statutory provisions		
MISSISSIPPI	71-1-47; Miss. Const. Art VII §198-A	The right to work shall not be denied or abridged because of membership or nonmembership in a labor union or organization.	Agreement or combination between employer and labor organization to make membership condition of employment or where union or organization acquires an employment monopoly; requirement to become or remain member; requirement to abstain or refrain from membership; requirement to pay dues.
MISSOURI	No statutory provisions		
MONTANA	No statutory provisions		
NEBRASKA	48-217, 911; Neb. Const. Art. XV §13	No person shall be denied employment because of membership, affiliation, resignation, or expulsion in or from a labor organization or because of refusal to join or pay fees.	Contracts between employer and labor organization to exclude because of membership or nonmembership; right to strike and right to work.
NEVADA	613.230, *et seq.*		Agreements prohibiting employment because of nonmembership in labor organization; strike or picketing to force or induce employer to make agreement; compelling person to join labor organization, strike, or leave employment; conspiracy to cause discharge or denial of employment or to induce refusal of work on basis of membership.

(Continued)

Table 17: Right to Work—Continued

State	Code Section	Policy	Prohibited Activity
NEW HAMPSHIRE	No statutory provisions		
NEW JERSEY	No statutory provisions		
NEW MEXICO	No statutory provisions		
NEW YORK	No statutory provisions		
NORTH CAROLINA	95-78, *et seq.*	The right to live includes the right to work. The right to work shall not be denied or abridged on account of membership or nonmembership in any labor union or organization.	Agreement or combination between employer and labor organization where nonmembers are denied right to work or where membership is made condition of employment or where organization acquires employment monopoly; membership status as condition of employment; payment of dues as condition of employment.
NORTH DAKOTA	34-01-14	The right of a person to work shall not be abridged or denied on account of membership or nonmembership in any labor union or organization.	All contracts in negation or abrogation of right to work are invalid; "agency shop" dues "check off" of nonmember of union as condition of employment or continuance.
OHIO	No statutory provisions		
OKLAHOMA	No statutory provisions		
OREGON	No statutory provisions		
PENNSYLVANIA	No statutory provisions		
RHODE ISLAND	No statutory provisions		
SOUTH CAROLINA	41-7-10, *et seq.*	The denial of the right to work because of membership or nonmembership in a labor organization is against public policy.	Agreements between employer and labor organization denying nonmembers right to work or requiring union membership; requirement of membership or to refrain from membership or payment of dues as condition of employment; deduction of dues from wages without authorization; contracts declared to be unlawful by §41-7-20 or 41-7-30.
SOUTH DAKOTA	60-8-3, *et seq.*; 60-10-10	The right of persons to work shall not be denied or abridged on account of membership or nonmembership in a labor union or organization.	Any agreement relating to employment denying free exercise of right to work; any coercion to enter into such agreement; coercion of employee to join union; interference with right to work by use of force or violence.
TENNESSEE	50-1-201, *et seq.*	It is unlawful to deny employment because of affiliation or nonaffiliation with a labor union.	Contracts for exclusion from employment because of affiliation or nonaffiliation with labor union; exclusion from employment for payment or failure to pay union dues.
TEXAS	Tex. Rev. Civ. Stat. Ann. Art. 5207a §§1, *et seq.*	No person shall be denied employment on account of membership or nonmembership in a labor union.	Any contract which requires membership or nonmembership; denial of right to work and bargain freely with employer, individually or collectively.

(Continued)

Table 17: Right to Work—Continued

State	Code Section	Policy	Prohibited Activity
UTAH	34-34-2, *et seq.*	The right of persons to work shall not be denied or abridged on account of membership or nonmembership in a labor union, labor organization, or any other type of association.	Agreement, understanding, or practice denying right to work based on membership in labor organization; compelling person to join or not join organization; employer cannot require union membership, abstinence from membership, or payment of dues or fees.
VERMONT	No statutory provisions		
VIRGINIA	40.1-58, *et seq.*	The right to work shall not be abridged or denied on account of membership or nonmembership in a labor union or organization.	Agreements between labor organization to deny nonmembers right to work or where membership is made condition of employment or where union acquires monopoly; requirement of membership, nonmembership, or payment of dues as condition of employment.
WASHINGTON	No statutory provisions		
WEST VIRGINIA	No statutory provisions		
WISCONSIN	No statutory provisions		
WYOMING	27-7-109, *et seq.*	No person is required to become a member of a labor organization or abstain therefrom as a condition of employment.	Requirement of membership or nonmembership or payment of dues as a condition of employment; requirement of connection with or approval from labor union.

V. FAMILY LAWS

18. ABORTION

The laws governing abortion are the most controversial in the United States today. The disunity among states regarding these laws, particularly those that define a legal abortion, reflects society's conflicting views toward abortion.

Abortion laws, as treated here, contain three main parts: a definition of an illegal abortion, a definition of a legal abortion, and a section dealing with consent and/or notice. There are also sections dealing with the penalties for violating the laws, residency requirements, waiting periods, and abortionists, licensing requirements. These sections are impossible to compare. Because the Supreme Court through inconsistent rulings has caused the laws regulating abortion to be so unsettled, many state legislatures are not enacting any legislation pending the outcome of various lawsuits and federal legislation. Therefore waiting periods, spousal notification, and other particulars mentioned below are *not* separately treated because the Court has virtually preempted the states' power to legislate in these areas. However, these sections are ancillary to those questions regarding the legality of the act itself.

Illegal Abortion

In no state is unrestricted abortion legal; indeed, virtually all states begin with the presumption that abortion is a crime, though all state statutes do have definitions of legal abortions. Twenty states define an illegal abortion in terms of the definition of a legal abortion; for example, Hawaii defines an illegal abortion as failure to meet the criterion of a legal abortion. (The definition of a legal abortion, in Hawaii, is simply the destruction of a nonviable fetus.) Seventeen states, however, predominately in the East and the South, do define illegal abortions without reference to legal instances of abortion. A few of these, interestingly, include in their definitions the provision that if the mother dies, *then* the abortion is illegal. But of these states, only some have specific statutes defining an illegal abortion; others merely define a legal

abortion and impose penalties for their violation. The remaining states have definitions that specifically mention the limits of when an abortion is acceptable. For example, West Virginia defines an illegal abortion as any activity "with intent to destroy an unborn child or produce abortion [or] if mother dies."

Legal Abortion

Legal abortion is universally defined in terms of the mother's convenience or health. Though few definitions mention the life or health of the fetus, many refer to its "viability" as a standard for when an abortion may be performed with impunity, and without further attempt to define the term. These definitions are objective in that specific time parameters are set, outside of which an abortion cannot legally be done, absent exigent circumstances. The most unrestrictive of all definitions occur in Hawaii and Alaska, where a legal abortion is an abortion on "any nonviable fetus." Interestingly, the definition of an illegal abortion in these two states is equally open; they say essentially that any act knowingly found to be contrary to the legal definition is illegal. After viability has been established, most states give additional instances when abortion may be legal: to save the life of the mother or if there are severe defects present in the fetus.

State of the Statutes

Prior to 1973 and the *Roe* v. *Wade* decision by the Supreme Court (410 U.S. 113 (1973)), the regulation of abortion was left to the states. In *Roe* v. *Wade,* the Supreme Court decided that the Constitution protected a woman's right to abortion, a novel right said to be found in the unstated right to privacy, from state regulation during the first trimester of pregnancy. However, the Court also held that the states have an "important and legitimate interest in protecting the potentiality of human life."

The abortion controversy has revolved around the states' consequent attempts to protect unborn life. The

Supreme Court's patchwork of opinions following *Roe* has left abortion a highly unsettled area of law. Many statutes reflect state attempts at balancing a woman's right to choose an abortion with the state's compelling interest in protecting fetal life.

The statutes in this chapter are as they currently appear in the State Codes. Interestingly enough, some of the statutes may be unconstitutional if challenged, based on prior Supreme Court rulings. Following are the general areas of abortion legislation and the Supreme Court's treatment of each:

- *Parental Consent.* States may require a minor seeking an abortion to obtain the consent of a parent or guardian as long as there is an adequate judicial bypass procedure.

- *Informed Consent.* A State may require a physician to provide a woman with such information such as alternatives to abortion, sources of financial aid, development of the child, and the gestational age of the child. Prior to 1992, informed consent provisions were unconstitutional.

- *Spousal Consent.* A State may not require a married woman to obtain her husband's consent before undergoing an abortion.

- *Abortion Method.* A State may not require the physician performing the abortion to use the technique providing for the best opportunity for the unborn child to survive the abortion.

- *Second Physician.* A State may not require that a second physician attend the abortion to take immediate control of the care of a child born alive on an abortion unless the provision has an exception for a situation when the health of the mother was endangered.

- *Waiting Period.* A twenty-four hour waiting period does not constitute an undue burden on a woman's decision to abort and, therefore, is constitutional. Prior to 1992, waiting period requirements were unconstitutional.

- *Parental Notice.* A State may require that one parent be notified of a minor's abortion, but not two.

- *Fetal Remains.* States may not require that the remains of the unborn child are disposed of in a "human and sane" manner as it may suggest a mandate for some sort of "decent burial."

Table 18: Abortion

State/Code Section	Statutory Definition of		Penalty	Consent	Residency	License
	Illegal Abortion	Legal Abortion				
ALABAMA 13A-13-7	By drug, substance, instrument which induces abortion or miscarriage	Purpose to preserve life, health of mother	Fine of $100 to $1,000 and imprisonment to 12 months			
ALASKA 18.16.010	Knowingly doesn't meet standards for legal abortion	Nonviable fetus	Fine to $1,000 and imprisonment 1 to 5 years	Of patient to guardian if unmarried patient less than 18	30 days before procedure	Licensed M.D., hospital or approved facility
ARIZONA 13-3603; 36-2152; 36-2153	By drug, instrument with intent to procure miscarriage	Necessary to preserve life of mother	Imprisonment 2 to 5 years	Written consent of parent or legal guardian if unmarried or unemancipated patient is under 18, except by court order or medical emergency		
ARKANSAS 5-61-101 to 102; 20-9-302; 20-16-601; 20-16-701 to 707; 20-16-801, *et seq.*	Intentional termination of pregnancy with intent other than to increase probability of live birth or to remove dead or dying fetus. Viable fetus defined as one which can live outside the womb; fetus is presumed nonviable prior to end of 25th week of pregnancy	No abortion of viable fetus other than as necessary to preserve life of mother, or where pregnancy is result of rape or incest of minor; written certification by licensed physician required	Class 4 misdemeanor; fine to $1,000 and imprisonment 1 to 5 years	Written consent of mother; if minor or incompetent, written notice to parent or guardian required at least 48 hours before procedure, except by court order, medical emergency, or upon declaration of child abuse or neglect		Clinics must be licensed and periodically inspected by State Department of Health; physicians must be licensed
CALIFORNIA Health & Safety §§25950 to 25958; Pen. §§274 to 276	By drugs, medicine, or instrument with intent to procure miscarriage	Continuation of pregnancy would greatly impair life or health of mother, or pregnancy result of rape or incest	Imprisonment in the state prison	In case of unemancipated minor, written consent of minor and one parent or legal guardian, or by order of petition to Juvenile Court		Approved health care facility, approval of medical board; certified physician/surgeon
COLORADO 18-6-101 to 105 (portions declared unconstitutional by *People* v. *Norton*, 181 Co. 47, 507 P.2d 862 [1973] although they have not been repealed)	Ends or causes pregnancy to be ended by any means other than justified medical	Continuation of pregnancy likely to result in death or permanent physical or mental impairment of mother, or child born with grave mental or physical retardation, or within first 16 weeks of pregnancy and pregnancy result of sexual assault or incest	Maximum 8 to 12 years imprisonment and 1 year parole (Class 2 felony) and fine of $5,000 to $1,000,000	Mother; mother and father, if married; mother and parent/guardian if under 18 years		Licensed physician using accepted medical procedures in a licensed hospital upon written certification by all the members of a special hospital board

(Continued)

Table 18: Abortion—Continued

State/Code Section	Statutory Definition of		Penalty	Consent	Residency	License
	Illegal Abortion	Legal Abortion				
CONNECTICUT 19a-600, *et seq.*	By giving, administering, advising, causing to take or use instrument with intent to procure abortion or miscarriage	Preserve life of mother or unborn child	Fine of $1,000 and/or imprisonment to 5 years			
DELAWARE Tit. 24 §§1790 to 1795; 24§1766	By drugs or act done with intent to cause miscarriage including acts by mother	Continuation of pregnancy would result in death or injury to mother; mental and/or physical retardation of child or pregnancy result of rape or incest, but must be performed within first 20 weeks	Felony; maximum fine of $5,000 and imprisonment 2 to 10 years	Written consent of mother with full explanation, 24 hour waiting period following consent; if unmarried and under 18, consent of parent	120 days before procedure unless employed in state or patient of state-licensed M.D.	Licensed M.D., national accredited hospital; approval of hospital review board
DISTRICT OF COLUMBIA 22-201	By means of instrument, drugs, or whatever attempts to or procures abortion	Necessary to preserve life or health of mother	Imprisonment 1 to 10 years; if mother dies (second degree murder), imprisonment 20 years to life			Under direction of competent licensed practitioner of medicine
FLORIDA 390.001, *et seq.*; 797.02; 797.03	Termination of pregnancy during last trimester which does not meet requirements of legal abortion	Regulated only in last trimester, necessary to save life or preserve health of mother	Second degree misdemeanor; fine to $500 and/or imprisonment to 60 days	Written informed consent of mother; if mentally incompetent, consent of guardian; if under 18 and unmarried, written consent of parent or guardian or order of court; husband must be given notice unless separated		Validly licensed hospital, abortion clinic, or physician's office; third trimester only in hospital
GEORGIA 26-1201 to 1204; 24A-4401 to 4409	By administering medicine, drugs, or substance or using instrument with intent to procure miscarriage or abortion	Preserve life or health of mother	Imprisonment 1 to 10 years	Written, informed consent of parent or guardian of unemancipated minor under the age of 18; parent must have 24-hour notice before scheduled abortion, unless waived		First trimester: licensed M.D. and licensed hospital; second trimester, M.D. and two consulting M.D.s certifying necessity of procedure
HAWAII 453-16	Failure to meet standards for legal abortion	Nonviable fetus	Fine to $1,000 and/or imprisonment to 5 years		90 days	Licensed M.D., licensed hospital

(Continued)

Table 18: Abortion—Continued

State/Code Section	Statutory Definition of		Penalty	Consent	Residency	License
	Illegal Abortion	Legal Abortion				
IDAHO 18-603 to 612	Provides, supplies, administers drugs or substances to woman, or uses instrument with intent to produce abortion		Fine to $5,000 and/or imprisonment 2 to 5 years; mother, fine to $5,000, and/or imprisonment 1 to 5 years	Mother must be informed including information about development of fetus, adoption and other services, risks, etc.		First trimester: consultation between licensed M.D. and mother and determination by M.D. that abortion is appropriate considering various mental, physical, family factors; second trimester: same as first except that procedure must be performed in licensed hospital; third trimester: same as second except requires consulting M.D. and procedure must be necessary to preserve life of mother or fetus
ILLINOIS 720 ILCS 510/1 to 520/10	Use of any instrument, drug, or any other device to terminate pregnancy of a woman known to be pregnant with an intention other than to increase the probability of a live birth, to preserve the life or health of the child after live birth, or to remove a dead fetus	If fetus nonviable and abortion not necessary to preserve mother's health, M.D. must certify nonviability; if fetus is viable, abortion must be medically necessary to preserve life, health of mother; M.D. must certify this necessity	Fine to $1,000 and/or imprisonment 3 to 7 years for M.D. (Class 2 felony); if fetus could have survived with or without support and M.D. does not use method to keep it alive: Class 3 felony	Parental consent required for unmarried woman under 18; consent of minor is required 48 hours prior to procedure; 24 hours notice to parents required if mother is unemancipated minor		Licensed M.D. determines abortion is "necessary"

(Continued)

Table 18: Abortion—Continued

State/Code Section	Statutory Definition of		Penalty	Consent	Residency	License
	Illegal Abortion	Legal Abortion				
INDIANA 35-1.58.5-1 to 35-1.58.5-7	Termination of human pregnancy with intent other than to produce live birth or remove dead fetus	During first trimester with mother's consent; after first trimester but before viability, permissible with mother's consent and if performed in hospital or surgical center; after viability, procedure necessary to prevent impairment of life, health of mother	Class C felony	Written consent of mother, not applicable in emergency; if unemancipated minor, consent of one parent or legal guardian is required; court can waive requirement; not applicable in emergency		First trimester: professional judgment of attending licensed M.D.; second trimester, before viability: same as first and licensed hospital; after viability: same as second and reasons for procedure regarding mother certified by M.D. to hospital.
IOWA 707.7; *et seq.*	"Feticide": Intentional termination of human pregnancy after end of second trimester	Necessary to preserve life or health of mother or fetus; after end of second trimester with every reasonable effort made to preserve life of viable fetus	Class C felony			Licensed M.D., every effort made (not inconsistent with preserving life of mother) to preserve life of viable fetus
KANSAS 21-3407 and 65-443 to 445	Purposeful and unjustifiable termination of pregnancy of any female other than by a live birth	Continuance would impair physical or mental health of mother, or child would be born with physical or mental defects; pregnancy result of rape or incest or mother under 16 years	Class D Felony: Fine to $10,000 and/or imprisonment, indefinite sentence, minimum 1 to 3 years, maximum 5 to 10 years			Licensed M.D.; three M.D.s certify in writing the necessity of termination, except in emergency situations
KENTUCKY 311.710 to 830; 436.026	Use of any means whatsoever to terminate the pregnancy of a woman known to be pregnant with intent to cause fetal death	Permissible during first trimester; after viability of fetus, necessary to preserve life or health of mother	Aborting when M.D. did not believe it necessary to receive a written referral or violating notice to spouse provisions is Class D felony; without private medical consultation, violating woman's consent provisions or aborting with reckless disregard of whether mother is minor is Class A misdemeanor	Written informed consent with two-hour waiting period of mother; of parents/ guardian if mother under 18 and unemancipated, except when medical emergency; doctor must notify spouse if possible prior to abortion, if not possible, within 30 days of abortion		First trimester: upon advice of licensed M.D.; after first trimester, same as first except must be in licensed hospital, except in medical emergency

(Continued)

Table 18: Abortion—Continued

State/Code Section	Statutory Definition of		Penalty	Consent	Residency	License
	Illegal Abortion	Legal Abortion				
LOUISIANA 14:87, *et seq.* 40:1299.35, *et seq.*; 40.1299.35.0 *et seq.*	Administration of drug or substance or use of instrument with intent of procuring premature delivery	After viability or third trimester, necessary to preserve life, health of mother and/or fetus or when pregnancy resulted from rape or incest and fetus is not viable	Fine to $1000 and/ or imprisonment maximum 2 years	Written informed consent of woman; if unemancipated minor, consent of parent or guardian or court, except in medical emergency		After first trimester, licensed M.D. must make judgment of advisability or necessity of abortion and procedure must be performed in licensed hospital
MAINE Tit. 22 §§1591 to 1599	Intentional interruption of a pregnancy by the application of external agents, whether chemical or physical, or the ingestion of chemical agents with an intention other than to produce a live birth or to remove a dead fetus	After viability, only when necessary to preserve life or health of mother	Class D Crime: M.D. failing to perform any action required: fine up to $1000 for each violation	In case of unemancipated minor, actual notice to parent or guardian at least 24 hours before procedure, except in medical emergency; if actual notice cannot be given, written notice by certified mail must be given at least 48 hours before abortion; consent of one parent/guardian required for minor; informed consent of mother required; information given to mother at least 48 hours before procedure except in medical emergency		Licensed M.D.

(Continued)

195

Table 18: Abortion—Continued

State/Code Section	Statutory Definition of		Penalty	Consent	Residency	License
	Illegal Abortion	Legal Abortion				
MARYLAND Health & Gen. §§20-210 to 214; 10-103	Sells or gives any drug, substance, or instrument for purpose of causing or inducing termination of human pregnancy or counsels for purpose of inducing abortion or assists in obtaining or performing abortion, except when licensed M.D. in licensed hospital	Continuation of pregnancy likely to result in death or impairment of physical or mental health of mother; fetus likely to be born with physical or mental retardation or pregnancy result of rape; also must be performed within first 26 weeks of pregnancy unless life of mother is threatened or fetus is dead	Fine to $5,000 for each offense and/or imprisonment to 3 years	Informed, written consent of mother required, except in medical emergency; M.D. may not perform an abortion on an unmarried minor unless M.D. first gives notice to parent or guardian, unless minor does not live with parent/guardian and reasonable efforts to give notice are unsuccessful or if in M.D.'s judgment notice to parent/guardian may lead to physical or emotional abuse, or the minor is mature and capable of informed consent or notice would not be in the best interest of minor		Licensed M.D., licensed hospital, approval of hospital board required
MASSACHUSETTS Ch. 112§§12J to 12U	Failure to meet standards for legal abortion; violation of procedural standards such as informed consent, medical procedure required, etc. Knowing destruction of the life of an unborn child or the intentional expulsion or removal of an unborn child from the womb other than for the principal purpose of live birth or removing a dead fetus	Under 24 weeks, abortion may be performed only by M.D. and only if in M.D.'s best judgment the abortion is necessary under the circumstances; after 24 weeks, if necessary to save life of mother or continuation will impose substantial risk if grave physical or mental impairment; no procedure can be used which destroys or injures fetus unless in M.D.'s opinion other available procedures would be greater risk to mother or future pregnancies	Failure to meet standards: imprisonment 1 to 5 years; violation of standards: fine of $500 to $1,000 and/or imprisonment 3 months to 5 years	Written informed consent within 24 hours before procedure; if mother less than 18 years and unemancipated, consent of parents or guardians or court, except in medical emergency		M.D. except in medical emergency; after 13th week, must be performed in licensed hospital

(Continued)

Table 18: Abortion—Continued

State/Code Section	Statutory Definition of		Penalty	Consent	Residency	License
	Illegal Abortion	Legal Abortion				
MICHIGAN MCL 750.14; MCL 722.901	Drug, substance, or instrument employed with intent to terminate pregnancy for a purpose other than to increase probability of a live birth, to preserve the health of the child, or to remove a dead fetus	After viability, necessary to preserve life of mother	Felony: fine to $2,000 and/or imprisonment to 4 years; if mother dies, manslaughter, fine to $7,500 and/or imprisonment to 15 years	No abortion may be performed on minor without her consent and that of one parent or guardian; court may waive parental consent if minor is mature and well-informed so as to be able to make the decision, or waiver is in minor's best interest		
MINNESOTA 145.411 to 424 and 617.20 to 22	Failure to meet standards of legal abortion; sale or manufacture of drug, substance, or instrument intended for unlawful use in abortion procedure; act, procedure, or use of any instrument, medicine, or drug which is supplied, prescribed for, or administered to a pregnant woman which results in the termination of pregnancy	After viability, necessary to preserve life, health of mother and procedure used will reasonably assure live birth	Felony	Informed consent of mother		Licensed M.D., in abortion facility or hospital after first trimester
MISSISSIPPI 97-3-3 to 5	By means of instrument, medicine, drug, or any other substance causing any pregnant woman to abort or miscarry	Necessary to preserve mother's life; pregnancy result of rape	Felony: imprisonment 1 to 10 years; if mother dies, murder; if M.D. convicted, license will be revoked			Licensed M.D.; advice of two licensed M.D.s required in writing

(Continued)

Table 18: Abortion—Continued

State/Code Section	Statutory Definition of		Penalty	Consent	Residency	License
	Illegal Abortion	Legal Abortion				
MISSOURI 188.010 to 220	Failure to meet standards for legal abortion	After viability, necessary to preserve life, health of mother; method used must be one most likely to preserve life, health of fetus unless greater risk to mother	Fine to $1,000 and imprisonment to 1 year; second degree murder to take the life of a child aborted alive; anyone not a physician attempting to perform an abortion is guilty of Class B felony	Informed, written consent of mother; if mother is less than 18 and unemancipated, informed written consent of one parent/guardian or court order		After viability, licensed M.D. must certify abortion necessary including medical indicators and method to be utilized with reasoning for decision; second M.D. must be in attendance to aid fetus; at 20 weeks, M.D. required to determine whether fetus is viable, using ordinary skill and care for testing
MONTANA 50-20-101 to 112	Performance of, assistance or participation in the performance of, or submission to an act or operation intended to terminate a pregnancy without a live birth	After viability, if necessary according to M.D. to preserve life or health of mother; procedure utilized must not negligently or intentionally endanger life of fetus unless to preserve mother's life	Violation of infant protection; violation of abortion practices by M.D.: felony, fine to $1,000 and/or imprisonment to 5 years; violation of consent provisions: misdemeanor, fine to $500 and/or imprisonment to 6 months	Informed consent of mother signed by her M.D. except when M.D. certifies necessary to preserve mother's life; if married, written notice of spouse; if under 18 years and unmarried, written notice of parent/guardian		Licensed M.D., after first 3 months in licensed hospital; after viability, M.D. must certify in writing necessity of procedure including grounds for decision plus two other M.D.s must confirm decision except when necessary to preserve mother's life

(Continued)

Table 18: Abortion—Continued

State/Code Section	Statutory Definition of		Penalty	Consent	Residency	License
	Illegal Abortion	Legal Abortion				
NEBRASKA 28-325 to 347; 71-6901, *et seq.*	Act, procedure, device, or prescription administered to a woman to produce premature expulsion, removal, or termination of the human life within the womb of the pregnant woman unless the child's viability is threatened by continuation of the pregnancy	After viability, to preserve life or health of mother	M.D.: Class IV felony; anyone not M.D. performing abortion: Class IV felony; using any method but accepted medical procedure: Class IV felony	Notice required of risks associated with procedure to be used and of agencies and services available for preventing pregnancies; parental consultation, informed consent, waiting periods, and abortion reporting declared unconstitutional. *Women's Services, PC* v. *Thone*, 636 F.2d 206 (8th Cir. 1980), affirmed on rehearing (8th Cir. 1982); waiting period repealed		Licensed M.D.
NEVADA §§442.240 to 270	Termination of a human pregnancy with an intention other than to produce the birth of an infant capable of sustained survival by natural or artificial support or to remove a dead fetus	Only within first 24 weeks unless necessary to preserve life, health of mother	Imprisonment 1 to 10 years and fine to $10,000; violation of notice or consent statutes: misdemeanor	Informed consent of mother, certified by M.D.; if mother under 18, unemancipated and unmarried, actual notice to parent/ guardian required before procedure; if actual notice is unsuccessful, then M.D. must delay abortion until s/he has notified parent by certified mail		Licensed M.D. must exercise "best clinical judgment"; licensed health care facility; records of mother must contain facts upon which M.D. based decision
NEW HAMPSHIRE 585:12 to 14	(1) Willfully administers substance to mother or employs instrument with intent to procure abortion; (2) if child is "quick"; (3) if mother dies	If child is "quick" must be malformed, difficult or protracted labor, necessary to preserve life, or advised by two M.D.'s to be necessary	(1) Fine to $1,000 and/or imprisonment to 1 year; (2) fine to $1,000 and/or imprisonment to 10 years; (3) imprisonment to life			
NEW JERSEY 2A:87-1, *et seq.* (Abortion) repealed effective September 1, 1979. No replacement statute enacted						

(Continued)

Table 18: Abortion—Continued

State/Code Section	Statutory Definition of		Penalty	Consent	Residency	License
	Illegal Abortion	Legal Abortion				
NEW MEXICO 30-5-1 to 3	(1) Failure to meet standards of justified termination; (2) if mother dies; (3) administering medical drug or other substance or means whereby an untimely termination of pregnancy is produced with intent to destroy fetus and not a justified medical termination	Continuation likely to result in death or impairment of mother's health or fetus likely to result in death or impairment of health of mother or fetus likely to be physically or mentally retarded; or pregnancy result of rape or incest	Criminal abortion: fourth degree felony; abortion resulting in woman's death: second degree felony	Mother must "request" procedure; if under 18 the procedure must be requested by her and parent/guardian		Licensed M.D., licensed hospital, written certification of hospital board required
NEW YORK Penal §125.05; Exec. §291; Pub. Health §4167	(1) Failure to meet standards for legal abortion; (2) if mother dies; (3) if not within first 24 weeks	Within first 24 weeks or necessary to preserve mother's life; if mother performs abortion it must be on the advice of M.D. within the first 24 weeks or to preserve her own life				
NORTH CAROLINA 14-44 to 46	Willfully administer to mother, prescribe, advise, procure substance or instrument with intent to destroy child	First 20 weeks of pregnancy no medical requirements regarding mother or fetus; after 20 weeks, must be substantial risk that would threaten life, health of mother	Class H felony: Fine and/or imprisonment up to 10 years; Class I felony: Fine and/or imprisonment up to 5 years			Licensed M.D., licensed hospital or clinic

(Continued)

Table 18: Abortion—Continued

State/Code Section	Statutory Definition of		Penalty	Consent	Residency	License
	Illegal Abortion	Legal Abortion				
NORTH DAKOTA 14.02.1-01 to 12	(1) Non-licensed person performs abortion; (2) if licensed M.D. but doesn't conform to standards for legal abortion; termination of human pregnancy with an intention other than to produce a live birth or to remove a dead embryo or fetus	After viability, necessary to preserve life of mother or continuance would impair her physical or mental health	M.D.: Class A misdemeanor; anyone not M.D. who performs abortion: Class B felony; if M.D. does not take proper care to preserve life of unborn or born viable fetus: Class C felony	Informed consent of mother as certified by M.D. within 30 days to 24 hours before procedure; before viability, if mother is unemancipated minor M.D. must inform both parents or guardian at least 24 hours before minor's consent; after viability, husband's written consent or consent of both parents/guardian if mother is less than 18 years and unmarried, unless procedure is necessary to preserve life, health of mother; court can authorize abortion on minor without parental consent		Licensed M.D. using medical standards applicable; licensed hospital required after first 12 weeks of pregnancy; M.D. must certify facts unless medical emergency
OHIO 2919.11 to 14	(1) Failure to obtain informed consent; (2) taking life of fetus born alive or failing to provide reasonable medical attention to same; purposeful termination of a human pregnancy by any person with the intention other than to produce a live birth or remove a dead fetus		Violators guilty of unlawful abortion: first degree misdemeanor; second violation: fourth degree felony	Informed consent of mother; if mother is unmarried minor, parental informed consent also required; court may authorize minor to consent without parental notification; other family members may issue consent if minor in danger of physical, sexual, or emotional abuse from parent; constructive notice by mail allowed		

(Continued)

Table 18: Abortion—Continued

State/Code Section	Statutory Definition of		Penalty	Consent	Residency	License
	Illegal Abortion	Legal Abortion				
OKLAHOMA Tit. 63§§1-730 to 741; 21§§713 to 714; 21§861	(1)Non-licensed person performs abortion; (2) failure to meet standards for legal abortion; (3) taking life of viable fetus unless necessary to preserve life, health of mother or failure to provide medical aid to fetus; purposeful termination of a human pregnancy with intent other than to produce a live birth or remove a dead fetus	After viability, necessary to preserve life, health of mother (viability presumed after 24th week)	Woman soliciting or submitting to abortion unless necessary to preserve her life: imprisonment up to 1 year and/or fine up to $1000; person not M.D. performing abortion: 1 to 3 years in state penitentiary; anyone aborting viable fetus not to prevent mother's death or health impairment: homicide			Licensed M.D.; approved hospital required after first trimester; M.D. must certify necessity of procedure after viability, including factors considered; after viability M.D. required for fetus, except in medical emergency
OREGON 435.485				No M.D. is required to give advice with respect to or participate in any abortion if refusal is based on election not to do so and M.D. so advises patient; no hospital employee or member of medical staff is required to participate in abortions if individual notifies hospital of such election		
PENNSYLVANIA Tit. 18§§3201 to 3220	(1) Failure to obtain informed consent of woman; (2) failure to meet standards for legal abortion; (3) using any means to cause the death of an unborn child but not meaning use of intrauterine device or the birth control pill	Abortion must be necessary; after viability, necessary to preserve life of mother	(1) Person inducing abortion or failing to adequately care for viable fetus guilty of third degree felony; (2) physician violating provisions of informed consent or medical consultation sections: License may be revoked; first offense: summary offense; second: third degree misdemeanor	Except for medical emergency, physician must give written information to mother at least 24 hours before abortion; if mother under 18 years and not emancipated, parent/guardian consent required		Licensed M.D., licensed hospital facility

(Continued)

Table 18: Abortion—Continued

State/Code Section	Statutory Definition of		Penalty	Consent	Residency	License
	Illegal Abortion	Legal Abortion				
RHODE ISLAND 23-4.7-1 to 5; 11-9-18	(1) Failure to obtain informed consent; (2) failure to provide for any fetus born alive (unless necessary to preserve life of mother); administering to pregnant woman medicine, drug, instrument, etc. with intent to terminate pregnancy		(1) Physician who violates consent provisions guilty of unprofessional conduct; (2) fine to $5,000 and/or imprisonment to 5 years; (3) failure to care for infant born alive: fine up to $5000 and/or imprisonment 5 years; charge of manslaughter if baby dies	Informed consent after written disclosures; if mother under 18 years and unemancipated, parental consent required; court can consent; if married, husband must be notified if possible		
SOUTH CAROLINA 44-41-10 to 80	(1) Failure to meet standards for legal abortion; (2) self-abortion that does not meet standards for legal abortion; (3) use of instrument, medicine, drug, or other substance or device with intent to terminate pregnancy for reasons other than to increase probability of a live birth, preserve child's life or health, or to remove a dead fetus	Third trimester, necessary to preserve life or health of mother; if basis is mental health must be so certified by two consulting M.D.s	(1) Fine to $5,000 and/or imprisonment 2 to 5 years; (2) fine to $1,000 and/or imprisonment to 2 years for mother having abortion when life not endangered; failure to obtain required consent is prima facie evidence of interference with family relations in civil actions; parents have common law rights	Mother's written consent required; if mother married and third trimester, husband's consent is required; if mother under 17 years and unmarried, parental/guardian consent required, except in medical emergency		First trimester on advice of licensed M.D.; second trimester must be performed by licensed M.D. in licensed hospital; third trimester, second M.D.'s recommendation required, facts and reasons supporting recommendations must be certified by both M.D.s
SOUTH DAKOTA 22-17-5; 34-23A-1 to 21	(1) Failure to meet standards for legal abortion; (2) failure of M.D. to obtain informed consent; (3) termination of human pregnancy with intent other than to produce a live birth or remove a dead fetus	After 24th week, necessary to preserve life, health of mother	Violating informed consent statutes: misdemeanor, fine of $100 and/or imprisonment 30 days; any unauthorized abortion: Class 6 felony, fine to $2000 and/or imprisonment 2 years	Written informed consent of mother 24 hours before procedure; if mother unmarried minor, parent/guardian consent also required; if mother is married minor, husband's consent is required		First 12 weeks, licensed M.D., solely medical judgment; between 12 and 24 weeks, licensed M.D., licensed hospital; after 24th week, licensed M.D. and hospital

(Continued)

Table 18: Abortion—Continued

State/Code Section	Statutory Definition of		Penalty	Consent	Residency	License
	Illegal Abortion	Legal Abortion				
TENNESSEE 39-15-201 to 208; 37-10-301, *et seq.*	(1) Failure to meet standards for legal abortion including residency requirement; (2) attempted criminal abortion; (3) coerced or compelled abortion; (4) administering to pregnant woman medicine, drug, or any substance or instrument with intent to destroy such child	After viability, necessary to preserve life, health of mother	Impermissible abortion: Class C felony; mother attempting to procure a miscarriage: Class E felony; M.D. fails to use due care to preserve life of baby born alive: Class E felony; violation of 48-hour waiting period: Class E felony; M.D. performs abortion on minor violating consent statute: misdemeanor	Informed, written consent of mother, 48-hour waiting period between M.D. giving mother information and consent; after viability, same as first trimester except M.D. must certify in writing to the hospital that procedure was necessary; both parents must consent to abortion to be performed on minor; minor may petition court for waiver	Mother must produce to M.D. evidence she is bona fide resident prior to procedure except in medical emergency, but M.D. must still give information to mother	First trimester, licensed M.D. upon his medical advice; after first trimester to viability, licensed M.D., licensed hospital
TEXAS Civ. Stat. §§4512.5, .7, .8; 4995b	(1) Destroys the vitality or life of child in birth or before (which otherwise would have been born alive); (2) operating a facility without license, failure to meet Board of Health standards, or failure to make reports to Department of Health; (3) act involving instrument, medicine, drug, devise to terminate pregnancy other than to increase probability of live birth, preserve child's life, or health or remove dead fetus	Abortion during third trimester of viable child permissible only if necessary to prevent substantial risk of serious impairment to woman's physical or mental health, or if fetus has severe and irreversible abnormality	Abortion of viable fetus: imprisonment 5 years to life; operating facility without license: fine $100 to $500			Licensed physician; at licensed facility unless necessary to protect life, health of mother

(Continued)

Table 18: Abortion—Continued

State/Code Section	Statutory Definition of		Penalty	Consent	Residency	License
	Illegal Abortion	Legal Abortion				
UTAH 76-7-301 to 324	(1) Failure to meet standards for legal abortion; (2) coerce someone to have abortion (3) intentional termination of human pregnancy including all procedures undertaken to kill alive, unborn child or produce a miscarriage	Before 20 weeks, abortion may be performed to save mother's life or health, if woman was raped or incest committed, or child has grave defects; after viability, necessary to preserve health, life of mother or if child would be born with grave defects	Failure to meet standards: fine to $10,000 and/or imprisonment 1 to 15 years; coercion: fine to $5,000 and/or imprisonment 5 years; person performing unauthorized abortion: third degree felony	Notice, if possible, to parents/guardian if minor unmarried, mother or husband if married; informed consent of mother required		Licensed M.D.; after first trimester, licensed hospital; M.D. must provide mother with information regarding abortion at least 24 hours before procedure except in medical emergency
VERMONT Tit.13 §§101 to 104	(1) Willfully administers, advises any thing or any means with intent to procure miscarriage; (2) if mother dies; (3) if mother does not die (mother not liable)	Necessary to preserve mother's life	If mother dies: imprisonment 5 to 20 years; if mother does not die: imprisonment 3 to 10 years; advertising/ dealing in information about procuring miscarriages: imprisonment 3 to 10 years; person selling or giving anything to produce miscarriage: imprisonment 1 to 3 years and/or fine of $200 to $500; mother not liable to the penalties			
VIRGINIA 18.2-71 to 76.2	Failure to meet standards for legal abortion	First and second trimester, no restrictions; third trimester, continuation of pregnancy likely to result in death, physical or mental impairment of mother	Class 4 felony: imprisonment 2 to 10 years and/or fine to $100,000	Informed, written consent of mother		Anytime, licensed M.D.; second and third trimesters, licensed hospital; third trimester, attending M.D. and two consulting M.D.s certify medical necessity; if necessary to save mother's life, no condition applies except licensed M.D.

(Continued)

Table 18: Abortion—Continued

State/Code Section	Statutory Definition of		Penalty	Consent	Residency	License
	Illegal Abortion	Legal Abortion				
WASHINGTON 9.02	Any medical treatment intended to induce the termination of a pregnancy except for the purpose of producing a live birth	"The state may not deny or interfere with a woman's right to choose to have an abortion prior to viability of the fetus or to protect her life or health."	Unauthorized abortion performed: Class C felony			Licensed M.D., licensed hospital, except when medical emergency
WEST VIRGINIA 61-2-8; 16-2F-1, *et seq.*	(1) Administer substance or use means with intent to destroy unborn child or produce abortion; (2) if mother dies	Necessary to save life of mother or fetus	Performing abortion: imprisonment 1 to 10 years and/or fine to $10,000	24 hours actual notice or 48 hours constructive notice to parent/guardian of minor		
WISCONSIN 940.04	(1) Intentionally destroys life of unborn child (other than mother); (2) causes death of mother during procedure; (3) mother intentionally destroys unborn child or consents to same; (4) mother intentionally destroys life of unborn quick child or consents to same	Necessary to save life of mother or advised by two consulting M.D.s as necessary	Person other than mother performs abortion: imprisonment 1 to 3 years and/or fine to $5,000; mother dies: imprisonment to 15 years; mother performs or consents to abortion: imprisonment to 6 months and fine to $200; mother performs or consents to abortion on quick child: imprisonment to 2 years			Licensed M.D., licensed maternity hospital except in medical emergency

(Continued)

Table 18: Abortion—Continued

State/Code Section	Statutory Definition of		Penalty	Consent	Residency	License
	Illegal Abortion	Legal Abortion				
WYOMING 35-6-101 to 117	(1)Any procedure after viability that is not "necessary," M.D. who intentionally terminates viability of unborn fetus during legal abortion; (2) use of other than accepted medical procedures, other than licensed M.D. (including pregnant woman) performs act, procedure, prescription administered to produce premature expulsion, removal, or termination of fetus except when continuation of pregnancy threatens fetus's viability	After viability, necessary to preserve health, life of mother	M.D. aborting viable fetus: felony, imprisonment for 14 years; use of other than accepted medical procedures: imprisonment 1 to 14 years; person other than M.D. performing abortion: felony, imprisonment 1 to 14 years	Woman's consent required; one of minor's parents must be notified 48 hours before abortion; M.D. must have one parent's consent or court order		Licensed M.D.

19. ADOPTION

There is great variety among states regarding adoption laws, perhaps due to the very personal nature of these laws. A long legal tradition did not surround family law, and as state governments began to take responsibility for regulating family relationships, they tended to develop very unique and regional variations on aspects of family law, including adoption. These variations spawned difficult legal conflicts as modern families grew more mobile, and these conflicts gave rise to the desire to standardize laws among the states into Model Acts and Uniform Laws. The need for adoption standardization is so strong that, to date, only nine states have not adopted the Uniform Adoption Act.

Any adult may adopt any other person with only minor logical restrictions. A married person must apply for adoption jointly with his or her spouse, for example, and, if the child in certain states is over the age of ten, twelve, or fourteen, the state will require his or her consent as well (except in Louisiana and Wisconsin, where the child's consent is not required). Objective standards, like Mississippi's and Hawaii's requirement of a "proper" adopter, or Illinois's "reputable" one, and Virginia's "natural" one, also are present, as are specific requirements, for example, that the adopter be at least ten years older than the adoptee. Sometimes the adoptee must be a minor, sometimes not. In Florida homosexuals are, from the face of the statute, specifically excluded from adopting; it is unclear whether terms such as "proper," "reputable," or "natural" refer to a prospective parent's sexual orientation.

The laws of adoption, as are the laws of the family in general, are changing as society's traditional values are increasingly scrutinized. There is a growing trend to recognize the rights and opinions of children at younger ages, and to recognize the rights of non-traditional individuals. Indeed, same-sex couples are recognized as adoptive parents in a number of states. Also, some states appear headed in the direction of "open" adoption, whereby any individual may adopt any other individual for any reason.

Federal Law

Federal law has preempted the entire scope of the laws of adoption regarding Native Americans, provoking no small amount of controversy over a non-Native American family's ability to adopt a Native American. When a member of the Aleut tribe had a baby out of wedlock, a non-Native couple living in Vancouver, British Columbia, adopted the child. The tribe sued and won the right to intervene in the adoption after claiming that they had a vital interest in preserving the child's Indian heritage. A California court, in this 1991 case, upheld the tribe's right to intervene, but in the child's interest let her remain with her adoptive parents because she had been living with them for nearly two years.

Table 19: Adoption

State/Code Section; Uniform Act	Who May Be Adopted	Child's Consent	Who May Adopt	Adoptive Home Residency Prior to Decree	State Agency/ Court	Statute of Limitation to Challenge
FEDERAL 25 U.S.C. §§1901-1023 Indian Child Welfare Act				Placement preferences	Indian Tribe exclusive jurisdiction/Tribal	2 years
ALABAMA 26-10A-1 to 26-10A-38; No	Any minor	14 years and older	No rule or regulation of Department of Human Resources shall prevent adoption by single parent.	60 days	Dept. of Human Resources/Probate	5 years
ALASKA 25.23.010 to 25.23.240; Yes	Any person	10 years and older	Husband and wife together; unmarried adult, including father or mother of person to be adopted; married person without other spouse joining if other spouse is parent of adoptee and consents or need for consent is excused by court or spouses are legally separated.	Yes	Health & Social Services/Superior	1 year
ARIZONA 8-101 to 8-145; No	Any child under 18 years of age or foreign born person under age 21 who is not illegal alien	12 years and older	Husband and wife may jointly adopt children. Adults may adopt adult relatives.	No	Economic Security/Superior	1 year
ARKANSAS 9-9-101; 9-9-201 to 223; 9-9-301 to 304; 9-9-402 to 412; 9-9-501 to 508; Yes	Any person	10 years and older		6 months	Human Services/ Probate	1 year
CALIFORNIA Civ. §§221-230; No	Any unmarried minor child at least 10 years younger than petitioner and any younger adult	12 years and older	Any adult	No	Social Services/ Superior	Procedural: 3 years; other: 5 years

(Continued)

Table 19: Adoption—Continued

State/Code Section; Uniform Act	Who May Be Adopted	Child's Consent	Who May Adopt	Adoptive Home Residency Prior to Decree	State Agency/ Court	Statute of Limitation to Challenge
COLORADO 14-1-101; 19-5-201 to 304; No	Any person	12 years and older	Minor with court approval or any person over 21. Married person must petition jointly with spouse unless such spouse is natural parent of or has previously adopted child.	No	Social Services/ Juvenile	2 years
CONNECTICUT 45a-706 to 765; No	Any person	14 years and older	Married persons must join in adoption unless court finds sufficient reason for nonjoinder.	No	Children and Youth Services/ Probate	Not specified
DELAWARE Tit. 13-901 to 930; No	Any person	14 years and older	Unmarried person; divorced or legally separated person; husband and wife who are living together. Must be legal resident in Delaware and over 21.	1 year	Dept. of Services for Children, Youth & Families/ Family	2 years
DISTRICT OF COLUMBIA 16-301 to 315; No	Any person	14 years and older	Any person, provided spouse (if any) joins in petition or (if spouse is natural parent of adoptee) consents thereto.	No	Mayor or licensed agency/Superior	1 year
FLORIDA Ch. 63; No	Any person	12 years and older	Any adult or unmarried natural parent except homosexuals. Married person must be joined by spouse unless such spouse is parent and consents, or failure to join or consent is excused.	No	Health & Rehabilitative Services/Circuit	1 year
GEORGIA 19-8-1 to 26; No	Any child 10 years younger than petitioner; any adult.	14 years and older	Any adult at least 25 years of age or married and living with spouse.	No	Human Resources/ Superior	Not specified
HAWAII 578-1 to 17; No	Any person	10 years and older; if married adult, consent of spouse also	Any proper adult person, not married, or married to legal parent of minor, or husband and wife jointly.	No	Human Services/ Family	1 year

(Continued)

Table 19: Adoption—Continued

State/Code Section; Uniform Act	Who May Be Adopted	Child's Consent	Who May Adopt	Adoptive Home Residency Prior to Decree	State Agency/ Court	Statute of Limitation to Challenge
IDAHO 16-1501; No	Any child; any adult if adoption during minority was overlooked due to inadvertence, mistake, or neglect and person adopting has sustained relation of parent.	12 years and older	Any adult resident of Idaho who is either 15 years older than child or 25 years of age or older; spouse of natural parent may adopt without above age restriction. No married person can adopt without consent of spouse.	No	Health & Welfare/ District	Not specified
ILLINOIS 750 ILCS 50/1 to 50/24; No	Any child; any adult residing in home 2 years, or a relative.	14 years and older	Any reputable person of legal age who has resided continually in Illinois for at least 6 months. Residency requirement waived in adoption of relative. If petitioner is married, husband or wife must join in petition. Minor may also petition by leave of court upon good cause shown.	6 months	Department of Children and Family Services/ Circuit	1 year to challenge for failure of notice to putative father
INDIANA 31-3-1-1; No	Any person	14 years and older	Any resident of state. If married, spouse must join. Spouse must consent if such spouse is natural or adoptive parent. Nonresidents of state may adopt hard to place child as defined in §31-3-3-1.	No	Public Welfare/ Probate	Not specified
IOWA 600.1, *et seq.*; No	Any person	14 years and older	Unmarried adult; husband and wife together; husband or wife separately under certain circumstances.	180 days	Human Services/ District	Not specified
KANSAS 59-2101, *et seq.*; No	Any person	14 years and older	Any adult, or husband and wife jointly, except one spouse cannot adopt without consent of other.	Not required	Social & Rehabilitative Services/District	30 days
KENTUCKY 199.470; No	Any person	12 years and older	Any person over 18 who is a resident of or who has resided in Kentucky for 12 months immediately preceding filing.	3 months for children under 16	Department for Social Services within Cabinet for Human Resources/ Circuit	Procedural: 2 years; ethnic difference: 5 years

(Continued)

Table 19: Adoption—Continued

State/Code Section; Uniform Act	Who May Be Adopted	Child's Consent	Who May Adopt	Adoptive Home Residency Prior to Decree	State Agency/ Court	Statute of Limitation to Challenge
LOUISIANA Ch. C. Art. 1167-1270; No	Any child or adult	Not required	Any single person 18 years of age or older, or married couple jointly. Special procedures exist to adopt adult.	1 year	Dept. of Social Services/Juvenile	6 months for fraud or duress
MAINE Tit. 19 §§531 to 538; No	Any person	14 years and older		1 year may be required at discretion of court	Human Services/ Probate	Not specified
MARYLAND Fam. Law §5-301, *et seq.*; No	Any person	10 years and older	Any adult, even though single or unmarried. Married persons must act jointly unless legally separated or if one spouse is natural parent of adoptee or spouse is incompetent.	Not required	Social Services Administration/ Circuit or Equity	1 year
MASSACHUSETTS Ch. 210; No	Any person younger than adopter; Department of Social Services must verify that child under 14 not registered as missing person.	12 years and older	Any person of full age, his spouse joining, may, subject to certain exceptions, petition to adopt any person younger than himself (other than petitioner's spouse, brother, sister, aunt, or uncle of whole or half blood).	6 months if adoptee is under 14	Social Services Probate	Not specified; 1 year for appeal
MICHIGAN MCL §555.21; No	Any person	14 years and older	Any person; if married, spouse must join.	Not required	Social Services/ Probate	20 days from entry of order or denial of petition for rehearing
MINNESOTA 259.21; No	Any person	14 years and older	Any person who has resided in the state for more than one year, unless residence requirement waived.	3 months; may be waived by court	Human Services/ Juvenile	Not specified

(Continued)

Table 19: Adoption—Continued

State/Code Section; Uniform Act	Who May Be Adopted	Child's Consent	Who May Adopt	Adoptive Home Residency Prior to Decree	State Agency/ Court	Statute of Limitation to Challenge
MISSISSIPPI 93-17-1, *et seq.*; No	Any person	14 years and older	Any proper unmarried adult, or husband and wife jointly. Must be Mississippi resident for 90 days preceding filing except under certain circumstances.	6 months; waiting period may be shortened if child resided in adoptive home prior to entry of interlocutory decree.	Public Welfare/ Chancery	6 months to challenge interlocutory decree; 6 months to challenge final decree
MISSOURI 453.010 to 170; No	Any person	14 years and older		9 months	Social Services, Family Services Division/Juvenile	1 year
MONTANA 40-8-101, *et seq.;* Yes	Any person	12 years and older		6 months	Department of Family Services/ District or Tribal	Not specified
NEBRASKA 43-101 to 43-160; No	Any child. Adoption of American Indian children is govered by the Nebraska Indian Child Welfare Act (§43-1501).	14 years and older	Any adult person may adopt minor child; adult child may be adopted by spouse of such child's parent. Husband and wife must jointly adopt child, unless he or she is parent of child.	6 months	Department of Social Services/ County	2 years
NEVADA 127; Yes	Any person	14 years and older	Minor: Any adult who is 10 years older than adoptee. If petitioner is married, spouse must join. Must have resided in state during 6 months preceding adoption. Adult: Any adult may adopt younger adult.	6 months	Human Resources, Welfare Division/ District	4 years
NEW HAMPSHIRE 170-B; No	Any person	12 years and older	Any person age 18 or older may petition to adopt any other individual except his or her spouse.	6 months	Division for Children and Youth Services/ Probate	1 year
NEW JERSEY 9:3; 2A:22-1; No	Any person 10 years younger than petitioner	10 years and older	Any person of full age. If petitioner is married, spouse must consent or application may be made jointly. Court may waive any of these requirements.	6 months	Human Services/ Superior or County	2 years

(Continued)

Table 19: Adoption—Continued

State/Code Section; Uniform Act	Who May Be Adopted	Child's Consent	Who May Adopt	Adoptive Home Residency Prior to Decree	State Agency/ Court	Statute of Limitation to Challenge
NEW MEXICO 40-7; Yes	Any person	10 years and older.	Any adult. If petitioner is married, spouse must join unless natural parent of adoptee or legally separated or excused from joining by court.	90 days if less than one year old when placed; 180 days if more than one year old when placed.	Human Services, Social Services Division/District	1 year
NEW YORK Dom. Rel. §109-117	Any person	14 years and older.	Adult unmarried person or adult husband and wife together unless legally separated. Adult or minor husband and wife, together or separately, may adopt child either born in or out of wedlock.	6 months	As defined by social services law/Family	45 days
NORTH CAROLINA 48; No	Any person	12 years and older	Any proper adult person, or husband and wife jointly. Must have resided in North Carolina for six months next preceding filing of petition. Residency requirement waived under certain circumstances.	1 year	Social Services, Human Resources/ Superior	3 years
NORTH DAKOTA Ch. 14-15; Yes	Any person	10 years and older		6 months	Human Services or County Social Services Board/ District	1 year
OHIO 3107; Yes	Any child; certain adults only.	12 years and older	Unmarried adult; unmarried minor parent of adoptee; husband and wife (at least one of whom is adult) together, unless legally separated or under certain other circumstances.	6 months	Human Services/ Probate	1 year
OKLAHOMA Tit.10 §§55, 60.1; Yes	Any person	12 years and older.	Husband and wife, or either if other spouse is parent of child; unmarried person 21 years or older; married person 21 years or older who is legally separated from spouse; unmarried father or mother of illegitimate child.	6 months, discretionary	Department of Human Services/ District	1 year

(Continued)

Table 19: Adoption—Continued

State/Code Section; Uniform Act	Who May Be Adopted	Child's Consent	Who May Adopt	Adoptive Home Residency Prior to Decree	State Agency/ Court	Statute of Limitation to Challenge
OREGON 109.305, *et seq.*; No	Any person	14 years and older	Any person. Petitioner, consenting party, or child must be resident of Oregon. If petitioner is married, spouse must join. Compliance with Indian Child Welfare Act required if applicable.	Not required	Children's Services Division/ Probate or Circuit	1 year
PENNSYLVANIA Tit. 23 §§2101 to 2910; No	Any person	12 years and older	Any person	Not required	Pennsylvania Adoption Cooperative Exchange (PACE) in Dept. of Public Welfare/Common Pleas	Not specified
RHODE ISLAND 15-7; Yes	Any person	14 years and older	Any person residing in state may adopt any person younger than himself. If petitioner is married, spouse must join; however, requirement may be waived if it can be shown adoption would be in child's best interest. Nonresident may petition under certain circumstances.	6 months, but court may waive for good cause	Child Welfare Services Dept. for Children and their Families/Family	20 days
SOUTH CAROLINA 20-7-1646 to 1890; No	Any person	14 years and older	Any South Carolina resident may petition court to adopt child. Any adult person may adopt any other adult person.	6 months	Children's Bureau, pending transfer of operations to Social Services/ Family	1 year
SOUTH DAKOTA 25-6; No	Any person	12 years and older	Any adult person may adopt any child at least 10 years younger. Any adult may adopt another adult with the latter's consent.	6 months	Social Services/ Circuit	Not specified
TENNESSEE 36-1; No	Any person	14 years and older	Any person over 18 years of age who has been Tennessee resident for one year. Residency requirement may be waived under certain circumstances.	1 year	Human Services/ Chancery	1 year

(Continued)

Table 19: Adoption—Continued

State/Code Section; Uniform Act	Who May Be Adopted	Child's Consent	Who May Adopt	Adoptive Home Residency Prior to Decree	State Agency/ Court	Statute of Limitation to Challenge
TEXAS Fam. Ch. 11, 16; No	Any person	12 years and older	Any adult. If petitioner is married, spouse must join.	6 months	Human Services/ District	2 years
UTAH 78-30; No	Any person 10 years younger than petitioner	12 years and older	Any adult.	6 months	Family Services/ District or Juvenile	4 years
VERMONT Tit.15 §§431, *et seq.*; No	Any person	14 years and older	Any proper person of full age and sound mind. If petitioner is married, spouse must consent.	6 months	Social & Rehabilitation Services/Probate	1 year for child's dissent after reaching majority
VIRGINIA 63.1-220, *et seq.*; No	Any child; adult under certain conditions	14 years and older	Any natural person may petition to adopt minor child. If petitioner is married, spouse must join. Any natural person may adopt another adult under certain conditions (see §63.1-222).	6 months	Public Welfare or Social Services/ Circuit	6 months
WASHINGTON 26.33; No	Any person	14 years and older	Any legally competent person, 18 years of age or over.	Not required	Social & Health Services/Superior	1 year
WEST VIRGINIA 48-4	Any person	12 years and older	Any person not married or any person with his or her spouse's consent or husband and wife jointly.	6 months	Department of Human Services/ Circuit	1 year
WISCONSIN 48.81, *et seq.*; No	Any person	No child's consent required; however, minors 12 and older must attend hearing unless court orders otherwise.	Unmarried adult, husband and wife jointly, spouse of minor's parent may adopt minor. Must be Wisconsin residents and (if practicable and if requested by birth parent) of same religion as adoptee's natural parents. Any resident adult may adopt any other adult.	6 months	Department of Health & Social Services/Circuit	40 days
WYOMING 1-22-101; No	Any person	14 years and older	Any adult person who has resided in state during 60 days immediately preceding filing of petition and who is determined by court to be fit and competent to be a parent.	6 months	Department of Family Services/ District	10 years

217

20. ANNULMENT AND PROHIBITED MARRIAGE

Annulment

Annulment differs from divorce in that it addresses defects in a marital relationship occurring at the time of the formation of that relationship. Thus, if a marriage is illegally formed, when it is annulled the parties regain their legal rights and responsibilities as they existed before the marriage occurred. By contrast, a divorce deals with problems in a marital relationship arising after the marriage is formed. Traditionally, after a divorce the parties have continuing legal status as ex-spouses involving division of property, custody of children, and alimony.

Annulments are becoming similar to divorces in that with annulments courts may now divide marital property, order the payment of spousal support or alimony, or decree nearly anything that would be common upon a decree of divorce. Unlike with divorce, however, certain rights or entitlements such as worker's compensation benefits or alimony from a previous marriage that may have ended upon marriage will be restarted upon annulment, because the decree legally makes the marriage nonexistent.

Grounds for annulments and prohibited marriages are varied. Insanity, fraud, force, duress, impotency, being underage, and polygamy are all leading grounds for annulment. There are also a few more creative grounds. Colorado, for instance, has an annulment provision considering if the act were done as "Jest or Dare." A couple of states will also make a marriage void or voidable if a party is found to have AIDS or venereal disease.

Prohibited Marriage

Many states prohibit marriage between parties more closely related than second cousins, though in some states first cousins may marry. In three states that prohibit marriages of first cousins, an exception is made for elderly parties: in Arizona and Indiana if parties are over 65 and one is sterile, or in Wisconsin if the woman is over 55 and one party is sterile. Only in Rhode Island do special exceptions exist for a particular religious group: Jews are permitted to marry according to religious law exclusive of state rules. It is interesting to note that five states specifically list same-sex marriages as prohibited, and one state, Louisiana, lists "purported" same-sex marriages as having no civil effect. This specific prohibition is an apparent effort to reinforce the recognition of heterosexual relationships as the only ones that are legitimate.

Table 20: Annulment and Prohibited Marriage

State	Code Section	Grounds	Time Limitation	Legitimacy of Children	Prohibited Marriages
ALABAMA	13A-13-1; 30-1-3	Insanity at marriage (28 Ala. 565); fraudulent intent not to perform marriage vows (2 So.2d 443); bigamy (16 So.2d 401); incest (180 So. 577); under age of consent (78 So. 885)		Issue of incestuous marriage before annulment is legitimate	Bigamous
ALASKA	25.05.021,031, 050	Underage; insufficient understanding for consent; consent was obtained by force or fraud; party fails to consummate		Children legitimate if parents subsequently marry	Either party has living spouse at time; parties related closer than fourth degree of consanguinity
ARKANSAS	9-12-201; 9-11-106	Incapable of consent due to age or understanding; incapable for physical causes; if consent obtained by fraud or force	Action to annul on ground of non-age must be brought before legal age is attained (24 S.W. 2d 807)		Between parents and child, brother and sister (half-blood included), uncle and niece, aunt and nephew, first cousins
ARIZONA	25-101, 125, 301	Superior courts may dissolve and adjudge marriage null and void when cause alleged constitutes impediment rendering it void	Common law rules apply		Between parents and children, grandparents and grandchildren, brothers and sisters, (half and whole), aunt and nephew, uncle and niece, first cousins unless both are over 65 or one is not able to reproduce; same sex
CALIFORNIA	Civ. §4400; 4401; 4425; 4426	Party did not have capability to consent; another living spouse; unsound mind; consent obtained by force or fraud; physically incapable of entering marriage state	Age of consent: Underage party within 4 yrs. of reaching age of consent or by parent before party has reached age; Fraud: Within 4 yrs. by injured party; Husband/Wife living: Either party during life or by former spouse; Unsound Mind: Any time before death; Consent by Force: Within 4 yrs. by injured party; Physical Incapability: Within 4 yrs. by injured party		Ancestor and descendant of any degree, brother and sister (half-blood included), uncle and niece, aunt and nephew; bigamy and polygamy
COLORADO	14-10-111, *et seq.*	Consent lacking; mental incapacity; alcohol; drugs; underage; jest or dare; duress; fraudulent act; physical incapacity to consummate	Lacking capacity: 6-24 months after knowledge of condition depending on grounds	Children of invalid marriage are legitimate	Prior marriage still valid; between ancestor and descendant, brother and sister, uncle and niece, aunt and nephew

(Continued)

Table 20: Annulment and Prohibited Marriage—Continued

State	Code Section	Grounds	Time Limitation	Legitimacy of Children	Prohibited Marriages
CONNECTICUT	46b-40, 60	Lack of mutual consent (460 A.2d 945); physical incapacity to consummate (11 Conn. Sup. 361); bigamous marriage is a nullity (18 Conn. Sup. 472)		Children of void marriage are legitimate	
DELAWARE	Tit. 13 §1506	Innocent party may demand for unsoundness of mind, influence of alcohol, drugs, etc.; physical incapacity to consummate; underage without consent of parents; fraud; duress; jest; dare; bigamy; polygamy; incestuous	Lack of capacity, fraud, duress, jest or dare: Within 90 days of obtaining knowledge; Inability to consummate: 1 yr. after knowledge obtained; Underage: Within 1 yr. of marriage; Prohibited: Anytime before death of either party	Children born of annulled marriage are legitimate	Between person and ancestor, descendant, brother, sister, uncle, aunt, niece, nephew, first cousin
DISTRICT OF COLUMBIA	30-101, 103; 16-907, 908	Marriage of an idiot or adjudged lunatic; consent by force or fraud; physical incapacity; underage		Children born in or out of wedlock are legitimate children of father and mother and their blood and adopted relatives	Marriage to one whose previous marriage has not been terminated by death or divorce; between ancestor and descendant, uncle and niece, aunt and nephew, brother and sister and corresponding in-law relationships
FLORIDA	741.21	No statutory provisions			No marriage between persons related by lineal consanguinity, sister, aunt, niece, brother, uncle, nephew
GEORGIA	19-3-3, 5; 19-4-1	Unable to consummate; unwilling or fraudulently induced; no annulment granted where children are born or are to be born of marriage		Issue of void marriage is legitimate	Related by blood or marriage, father and daughter or stepdaughter, mother and son or stepson, brother and sister (whole- or half-blood), grandparent and grandchild, aunt and nephew, uncle and niece (penalty of prison 1-5 yrs.)
HAWAII	580-21	Underage; spouse still living; lacking mental capacity; consent obtained by force, duress, fraud and no subsequent cohabitation; party afflicted with loathsome disease			Between ancestor and descendant, brother and sister, uncle and niece, aunt and nephew

(Continued)

Table 20: Annulment and Prohibited Marriage—Continued

State	Code Section	Grounds	Time Limitation	Legitimacy of Children	Prohibited Marriages
IDAHO	32-205, 206, 501 to 503	Underage; former spouse living; unsound mind; consent obtained by fraud or force; party physically incapable of consummating	Underage: Anytime before majority reached; Spouse living: Anytime during life; Unsound mind: Anytime before death; Fraud: Within 4 yrs. of discovery; Force: Within 4 yrs. of marriage; Incapacity to consummate: 4 yrs. from marriage	Not affected by annulment unless grounds is fraud, that woman was pregnant with another man's child	Incestuous; between ancestor and descendant, brother and sister, uncle and niece, aunt and nephew, first cousin
ILLINOIS	750 ILCS 5/212, 5/301, 5/303	Capacity lacking (infirmity, alcohol, drugs, force, duress, fraud); physically incapable of consummating; underage; prohibited		Children born of annulled marriage are legitimate	Former marriage undissolved; between ancestor and descendant, brother and sister, uncle and niece, aunt and nephew, first cousins, unless no chance of reproduction
INDIANA	31-7-7, *et seq.*	Underage or mentally incompetent to consent; obtained by fraud		Children of incestuous marriage are legitimate; child conceived before marriage is annulled is legitimate	More closely related than second cousin unless first cousins married after September 1, 1977, and both 65 at marriage
IOWA	595.19; 598.29, 31	Prohibited; impotency; prior marriage undissolved; lacking capacity to consent or underage		Children of annulled marriage are legitimate	Undissolved prior marriage; between descendant and ancestor, brother and sister, aunt and nephew, uncle and niece, first cousins
KANSAS	23-102; 60-1602	Induced by fraud; mistake of fact; lack of knowledge of a material fact or any other reason justifying rescission			Between ancestor and descendant, brother and sister, uncle and niece, aunt and nephew, first cousins
KENTUCKY	391.100; 402.020, 070; 403.120;	Capacity lacking (drugs, alcohol, force, duress, fraud); physical capacity for marriage lacking; underage; prohibited	Underage: Must be annulled before cohabitation after eighteenth birthday; No consent; physical incapacity: Within 90 days of knowledge; Prohibited: No later than 1 yr. after discovery	Children born of unlawful or void marriages are legitimate	Any kin closer than second cousin; with person mentally disabled; living spouse; underage; solemnized before one without authority unless parties believed he had authority
LOUISIANA	Civ. §§94 to 96	Null without marriage ceremony; consent not freely given; purported marriage between same sex has no civil effects		Child of marriage contracted in good faith is legitimate	

(Continued)

Table 20: Annulment and Prohibited Marriage—Continued

State	Code Section	Grounds	Time Limitation	Legitimacy of Children	Prohibited Marriages
MAINE	Tit. 19 §§32-33	Incapable of contracting marriage; mental illness/ retardation of sufficient degree; polygamous marriage		If marriage is annulled because of consanguinity or affinity of parties, issue is illegitimate; if because of nonage, mental illness, or idiocy, issue is legitimate issue of parent capable of contracting marriage; if because of prior marriage still in existence, children are legitimate issue of parent capable of contracting	Between ancestor and descendant, brother and sister, aunt and nephew, uncle and niece, first cousins unless cousins obtain physician's certificate of genetic counseling
MARYLAND	Md. Rules SP P Rule S76; Md. Fam. §2-202	Bigamy or prohibited marriage			
MASSACHUSETTS	1 to 5; 14 to 16	Determining validity; nonage; insanity		Issue of relationship in consanguinity or affinity is illegitimate	Polygamous; man cannot marry his ancestors or descendants, sister, stepmother, grandfather's wife, wife's ancestors or descendants, niece, aunt; woman cannot marry ancestors or descendants, brother, stepfather, grandmother's husband, daughter's husband, granddaughter's husband, husband's grandfather, husband's son, husband's grandson, nephew, uncle; these provisions continue even after dissolution, by death or divorce, of marriage by which affinity was created unless divorce was given because original marriage was unlawful or void
MICHIGAN	MCL 552.34, *et seq.*	Underage; insanity; physical incapacity to consummate	Underage: Unless they cohabit upon reaching majority: Incapacity: 2 years from marriage		Provisions repealed (MCL 551.3-551.6)

(Continued)

Table 20: Annulment and Prohibited Marriage—Continued

State	Code Section	Grounds	Time Limitation	Legitimacy of Children	Prohibited Marriages
MINNESOTA	518.02	Lacking capacity to consent (mental, alcohol, drugs, force, fraud); no capacity to consummate; underage; marriages within prohibited decrees and bigamous are void			Previously undissolved marriage; between ancestor and descendant, brother and sister, uncle and niece, aunt and nephew, first cousins
MISSISSIPPI	93-1-1; 93-7-3, 5	Incurable impotency, insanity, or idiocy; incapable of consent from lack of understanding, force, fraud; pregnant by another man and husband did not know	Insanity, lack of consent, pregnancy: Within 6 months of marriage	Void or annulled marriage's issue is legitimate, but issue of incestuous marriage is not	Bigamous and incestuous marriages are void; between ancestor and descendant, brother and sister, aunt and nephew, uncle and niece, first cousins by blood, daughter or son-in-law to father or mother-in-law
MISSOURI	451.020, 030	No statutory provisions			Between ancestor and descendant, brother and sister, uncle and niece, aunt and nephew, first cousins; between persons lacking capacity to consummate; previous marriage undissolved
MONTANA	40-1-401, 402	Lacking consent (mental, alcohol, duress, fraud, force); no physical capacity to consummate; underage; prohibited	Mental infirmity: Within 1 yr. after knowledge; Alcohol, drugs: 1 yr. after knowledge; Force, duress, fraud: 2 yrs. after knowledge; Physical incapacity: Party must not know at time of marriage and must bring within 4 yrs.; Underage: Until age of majority; Prohibited: Anytime	Children born of prohibited marriages are legitimate	Previous marriage undissolved; between ancestor and descendant, brother and sister, first cousins, uncle and niece, aunt and nephew
NEBRASKA	42-103, 118, 374, 377	Underage, if separate during such nonage and no cohabitation thereafter; consent obtained by force or fraud and no voluntary cohabitation thereafter; impotency; previous marriage undissolved; mental illness or retardation at marriage or force or fraud			Marriage void when previous marriage undissolved; either party at marriage is mentally incompetent to enter marriage relation; between ancestor and descendant, brother and sister, first cousins, uncle and niece, aunt and nephew

(Continued)

Table 20: Annulment and Prohibited Marriage—Continued

State	Code Section	Grounds	Time Limitation	Legitimacy of Children	Prohibited Marriages
NEVADA	125.300 to 350	Underage; lack of understanding to consent; insanity; fraud; where grounds to void the contract in equity	Underage: Within 1 yr. after 18; Fraud: May not annul if after discovery parties voluntarily cohabit	Not affected by annulment	Previous marriage undissolved; not nearer in kin than second cousins
NEW HAMPSHIRE	457:1, *et seq.*; 458:1, 23	Underage until confirming marriage upon reaching age; bigamy		Issue of incestuous marriage are treated as children of unwed unless while married it was valid, then children are legitimate; legitimacy not affected by annulment	Between ancestor and descendant, brother and sister, uncle and niece, aunt and nephew, cousins; same sex; previous marriage undissolved
NEW JERSEY	2A:34-1, 20; 37:1-1	Previous marriage undissolved; impotency; lack of consent due to alcohol, understanding capacity, drugs, duress, fraud, underage		Children of annulled marriage are legitimate	Between ancestor and descendant, brother and sister, uncle and niece, aunt and nephew
NEW MEXICO	40-1-9	Underage	Underage: Anytime until age of majority	Children are legitimate if marriage declared void	Between ancestor and descendant, brother and sister, uncle and niece, aunt and nephew
NEW YORK	Dom. Rel. §5, 24, 140	Undissolved previous marriage; underage; mental illness or retardation; physical incapacity; consent by force, duress or fraud	Undissolved: Anytime; Underage: Until majority and cohabitation; Mental: Anytime as illness continues; Physical incapacity: Within 5 yrs. of marriage if unknown at marriage; Physical incapacity: Within 5 yrs. of marriage if unknown at marriage; Force, duress, fraud: Within civil statute of limitations unless voluntary cohabitation after discovery	Children of annulled or void marriages are legitimate	Between ancestor and descendant, brother and sister, uncle and niece, aunt and nephew
NORTH CAROLINA	51-3	Underage; previously undissolved marriage; impotent; lack of consent due to lack of will or understanding; under 16	Age: Marriage will not be declared void if girl is pregnant (§51-3) or if cohabitation after 16 (10 S.E.2d 807)		Bigamy; between double first cousins or nearer in kin than first cousin

(Continued)

Table 20: Annulment and Prohibited Marriage—Continued

State	Code Section	Grounds	Time Limitation	Legitimacy of Children	Prohibited Marriages
NORTH DAKOTA	14-04-01, *et seq.*	Underage; previous marriage undissolved; unsound mind; fraud; force; physically incapable; incestuous	Previous marriage undissolved: Anytime; Underage: Within 4 yrs. of age of consent; Unsound mind: Anytime; Fraud, force or physically incapable: 4 yrs.; Incestuous: Anytime	Issue of annulled or prohibited marriages are legitimate	Between ancestor and descendant, brother and sister, uncle and niece, aunt and nephew, first cousins; marriage by woman under 45 or man of any age (unless he marries woman over 45) is prohibited if man or woman is institutionalized as severely retarded
OHIO	3101.01; 3105.31	Underage; previous marriage undissolved; mental incompetence; consent obtained by fraud or force; never consummated	Underage: Within 2 yrs. of age of consent; Previous marriage undissolved: Anytime; Mental: Anytime before death; Fraud: Within 2 yrs. of discovering fraud; Force: 2 yrs. after marriage; No consummation: 2 yrs. from marriage		Between persons nearer in kin than second cousins; previous marriage undissolved
OKLAHOMA	Tit. 43 §§2, 128	Lack of age or understanding		Issue of annulled marriage are legitimate	Between ancestor and descendant, stepparent and stepchild, uncle and niece, aunt and nephew, brother and sister, first cousins (but will recognize marriage of first cousins married in state where it is legal)
OREGON	106.020, 190; 107.015	Incapable of consent for age or lack of understanding; consent obtained by force or fraud		Issue of prohibited marriage is legitimate	Previous marriage undissolved; between first cousins or any persons nearer in kin (unless parties are first cousins by adoption only)
PENNSYLVANIA	Tit. 23 §§1304, 3304, 5102	Previous marriage undissolved; within consanguinity lines prohibited; lacked capacity by insanity or did not intend to consent; underage; one party is weak-minded or under influence of alcohol or drugs		Pennsylvania no longer recognizes status of being illegitimate	Between ancestor and descendant, aunt and nephew, brother and sister, uncle and niece, first cousins

(Continued)

Table 20: Annulment and Prohibited Marriage—Continued

State	Code Section	Grounds	Time Limitation	Legitimacy of Children	Prohibited Marriages
RHODE ISLAND	15-1-1, *et. seq.*	Remedy is by divorce: No statutory provision for annulment		Issue of idiot or lunatic is illegitimate	Marriage of idiot or lunatic absolutely void; between ancestor and descendant, stepparent and stepchild, parent-in-law and son- or daughter-in-law; parent or parent-in-law and son- or daughter-in-law, brother and sister, uncle and niece, aunt and nephew; special exceptions for Jewish marriages allowed by Jewish religious law
SOUTH CAROLINA	20-1-10, 80, 90, 530, 550	Marriage invalid without cohabitation		Parties entering bigamous marriage in good faith have legitimate children	Mental incompetent; between ancestor and descendant, spouse of ancestor or descendant, uncle and niece, aunt and nephew; bigamous marriages are void unless former spouse absent and unheard of for 5 yrs.
SOUTH DAKOTA	25-3-1, *et seq.*	Underage; previous marriage undissolved; either party of unsound mind; consent by fraud; physical incapacity	Underage: Until couple cohabits after reaching age of consent; Previous marriage undissolved: Anytime; Unsound mind: Anytime; Fraud: Within 4 yrs. of discovery; Physical incapacity: 4 yrs. after marriage	Children are legitimate when marriage is annulled for reasons of mental illness or previously undissolved marriage	Between ancestor and descendant, brother and sister, uncle and niece, aunt and nephew, cousins, stepparent and stepchild
TENNESSEE	36-3-101; 36-4-125			Annulment shall not affect the legitimacy of children	Between ancestor and descendant, brother and sister, uncle and niece, aunt and nephew
TEXAS	Fam. §§2.41, *et seq.*	Underage; under influence of alcohol and drugs; impotency; fraud; duress, or force; mental incompetence; concealed divorce; marriage took place within 72 hours after marriage license	Underage: Suit to annul must be brought within 90 days of fourteenth birthday		Between ancestor and descendant, brother and sister, aunt and nephew, uncle and niece, spouse of ancestor or descendant, descendant of husband or wife

(Continued)

Table 20: Annulment and Prohibited Marriage—Continued

State	Code Section	Grounds	Time Limitation	Legitimacy of Children	Prohibited Marriages
UTAH	30-1-1, 2; 17.1	When marriage prohibited and grounds existing at common law			Between ancestor and descendant, brother and sister, uncle and niece, aunt and nephew, first cousins, or between relations within but not including fifth degree of consanguinity; person with AIDS, syphilis, gonorrhea; previous marriage undissolved; underage; same sex
VERMONT	Tit. 15 §§512, *et seq.*	Under 16; idiocy or lunacy; physically incapable of marriage state; consent had by force or fraud	Underage: Until parties obtain legal age and cohabit; Idiocy: Anytime during their life; Physical incapacity: 2 yrs. from marriage; Consent by force or fraud: Anytime unless parties after commencement of action cohabit	Children of annulled marriage are legitimate	Between ancestor and descendant, brother and sister, aunt and nephew, uncle and niece; prohibitions apply even after divorce has dissolved relationship unless marriage was void or unlawful
VIRGINIA	20-38.1; 20-43; 20-45.1, 2; 20-48, 49; 20-89.1	Mentally incapacitated; fraud; duress; impotency; either convicted of felony before marriage; if without other's knowledge: wife pregnant by another man, husband fathered another child born within 10 months after marriage; either had been a prostitute; no annulment allowed for fraud, duress, mental incapacity, felony, pregnancy or fathering if parties cohabited after knowledge	All actions must be brought within 2 yrs. of marriage		Previous marriage undissolved; between ancestor and descendant, brother and sister, uncle and niece, aunt and nephew; same sex; bigamous; parties under 18 and have not complied with consent provisions
WASHINGTON	26.04.020, 130	Annulment provisions have been repealed			Previous marriage undissolved; between persons closer in kin than second cousins; voidable marriages: underage or without sufficient understanding; consent gained by fraud or duress voidable by party laboring under disability or upon whom force or fraud was imposed

(Continued)

Table 20: Annulment and Prohibited Marriage—Continued

State	Code Section	Grounds	Time Limitation	Legitimacy of Children	Prohibited Marriages
WEST VIRGINIA	42-1-7; 42-2-2; 48-1-2, 3	Previous marriage undissolved; within line of prohibited consanguinity; party insane; venereal disease; impotency; underage; convicted of infamous offense prior to marriage; wife with child of another man or had been a prostitute; husband had been a licentious person		Children of annulled or prohibited marriage are legitimate	Between ancestor and descendant, brother and sister, half-brother and half-sister, aunt and nephew, uncle and niece, first cousins, double cousins (unless solely by adoption)
WISCONSIN	767.03, 60	Consent lacking; underage; mental infirmity; alcohol; drugs; force; duress; fraud; lack capacity to consummate	Underage: Within 1 yr. of marriage; Mental infirmity, alcohol, drugs, force, duress, fraud, no capacity to consummate: Within 1 yr. of knowledge	Issue of void marriage is legitimate	Previous marriage undissolved; between persons no closer in kin than second cousins (unless woman is 55 or one party is sterile and they are first cousins); one lacking understanding to consent
WYOMING	20-2-101, 117	Prohibited marriages; underage; physical incapacity	Underage: Until couple cohabits upon reaching age of consent; Physical incapacity: Until 2 yrs. after marriage	Legitimacy not affected by dissolution	Previous marriage undissolved; party mentally incompetent; between ancestor and descendant, brother and sister, uncle and niece, aunt and nephew, first cousins

21. CHILD CUSTODY

Because of the importance of the laws regarding child custody, all fifty states and the District of Columbia have adopted the Uniform Child Custody Act.

Prior to the twentieth century it was standard that the father would take sole custody of the children upon divorce. In the twentieth century, however, it became common practice to award custody of children "of tender years" to the mother. It is now most common to award custody to both parents at the same time, in an arrangement known as "joint custody," under which custody of the children is divided into legal and physical custody, with both parents sharing responsibility for the children simultaneously. But joint custody does not necessarily mean equal custody. Rather, it merely means custody co-exists between parents with the physical arrangements coordinated in the best interests of the children. All but nine states recognize the joint custody arrangement in child custody matters. Eleven states, apparently feeling the need to remove the children from the pressures of having to make difficult and emotional decisions, do not consider the wishes of the children when awarding custody. However, it is safe to say that judges will never completely ignore children's wishes in considering custody matters, just as they will not make them bear the brunt of the responsibility for a decision when answering the objections of a parent.

Until ten years ago, only a few states recognized a grandparent's desire to visit his or her grandchildren as a *right*. Now, all except the District of Columbia recognize visitation rights of grandparents.

Table 21: Child Custody

State	Code Section	Year Uniform Child Custody Act Adopted	Joint Custody	Grandparent Visitation	Child's Wishes Considered
ALABAMA	30-3-1 to 99	1980	No	Yes, §30-3-4	Yes
ALASKA	25.24.150	1977	No	Yes, §25.24.150	Yes
ARIZONA	25-331, *et seq.*	1978	Yes, §25-332	Yes, §25-337.01	Yes
ARKANSAS	9-13-101, *et seq.*	1979	No	Yes, §9-13-103	No
CALIFORNIA	Civ. §4600	1973	Yes, Civ. §4600.5	Yes, Civ. §§197.5; 4601	Yes
COLORADO	14-10-123	1973	Yes, §14.10.123.5	Yes, §19-1-117, *et seq.*	Yes
CONNECTICUT	46b-56	1978	Yes §46b-56a	Yes, §46b-56, 46b-59	Yes
DELAWARE	Tit. 13 §§721, *et seq.*	1976	Yes, Tit. 13 §§727, 728	Yes, Tit. 13 §727	Yes
DISTRICT OF COLUMBIA	16-911(5); 16-914	1983	No	No	Yes
FLORIDA	61.13	1977	Yes, §61.13(2)(b)2	Yes, §61.13(2)(c)	Yes
GEORGIA	19-9-1	1978	Yes, §19-9-3	Yes, §19-7-3	Yes
HAWAII	571-46	1973	Yes, §571-46.1	Yes, §571-46(7)	Yes
IDAHO	32-717	1977	Yes, §32-717B	Yes, §32-1008	Yes
ILLINOIS	750 ILCS 5/601	1979	Yes, 750 ILCS 5/602.1	Yes, 750 ILCS 5/607	Yes
INDIANA	31-1-11.5-21	1977	Yes, §31-1-11.5-21	Yes, §31-1-11.7, *et seq.*	Yes
IOWA	598.41	1977	Yes, §598.41(2)	Yes, §598.35	Yes
KANSAS	60.1610	1978	Yes, §60.1610(4)(A)	Yes, §§38-129; 60.1616	Yes
KENTUCKY	403.270	1980	Yes, § 403.270(3)	Yes, §465.021	Yes
LOUISIANA	Civ. Art. 131; Rev. Stat. §9:572	1978	Yes, Civ. Art. 131, 146	Yes, Rev. Stat. Art. IX: 572	Yes
MAINE	Tit. 19 §752	1979	Yes, Tit. 19 §752	Yes, Tit. 19 §1001, *et seq.* Repeal effective July 31, 1994.	Yes
MARYLAND	Fam. §5-203	1975	Yes, §5-203	Yes, §9-102	No
MASSACHUSETTS	208:28	1983	Yes, §208: 31; 209C: 10	Yes, Ch. 119 §39D	No
MICHIGAN	722.21	1975	Yes, §722.26(a)	Yes, §722.27(b)	Yes
MINNESOTA	518.155	1977	Yes, §518.17	Yes, §257.022	Yes
MISSISSIPPI	93-5-23	1982	Yes, §93-5-24	Yes, §93-16-1, *et seq.*	No
MISSOURI	452.375	1978	Yes, §452.375	Yes, §452.402	Yes
MONTANA	40-4-211	1977	Yes, §40-4-222, 224	Yes, §40-4-217; 40-9-102	Yes
NEBRASKA	42-364	1979	Yes, §42-364(3)	Yes, §43-1802, *et seq.*	Yes
NEVADA	125.450	1979	Yes, §125.480, 490, 510	Yes, §125A.330	Yes
NEW HAMPSHIRE	458: 17	1979	Yes, §458: 17	Yes, §458.17	Yes
NEW JERSEY	2A: 34-23	1979	Yes, §9: 2-4	Yes, §9-2-7.1	Yes

(Continued)

Table 21: Child Custody—Continued

State	Code Section	Year Uniform Child Custody Act Adopted	Joint Custody	Grandparent Visitation	Child's Wishes Considered
NEW MEXICO	40-4-9	1981	Yes, §40-4-9.1	Yes, §40-9-2 to 4	Yes
NEW YORK	Dom. Rel. §240	1977	Yes, Dom. Rel. §240	Yes, Dom. Rel. §240	No
NORTH CAROLINA	50-11.2	1979	Yes, §50-13.2	Yes, §50-13.2	No
NORTH DAKOTA	14-05-22	1969	No	Yes, §14-09-05.1	Yes
OHIO	3109.03, 3105.21	1977	Yes, §3109.04(A)	Yes, §3109.051	Yes
OKLAHOMA	Tit. 43 §112	1980	Yes, 43§109	Yes, 10§5	Yes
OREGON	107.105	1973	Yes, §§107.095(1)(b), 105, 169, 179	Yes, §109.119, 121, 123	No
PENNSYLVANIA	Tit. 23 §5301	1977	Yes, Tit. 23 §5304	Yes, Tit. 23 §§5311, 5312	No
RHODE ISLAND	15-5-16	1978	No, §15-5-16(e)	Yes, §§15-5-24.1 to 24.3	No
SOUTH CAROLINA	20-3-160	1981	No	Yes, § 20-7-420(33)	No
SOUTH DAKOTA	25-4-45	1978	Yes, §25-5-7.1	Yes, §§25-4-52, 53	Yes
TENNESSEE	36-6-101, 102	1979	Yes, §36-6-101(a)	Yes, §36-6-301	Yes
TEXAS	Fam. §3.55; 14.01	1983	Yes, Fam. §§14.01, 14.021	Yes, Fam. §14.03(e)	Yes
UTAH	30-3-10	1980	Yes, §§30-3-10.1, *et seq.*	Yes, §30-5-2	Yes
VERMONT	Tit. 15 §665	1979	Yes, Tit. 15 §664(A)	Yes, Tit. 15 §§1101, *et seq.*	No
VIRGINIA	20-107.2	1979	Yes, §§16.1-336, 20.107.2	Yes, §20-107.2	Yes
WASHINGTON	26.09.050	1979	No	Yes, §26.09.240	Yes
WEST VIRGINIA	48-2-15	1981	No	Yes, §48-2-15(b)(1)	Yes
WISCONSIN	767.24	1975	Yes, §767.24(2)(b)	Yes, §767.245	Yes
WYOMING	20-2-113	1973	No	Yes, §20-2-13(c)	Yes

22. GROUNDS FOR DIVORCE

The bond of marriage and the nuclear family unit were thought to be sacred unions to be preserved at all costs. Divorce was a stigma and a "bad" marriage was a thing to be endured for the sake of the family and, in particular, the children. However, the last forty years has seen a remarkable shift in emphasis in the area of divorce.

Originally, in order to obtain a divorce the pleading party had to show fault on the other side of the marriage, proving that the spouse had committed some act or activity believed ruinous to the marital relationship, such as adultery, cruelty, or desertion. The other party could then counter by proving fault in the pleading spouse or that the alleged activity did not occur. Fault was important not only in obtaining the divorce, but also in factoring property divisions and alimony.

No-fault divorce is the relatively recent invention of legislators who deemed it necessary in order to allow women to free themselves from destructive marriages. Under no-fault divorce a party does not need to prove any fault; all that is required is to claim that there exists irretrievable breakdown or irreconcilable differences between the spouses or desertion. The pleading party in a divorce action merely needs to claim that she or he is so unhappy that leaving home (or "constructive desertion") or dissolving the marriage is the only solution.

All states have adopted no-fault divorce, either as the only grounds for divorce or as an additional ground. As a practical matter, however, the other grounds are seldom used owing to the difficulty of proving things like adultery, mental cruelty, and the like. These are only used in situations where proof of fault will affect the court's decisions with regard to the distribution of property, alimony, or child custody. Thus, only about 10 percent of divorces actually go to trial today.

In the accompanying table, the No-Fault column lists the particular type of no-fault statute that exists in the state. If there are no items listed under Grounds, then no-fault is the only ground for divorce in that state. If grounds are listed, no-fault is simply an additional available ground.

Table 22: Grounds for Divorce

State	Code Section	Residency	Waiting Period	No Fault	Defenses	Grounds
ALABAMA	30-2-1 to 12, 30, 31	Personal appearance will not confirm jurisdiction; at least one party must be resident; one party must have resided 6 months if other is a nonresident.		Irretrievable breakdown; separation.	Recrimination, condonation, or husband's knowledge/ connivance when ground is adultery.	Adultery; cruelty or violence; desertion; drug/ alcohol addiction; nonsupport; insanity; pregnant at time of marriage; unexplained absence; conviction of crime; crime against nature before or after marriage; incompatible temperaments; divorce from bed or board when wife lived apart for 2 years without husband's support.
ALASKA	25.24.050; 25.24.080; 25.24.120, 130, 200	When marriage solemnized in state and plaintiff is resident, divorce action may be brought; may also use spouse's residency for marriage not solemnized in Alaska.	Final decree entered on determination but 30 days must elapse between filing and trial.	Separation.	For adultery, procurement, connivance, express or implied forgiveness, dual guilt, or waiting over 2 yrs. to bring action; procurement or express forgiveness is defense to any other ground.	Adultery; cruelty or violence; desertion; drug/ alcohol addiction; insanity; conviction of crime; failure to consummate; incompatible temperament.
ARIZONA	Uniform Marriage and Divorce Act §§25-311 to 25-381	One party must be Arizona domiciliary and presence has been maintained 90 days prior to filing for divorce.	Before filing for divorce, either may file in conciliation court; no trial until 60 days after service of process.	Irretrievable breakdown; separation (both parties must consent and relationship must be irretrievably broken).		Only requirement is that relationship is irretrievably broken and the court has made provisions for child custody, support, disposition of property, and support of spouse.

(Continued)

Table 22: Grounds for Divorce—Continued

State	Code Section	Residency	Waiting Period	No Fault	Defenses	Grounds
ARKANSAS	9-12-301, 307, 310	One party must be resident at least 60 days before action and a resident 3 months before decree.	30 days from filing for decree.	Separation:- same grounds as divorce although grounds need not be sufficient for divorce.		Adultery; cruelty or violence; desertion; drug/ alcohol addiction; impotency; nonsupport; insanity; unexplained absence; conviction of crime; separation of 18 months or longer.
CALIFORNIA	Civ. §§4506, *et seq.*	One party must have been resident 6 months and for 3 months in county where action is filed.	If it appears there is a reasonable possibility of reconciliation, proceeding may halt for 30 days; no decree is final until 6 months from service or respondent's appearance, whichever is first.	Irretrievable breakdown; separation; irreconcilable differences and consent of both parties; incurable insanity.		
COLORADO	Uniform Marriage and Divorce Act §§14-10-106, 120	One spouse domiciliary for 90 days preceding commencement of action.		Irretrievable breakdown.	Lack of jurisdiction and failure to establish a case.	
CONNECTICUT	46b-40, 44, 67	Resident for 12 months before filing or 1 party domiciliary at time of marriage and returned with intent to stay or the cause for dissolution occurred after either moved to the state.	90 days.	Irretrievable breakdown; separation.		Adultery; cruelty or violence; desertion; drug/ alcohol addiction; insanity; unexplained absence; conviction of crime; fraudulent contract.

(Continued)

Table 22: Grounds for Divorce—Continued

State	Code Section	Residency	Waiting Period	No Fault	Defenses	Grounds
DELAWARE	Uniform Act partially adopted Tit. 13 §§1503, *et seq.*	Action brought where either party is a resident for 6 months or longer.	Decree final when entered subject to right of appeal.	Irretrievable breakdown; separation.	Defenses of condonation; connivance, recrimination, insanity and lapse of time are preserved only for a marriage that is separated and the separation caused by misconduct.	Adultery; cruelty or violence; desertion; drug/alcohol addition; nonsupport; insanity; bigamy; conviction of crime; homosexuality; venereal disease; refusing to perform marital obligations; incompatibility.
DISTRICT OF COLUMBIA	16-901, *et seq.*	One party resident for 6 months.	Divorce not final until time for appeal is up.	Separation (6 months).		Adultery; cruelty or violence; voluntary separation.
FLORIDA	61.021, 031, 052, 19	Petitioner must have residence in Florida 6 months before filing suit.	20 days after petition filed.	Irretrievable breakdown.		Insanity; Florida courts cannot grant separation.
GEORGIA	19.5-1, *et seq.*	One party resident for 6 months before action.	Decree in effect immediately.	Irretrievable breakdown.		Adultery; cruelty or violence; desertion; drug/alcohol addiction; impotency; insanity; pregnant at time of marriage; conviction of crime; force or fraud in obtaining marriage; irreconcilable differences; intermarriage in line.
HAWAII	580	One party domiciled or physically present 6 months before filing.	Court fixes time after decree that it is final but not over 1 month.	Irretrievable breakdown; separation.		

(Continued)

Table 22: Grounds for Divorce—Continued

State	Code Section	Residency	Waiting Period	No Fault	Defenses	Grounds
IDAHO	32-603, 608, 610, 616; 32-901	Plaintiff must be resident for 6 full weeks before commencing action.	Decree entered immediately on determination of issues.	Separation (5 yrs.); irreconcilable differences.	Collusion; condonation; recrimination or limitation and lapse of time.	Adultery; cruelty or violence; desertion; drug/alcohol addiction; nonsupport; insanity; conviction of crime; separation over 3 yrs.; irreconcilable differences.
ILLINOIS	750 ILCS 5/401, *et seq.*	One spouse must be resident of Illinois for 90 days before commencing action.	Final when entered subject to right of appeal.	Irretrievable breakdown; separation (2 yrs.).	Collusion.	Adultery; cruelty or violence; desertion; drug/alcohol addiction; impotency; unexplained absence; conviction of crime; venereal disease; 2-yr. separation by irreconcilable differences; undissolved prior marriage.
INDIANA	31-1-11.5-1 to 31-1-11.5-28	One party at filing must be resident for 6 months.	Hearing no sooner than 60 days after filing; continue matter for 45 days if possibility for reconciliation; after 45, judge may enter decree upon request; if no request after 90 days, matter is dismissed.	Irretrievable breakdown.		Impotency; insanity; conviction of crime.
IOWA	598.6, 17, 19	Unless respondent is a resident and given personal service, petitioner must have been resident for last year.	90 days after service of notice.	Irretrievable breakdown; separation.		Irretrievable breakdown.

(Continued)

Table 22: Grounds for Divorce—Continued

State	Code Section	Residency	Waiting Period	No Fault	Defenses	Grounds
KANSAS	60-1601, *et seq.*	One party must have been resident for 60 days before filing.	Hearing not for 60 days after filing.	Incompatibility.		Nonsupport; insanity; incompatibility.
KENTUCKY	403	One party must be resident of state and have been for 180 days before filing.	Final when entered.	Irretrievable breakdown.	All previous defenses abolished.	
LOUISIANA	Civ. Code §§102, 104	One spouse must be domiciled in state at time of filing.		Separation.	Reconciliation.	Adultery; conviction of crime.
MAINE	Tit. 19 §§661 to 752	Parties must have been married there, cohabited there after marriage, or resided there when cause of action accrued; plaintiff resides there in good faith 6 months prior; defendant is resident.	Court may make it final immediately, but otherwise it is subject to an appeal period.	Separation; irreconcilable differences.	Collusion; recrimination is comparative not absolute defense; sometimes condonation in court's discretion.	Adultery; cruelty or violence; desertion; drug/alcohol addiction; impotence; nonsupport; insanity; irreconcilable differences.
MARYLAND	Fam. Law §7-103	If grounds occurred outside the state, one party must have resided in state 1 yr. before filing.	Upon meeting requirements, absolute divorce granted.	Separation (voluntary for 12 months); limited divorce for cruelty, separation; desertion.	Condonation is factor but not absolute bar.	Adultery; desertion; insanity; conviction of crime; cruelty; voluntary separation grounds for limited divorce.
MASSACHUSETTS	Ch. 208	Parties must have lived together in the commonwealth unless plaintiff lived there 1 yr. before filing or cause occurred in the commonwealth and plaintiff filed when living there.	90 days unless court orders otherwise.	Irretrievable breakdown.	No defense.	Adultery; cruelty or violence; desertion; drug/alcohol addiction; impotency; nonsupport; conviction of crime.
MICHIGAN	MCL 552.1, *et seq.* and Rules 721 to 31	One party must have resided in Michigan for 180 days before filing.	No final decree entered upon determining plaintiff entitled to divorce.	Irretrievable breakdown.		

(Continued)

240

Table 22: Grounds for Divorce—Continued

State	Code Section	Residency	Waiting Period	No Fault	Defenses	Grounds
MINNESOTA	518	One party must have resided in state for 180 days before filing.	Decree entered immediately upon finding irretrievable breakdown, subject to appeal.	Irretrievable breakdown.	All abolished by §518.06.	
MISSISSIPPI	93-5-1, *et seq.*	One party actual, bona fide resident for 6 months before suit.	Final decree entered immediately but may be revoked at any time by granting court upon request of parties.	Irreconcilable differences (only if uncontested).	Recrimination not absolute bar.	Adultery; cruelty or violence; desertion; drug/ alcohol addiction; impotency; insanity; pregnant at time of marriage; conviction of crime; prior marriage undissolved; in line of consanguinity.
MISSOURI	452	Either party must be a resident.	No decree immediately final.	Irretrievable breakdown.	Abolished by §452.310.	
MONTANA	40-4-101 to 220	One party must be domiciled in Montana for 90 days.	Decree is final, subject to appeal.	Irretrievable breakdown; separation (180 days); serious marital discord.	Abolished by §40-4-105.	
NEBRASKA	§§42-341 to 823	Marriage solemnized in the state or one party has resided in-state for 1 yr. before filing.	Decree not final for 6 months except for purposes of appeal.	Irretrievable breakdown.		
NEVADA	125.010	Unless grounds accrued in county where action brought, one party must have been a resident at least 6 weeks before filing.	Decree is final when entered.	Separation; incompatibility.		Insanity.

(Continued)

Table 22: Grounds for Divorce—Continued

State	Code Section	Residency	Waiting Period	No Fault	Defenses	Grounds
NEW HAMPSHIRE	458	Both parties domiciled or plaintiff was domiciled and defendant was served in-state or plaintiff domiciled in state at least 1 yr.	Upon due cause, decree is immediately final; otherwise, it becomes final on the last day of the term in which the case is heard.	Irretrievable breakdown; separation.	Condonation and recrimination exist as in common law.	Adultery; cruelty or violence; drug/alcohol addiction; impotency; nonsupport; unexplained absence; conviction of crime; joining religious group believing "relations" unlawful.
NEW JERSEY	2A:34	Either party a bona fide resident of New Jersey.	Decree immediately final, except for 45 days following, it is appealable.	Separation (18 months).	Abolished by §2A:34-7.	Adultery; cruelty or violence; desertion; drug/alcohol addiction; insanity; conviction of crime; deviant sexual behavior without plaintiff's consent.
NEW MEXICO	40-4-1, *et seq.*	New Mexico domicile required plus 6 months residency.	No special provision.	Separation (permanent); incompatibility.		Adultery; cruelty or violence; desertion.
NEW YORK	Dom. Rel. §§170, 202, 230, 231	Were married in state and either party has been resident 1 yr. before commencing suit; resided in New York and either has been there 1 yr.; cause occurred in New York and either is 1-yr. resident; either has been resident for 2 yrs.		Separation (1 yr.).	Offense committed with plaintiff's connivance; offense forgiven, 5 yrs. has passed; plaintiff also guilty of adultery; defendant may set up misconduct of plaintiff.	Adultery; cruelty or violence; desertion; conviction of crime.
NORTH CAROLINA	50	Either party a bona fide resident for 6 months before bringing action.	Decree final immediately.	Separation.		Adultery; cruelty or violence; desertion; drug/alcohol addiction; insanity.

(Continued)

Table 22: Grounds for Divorce—Continued

State	Code Section	Residency	Waiting Period	No Fault	Defenses	Grounds
NORTH DAKOTA	14-05-03, *et seq.*	Plaintiff resident for 6 months before commencement of action or entry of divorce decree.	Final immediately.	Irreconcilable differences.	Connivance; collusion; condonation; lapse of time.	Adultery; cruelty or violence; desertion; drug/ alcohol addiction; nonsupport; insanity; conviction of crime.
OHIO	3105	Plaintiff must have been resident 6 months.	Decree immediately final, but court may order conciliation period for up to 90 days.	Separation; incompatibility.	Abolished by §§3105.62 to 3105.65.	Adultery; cruelty or violence; desertion; drug/ alcohol addiction; nonsupport; conviction of crime; prior marriage undissolved; fraudulent contract; other party procures a divorce out of state.
OKLAHOMA	Tit. 43 §§101, *et seq.*	One party must have been resident in good faith for 6 months before filing.	Final immediately unless appealed, but neither may marry for 6 months.	Incompatibility.		Adultery; cruelty or violence; desertion; drug/ alcohol addition; impotency; nonsupport; insanity; pregnant at time of marriage; conviction of crime; fraudulent contract; procuring divorce out of state not releasing one party.
OREGON	107	One party resident for 6 months prior unless marriage solemnized in state and either is resident at time of filing.	Decree final immediately but marital statute unaffected for 30 days or determination of any appeal; no trial until 90 days after service.	Irretrievable breakdown.	Abolished by §107.036.	

(Continued)

243

Table 22: Grounds for Divorce—Continued

State	Code Section	Residency	Waiting Period	No Fault	Defenses	Grounds
PENNSYLVANIA	Tit. 23 §§3101 to 3707; Pa. R. Civ. P. 400; 1920.1-1920.92	Bona fide residency by one party at least 6 months before filing.	Immediately final, subject to appeal.	Irretrievable breakdown; separation.	Collusion defense to all grounds but irretrievably broken marriage; rest abolished.	Adultery; cruelty or violence; desertion; insanity; bigamy; conviction of crime.
RHODE ISLAND	15-5-1 to 28	One party resident 1 yr.; if based on defendant's residency, he must be personally serviced with process.	Final decree entered anytime within 30 days or 3 months from decision date.	Irretrievable breakdown; separation.	Collusion.	Adultery; cruelty or violence; desertion; drug/alcohol addiction; impotency; nonsupport; any other gross/repugnant behavior.
SOUTH CAROLINA	20-3-10 to 440	One party resident 1 yr.; if both residents when action commenced, then only 3 month requirement.	Decree cannot be entered until 3 months after filing unless divorce sought on grounds of separation or desertion.	Separation (for 1 yr. continuously).	Collusion.	Adultery; cruelty or violence; desertion; drug/alcohol addiction.
SOUTH DAKOTA	25-4-2, *et seq.*	Plaintiff, at time action is commenced, must be a resident.	Final immediately.	Irreconcilable differences.	Connivance; collusion; condonation; limitation or lapse of time.	Adultery; cruelty or violence; desertion; impotency; nonsupport; insanity; conviction of crime.
TENNESSEE	36-4-101, *et seq.*	No residency required if acts committed while plaintiff was resident; or if grounds arose out of state and plaintiff or defendant has resided in state 6 months next to filing.		Separation; irreconcilable differences.		Adultery; cruelty or violence; desertion; drug/alcohol addiction; impotency; pregnant at time of marriage; unexplained absence; conviction of crime; previous marriage unresolved.

(Continued)

Table 22: Grounds for Divorce—Continued

State	Code Section	Residency	Waiting Period	No Fault	Defenses	Grounds
TEXAS	Fam. 3.01, *et seq.*	One party domiciliary for preceding 6 months.	Absolute upon entry.	Separation (3 yrs.); irreconcilable differences.	Defense of recrimination abolished; condonation is defense only when reasonable expectation of reconciliation; defense of adultery abolished.	Adultery; cruelty or violence; desertion; insanity; conviction of crime.
UTAH	30-3	One party bona fide resident 3 months before commencing action.	Except for good cause, no hearing for 90 days after filing; decree becomes absolute on day signed by court.	Separation; irreconcilable differences.		Adultery; cruelty or violence; desertion; drug/ alcohol addiction; impotency; nonsupport; insanity; conviction of crime.
VERMONT	Tit. 15 §§551, 554, 562, 563, 592, 631	6 months before commencing action and 1 yr. before final hearing.	Decree not final for 3 months; court may fix earlier date.	Separation (6 months).	Recrimination and condonation not defenses.	Adultery; cruelty or violence; desertion; nonsupport; insanity; unexplained absence; conviction of crime.
VIRGINIA	20	One party resident and domiciled 6 months before suit.	Decree immediate on determination of issues.	Separation (1 yr.).		Adultery; cruelty or violence; desertion; conviction of crime; sodomy; buggery.
WASHINGTON	26.09.030	Plaintiff must be a resident.	90 days must elapse from point of filing petition; decree is final subject to right of appeal.	Irretrievable breakdown.		

(Continued)

Table 22: Grounds for Divorce—Continued

State	Code Section	Residency	Waiting Period	No Fault	Defenses	Grounds
WEST VIRGINIA	48-2	If ground other than adultery, one party must be resident at time the cause arose or since then has become a resident and lived in state 1 yr. before action; if parties married in West Virginia, then only one must be resident upon filing—no specified length of time.		Irretrievable breakdown; separation (1 yr.).	Condonation; connivance; plaintiff's own misconduct; collusion is not a bar.	Adultery; cruelty or violence; desertion; drug/alcohol addiction; nonsupport; insanity; conviction of crime; abuse of child.
WISCONSIN	767.001, *et seq.*	Either party bona fide resident at least 6 months.	Judgment effective immediately, except parties cannot remarry for 6 months.	Irretrievable breakdown.		
WYOMING	20-2-101, *et seq.*	Plaintiff must have resided 60 days before filing.	Final decree upon issue of determination but never issued less than 20 days from when complaint filed.	Irreconcilable differences.		Insanity; undissolved prior marriage.

23. MARITAL PROPERTY

Marital property is generally considered to be all property acquired by a couple during their marriage or earned by either spouse during their marriage. It is all property owned by the marital estate. Generally, gifts or inheritances to either spouse along with any money or property earned prior to the marriage are the separate property of that spouse unless it is somehow "converted" into marital property.

There are two general categories that define marital property: community property and not community property. Nine states recognize community property. In these states, all property or income acquired by either spouse during marriage is considered equally owned by both spouses for purposes of the division of the property upon death or divorce or for purposes of business transacted by either spouse. This property ownership scheme has its roots in Spanish Law. Consequently, community property laws are found generally in those states that were originally possessions of or which in some way owe some of their legal heritage to colonial Spain.

If a state is not a community property state, various rules and schemes apply to define the nature of marital property. For example, there are a number of legal options from which a couple may choose when they decide to acquire property together. They may choose joint tenancy, tenancy by the entirety, or tenancy-in-common. In most states, the character of the property in question is determined by the nature of the property itself, the nature of the event giving rise to the need for the particular characterization of property ownership, and the manner, agreement, and instrument by which it was acquired. If the event giving rise to the need for the characterization is divorce, a set of rules will apply to each portion of the marital property, depending on how it was acquired and what kind of property it is: bank account, primary home, automobile, etc.

Upon an individual's death, property will be distributed subject to the individual's legal will or trust, the rules of marital property, and/or intestate succession. A very old common law scheme of division of marital property is known as "dower and curtesy." Dower was a way that a woman, who traditionally was not given the opportunity to own property while married, was given a share of her husband's estate upon his death. Dower generally preserved a percentage share of the value of the estate. Curtesy is essentially the same system in reverse, giving the husband a percentage share of his wife's estate. However, dower and curtesy has generally become obsolete in the modern world. Laws of descent and distribution, divorce and property distribution, and use of joint tenancies, tenancies-in-common, and tenancies by the entirety have largely made it unnecessary to be concerned with the surviving spouse being left with no part of the marital property.

Table 23: Marital Property

State	Community Property	Dower And Curtesy
ALABAMA	No	Dower and curtesy abolished (§43-8-57)
ALASKA	No	Curtesy: Uniform Probate Code adopted (§13.06-16); dower has been abolished
ARIZONA	Yes (§25-211)	Dower and curtesy abolished (§1-201)
ARKANSAS	No	Dower (§§28-11-301, *et seq.*); common law curtesy abolished; statutory allowance called curtesy provided (§28-11-301)
CALIFORNIA	Yes (Civ. C. §§5107, *et seq.*)	No estate by dower or curtesy (Prob. C. §6412)
COLORADO	No	No tenancy by curtesy (§15-11-113); dower abolished (§15-11-113)
CONNECTICUT	No	No dower or curtesy when marriage occurred after April 20, 1877
DELAWARE	No	Dower and curtesy abolished (§12-511)
DISTRICT OF COLUMBIA	No	Curtesy abolished with respect to wife dying on or after November 29, 1957 (§19-102); dower in case of wife intermarried to deceased husband before November 29, 1957, or in case of both husband and wife if spouse dies on or after March 16, 1962 (§19-102)
FLORIDA	No	Dower and curtesy abolished (§732.111); statutory right to elective share recognized (§732.201, *et* seq.)
GEORGIA	No	No tenancy by curtesy (§53-1-2); dower completely abolished by Georgia Laws 1969 p. 123, repealing Title 31
HAWAII	No	Dower and curtesy: Uniform Probate Code adopted with exceptions (Ch. 560)
IDAHO	Yes (§32-906)	Curtesy abolished (§32-914); dower does not exist (§32-912)
ILLINOIS	No	Dower and curtesy abolished (755 ILCS 5/2-9)
INDIANA	No	Dower and curtesy abolished (IC §29-1-2-11)
IOWA	No	Curtesy abolished (§636.5); dower abolished (§633.211)
KANSAS	No	Dower and curtesy abolished (§59-505)
KENTUCKY	No	Dower and curtesy: Yes, with exceptions (KRS §392.010, *et seq.*)
LOUISIANA	Yes, with considerable exceptions (CC Art. 2334, *et seq.*)	Dower and curtesy: Unknown to the law of Louisiana
MAINE	No	Dower and curtesy abolished (T.18-A, §2-113)
MARYLAND	No	Dower and curtesy abolished as to person dying on or after January 1, 1970 (Est. & Tr. Art.§3-302)
MASSACHUSETTS	No	Curtesy abolished (Ch. 189, §1), but certain dower and curtesy rights (merged and together called "dower") remain
MICHIGAN	No	Dower (§§558.2, *et seq.*) and curtesy abolished (§§557.1-.5)

(Continued)

Table 23: Marital Property—Continued

State	Community Property	Dower And Curtesy
MINNESOTA	No	Dower and curtesy abolished (§519.09)
MISSISSIPPI	No	Dower and curtesy abolished (§93-3-5)
MISSOURI	No	Dower and curtesy abolished (§474.110); widow and widower have same rights of inheritance, allowances, and exemptions
MONTANA	No	Dower abolished (§72-2-701); no right of curtesy (§72-2-701)
NEBRASKA	Repealed	Dower and curtesy abolished (§30-104)
NEVADA	Yes (§§123.130, 230)	Dower and curtesy abolished (§123.020)
NEW HAMPSHIRE	No	Dower and curtesy abolished (Ch. 560 §3)
NEW JERSEY	No	Dower and curtesy abolished as to all property obtained after May 28, 1980 (Tit. 3, Ch. 28 §2); some rights exist re property obtained before that date (Tit. 3B, Ch. 28 §1, *et seq.*)
NEW MEXICO	Yes (§§40-3-4, *et seq.; 45-2-102*)	Dower and curtesy abolished
NEW YORK	No	Certain dower rights for widow of marriage before September 1, 1930 (RPL §§190, 190b); curtesy abolished (RPL §189), certain rights remain for widower of woman who died on or before August 31, 1930
NORTH CAROLINA	No, however Uniform Disposition of Community Property Rights at Death Act adopted (§§31C-1, *et seq.*)	Dower and curtesy abolished by Intestate Succession Act (Ch. 29) effective July 1, 1960; surviving spouse may elect to take interest similar to common law dower or curtesy in estate of deceased spouse in lieu of intestate or testamentary share
NORTH DAKOTA	No	Dower abolished (§56-01-02); no estate by curtesy (§14-07-09)
OHIO	No	Dower (§§2103.02; 2103.041; 3105.10); curtesy abolished (§2103.09), husband has dower interest
OKLAHOMA	Repealed June 2, 1949 (§32-83)	Dower and curtesy abolished (§§84-214; 32-3, 8)
OREGON	Repealed effective April 11, 1949 (§108.520)	Dower and curtesy abolished for surviving spouse of person who dies after July 1, 1970 (§112.685-695)
PENNSYLVANIA	State Supreme Court held community property law (§§48-201, *et seq.*) invalid under state constitution (337 Pa. 581, 55 A.2d 521)	Share of spouse's estate which is allotted to surviving spouse by rules of intestate succession or by election against will is in lieu and full satisfaction of dower or curtesy at common law (§§20-2102, 2105, 2203)
RHODE ISLAND	No	Dower and curtesy abolished (§33-25-1)
SOUTH CAROLINA	No	Dower and curtesy abolished by statute May 31, 1985 (§21-5-10)
SOUTH DAKOTA	No	Dower and curtesy abolished (§§25-2-9; 29-1-3)
TENNESSEE	No	Dower and curtesy, unless vested, abolished as of April 1, 1977 (§31-2-102)
TEXAS	Yes (Fam. C. §§5.01b, 5.02, 5.61; Prob. C. §§38, 45)	Does not exist

(Continued)

Table 23: Marital Property—Continued

State	Community Property	Dower And Curtesy
UTAH	No	No dower and curtesy rights (§75-2-113)
VERMONT	No	Dower and curtesy rights set forth in §§ 14-461 to 474
VIRGINIA	No	Dower and curtesy abolished unless vested before January 1, 1991 (§64.1-19.2)
WASHINGTON	Yes (§26.16.030)	Dower and curtesy abolished (§11.04.060)
WEST VIRGINIA	No	Dower rights set forth at Ch. 43, Art. 1, §§1, *et. seq.*; curtesy abolished but surviving husband has dower rights (Ch. 43, Art. 1 §18)
WISCONSIN	Adopted Uniform Marital Property Act with variations on January 1, 1986 (§§766.31)	No dower or curtesy rights exist
WYOMING	No	Dower and curtesy abolished (§2-4-101)

24. MARRIAGE AGE REQUIREMENTS

The laws regulating marriage are quite uniform. The right to marry is considered very personal, and once the "age of majority," or when one can marry without the permission of a parent or guardian, is reached, it is the couple's sole decision whether or not to marry. However, below this age, parental consent is required (though states do not require the consent of a parent or guardian who is not present in the country or who has abandoned his or her child). The age of majority is now universally eighteen, except in Mississippi, where the parties need to be twenty-one, and Arkansas, where the female needs only to be sixteen.

While only two states, California and Kentucky, have no statutory minimum age under which marriage licenses will not be issued, many states with a minimum age requirement *do* permit marriages between minors under that age. Virtually all states allowing the marrying of minors require court approval in addition to parental consent. A growing number of states now require counseling for minors seeking to marry. Provisions for underage marriages exist in order to permit pregnant minor females and/or couples to marry, and prevailing code language still clearly reflects that bias. Ohio has the most explicit rule on this issue. In that state, the juvenile court is authorized to grant official consent to the marriage of underage persons, and the probate court issues the license. According to Ohio statutes, the probate court may delay issuing the license until the court is convinced that the female is pregnant and will carry the child to term or may even delay issuance of the license until the baby is born.

In addition to minimum age, marriage laws also require that couples seeking to marry also be of opposite sex. To date, no state has yet recognized same-sex marriages. However, a few other government or quasi-government agencies such as the City of San Francisco, California, and the Bay Area Rapid Transit District (BART), a coalition of counties that operate a regional rapid transit service around San Francisco now recognize registered same-sex unions, called "Domestic Partnerships." This was done for a variety of purposes, most importantly to provide for health and other benefits usually extended to spouses of city or BART employees.

Table 24: Marriage Age Requirements

State	Code Section	Minimum Legal Age With Parental Consent	Minimum Legal Age Without Parental Consent	Comments
ALABAMA	30-1-4	Male: 14; Female: 14	Male: 18; Female: 18	Marriage under 14 is voidable, not void. Marriage between 14 and 18 without parental consent is not grounds for annulment.
ALASKA	25.05.171	Male: 16; Female: 16	Male: 18; Female: 18	Superior court judge may grant permission for person over 14.
ARIZONA	25.102	Male: 16; Female: 16	Male: 18; Female: 18	Minors under 16 may be allowed to marry with parental consent and approval of superior court judge.
ARKANSAS	9-11-102 to 105	Male: 17; Female: 16	Male: 18; Female: 18	Minors under minimum age may obtain license in case of pregnancy or birth of child, with parental consent and judicial order.
CALIFORNIA	Civ. §4101-4102	Male: No age limit; Female: No age limit	Male: 18; Female: 18	
COLORADO	14.2.106 to 108	Male: 16; Female: 16	Male: 18; Female: 18	Minors under 16 may be allowed to marry with parental consent and approval of juvenile court judge.
CONNECTICUT	46b-30	Male: 16; Female: 16	Male: 18; Female: 18	Minors under 16 may be allowed to marry with parental consent and consent of probate judge.
DELAWARE	Tit. 13 §123	Male: 18; Female: 16	Male: 18; Female: 18	Minors under minimum age may obtain license in case of pregnancy or birth of child.
DISTRICT OF COLUMBIA	§30-103, 111	Male: 16; Female: 16	Male: 18; Female: 18	Parental consent not required if minor was previously married.
FLORIDA	741.0405	Male: 16; Female: 16	Male: 18; Female: 18	Parental consent not required if minor was previously married. Under age 16, a county judge has discretion whether or not to give license if the couple has a child or is expecting one.
GEORGIA	19-1-1; 19-3-2, 36-37	Male: 16; Female: 16	Male: 18; Female: 18	Minors under minimum age may obtain license without parental consent in case of pregnancy or birth of child.
HAWAII	572.1-2	Male: 16; Female: 16	Male: 18; Female: 18	In certain circumstances, 15 year olds may obtain license, but never under 15.
IDAHO	32.202	Male: 16; Female: 16	Male: 18; Female: 18	Minors under age 16 may obtain license with parental consent and order of the court.
ILLINOIS	750 ILCS 5/208	Male: 16; Female: 16	Male: 18; Female: 18	No provisions for marriage under age 16.

(Continued)

Table 24: Marriage Age Requirements—Continued

State	Code Section	Minimum Legal Age With Parental Consent	Minimum Legal Age Without Parental Consent	Comments
INDIANA	31-7-1-5 to 31-7-2-3	Male: 17; Female: 17	Male: 18; Female: 18	Minors ages 15-17 may obtain license in case of pregnancy, birth of child, or with approval of judge of superior or county court.
IOWA	595.2-4	Male: 16; Female: 16	Male: 18; Female:18	Minors 16-17 may obtain license without parental consent with approval of court.
KANSAS	23.106	Male: 14; Female: 12	Male: 18; Female: 18	No statutory provision for minimum age with consent. Common law prevails. See *State v. Wade,* 766 P. 2d 811 at 815.
KENTUCKY	402.020	Male: No minimum age; Female: No minimum age	Male: 18; Female: 18	Minors under age 18 may obtain license without parental consent in case of pregnancy or birth of child.
LOUISIANA	Children's Code Art. 1545, *et seq.*	Male: 16; Female: 16	Male: 18; Female: 18	Minor under 16 must obtain both parental consent and authorization of court.
MAINE	Tit. 19§62	Male: 16; Female: 16	Male: 18; Female: 18	Minors under 16 may be allowed to marry with parental consent and approval of court.
MARYLAND	Fam. Law 2-301	Male: 16; Female: 16	Male: 18; Female: 18	Minors under 16 may obtain license in case of pregnancy or birth of child.
MASSACHUSETTS	Ch. 207§7	Male: 14; Female: 12	Male: 18; Female: 18	No statutory provision for minimum age with consent. Common law prevails.
MICHIGAN	MCL §551.51 & 551.103	Male: 16; Female: 16	Male: 18; Female: 18	Minors under 16 may obtain license in case of pregnancy, birth of child, or other special circumstances.
MINNESOTA	517.02	Male: 16; Female: 16	Male: 18; Female: 18	
MISSISSIPPI	93.1.5	Male: 17; Female: 15	Male: 21; Female: 21	Minors under minimum age may obtain license with parental consent and approval of court.
MISSOURI	451.090	Male: 15; Female: 15	Male: 18; Female: 18	Minors under 15 may obtain license under special circumstances.
MONTANA	40.1.213	Male: 16; Female: 16	Male: 18; Female: 18	
NEBRASKA	42.102, 105	Male: 17; Female: 17	Male: 18; Female: 18	
NEVADA	122.010, 025	Male: 16; Female: 16	Male: 18; Female: 18	Minors under 16 may obtain license by parental consent and approval of court.

(Continued)

Table 24: Marriage Age Requirements—Continued

State	Code Section	Minimum Legal Age With Parental Consent	Minimum Legal Age Without Parental Consent	Comments
NEW HAMPSHIRE	457:4 to 457:6	Male: 14; Female: 13	Male: 18; Female: 18	Any marriage contracted by persons under 18 may, in discretion of superior court, be annulled at suit of the party who at the time of marriage was under 18. The parent or guardian can also annul, unless the parties confirm marriage upon reaching age of consent (18 years).
NEW JERSEY	37:1-6	Male: 16; Female: 16	Male: 18; Female: 18	Minors under 16 may obtain license by parental consent and approval of court.
NEW MEXICO	40-1-5 to 6	Male: 16; Female: 16	Male: 18; Female: 18	Minors under 16 may only obtain license by order of children's court or family division of district court. Courts may authorize marriage in settlement of action for support, to establish parentage, or in case of pregnancy.
NEW YORK	Dom. Rel. §§7, C7:1, 15	Male: 14; Female: 14	Male: 18; Female: 18	Minors under 16 must have approval of parents and court. Minors 16 and 17 must have only parental consent.
NORTH CAROLINA	51-2	Male: 16; Female: 16	Male: 18; Female: 18	Female minor 12-18 may obtain license with parental consent in case of pregnancy or birth of child.
NORTH DAKOTA	14-03-02	Male: 16; Female: 16	Male: 18; Female: 18	No license issued to persons under 16.
OHIO	3101.01 to 3101.04	Male: 18; Female: 16	Male: 18; Female: 18	Applicants under 18 must state that they have had marriage counseling. After all conditions are met, the court may delay issuance of consent for minors without parents' or guardians' consent until the female bears the child or the court is convinced she is pregnant and intends to carry the baby to term.
OKLAHOMA	Tit. 43 §3	Male: 16; Female: 16	Male: 18; Female: 18	Minors under 16 may obtain license in case of pregnancy or birth of child.
OREGON	106.010 to 106.060	Male: 17; Female: 17	Male: 18; Female: 18	
PENNSYLVANIA	Tit. 23 §1304(1) to (2)	Male: 16; Female: 16	Male: 18; Female: 18	Minors under 16 may obtain license with parental consent and approval of court.

(Continued)

Table 24: Marriage Age Requirements—Continued

State	Code Section	Minimum Legal Age With Parental Consent	Minimum Legal Age Without Parental Consent	Comments
RHODE ISLAND	15-2-11	Male: 18; Female: 16	Male: 18; Female: 18	Younger parties may obtain license in special circumstances.
SOUTH CAROLINA	20.1.210 to 20.1.300	Male: 16; Female: 14	Male: 18; Female: 18	Younger parties may obtain license in case of pregnancy or birth of child.
SOUTH DAKOTA	25.1.9 to 25.1.14	Male: 16; Female: 16	Male: 18; Female: 18	Minors under 16 may obtain license in case of pregnancy or birth of child.
TENNESSEE	36.3.104 to 107	Male: 16; Female: 16	Male: 18; Female: 18	Minors under 16 may obtain license in special circumstances.
TEXAS	Fᴀᴍ. 1.51 to 1.53	Male: 14; Female: 14	Male: 18; Female: 18	Minors under 16 may obtain license with parental consent and court order. Minors 16-18 may obtain license with parental consent or court order.
UTAH	30-1-2; 30-1-9	Male: 14; Female: 14	Male: 18; Female: 18	Counties are authorized to provide for premarital counseling as a requisite to issuance of license to persons under 19 and persons previously divorced. Parental consent not required if minor was previously married.
VERMONT	Tit. 18 §5142	Male: 16; Female: 16	Male: 18; Female: 18	Minors under 16 may obtain license with parental consent and court order. No persons under 14 may marry.
VIRGINIA	20-48, 49	Male: 16; Female: 16	Male: 18; Female: 18	Parental consent not required if minor was already married. Minors under 16 may obtain license in case of pregnancy or birth of child.
WASHINGTON	26.04.010	Male: 17; Female: 17	Male: 18; Female: 18	Minors under 17 may obtain license in special circumstances.
WEST VIRGINIA	48-1-1	Male: 16; Female: 16	Male: 18; Female: 18	Minors under 16 may obtain license with parental consent and court order.
WISCONSIN	765.02	Male: 16; Female: 16	Male: 18; Female: 18	
WYOMING	20-1-102	Male: 16; Female: 16	Male: 18; Female: 18	Minors under 16 may obtain license in special circumstances.

VI.   GENERAL CIVIL LAWS

25. CIVIL RIGHTS

Civil rights laws are among the most volatile and controversial in the American legal system. The force behind these laws is that certain groups of individuals in our society need protection from infringement on certain basic rights that are recognized under our legal system and are inherent in our form of government.

Civil rights are considered fundamental to all citizens under the Constitution of the United States. These rights include freedom of speech and association, freedom to seek employment, and freedom from discrimination on the basis of religious belief, race, or national origin. When certain groups have historically been denied any of these civil rights, the government has stepped in to make it illegal to interfere in that group's exercise of their rights. For example, African Americans historically have been excluded from certain types of activities in pursuit of their livelihoods. Thus civil rights laws have been enacted at both the federal and state levels to both guarantee African Americans their rights to freely seek employment in the workplace and to obtain an education in the institution of their choice without fear of discrimination on the basis of race and to provide a legal remedy for individuals who are discriminated against. Under civil rights law, acts by certain classes of people that deny others their civil rights can be either criminal in nature or actionable in civil court.

Federal civil rights laws may be enforced by the Justice Department. Usually, violations of the laws are punished by fines and/or injunctions. They may also serve as the basis for private lawsuits by individuals. Civil rights laws usually specify limits to the amount of recovery available in lawsuits filed under them. Also, they often require that a civil rights suit be filed under the available statute, rather than under general common law. This is called the doctrine of preemption, where civil rights laws preempt ordinary tort actions. Preemption is important because it caps the amount of damages for which a defendant may be liable.

Many states have gone even further than the federal laws in protecting civil rights. In those states that have established their own civil rights laws, most have authorized either the creation of new state agencies or have authorized existing agencies to handle the enforcement, administration, and/or investigation of violations of the laws. In some cases, the jurisdiction of the agencies is preemptive. For example, if a worker is fired because of his or her age, the firing may violate civil rights laws against age discrimination. If the state laws preempt private actions, the employee may only bring the complaint against the employer through the state agency or under the state law. In this case, the employee is bound by any restrictions regarding the type or size of the remedy. If the state law is not preemptive, or if the state law permits separate rights of action by the employee, the employee will be free to pursue his or her own course of action against the employer in court. The potential recovery for individual acts of discrimination or other civil rights infringements can be virtually limitless.

In many states civil rights laws may be very specifically divided in coverage and in agencies within state government. Housing and employment are the most frequent specific types of discrimination covered by state laws.

Table 25: Civil Rights

State	Code Section	Agency	Administrative Preemption	Private Action Permitted?	Attorney Fees	Statute of Limitation
ALABAMA	No statutory provisions					
ALASKA	18.80.200, *et seq.*	Commission for Human Rights	No	Yes	Discretionary	1 yr.
ARIZONA	41-1401, *et seq.*	Civil Rights Advisory Board	No	Yes	Yes	1 yr.; 180 days through the Civil Rights Division
ARKANSAS	21-3-201(Public Employment); 4-87-101 (Credit); 11-4-601 (Employment)	None	No	21-3-201: No; 4-87-101: Yes	4-87-105: Yes	4-87-102: 1 yr.
CALIFORNIA	Civ. §§51, *et seq.*; Civ. Proc. §338	Dept. of Fair Employment and Housing	No	Yes	Yes	3 yrs.
COLORADO	24-34-301, 306; 24-34-601 (Public accommodation)	Civil Rights Commission	24-34-301: Yes, with exception; 24-34-601: No	24-34-301: No, with exception for ill health; 24-34-601: Yes	Yes	90 days
CONNECTICUT	46a-51, *et seq.*; 46a-98 (credit)	Commission on Human Rights and Opportunities	46a-52: Yes; 46a-98: No	Yes	Yes; 46a-98: Not specified	180 days, except violation of §46a-80a: 30 days; 46a-98: 1 yr.
DELAWARE	Tit. 6 §4601 (Housing); Tit. 19 §710 (Employment)	Tit. 6 §4601: Human Relations Commission; Tit. 19 §710: Dept. of Labor	Yes	Tit. 6 §4601: No; Tit. 19 §710: Yes	Tit. 6 §4601: No; Tit. 19 §710: Yes	Tit. 6 §4601: 6 months; Tit. 19 §710: 90/120 days
DISTRICT OF COLUMBIA	1-2501 (Generally); 6-1701 (Handicapped)	Commission on Human Rights	No	Yes	Yes	1 yr.
FLORIDA	760.01, *et seq.*	Commission on Human Relations	Yes	No	Yes	180 days
GEORGIA	7-6-1 (Credit); 34-1-2 (Employment); 34-1-3 (Discrimination)	None	No	Yes	7-6-1: No; 34-1-2: Yes; 34-1-3: Yes	Not specified
HAWAII	378-1, *et seq.* (Employment); 515-3 (Realty)	378-1: Civil Rights Commission; 515-3: Dept. of Commerce and Consumer Affairs	Yes	No	Yes	90 days

(Continued)

Table 25: Civil Rights—Continued

State	Code Section	Agency	Administrative Preemption	Private Action Permitted?	Attorney Fees	Statute of Limitation
IDAHO	67-5901	Commission on Human Rights	No	Yes	No	2 yrs.
ILLINOIS	775 ILCS 5/1-101, *et seq.*	Human Rights Commission and Dept. of Human Rights	Yes	Yes, for temporary relief (775 ILCS 5/7A-104)	Yes	180 days
INDIANA	22-9-1-1, *et seq.*	Civil Rights Commission	No	Yes	No	Not specified
IOWA	601A.1, *et seq.*	Civil Rights Commission	Yes	Yes	Yes	180 days
KANSAS	44-1001 (Generally); 44-1015 (Housing); 44-1111 (Employment)	Commission on Civil Rights	Yes	44-1001: No; 44-1015: Yes; 44-1111: No	No	44-1001: 6 months; 44-1015: 180 days; 44-1111: Not specified
KENTUCKY	344.010	Commission on Human Rights	Yes	Yes	Yes	180 days
LOUISIANA	46:2253 (Handicapped)	None	No	Yes	Yes	180 days to 1 yr.
MAINE	Tit. 5 §§4551, *et seq.*	Human Rights Commission	Yes	Yes	Yes, with conditions	6 months
MARYLAND	Art. 49B§1	Commission on Human Relations	Yes	No	No	6 months
MASSACHUSETTS	Ch. 151B (Generally); Ch. 272 §§92A, 98 (Public Places)	Ch. 151B: Commission Against Discrimination; Ch. 272: None	151B: Yes; 272: No	151B: No; 272: Yes	151B: Yes; 272: No	151B: 6 months—agency 272: 3 yrs.—civil action (Ch. 260 §5B)
MICHIGAN	MCL 37.2601, *et seq.*	Civil Rights Commission	No	Yes	Yes	Not specified
MINNESOTA	363.01, *et seq.*	Dept. of Human Rights	No	Yes	Yes	1 yr.

(Continued)

Table 25: Civil Rights—Continued

State	Code Section	Agency	Administrative Preemption	Private Action Permitted?	Attorney Fees	Statute of Limitation
MISSISSIPPI	43-33-723, *et seq.* (Housing) NOTE: §25-9-149 provides that no person seeking employment in state service shall be discriminated against on the basis of race, color, religion, sex, national origin, age, or handicap.	Home Corporation Oversight Committee	Yes	No	No	Not specified
MISSOURI	Ch. 213 (Human Rights); Ch. 408.550 (Sex/Credit)	Ch. 213: Commission on Human Rights; Ch. 408.550: None	213: Yes; 408.550: No	213: No; 408.550: Yes	Yes	213: 180 days with commission; 2 yrs. civil action; 408.550: 1 yr.
MONTANA	49-2-101 (Generally); 49-4-101 (Handicapped)	49-2-101: Commission for Human Rights; 49-4-101: None	49-2-101: Yes; 49-4-101: No	49-2-101: No; 49-4-101: Yes	49-2-101: Separate action; 49-4-101: Yes	49-2-101: 180 to 300 days; 49-4-101: 2 yrs. (§27-2-211)
NEBRASKA	Ch. 20 (Generally); 48-1001 (Age)	Equal Opportunity Commission	Ch. 20: No; 48-1001: Yes	Yes	Ch. 20: Yes; 48-1001: No	180 days
NEVADA	613.310 (Employment); 651.050 (Public Housing); Ch. 598B.170	613.310: Equal Rights Commission or Labor Commission; 651.050: Equal Rights Commission; Ch. 598B.170: Banking Division	613.310: Yes; 651.050: No; Ch. 598B.170: No	Yes	613.310: No; 651.050: Yes; Ch. 598B.170: No	613.310: 180 days; 651.050: 1 yr.; Ch. 598B.170: 1 yr.
NEW HAMPSHIRE	Ch. 354A	Commission for Human Rights	No	Yes	No	180 days (Attorney General: 6 months)
NEW JERSEY	10:5-1	Division on Civil Rights	No	Yes	Yes	180 days
NEW MEXICO	Ch. 28-1-101	Human Rights Commission	Yes	Yes	Yes	180 days with commission/ 30 days for de novo appeal

(Continued)

Table 25: Civil Rights—Continued

State	Code Section	Agency	Administrative Preemption	Private Action Permitted?	Attorney Fees	Statute of Limitation
NEW YORK	Exec. §290 (Generally); Exec. §296-a (Credit); Civ. Rights §§18a to 47c	290: Division of Human Rights; 296-a: Banking Dept.; 18a-47c: State Human Rights Appeal Board	No	Yes	No	290: 1 yr.; 296-a: 1 yr.; 18a-47c: Not specified
NORTH CAROLINA	143-422.1	Human Relations Council	No	No	No	None
NORTH DAKOTA	14-02.4-01	Department of Labor	No	Yes	Yes	3 yrs.; 180 days (Housing)
OHIO	Ch. 4112 (Generally); 4112.02 (Housing); 4101.17 (Age); 4112.02.1 (Credit)	Civil Rights Commission	4112: Yes; 4112.02: No; 4101.17: No; 4112.02: No	4112: No; 4112.02: Yes; 4101.17: Yes; 4112.02: Yes	Yes	4112: 6 months with commission; 180 days with common pleas; 4112.01.1: 180 days; 4101.17: Not specified; 4112.02: 6 months with commission; 180 days with common pleas
OKLAHOMA	Tit. 25 §1101, 1505(7)	Human Rights Commission	Yes	No	Yes	180 days
OREGON	659.010	Bureau of Labor and Industries	No	Yes	Yes	1 yr.
PENNSYLVANIA	Tit. 43 §951	Human Relations Commission	No	Yes	No	180 days
RHODE ISLAND	34-37-1 (Housing); 28-5-1 (Employment); 28-6-18 (Sex); 42-87-1 (Handicapped)	42-87-1; 34-37-1; 28-5-1: Commission for Human Rights; 28-6-18: Department of Labor	42-87-1; 34-37-1; 28-6-18: No; 28-5-1: Yes	42-87-1: Yes; 34-27-1: Yes; 28-6-18: Yes; 28-5-1: No	No	34-37-1: 1 yr.; 28-5-1: 1 yr.; 28-6-18: Not specified; 42-87-1: Not specified
SOUTH CAROLINA	1-13-10	Human Affairs Commission	No	Yes	No	180 days
SOUTH DAKOTA	20-13-1; 60-12-15 (Sex)	20-13-1: Commission of Humanities; 60-12-15: None	20-13-1: Yes; 60-12-15: No	20-13-1: No; 60-12-15: Yes	20-13-1: No; 60-12-15: Yes	20-13-1: 180 days; 60-12-15: 2 yrs.

(Continued)

Table 25: Civil Rights—Continued

State	Code Section	Agency	Administrative Preemption	Private Action Permitted?	Attorney Fees	Statute of Limitation
TENNESSEE	4-21-101	Human Rights Commission	No	Yes	Yes	180 days for filing with agency; 1 yr. for direct action (§28-3-104)
TEXAS	Hum. Res. §121.004	Department of Human Resources	No	Yes	No	Not specified
UTAH	13-7-3 (Public Places); 34-35-1 (Employment)	13-7-3: None; 34-35-1: Antidiscrimination Division	13-7-3: No; 34-35-1: Yes	13-7-3: Yes; 34-35-1: No	No	13-7-3: 3 yrs. (§78-12-26); 34-35-1: 180 days
VERMONT	Tit. 9 §4501 (Public Places and Housing); Tit. 21 §495 (Employment)	None	No	Yes	Tit. 9 §4501: Yes; Tit. 21 §495: No	Tit. 9 §4501: Not specified; Tit. 21 §498: 6 yrs. (Tit. 12 §511)
VIRGINIA	36-86 (Housing); 40.1-28.6 (Sex/Pay)	36-86: Real Estate Commission; 40.1-28.6: None	No	Yes	36-86: Yes; 40.1-28.6: No	36-86: 180 days; 40.1-28.6: 2 yrs.
WASHINGTON	49.60.010	Washington State Human Rights Commission	No	Yes	Yes	6 months
WEST VIRGINIA	5-11-1	Human Rights Commission	No	Yes	Yes	180 days
WISCONSIN	101.22 (Housing and Education); 111.325 (Employment); 924.04 (Public Places)	101.22; 111.325: Dept. of Industry, Labor, and Human Relations; 924.04: None	101.22: No; 111.325: Yes; 924.04: No	101.22:Yes; 111.325: No; 924.04: Yes	101.22: Yes; 111.325: No; 924.04: No	101.22: 1 yr.; 111.325: 300 days; 924.04: 6 yrs. (§893.53)
WYOMING	27-9-101	Fair Employment Commission	Yes	No	No	Not specified

26. CIVIL STATUTES OF LIMITATION

The idea behind statutes of limitation is mainly one of general practicability and fairness. It is never fair to let a legal matter hang unfinished over someone's head indefinitely. There needs to be a distinct end to each legal conflict in order to let the parties involved move on with their lives. Particular legal matters may cause parties to cease certain business transactions or personal activity as they await the outcome.

A similar dynamic is at work with respect to statutes of limitation. The offending party in any legal dispute knows that he or she committed or may be accused of committing some wrong against the other party. In such a case, the wronged party must decide whether to press a lawsuit in order to recover for his or her wrong. The law will not tolerate a procrastinative plaintiff, a plaintiff who delays for effect, or one who is negligent or forgetful. After a period of time has passed, the chance to sue disappears.

How Long?

The lengths of time for statutes of limitation correspond roughly to the amount of notice that both parties have regarding the underlying injury or wrong. The more notice both parties have that there is a problem and the more likely it is that the injured party will sue, the longer the statute of limitation. The less likely it is that the offending party will be aware of his wrong or the more inconsequential it is likely to be, the shorter the statute of limitation.

The longest statutes of limitation are generally those regarding the recovery of judgments after a lawsuit. Obviously, the parties are clearly on notice in this situation. If the losing party refuses to pay his judgment, it should come as no surprise that he will be sued, even if it is as many as ten years later. On the other hand, if one person is physically injured by another person but does not sue within a year or two, it is reasonable to expect that the plaintiff either forgot about the injury or it was not as serious as originally suspected. In this case, the potential defendant is protected from a lawsuit that he may not even be aware is pending, especially more than a year or two after the accident that caused the injury occurred.

Where no statute is listed on the following chart, it is probable that there is simply not a specific statute governing the situation. In these cases, a general civil statute of limitation most likely applies. For example, in cases of medical malpractice, the statute of limitation may just as easily be covered by the statute governing personal injury.

From When to When?

There are many interesting controversies about when statutes of limitation begin and end. In many cases, the injured party may not even know he was wronged until a great while after the wrong was committed. This is often true in the case of breach of contract or fraud, and it often arises, perhaps surprisingly, in cases of personal injury or medical malpractice. In the case of certain surgical procedures, the party may not know that, for example, a sponge was left in his abdomen or something else was done improperly—until years later. There has also been much controversy, now largely settled by statute, about whether the statute should begin to run when the wrong was committed or when it was discovered. Court decisions have largely gone in favor of the injured party, allowing the statute to start running upon discovery of the injury or when the injury or act of negligence should "reasonably have been discovered."

Most states "toll," or stop, the statute of limitation upon the incapacity of the injured party. But there are a number of ways a person can be incapacitated. If the person has been committed to a mental hospital or is out of the country, these may toll the statute of limitation until they either regain their mental facilities or return from abroad.

Overall, the statutes of limitation are fair and reasonable limitations of potentially disruptive and always distracting legal action between parties. Dramatic stories about lawyers rushing to file papers before the statute runs out are almost always due to the injured party's (or the party's attorney's) procrastination or negligence.

Table 26: Civil Statutes of Limitation

Injury to Person	Libel/ Slander	Fraud	Injury to Personal Property	Professional Malpractice	Trespass	Collection of Rents	Contracts	Collection of Debt on Account	Judgments
				ALABAMA					
6 yrs. 6-2-34	2 yrs. 6-2-38(K)	2 yrs. from accrual of action (discovery) 6-2-3	6 yrs. §6-2-34	Medical: 2 yrs. §6-5-482	6 yrs. §6-2-34	6 yrs. §6-2-34(5)	Written: 10 yrs. if under seal; 6 yrs. if not §§6-2-33 to 6-2-34; Oral: 6 yrs. §6-2-34	6 yrs. stated liquidated account; 3 yrs. open unliquidated account §§6-2-34 and 6-2-37	20 yrs. §6-2-32
				ALASKA					
2 yrs. §09.10.070	2 yrs. §09.10.070		6 yrs. §09.10.050	Medical: 2 yrs. §09.10.070	6 yrs. §09.10.050		Written: 6 yrs. §09.10.050; Oral: 6 yrs. §09.10.050		
				ARIZONA					
Assault and Battery: 2 yrs.; False imprisonment; 1 yr. §12-541	1 yr. §12-541	3 yrs. §12-543(3)	2 yrs. §12-542	2 yrs. §12-542	2 yrs. §12-542(3)		Written: 6 yrs. §12-548; Oral (for indebtedness): 3 yrs. §12-543	3 yrs. §12-543(2)	4 yrs. foreign judgment §12-544(3)
				ARKANSAS					
1 yr. §16-56-104	Libel: 3 yrs. Slander: 1 yr. §§16-56-104, 105		3 yrs. §16-56-105		3 yrs. §16-56-105	3 yrs. §16-56-112	Written: 5 yrs. §16-56-111; Oral: 3 yrs. §16-56-105	3 yrs. if not written or under seal §16-56-105	10 yrs. §16-56-114

(Continued)

Table 26: Civil Statutes of Limitation—Continued

Injury to Person	Libel/ Slander	Fraud	Injury to Personal Property	Professional Malpractice	Trespass	Collection of Rents	Contracts	Collection of Debt on Account	Judgments

CALIFORNIA

Injury to Person	Libel/ Slander	Fraud	Injury to Personal Property	Professional Malpractice	Trespass	Collection of Rents	Contracts	Collection of Debt on Account	Judgments
1 yr. CIV. PROC. §340	1 yr. CIV. PROC. §340	3 yrs. CIV. PROC. §338	3 yrs. CIV. PROC. §338	Legal: 1 yr. from discovery, max. of 4 yrs. from the wrong; Vet.: 1 yr. for injury to animal CIV. PROC. §340.6	3 yrs. CIV. PROC. §338	4 yrs. CIV. PROC. §337.2	Written: 4 yrs. §337; Oral: 2 yrs. CIV. PROC. §339	4 yrs. (book and stated accounts) CIV. PROC. §337	10 yrs. CIV. PROC. §337.5

COLORADO

Injury to Person	Libel/ Slander	Fraud	Injury to Personal Property	Professional Malpractice	Trespass	Collection of Rents	Contracts	Collection of Debt on Account	Judgments
1 yr. §13-80-103(1)(a)	1 yr. §13-80-103(1)(a)	3 yrs.; 1 yr. for actions under §12-20-113 and 12-61-303 and 13-80-103(1)(f)(g) §13-80-101(1)(c)		Vet: 2 yrs. §13-80-102(1)(c)	2 yrs. §13-80-102	6 yrs. §13-80-103.5	Written: 3 yrs. §13-80-101; Oral: 3 yrs. §13-80-101	6 yrs. if contract §13-80-103.5	

CONNECTICUT

Injury to Person	Libel/ Slander	Fraud	Injury to Personal Property	Professional Malpractice	Trespass	Collection of Rents	Contracts	Collection of Debt on Account	Judgments
3 yrs. §52-577	2 yrs. §52-597	3 yrs. §52-577	2 yrs. from discovery; max. of 3 from act §52-584	2 yrs. from discovery; max. of 3 from wrong §52-584	3 yrs. §52-577		Written: 6 yrs. §52-576; Oral: 3 yrs. §52-581	6 yrs. §52-576	25 yrs. (variations for small claims judgments) §52-598

DELAWARE

Injury to Person	Libel/ Slander	Fraud	Injury to Personal Property	Professional Malpractice	Trespass	Collection of Rents	Contracts	Collection of Debt on Account	Judgments
2 yrs. Tit. 10 §8119	2 yrs. Tit. 10 §8119		2 yrs. Tit. 10 §8107		3 yrs. Tit. 10 §8106		Written: 3 yrs. Tit. 10 §8106; Oral: 3 yrs. Tit. 10 §8106	3 yrs. Tit. 10 §8106	5 yrs. Tit. 10 §5072

(Continued)

Table 26: Civil Statutes of Limitation—Continued

Injury to Person	Libel/ Slander	Fraud	Injury to Personal Property	Professional Malpractice	Trespass	Collection of Rents	Contracts	Collection of Debt on Account	Judgments

DISTRICT OF COLUMBIA

Injury to Person	Libel/ Slander	Fraud	Injury to Personal Property	Professional Malpractice	Trespass	Collection of Rents	Contracts	Collection of Debt on Account	Judgments
1 yr. §12-301(4)	1 yr. §12-301(4)		3 yrs. §12-301(3)(2)		3 yrs. §12-301(3)		Written: 4 yrs. (sale contract); 3 yrs. (simple contract) §§28-2-725 and 12-301(7)		12 yrs. §15-101; Foreign judgments according to law of foreign jurisdiction §12-307

FLORIDA

Injury to Person	Libel/ Slander	Fraud	Injury to Personal Property	Professional Malpractice	Trespass	Collection of Rents	Contracts	Collection of Debt on Account	Judgments
4 yrs. §95.11(3)(o)	4 yrs. §95.11(3)(o)	4 yrs. §95.11(3)(j)	4 yrs. §95.11(3)(h)	2 yrs.; Medical: 2-4 yrs. §95.11(4)(a) and (b)	4 yrs. §95.11(3)(g)		Written: 5 yrs. §95.11(2)(b), 1 yr. specific performance §95.11(5)(a) Oral: 4 yrs. §95.11(3)(k)		20 yrs. domestic §95.11(1); 5 yrs. foreign judgment §95.11(2)(a)

GEORGIA

Injury to Person	Libel/ Slander	Fraud	Injury to Personal Property	Professional Malpractice	Trespass	Collection of Rents	Contracts	Collection of Debt on Account	Judgments
2 yrs. §9-3-33	1 yr. §9-3-33	2 yrs. §9-3-33	4 yrs. §9-3-32	2 yrs., max. of 5 from act §9-3-71	4 yrs. §9-3-30		Written: 6 yrs. §9-3-24; Oral: 4 yrs. §9-3-26	4 yrs. §9-3-25	5 yrs. foreign judgment §9-3-20

HAWAII

Injury to Person	Libel/ Slander	Fraud	Injury to Personal Property	Professional Malpractice	Trespass	Collection of Rents	Contracts	Collection of Debt on Account	Judgments
2 yrs. §657-7	2 yrs. §657-4	2 yrs. §657-7	2 yrs. §657-7	Medical: 2 yrs. from reasonable discovery to max. of 6 §657-7.3	2 yrs. §657-7	6 yrs. §657-1	Written: 6 yrs. §657-1; Oral: 6 yrs. §657-1	6 yrs. §657-1	10 yrs. from ct. of record §657-5; 6 yrs. if judgment from a court not of record §657-1

(Continued)

Table 26: Civil Statutes of Limitation—Continued

Injury to Person	Libel/ Slander	Fraud	Injury to Personal Property	Professional Malpractice	Trespass	Collection of Rents	Contracts	Collection of Debt on Account	Judgments
IDAHO									
2 yrs. §5-219(5)	2 yrs. §5-219(5)	3 yrs. §5-218(4)	3 yrs. §5-218(3)	2 yrs. §5-219(4)	3 yrs. §5-218(2)	5 yrs. §5-204	Written: 5 yrs. §5-216; Oral: 4 yrs. §5-217		6 yrs. §5-215(1)
ILLINOIS									
2 yrs. 735 ILCS 5/13-202	1 yr. 735 ILCS 5/13-201		5 yrs. 735 ILCS 5/13-205		5 yrs. 735 ILCS 5/13-205		Written: 10 yrs. 735 ILCS 5/13-206; Oral: 5 yrs. 735 ILCS 5/13-205		Judgment may be revived within 20 yrs., 735 ILCS 5/13-218
INDIANA									
2 yrs. §34-1-2-2(1)	2 yrs. §34-1-2-2(1)	6 yrs. §34-1-2-1	2 yrs. §34-1-2-2(1)		6 yrs. §34-1-2-1	6 yrs. §34-1-2-1	Written: 10 yrs. §34-1-2-2(6); 6 yrs. for contract for payment of money §34-1-2-2(5); Oral: 6 yrs., 2 yrs. employ-ment agreements §§34-1-2-1 and 34-1-2-1.5	6 yrs. §34-1-2-1	10 yrs. §34-1-2-2(6)

(Continued)

Table 26: Civil Statutes of Limitation—Continued

Injury to Person	Libel/ Slander	Fraud	Injury to Personal Property	Professional Malpractice	Trespass	Collection of Rents	Contracts	Collection of Debt on Account	Judgments

IOWA

Injury to Person	Libel/ Slander	Fraud	Injury to Personal Property	Professional Malpractice	Trespass	Collection of Rents	Contracts	Collection of Debt on Account	Judgments
2 yrs. §614.1(2)	2 yrs. §614.1(2)	5 yrs. §614.1(4)	5 yrs. §614.1(4)	Medical: 2 yrs. from reasonable discovery; max. of 6 from act §614.1(9)	5 yrs. §614.1(4)		Written: 10 yrs. §614.1(5); Oral: 5 yrs. §614.1(4)		20 yrs.: judgment of court of record §614.1; (6); 10 yrs.: judgment of court not of record §614.1(5)

KANSAS

Injury to Person	Libel/ Slander	Fraud	Injury to Personal Property	Professional Malpractice	Trespass	Collection of Rents	Contracts	Collection of Debt on Account	Judgments
1 yr. §60.514(2)	1 yr. §60-514(1)	2 yrs. §60-513 (a)(3)	2 yrs. §60-513 (a)(2)	2 yrs. from reasonable discovery, 4 max. §60-513(a)(7), 60-513(c)	2 yrs. §60-513(a)(1)		Written: 5 yrs. §60-511(1); Oral: 3 yrs. §60-512(1)		

KENTUCKY

Injury to Person	Libel/ Slander	Fraud	Injury to Personal Property	Professional Malpractice	Trespass	Collection of Rents	Contracts	Collection of Debt on Account	Judgments
1 yr. §413.140 (1)(a)	1 yr. §413.140 (1)(d)	5 yrs. §413.120 (12)	5 yrs. §413.125	1 yr. §413.245	5 yrs. §413.120 (4)		Written: 15 yrs. §413.090 (2); Oral: 5 yrs. §413.120 (1)	5 yrs. §413.120	15 yrs. §413.090 (1)

LOUISIANA

Injury to Person	Libel/ Slander	Fraud	Injury to Personal Property	Professional Malpractice	Trespass	Collection of Rents	Contracts	Collection of Debt on Account	Judgments
1 yr. CIV. CODE ANN. §3492	1 yr. CIV. CODE ANN. §3492	1 yr. CIV. CODE ANN. §3492	1 yr. CIV. CODE ANN. §3492	1 yr. CIV. CODE ANN. §3492	1 yr. CIV. CODE ANN. §3492	3 yrs. CIV. CODE ANN. §3494	Written: 10 yrs. CIV. CODE ANN. §3499; Oral: 10 yrs. CIV. CODE ANN. §3499	3 yrs. CIV. CODE ANN. §3494(4)	Monetary judgments: 10 yrs. CIV. CODE ANN. §3501

(Continued)

Table 26: Civil Statutes of Limitation—Continued

Injury to Person	Libel/ Slander	Fraud	Injury to Personal Property	Professional Malpractice	Trespass	Collection of Rents	Contracts	Collection of Debt on Account	Judgments
				MAINE					
2 yrs. Tit. 14 §753	2 yrs. Tit. 14 §753	6 yrs. Tit. 14 §859		4 yrs. to 10 max. Tit. 14 §752-A			Written: 20 yrs. if under seal Tit. 14 §751		20 yrs. Tit. 14 §864
				MARYLAND					
1 yr. CTS. & JUD. PROC. §5-105	1 yr. CTS. & JUD. PROC. §5-105	3 yr. general limit CTS. & JUD. PROC. §5-101	3 yrs. generally CTS. & JUD. PROC. §5-101	Medical: 5 yrs. from injury or 3 yrs. from discovery, whichever is shorter (max. 7) CTS. & JUD. PROC. §5-109			Written: 3 yrs.; 12 yrs. if under seal CTS. & JUD. PROC. §5-101; 5-102(a)(5)	3 yrs. CTS. & JUD. PROC. §5-101	12 yrs. CTS. & JUD. PROC. §5-102 (a)(3)
				MASSACHUSETTS					
3 yrs. Ch. 260 §4	3 yrs. Ch. 260 §4		3 yrs. Ch. 260 §4	3 yrs. (personal injury) Ch. 260 §4	3 yrs. Ch. 260 §2A		Written: 20 yrs. if under seal; 6 yrs. others Ch. 260 §§1, 2; Oral: 6 yrs. Ch. 260 §2	6 yrs. Ch. 260 §2	6 yrs. Ch. 260 §2
				MICHIGAN					
2 yrs. §600.5805 (2)	1 yr. §600.5805 (7)	6 yrs. §600.5813	3 yrs. §600.5805 (8)	2 yrs. §600.5805 (4)	3 yrs. §600.5805 (8)		Written: 6 yrs. §600.5807 (8); Oral: 6 yrs. §600.5807 (8)		10 yrs. ct. of record; 6 yrs. ct. not of record §600.5809 (3)

(Continued)

Table 26: Civil Statutes of Limitation—Continued

Injury to Person	Libel/ Slander	Fraud	Injury to Personal Property	Professional Malpractice	Trespass	Collection of Rents	Contracts	Collection of Debt on Account	Judgments
				MINNESOTA					
2 yrs. §541.07(1)	2 yrs. §541.07(1)	6 yrs. §541.05(6)	6 yrs. §541.05(4)	Medical and veterinary: 2 yrs. §541.07(1)	6 yrs. §541.05 (3)		Written: 6 yrs. §541.05(1); Oral: 6 yrs. §541.05(1)		10 yrs. §541.04
				MISSISSIPPI					
1 yr. §15-1-35	1 yr. §15-1-35			2 yrs. from act or discovery §15-1-36			Oral: 3 yrs.; unwritten contract based on employment: 1 yr. §15-1-29	3 yrs. §15-1-29	7 yrs. domestic and foreign judgments §§15-1-43, 45
				MISSOURI					
2 yrs. §516:140	2 yrs. §516:140	10 yrs. §516:120 (5)	5 yrs. §516:120 (4)	Medical: 2 yrs. from discovery, max. 10. §516:105	5 yrs. §516:120 (3)		Written: 5 yrs; for payment of money, 10 yrs. §516:120 (1); 516:110; Oral: 5 yrs. §516:120 (1)	10 yrs. if in writing §516:110 (1)	10 yrs. §516:350
				MONTANA					
2 yrs. §27-2-204(3)	2 yrs. §27-2-204(3)	2 yrs. §27-2-203	2 yrs. §27-2-207(2)	Legal: 3 yrs. from discovery, max. 10 yrs. §27-2-206; Medical: 3 yrs., max. 5 yrs. §27-2-205	2 yrs. §27-2-207		Written: 8 yrs. §27-2-202(1); Oral: 5 yrs. §27-2-202(2)	3 yrs. obligation or liability other than contract not in writing §27-2-202(3)	10 yrs. judgment of ct. of record; 5 yrs. otherwise §27-2-201(2)

(Continued)

Table 26: Civil Statutes of Limitation—Continued

Injury to Person	Libel/ Slander	Fraud	Injury to Personal Property	Professional Malpractice	Trespass	Collection of Rents	Contracts	Collection of Debt on Account	Judgments
NEBRASKA									
1 yr. §25-208	1 yr. §25-208	4 yrs. §25-207(4)	4 yrs. §25-207(2)	2 yrs. or 1 yr. from discovery §25-222	4 yrs. §25-207(1)		Written: 5 yrs. §25-205: Oral: 4 yrs. §25-206		5 yrs. (foreign) §25-205
NEVADA									
2 yrs. §11.190-4(c)	2 yrs. §11.190-4(c)	3 yrs. §11.190-3(d)	3 yrs. §11.190-3(c)	Accountant, Attorney, Veterinarian: 4 yrs.; Medical: 2 yrs. after discovery or 4 yrs. after act §11.207	3 yrs. §11.190-3(b)		Written: 6 yrs. §11.190-1(b); Oral: 4 yrs. §11.190-2(c)	4 yrs. §11.190-2(a)	6 yrs. §11.190(1) (a)
NEW HAMPSHIRE									
3 yrs. §508:4		3 yrs. §508:4	3 yrs. §508:4	3 yrs. §508:4	2 yrs. §539:8		Written: 20 yrs. under seal §508:5		20 yrs. §508:5
NEW JERSEY									
2 yrs. §2A:14-2	1 yr. §2A:14-3		6 yrs. §2A:14-1	2 yrs. §2A:14-2	6 yrs. §2A:14-1	16 yrs. §2A:14-4	Written: 6 yrs. §2A:14-1; Oral: 6 yrs. §2A:14-1	6 yrs. §2A:14-1	6 yrs. §2A:14-5
NEW MEXICO									
3 yrs. §37-1-8	3 yrs. §37-1-8	4 yrs. §37-1-4	4 yrs. §37-1-4		4 yrs. §37-1-4		Written: 6 yrs. §37-1-3; Oral: 4 yrs. §37-1-4	4 yrs.§37-1-4	14 yrs. from ct. of record; 6 yrs. otherwise §37-1-2, 3

(Continued)

Table 26: Civil Statutes of Limitation—Continued

Injury to Person	Libel/ Slander	Fraud	Injury to Personal Property	Professional Malpractice	Trespass	Collection of Rents	Contracts	Collection of Debt on Account	Judgments
				NEW YORK					
1 yr. N.Y. Civ. Prac. L. & R. §215	1 yr. N.Y. Civ. Prac. L. & R. §215	6 yrs. N.Y. Civ. Prac. L. & R. §213	3 yrs. N.Y. Civ. Prac. L. & R. §214	3 yrs.; medical: 2 1/2 yrs.; foreign object in body of patient 1 yr. N.Y. Civ. Prac. L. & R. §214(6)	3 yrs. N.Y. Civ. Prac. L. & R. §214		Written: 6 yrs. N.Y. Civ. Prac. L. & R. §213; Oral: 6 yrs. N.Y. Civ. Prac. L. & R. §213		20 yrs. N.Y. Civ. Prac. L. & R. §211(b)
				NORTH CAROLINA					
3 yrs. §1-52(5)	3 yrs. §1-52(5)	3 yrs. §1-52(9)	3 yrs. §1-52(4)		3 yrs. §1-52(3)		Written: 3 yrs. §1-52(1); Oral: 3 yrs. §1-52(1)		
				NORTH DAKOTA					
2 yrs. §28-01-18	2 yrs. §28-01-18	6 yrs. §28-01-16(6)	6 yrs. §28-01-16(4)	Medical: 2 yrs.; 6 max. §28-01-18	6 yrs. §28-01-16(3)		Written: 6 yrs. §28-01-16(1); Oral: 6 yrs. §28-01-16(1)		10 yrs. §28-01-15
				OHIO					
1 yr. or 2 yrs. if bodily injury §§2305.11 (a); 2305.10	1 yr. §2305.11 (a)	4 yrs. §2305.09 (c)	2 yrs. §2305.10	1 yr.; Medical: 1 yr. to give notice which extends time 180 days after notice, max. 4 yrs. §2305.11(a)	4 yrs. §2305.09 (a)		Written: 15 yrs. §2305.06; Oral: 6 yrs. §2305.07	6 yrs. §2305.07	21 yrs. §2325.18

(Continued)

Table 26: Civil Statutes of Limitation—Continued

Injury to Person	Libel/ Slander	Fraud	Injury to Personal Property	Professional Malpractice	Trespass	Collection of Rents	Contracts	Collection of Debt on Account	Judgments
OKLAHOMA									
1 yr. Tit. 12 §95(4)	1 yr. Tit. 12 §95(4)	2 yrs. Tit. 12 §95(3)	2 yrs. Tit. 12 §95(3)		2 yrs. Tit. 12 §95(3)		Written: 5 yrs. Tit. 12§95(1); Oral: 3 yrs. Tit. 12 §95(2)		3 yrs. foreign judgment Tit. 12 §95(2)
OREGON									
2 yrs. §12.110	2 yrs. §12.110	2 yrs. from discovery §12.110	6 yrs. §12.080	Medical: 2 yrs. from act or reasonable discovery §12.110	6 yrs. §12.080 (3)	1 yr. §12.125	Written: 6 yrs. §12.080; Oral: 6 yrs. §12.080		10 yrs. §12.070
PENNSYLVANIA									
2 yrs. Tit. 42§5524(1)	1 yr. Tit. 42§5524(7)	2 yrs. Tit. 42§5524(7)	2 yrs. Tit. 42§5524(3)	2 yrs. Tit. 42 §5524(7)	2 yrs. Tit. 42 §5524(4)	21 yrs. Tit. 42§5530(2)	Written: 20 yrs. under seal; 4 years other Tit. 42 §5529(b); 5525(8); Oral: 4 yrs. Tit. 42§5525(3)		6 yrs. Tit. 42 §5527(1)
RHODE ISLAND									
3 yrs. §9-1-14	Slander: 1 yr. §9-1-14			Medical: 3 yrs. §9-1-14.1; Legal: 3 yrs. §9-1-14.3			Written: 20 yrs. under seal; 4 yrs. sale of goods §§6A-2-725; 9-1-17		20 yrs. §9-1-17

(Continued)

Table 26: Civil Statutes of Limitation—Continued

Injury to Person	Libel/ Slander	Fraud	Injury to Personal Property	Professional Malpractice	Trespass	Collection of Rents	Contracts	Collection of Debt on Account	Judgments

SOUTH CAROLINA

Injury to Person	Libel/ Slander	Fraud	Injury to Personal Property	Professional Malpractice	Trespass	Collection of Rents	Contracts	Collection of Debt on Account	Judgments
2 yrs. §15-3-550	2 yrs. §15-3-550	6 yrs. §15-3-530	6 yrs. §15-3-530	Medical: 3 yrs. from act or reasonable discovery §15-3-545	6 yrs. §16-3-530		Written: 20 yrs. under seal; 6 yrs. others §§15-3-520, 530; Oral: 6 yrs. §15-3-530		

SOUTH DAKOTA

Injury to Person	Libel/ Slander	Fraud	Injury to Personal Property	Professional Malpractice	Trespass	Collection of Rents	Contracts	Collection of Debt on Account	Judgments
2 yrs. §15-2-15	2 yrs. §15-2-15	6 yrs. §15-2-13	6 yrs. §15-2-13	Medical: 2 yrs. §15-2-14.1; Legal: 3 yrs. §15-2-14.2; CPA 4 yrs. §15-2-15.4	6 yrs. §15-2-13		Written: 20 yrs. under seal; 6 yrs. others §§15-2-6, 13; Oral: 6 yrs. §15-2-13		20 yrs. domestic judgments; 10 yrs. foreign §§15-2-6, 8

TENNESSEE

Injury to Person	Libel/ Slander	Fraud	Injury to Personal Property	Professional Malpractice	Trespass	Collection of Rents	Contracts	Collection of Debt on Account	Judgments
1 yr. §28-3-104	Libel: 1 yr.; Slander: 6 mos. §§28-3-103, 104		3 yrs. §28-3-105	Legal: 1 yr. CPA: 1 yr. §28-3-104	3 yrs. §28-3-105	6 yrs. §28-1-109(1)	Written: 6 yrs. §28-3-109(3); Oral: 6 yrs. §28-3-109		10 yrs. §28-3-110(2)

TEXAS

Injury to Person	Libel/ Slander	Fraud	Injury to Personal Property	Professional Malpractice	Trespass	Collection of Rents	Contracts	Collection of Debt on Account	Judgments
2 yrs. Civ. Prac. & Rem. §16.003	1 yr. Civ. Prac. & Rem. §16.002		2 yrs. Civ. Prac. & Rem. §16.003		2 yrs. Civ. Prac. & Rem. §16.003		Written: 4 yrs. real property Civ. Prac. & Rem. §16.004	4 yrs. Civ. Prac. & Rem. §16.004	

UTAH

Injury to Person	Libel/ Slander	Fraud	Injury to Personal Property	Professional Malpractice	Trespass	Collection of Rents	Contracts	Collection of Debt on Account	Judgments
1 yr. §78-12-29(4)	1 yr. §78-12-29(4)	3 yrs. §78-12-26(3)	3 yrs. §78-12-26(2)	Medical: 2 yrs. §78-14-4	3 yrs. §78-12-26(1)	6 yrs. §78-12-23	Written: 6 yrs. §78-12-23; Oral: 4 yrs. §78-12-25(1)	4 yrs. §78-12-25(1)	8 yrs. §78-12-22

(Continued)

Table 26: Civil Statutes of Limitation—Continued

Injury to Person	Libel/ Slander	Fraud	Injury to Personal Property	Professional Malpractice	Trespass	Collection of Rents	Contracts	Collection of Debt on Account	Judgments
VERMONT									
3 yrs. Tit. 12 §512	3 yrs. Tit. 12 §512	3 yrs. Tit. 12 §512	3 yrs. Tit. 12 §512	Medical: 3 yrs. from incident or 2 from reasonable discovery Tit. 12 §521			Written: 8 yrs. under seal; 6 yrs. others; 4 yrs. sales Tit. 12 §507; 9A §2-725; 12 §511; Oral: 6 yrs. Tit. 12§511	6 yrs., Tit. 12 §511	8 yrs. ct. of record; 6 yrs. not ct. of record Tit. 12 §506; Tit. 12 §511
VIRGINIA									
2 yrs. §8.01-243(a)	2 yrs. §8.01-243(a)	2 yrs. §8.01-243(a)	5 yrs. §8.01-243(b)	Health care providers: 2 yrs.; 10 max. §8.01-243.1	5 yrs. §8.01-243(b)		Written: 5 yrs. §8.01-246(2); Oral: 3 yrs. §8.01-246(4)		20 yrs.; 10 yrs. to enforce lien §8.01-251(a), (c)
WASHINGTON									
2 yrs. §4.16.100 (1)	2 yrs. §4.16.100 (1)	3 yrs. §4.16.080 (4)	3 yrs. §4.16.080 (2)		3 yrs. §4.16.080 (1)	6 yrs. §4.16.040 (2)	Written: 6 yrs. §4.16.040 (1); Oral: 3 yrs. §4.16.080 (3)	3 yrs. §4.16.040	10 yrs. §4.16.020 (2)
WEST VIRGINIA									
2 yrs. §55-2-12(b)	2 yrs. §55-2-12(c)		2 yrs. §55-2-12	2 yrs. §55-2-12(b)	2 yrs. §55-2-12	5 yrs. §55-4-21	Written: 10 yrs. §55-2-6; Oral: 5 yrs. §55-2-6		10 yrs. foreign judgment §55-2-13

(Continued)

Table 26: Civil Statutes of Limitation—Continued

Injury to Person	Libel/ Slander	Fraud	Injury to Personal Property	Professional Malpractice	Trespass	Collection of Rents	Contracts	Collection of Debt on Account	Judgments
				WISCONSIN					
2 yrs. §893.57	2 yrs. §893.57	6 yrs. §893.93(1)(b)	6 yrs. §893.52	Medical: the later of 3 yrs. from incident or 1 yr. from discovery §893.55(1), (2)	6 yrs. §893.52	6 yrs. §843.13(1)	Written: 6 yrs. §893.43; Oral: 6 yrs. §893.43		20 yrs.; 6 yrs. ct. not of record §§893.40, 893.42
				WYOMING					
1 yr. §1-3-105(v)(b), (c)	1 yr. §1-3-105(v)(a)	4 yrs. §1-3-105(a)(iv)(d)	4 yrs. §1-3-105(a)(iv)(b)		4 yrs. §1-3-105(a)(iv)(a)		Written: 10 yrs. §1-3-105(a)(i); Oral: 8 yrs. §1-3-105(a)(ii)(a)		5 yrs. foreign judgment §1-3-105(a)(iii)

27. LEGAL AGES

The law only recognizes as legal the acts of persons who possess the capacity to form the proper intent to perform the particular acts. Two aspects of "capacity" are recognized: the mental capacity to form the intent to commit an act, and maturity, or the roughly objective measure of the ability to form a legal intent. It is maintained that when a child reaches a certain age his or her capacity to form the proper intent matures. At this point a child can be held accountable for his or her actions.

The variation of age limits for different activities, such as marrying, voting, or consuming alcohol, illustrates the values a society places on certain types of activities and how a society values individual responsibility and accountability. For instance, when a minor intentionally injures another or damages property, he or she may be held liable for the act at age fourteen, and even earlier, in some instances, in certain courts. But he or she may not be allowed to drink or vote until age 21 or 18.

The limitations on a minor's ability to contract, however, are established to protect innocent third parties and ignorant or immature first parties. If a minor makes a foolish business decision out of immaturity or ignorance, the contract may be voided on the basis of a lack of capacity to contract.

Table 27: Legal Ages

State	Age of Majority	Emancipation	Contracts	Ability to Sue	Consent to Medical Treatment
ALABAMA	19 (§26-1-1)	18 (§26-13-1)	Minor 15 or more at nearest birthday may contract for life, health, accident, annuity insurance; however, not bound by any unperformed agreement to pay premium (§27-14-5)	May sue through personal representative, next friend, or guardian *ad litem;* if 14 or over has 30 days to choose guardian *ad* litem (ARCP 17)	
ALASKA	18 (§25.20.010)		May receive and give full discharge and acquittance for insurance payments up to $3000 if 16 or over (§21.42.290)		
ARIZONA	18 (§1-215); 21 years of age to consume alcohol	If veteran under Serviceman's Readjustment Act of 1944 (§44-131)	Governed by common law (§47-1103); at 16 or over may contract for educational loans (§44-140)	By guardian, guardian *ad litem,* next friend (§14-403; Civ. 17(g))	Can contract for diagnosis and treatment of VD; hospital, medical, surgical care if emancipated, homeless, or married (§§44-132, et *seq.*); if under influence, consent assumed at 12 and over (§44-133.01)
ARKANSAS	18 except 21 for sale of alcohol under Uniform Gifts to Minors Act (§9-25-101)	16 (§9-26-104)	Rescission by infant 18 or over permitted only upon full restitution; promise made after full age to pay debt contracted during infancy must be in writing (§§9-26-101; 4-59-101)	Next friend or guardian (§16-61-103, 104)	
CALIFORNIA	18 (Civ. Code §25.1)	If has entered valid marriage, is on active duty in the armed forces, or has received declaration pursuant to Civ. Code §64; if minor is 14 or over and is living apart from parent or guardian and otherwise legally qualified, application for emancipation must be sustained unless contrary to minor's interests	Yes (Civ. Code §63)	Yes (Civ. Code §63)	Yes (Civ. Code §63)

(Continued)

Table 27: Legal Ages—Continued

State	Age of Majority	Emancipation	Contracts	Ability to Sue	Consent to Medical Treatment
COLORADO	21, except as otherwise provided (2-4-401(6)		18 (§2-4-401(6))	18 (§2-4-401(6))	18 (§2-4-401(6))
CONNECTICUT	18; 21 re alcohol; 21 re Uniform Gifts to Minors Act (§1-1d)	If veteran under Service Readjustment Act (§36-4)	Common law; at 15, individual may contract for life, health, accident insurance (§38-157)	May sue parent for tort in motor vehicle (§52-572(c)); if married, may sue only regarding marriage itself (§46b-33)	
DELAWARE	18, including Uniform Gifts to Minors Act; 21 re alcohol (Tit. 12 §4501)	18 (Tit. 1 §701)	18 (Tit. 6 §2705)	18 (Tit. 10 §3923)	
DISTRICT OF COLUMBIA	18, including minor married women (§30-401)		Common law; cannot be charged unless promise made in writing after age of majority (§28-35.05)	Through appointed representative, if not available, next friend or guardian *ad litem* (§13-332)	If connected to pregnancy, substance abuse, psychological disturbance, or sexually transmitted disease (22 DCMR §600.7)
FLORIDA	18; 21 re alcohol; if minor marries, disabilities removed (§743.01, 07)	If legal marriage occurs (§743.07)	May contract for higher education financing if 16 or over (§743.05); may contract generally if married (§743.01)	By next friend or court appointed guardian; can sue for injuries by neglect to natural or adopted parents (§768.0415; RCP §1.210(b))	
GEORGIA	18 (§39-1-1), except 14 to make a will (§53-2-22); 21 re alcohol (§3-3-23)	Marriage with or without parental consent	Generally voidable; however, if benefits continue after age of majority, contract is valid (§13-3-20)	Through guardian or guardian *ad litem* (§29-4-7); suit started by infant alone not void but guardian must be appointed before verdict (§9-2-28)	18 for treatment in general (§31-9-2); if treatment is for VD, minor may consent; female minor has valid consent for treatment in connection with pregnancy
HAWAII	18	Legal marriage (§577-25)	Disaffirmance must be made within reasonable time after reaching age of majority	Guardian *ad litem* (§551-2)	

(Continued)

Table 27: Legal Ages—Continued

State	Age of Majority	Emancipation	Contracts	Ability to Sue	Consent to Medical Treatment
IDAHO	18 (§32-101)	Marriage (§32-101)	Cannot disaffirm otherwise valid contract to purchase necessities (§§32-101, *et seq.*); if 15 or over, may enter into insurance contract (§41-1807)	Through guardian, conservator, or like fiduciary, or infant may sue through guardian *ad litem* or next friend appointed by court (FRCP 17)	Age 14; treatment of infectious, contagious, communicable diseases (§39-3801)
ILLINOIS	18, except re alcohol (21)(235 ILCS 5/6-16); Uniform Gift to Minors Act (21)(755 ILCS 5/11-1)	Minors between 16 and 18 may apply if no parental objection (§§750 ILCS 30/1, *et seq.*)	Voidable unless for necessities; executing contract binding only if ratified after 18; executed contract binding unless disaffirmed within reasonable time after age 18; minor may enter into contract for promissory note for attendance at Illinois college/university	Guardian *ad litem* must be appointed	18 or over; medical or surgical procedures
INDIANA	18; 21 re alcohol (§7.1-1-3-25); 21 re Uniform Gift to Minors Act (§30-2-8-1, *et seq.*)		If under 18, child is not able to contract except for necessities and higher education expenses (§20-12-21.3-1); contracts are voidable, rather than void (§29-1-18-41); minors 16 or older may contract for life, accident, sickness insurance and annuities (§27-1-12-15)	Through guardian *ad litem*, court has discretion as to whether to honor request for infant's choice (Trial Procedure Rule 17(C))	
IOWA	18 or through marriage (§599.1)		For necessities; for other contracts, minor is bound unless disaffirmed after reasonable time of attaining majority and restoration made of money and property received (§599.2)	By minor's guardian or by next friend; court may substitute at its discretion (RCP 12)	

(Continued)

Table 27: Legal Ages—Continued

State	Age of Majority	Emancipation	Contracts	Ability to Sue	Consent to Medical Treatment
KANSAS	18, 16 if married (§38-101); 21 re alcohol (§§41-102, 175); 21 re Uniform Gifts to Minors Act (§38-1702)	At discretion of the court (§38-109)	Valid for necessities; also for other contracts unless disaffirmed in reasonable time after majority is obtained and money, property restored (§38-102); may consummate insurance contracts but must have consent of parents and cosignature of party over age 18 (§40-237)	Through infant's representative; if no representative, then through next friend or guardian *ad litem* (§§60-217; 59-2205)	
KENTUCKY	18; if mentally handicapped, parents entitled to services or earnings until emancipated (§§2.015; 405.010)	Marriage does not remove infant disability	Valid for necessities; otherwise, common law generally governs; exception made for war veterans under §384.090 (18) and for borrowing for educational purpose with parental consent (§287.385)	May sue by guardian or next friend if unmarried (CR 17.03); if married, may sue on his or her own	
LOUISIANA	18 (CC §29); if mentally handicapped, minor status may be continued by court order (CC §§355, 358)	(1). Through notarial act by father or mother, if no father, at age 15; has right to full administration of estate but may not be bound to amount of money greater than 1 year's revenue (CC §§370-373) (2). through marriage, no specific age given; cannot be revoked; if under 16, minor may not deal in selling or affecting real property without court consent (CC §§379-384); (3). minor 16 or over may be judicially emancipated (CC §385)	Yes, if made with consent of tutors; if no tutor or one who neglects to supply necessaries, such contract for benefit of the minor is valid (CC §1922)	Through father, then mother or court appointed tutor if one or both parents are dead or parents divorced (CC §683)	May consent without parental consent (T.40 §§1095-6)

(Continued)

Table 27: Legal Ages—Continued

State	Age of Majority	Emancipation	Contracts	Ability to Sue	Consent to Medical Treatment
MAINE	18; 21 re alcohol (Tit. 22, §2)	Not by marriage; however, married person of any age may handle real or personal property (Tit. 19, §161)	No, unless minor or authorized person ratified it at age of 18; exceptions are necessaries or real estate to which minor has title and retains benefit; contracts of minors re higher education are valid (Tit. 33 §52)	Through next friend or guardian *ad litem*, except in bastardy process	
MARYLAND	18 (Art. 1, §24); 21 re alcohol (Art. 2B §118)	Married minor may buy or sell property and to join in deed, mortgage, lease, notes if spouse is of age (Est. & Tr. Art. 13 §503(a)); age 15 re insurance and cannot repudiate on basis of minority (Est. & Tr. Art. 13 §503(c))	If not beneficial to minor, void *ab initio,* not ratifiable; if beneficial to minor or uncertain as to benefit or prejudice, voidable by infant, may be ratified at age 18; ratification may be express or through acceptance of benefits; voidable contract may be disaffirmed by minor during minority or reasonable time after age 18 (Art. 1 §103)	By guardian or next friend (R.P. Art. 2 §202[b][c])	If married or a parent or seeking help with drug use, alcoholism, VD, pregnancy, contraception falling short of sterilization, or if seeking consent would be life threatening (Health Gen. Art. 20 §§102, 104); minor 16 or older can consent to treatment for emotional disorder (Health Gen. Art. 20 §104); generally abortion cannot be performed on unmarried minor without notice to parents (Health Gen. Art. 20 §103)

(Continued)

Table 27: Legal Ages—Continued

State	Age of Majority	Emancipation	Contracts	Ability to Sue	Consent to Medical Treatment
MASSACHUSETTS	18 (Ch. 4 §7; Ch. 231 §85P)	18 unless legally incapacitated for reason other than age (Ch. 231 §85P)	No, except for necessaries and education; 16 or over for motor vehicle liability insurance; 15 or over for life insurance (Ch. 175 §§113K, 128)	By guardian or next friend; no court appointment needed; by court appointed guardian *ad litem*, next friend upon request (Ch. 201 §1)	If 12 or over and certified to be drug dependent, may consent to appropriate medical care (Ch. 112 §12e); minor may also consent to emergency care when: married, widowed, divorced; is a parent; is a member of armed forces; lives separately from parents and manages own financial affairs; reasonably believes he has come into contact with dangerous public health disease; and reasonably believes she is pregnant (Ch. 112 §12F)
MICHIGAN	18 (MSA 772.5, *et seq.*	Through marriage (§551.251)	For necessities only; 16 for life/disability insurance contracts	By next friend or guardian of estate; if age 14 or over, can select own (§201.5)	
MINNESOTA	18; 21 re Uniform Gift to Minors Act (§645.451); if married may join in conveyance of realty prior to age 18 (§507.02)		For necessities only; other contracts voidable	At 14 by general guardian *ad litem* appointed by court; otherwise by general guardian, relative, or friend, by default (RCP §17.02)	
MISSISSIPPI	21	If married, treated as adult for divorce and custody claims (§§93-19-11; 93-5-9)	18 for personal property; ratification must be signed in writing (§15-3-11); married minors 18 or over can execute homestead agreements (§93-3-11)	18 to settle personal injury claims; married minor may file in marital matters; court appoints guardian *ad litem*	Family planning information

(Continued)

Table 27: Legal Ages—Continued

State	Age of Majority	Emancipation	Contracts	Ability to Sue	Consent to Medical Treatment
MISSOURI	18; 21 re Uniform Gift to Minors Act (§§431.055; 442.020; 507.115)	If married, minor may convey or encumber real estate if spouse is of age (§442.040)	May be ratified after 18 (§431.060); for real property, may be disaffirmed within 2 years (§442.080)	By guardian or next friend, court appointed (CR §52.02; §§507.110, *et* seq.)	
MONTANA	18 (§41-1-101); 19 re alcohol (§16-6-305)	Occurs upon marriage (§40-6-234)	Contracts subject to power to disaffirm (§41-1-302); disaffirm through consideration within reasonable time after age of majority (§41-1-304); for necessities and may not be disaffirmed (§41-1-305); contract to borrow money for higher education (§41-1-303); contracts authorized by statute; if granted emancipation (§41-1-306)	Through general guardian or guardian *ad* litem (§41-1-202)	Yes, if emancipated; separated from parents and self-supporting; pregnant; has a communicable disease; or addicted to alcohol or drugs (§41-1-402)
NEBRASKA	19 (§43-2101); 21 re alcohol (§53-103[24])	Marriage (§43-2101)	Common law applies	By guardian or next friend (§38-114)	
NEVADA	18 (§129.010); 21 re alcohol (§202.020)	16 by court order (§129.080)	Common law; valid if emancipated (§129.130)	General guardian or guardian *ad litem* (§12.050)	If emancipated (§129.130)
NEW HAMPSHIRE	18; 21 re alcohol and Uniform Gift to Minors Act (Ch. 175 §6)		Bound with sureties by recognizances (Ch. 597 §14); can join with spouse in release of homestead interests (Ch. 460 §4)	Next friend; court may appoint guardian *ad litem*; settlement above $1500 must be court approved (Ch. 464-A §42)	
NEW JERSEY	18 (Tit. 9, Ch. 17B, §3); 21 re alcohol and Uniform Gifts to Minors (Tit. 9, Ch. 17B §1)		17 for sale of property (Tit. 37, Ch. 2 §30); 15 for insurance contracts (Tit. 17B, Ch. 24 §2)	By guardian or guardian *ad* litem (Rule 4:26-2)	

(Continued)

Table 27: Legal Ages—Continued

State	Age of Majority	Emancipation	Contracts	Ability to Sue	Consent to Medical Treatment
NEW MEXICO	28; 21 re alcohol (§28-6-1)	Through marriage, death, adoption, majority of minor as well as death, resignation, or removal of guardian (§45-5-210)	Common law applies	By guardian, guardian *ad litem,* or next friend; married minor may sue in action against him or spouse without a guardian; infant may request guardian ad litem if 14 or over	
NEW YORK	18 (Dom. Rel. §2); 21 re alcohol (Alco. Bev. Cont. §65)		May disaffirm most contracts if disaffirmed within reasonable time after reaching majority; exceptions: (1). certain loans; (2). married infant buying home; (3). providing medical care for self/ child; (4). for performing athletic or arts services if court-approved; (5). life insurance if 15 or over (Gen. Oblig. §§3-101, *et seq.*)	Through guardian or parent, adult spouse, guardian *ad litem* appointed by court or by infant if over 14 (Civ. Prac. L. & R. §1201)	
NORTH CAROLINA	18; 21 re alcohol, gift tax exemption; running for public office; Uniform Gifts to Minors Act (§48A-1, 2)	Upon marriage or becoming 18; may petition court if 16 or over (§§7A-726, *et seq.*)	Voidable subject to making restitution at common law; if 17 or over, may enter into contract to finance higher education; may be ratified by silence after 3 years subsequent to age of majority	By guardian, testamentary guardian, guardian *ad litem* (1A-1, R. 17(b)	VD, pregnancy, drug abuse, or emotional disturbance; any emancipated minor may consent to medical, dental, or health treatment for himself or child (§90-21.5)
NORTH DAKOTA	18; 21 re alcohol (§§14-09-01, *et seq.*)	Marriage; upon age 18, appointment of guardian or parent may relinquish to minor right of control and to earnings (§14-09-20)	May be disaffirmed upon age of majority or within 1 year thereafter; exception contract for reasonable value of necessary support; cannot make contracts re personal or real property not in immediate possession or control, otherwise may contract subject to disaffirmance (14-10-09 to 10-13)	May sue or be sued, but court must appoint guardian *ad litem* (14-10-03, 04)	

(Continued)

Table 27: Legal Ages—Continued

State	Age of Majority	Emancipation	Contracts	Ability to Sue	Consent to Medical Treatment
OHIO	18; 21 re alcohol and Uniform Gift to Minors Act (§§3109.01; 2111.181)	Upon application to probate court (2111.18.1)	Voidable; may be disaffirmed at infancy or within reasonable time after age of majority; exception for necessaries (3109.01)	Through personal representative or otherwise may sue by next friend or defend by guardian *ad litem;* minor not represented must have court appoint guardian *ad litem* (2111.23, 2151.28.1)	
OKLAHOMA	18; 21 re alcohol and Uniform Gift to Minors Act (58 §1201, *et seq.*)	Through court order; upon marriage (10 §10; 10 §91, *et seq.*)	Voidable when done within one year after age of majority; exception: contracts for necessaries (15 §13, *et seq.*)	Guardian or next friend	Either parent may consent to medical treatment under certain circumstances; minor may consent to own treatment (63 §2601, *et seq.*)
OREGON	18; 21 re alcohol and Uniform Gifts to Minors Act (§109.510, *et seq.*)	By marriage, parent, or court decree (419.523; 109.555; 109.510, *et seq.*)	Valid for necessaries and education; any others voidable upon attaining majority	By guardian or conservator of estate; if none available, guardian *ad litem* (417.660)	15 or over; no minimum for treatment of VD (109.610 *et seq.*)
PENNSYLVANIA	21; 18 re matters under Probate, Estates, Fiduciary Code	Marriage	Voidable except for necessaries until age 18	18 or older may sue or be sued as adult; infant may be represented by guardian, guardian ad litem, next friend	18, married or pregnant or upon graduation from high school
RHODE ISLAND	18; (§15-21-1); 21 re alcohol (3-8-1, *et seq.*); Uniform Transfers to Minors Act (18-7-1, *et seq.*)	Common law applies, *Pardey v. American Ship Windlass Co.* 34 A. 737 (1896)	Voidable except for necessaries, *Jacobs v. United Elec. Rys. Co.* 125 A. 286 (1924)	May sue through next friend; when sued, court-appointed guardian *ad litem, Keenan v. Aanagan* 147 A 617 (1929) *Vaughn v. Carr* 95 A 569 (1915)	
SOUTH CAROLINA	18 ; 21 re alcohol (§61-13-290, 61-9-40, 61-9-410); Uniform Gifts to Minors Act (20-7-140, *et seq.*)		No, except for necessaries and if contract is signed in writing promising ratification after age 18 (20-7-250, *et seq.*)		

(Continued)

Table 27: Legal Ages—Continued

State	Age of Majority	Emancipation	Contracts	Ability to Sue	Consent to Medical Treatment
SOUTH DAKOTA	18 (§26-1-1); 21 re alcohol (35-9-1); Uniform Transfer to Minors Act (55-10A)	Upon marriage or age of majority; by express agreement if no longer dependent for support (25-5-19; 25-5-24)	Contracts binding unless minor disaffirms as permitted; may make contract except re real property or personal property not under immediate control; may be disaffirmed if minor under 16 before age of majority or within one year afterwards; if 16 or older, can only disaffirm with restoration of consideration plus interest (26-2-1)	Only through general guardian or guardian *ad litem* (15-6-17(c))	
TENNESSEE	18; 21 re alcohol (1-3-113); Uniform Gifts to Minors Act (67-8-101)	No provision through marriage	May disaffirm within reasonable time after attaining age of majority; may also ratify expressly or by failure to disaffirm within reasonable time	May sue by guardian, next friend, or pauper's oath; defense by guardian *ad litem* (20-12-129; 21-1-70; 29-15-106)	
TEXAS	18 (Civ. Prac. & Rem. §129.003); Uniform Gifts to Minors Act (Prop. §141 *et seq.*)	16 if living apart from guardian or parents and is self supporting or by marriage (Fam. §31.01)	Must disaffirm within reasonable time after reaching age of majority	Guardian, next friend, guardian *ad litem* (Tex. R. Civ. P. v. 44, 173)	Treatment for VD, drug dependency, pregnancy with exception of abortion (Fam. §35.03)
UTAH	18 (§15-2-1) Uniform Transfers to Minors Act (75-5a-601 *et seq.*)	Marriage (15-2-1)	Bound for necessaries; otherwise, contracts valid unless disaffirmed within reasonable time after reaching age of majority and restoration of consideration (15-2-2, *et seq.*); minor 16 or over may contract for insurance (31A-21-103)	By guardian only (UT Rules of Civ. P. 17(b))	Informed consent of parent, guardian or authorized person must be obtained (78-14-5)
VERMONT	18 (§1-173); 21 re alcohol (7-2 (25)); Uniform Gifts to Minors Act (14-3201)		Voidable, subject to making restitution where possible	May sue by next friend; defendant infant represented by guardian *ad litem* (14-2657)	

(Continued)

Table 27: Legal Ages—Continued

State	Age of Majority	Emancipation	Contracts	Ability to Sue	Consent to Medical Treatment
VIRGINIA	18 (§1-13.42); 21 re alcohol (4-62); Uniform Transfers to Minors Act (31-37, *et seq.*)		Voidable as at Common Law subject to making restitution when possible with various exceptions for necessities	Next friend; defendant infant represented by guardian *ad litem* (8.01-8)	
WASHINGTON	18 (§26.28.010, *et seq.*); Uniform Transfers to Minors Act (11.114)		Bound for contracts for necessities; other contracts valid unless disaffirmed within reasonable time after reaching age of majority and restitution where possible of consideration (26.28.030, *et seq.*)	By guardian; if 14 or over may apply himself for court-appointed guardian; if under 14 application must be made to court through relative or friend (4.08.050)	
WEST VIRGINIA	21 (Ch. 36, Art. 7, §1; Ch. 60, Art. 3, §22); Uniform Transfers to Minors Act (Ch. 36 Art. 7, §1)	By marriage, if under 16; if over 16 unmarried may apply to court; must show ability to support oneself and make decisions (Ch. 49 Art. 7 §27)	Common law governs; ratification must be in writing and signed by charged party (Ch. 55, Art. 1, §1)	In own name, next friend, or guardian; defends by guardian *ad litem* (Ch. 56, Art. 4, §9)	
WISCONSIN	18 (§990.01(3)); Uniform Transfers to Minors Act (880.61)	By marriage (880.04(1))	Valid only for necessaries; necessaries contracts not valid if no implied or express provision for payment exists; contract made by infant may be ratified by acts or words after reaching age of majority, *Halbman v. Lemke* 298 NW2d 562 (1980); *Madison General Hosp. v. Haack*, 369 NW2d 663 (1985); *In re Kane's Estate*, 168 NW 402 (1918)	By guardian or guardian *ad litem* (803.01(3))	

(Continued)

Table 27: Legal Ages—Continued

State	Age of Majority	Emancipation	Contracts	Ability to Sue	Consent to Medical Treatment
WYOMING	19 (§14-1-101) Uniform Transfers to Minors Act (34-13-114, *et seq.*)	Through marriage, military service, or at age 17 if living separate, apart from parents; parents consent to living arrangement; minor deemed capable of handling financial affairs; and income is lawfully derived (14-1-201, *et seq.*)		General guardian, committee, conservator; otherwise by next friend or guardian *ad litem*, Wy Rule of Civil Proc. 17(c)	

28. MEDICAL RECORDS

Federal, state, and local governments are responsible for protecting and safeguarding the public health and welfare. Accordingly, during terms of various epidemics the state has required the registration of infected persons in order to treat and/or quarantine them and to study the spread of the disease to ultimately control and eradicate it. Thus, although access to medical records is highly guarded, the reporting of diseases is widely practiced at all levels of government. The Center for Disease Control, for example, publishes *The Morbidity and Mortality Weekly Report*, containing a comprehensive list of all reported illnesses by both state and region that benefits the family practice doctor as well as the epidemiologist. The reports of cases that are reported, from the flu to various venereal diseases to AIDS (acquired immunodeficiency syndrome), are given in confidence, and access to the records is forbidden for most other purposes.

The outbreak of AIDS has sparked controversy over the confidentiality of medical records and diagnoses. Some employers and insurance companies have sought to have individuals tested for the HIV virus, which can lead to AIDS, before hiring in order to prevent considerable expenses in the future as the employee's health fails. Often these same parties argue for access to medical records for background checks as part of the interview process. The great tension regarding the rights of individuals with the HIV virus or AIDS, the public's interest in controlling and fighting the epidemic, and the interest of employers, insurers, and health officials in providing adequate and affordable medical care has created a very dynamic ethical and legal dilemma that will not soon be resolved.

The laws controlling and regulating access to medical records vary greatly from state to state, although the basic protection is always there: a person's medical records are personal and private. As is historically the case, the federal government has gotten increasingly involved in the area of individual rights and has enacted a number of pieces of privacy legislation. For example, the Federal Privacy Act of 1974 requires the release of information in federal files to the subject individual upon request, although some government agencies have established regulations allowing the release of information to a physician chosen by the requesting individual (5 U.S.C. 552a(f)(3)). Federally funded community mental health and mental retardation centers must maintain safeguards to preserve confidentiality and protect the rights of patients (52 U.S.C. 2689(d)(2)), and the Department of Defense may not use for any adverse personnel decision any personal information obtained in interviews with members of the service who are HIV positive (PL 49-661 §705(c)).

This chapter treats all statutes that could be found concerning privacy and medical records. It must be noted, however, that this emerging field is increasingly subject to revision and new legislative attention. In addition, in certain areas such as AIDS information, the courts may have construed other statutes as protecting or not protecting AIDS victims. In these cases the courts may be awaiting or inviting legislative action. Spaces on the chart that are left blank are those situations where specific laws cannot be found; this does not necessarily mean that an individual is without protection in these areas.

Table 28: Medical Records

State	Who Has Access	Privilege	Mandatory Reporting	Patient Waiver	Insurance Purposes	AIDS
ALABAMA	Notifiable disease records confidential (§22-11A-2)		Physicians must file confidential reports on venereal disease (§§22-16-2, 4)	Waiver of record of disease or sexually transmitted disease by written consent (§22-11A-22)		
ALASKA	Any agent authorized by the principal, custodial, or non-custodial parent (§25.20.130; 13.26.344); Dept. of Social Services for medical assistance beneficiaries (§47.07.074)			Mental health records may be disclosed only with patient consent or court order (§47.30.260)		
ARIZONA		Physicians and surgeons in most cases (§12-2235)	Nonaccidental injuries, malnourishment, and sexual abuse are confidential and may only be used judicially (§13-3620); abused incapacitated adult (§46-454)			
ARKANSAS	Not open to public (§25-19-105); patient (§23-76-129); attorney (§16-46-106)	Psychiatrists, physicians, surgeons, trained nurses (§72-1616; 28-607); doctors may deny giving patients their records on adequate showing of detrimentality (§16-46-106)		Express consent (§23-76-129)		
CALIFORNIA	Patient, but mental health professional may refuse if disclosure would have adverse effect on patient; in that case, patient may designate another professional to inspect records on his/her behalf (H&S §25250); Doctor, dentist, nurse, psychologist, lab, or pharmacy must give copy of individual's medical record to attorney for that individual (H&S §25250); those with responsibility for health care decisions for others have access (H&S §25250); minor's representative has no right to access if minor does (H&S §25253)	Doctors, including psychiatrists (Ev. §1010); patient must waive doctor-patient confidentiality when plaintiff in civil suit (Ev. §1016)		Patient must waive doctor-patient confidentiality when plaintiff in civil suit (Ev. §1016); other: Civ. Code §56.	Insurer may obtain (Civ. Code §56.10(c)(2))	Blood testing must be anonymous and test results may not disclose identities of persons tested even through subpoena (H&S §199.20)

(Continued)

Table 28: Medical Records—Continued

State	Who Has Access	Privilege	Mandatory Reporting	Patient Waiver	Insurance Purposes	AIDS
COLORADO	Patient or designated representative with written authority, except for psychiatric records that would have significant negative psychological impact, in which case patient is entitled to summary (§25-1-801); both parents in joint custody (§14-10-123.5)		Venereal disease to health authorities (§25-4-402)			
CONNECTICUT	Patient may see and copy (§4-105); state law limits disclosure of mental health data about a patient by name or other identifier (§52-146h); state institutions may release to third parties only that information necessary to determine funding (§17-295c)					
DELAWARE	Venereal disease reports strictly confidential (Tit. 16 §701)	Not in child abuse cases; then only attorney-client privilege (Tit. 16 §907, 908)	Venereal disease (Tit. 16 §702)			
DISTRICT OF COLUMBIA	Person of record or his legal representative (§14-307); many others with consent of patient (§32-502); public mental health facility must make patient records available to patient's attorney or personal physician (§21-562)	Yes, with exceptions (§14-307)				
FLORIDA	Patient or his/her legal representative or health care provider (§455.241); patient's guardian, curator, anyone authorized in writing (§395.019)	Psychiatrist-patient (§455.241)		Patient must consent to release of records except by subpoena (§395.017)		Results may be disclosed with consent
GEORGIA	Disclosure of medical records in court or as required by statute does not destroy confidential nature (§24-9-42)	Psychiatrist (§24-9-21); physician (§24-9-42)	Venereal disease and suspected child abuse (§§19-7-5; 31-7-2)			
HAWAII	Patient or his attorney, but doctor may refuse if detrimental to patient's health (§622-57); medical records in court are covered by §622-51			Identity of individuals in tumor registries is confidential; no person providing such information is liable for it (§§324-11 and 12)		

(Continued)

Table 28: Medical Records—Continued

State	Who Has Access	Privilege	Mandatory Reporting	Patient Waiver	Insurance Purposes	AIDS
IDAHO	Patient or agent by subpoena (§9-420); custodian and non-custodial parent of minor child (§32-717A); in some civil actions records may be open to discovery (§39-1392(e))	Physician (§9-203(4))	Child abuse cases (§16-1619)	Patient or doctor or nurse responsible for entries in hospital record may request protective order to deny access (§9-420)		
ILLINOIS			Child abuse (325 ILCS 5/4)		AIDS test information must be kept confidential (410 ILCS 305/1)	No disclosure of AIDS test information without consent or court order
INDIANA	Patient, anyone patient authorizes, physicians, anyone by court order, coroner (§34-3-15.5-4)	Doctor-patient information not divulgable (§34-1-14-5)	Child abuse must be reported by physicians and non-physicians immediately (§31-6-11-4)			
IOWA	Medical records held by social services may be disclosed to public officials (§217.30(4)(b)		Confidential reports of venereal disease must be filed (§140.1-4)	Patient may waive so that person in confidence may disclose at trial		
KANSAS	Patient or other with patient's written consent or with consent of the head of the treatment facility (§59-2931)	Doctor-patient (with exceptions) (§§60-427; 65-2837(f); 74-5323)		Mental health records may not be disclosed except with patient's consent or court order (§59-2931)		
KENTUCKY		Narrow physician privilege; psychiatrist privilege (§§213.200; 422.330)		May ask to prohibit or limit use (§422.315)		
LOUISIANA	State hospitals must provide copies of records upon patient's request subject to subpoena (§40:1299-96)	Physician-patient, except when physician appointed by the court to investigate patient's physical or mental condition (§15:476)				

(Continued)

Table 28: Medical Records—Continued

State	Who Has Access	Privilege	Mandatory Reporting	Patient Waiver	Insurance Purposes	AIDS
MAINE	Patient after discharge unless doctor thinks it would be detrimental to his health or an authorized representative (22 §1711); attorney general in a criminal proceeding (5 §200-E)	Doctor-patient				Blood tests may not be conducted without consent and results must be kept confidential within health community
MARYLAND	Records of Secretary of Health & Mental Hygiene must be kept confidential. It is unlawful to disclose them except for research (Health-Gen §4-101, *et seq.*)	Psychiatrist-Patient (Cts. & Jud. Proc. §9-109)	Doctor allowed to report to Motor Vehicle Administration data on patients whose driving may be impaired for medical reasons (Transp. §16-118)		When insurance company compiles medical file, they must permit claimant or applicant to inspect file except information provided by doctor not available for 5 years unless doctor authorizes release (Art. 48A §490c)	
MASSACHUSETTS	Patient has right to confidentiality of all records and communications to extent provided by law and to inspect and receive copy of medical records (Ch. 112 §12CC); employer requiring physical exam of any employee shall upon request furnish copy of medical report (Ch. 111 §70T); attorneys for mental patient or patient himself may in some cases see record at discretion of mental health commissioner (Ch. 123 §36)		Any injury from discharge of gun or a burn affecting over 5% of the body (Ch. 112 §12A)			Labs and hospitals that conduct blood tests for AIDS must not disclose results to outsiders without consent of patients (Ch. 111 §70F)
MICHIGAN	Any review entity (331.531)	Privilege is recognized (§600.2157)				
MINNESOTA	Patient, patient's representative, or minor's parent or guardian has right to copy doctor's and hospital records about themselves (§144.335); mentally committed patients have access (§353B.03)	Physician may not disclose confidential information acquired in professional capacity (§595-02(4))				
MISSISSIPPI	Medical or dental review committee (§41-63-1, 2)	Doctor-patient (§13-1-21)	Reporting of cancer patients to Tumor Registry Agency required (§41-3-25)	Patient waiver of doctor's privilege (§13-1-21)		

(Continued)

Table 28: Medical Records—Continued

State	Who Has Access	Privilege	Mandatory Reporting	Patient Waiver	Insurance Purposes	AIDS
MISSOURI		Physician and surgeon (§491.060)				
MONTANA		Physician (§93-701-4(4)	Child abuse and Venereal disease (§§10-902; 69-4604)			
NEBRASKA	Patient (§44-2842); long-term care ombudsman (§81-2214.01); counsel for mentally ill patient (§83-1053); mental patient's records available to patient, counsel, parents or guardian if minor or legally incompetent, person authorized by the court or patient (§83-1068)		Reporting of patients with cancer to Dept. of Health upon its request (§81-642)	Privileged communications waived by patient consent and court of record		
NEVADA	Patient has right to inspect and copy both doctor's and hospital's records (§629.061); patient's representative, attorney general or grand jury if investigating certain crimes; between medical facilities (§§433.332; 449.705)			Patient may refuse to disclose or forbid any other person (including family members) from disclosing medical information (§49.215-245); right does not extend to mental patient (§49.245)		
NEW HAMPSHIRE	Records are deemed property of patient (§332:I-1); anyone with power of attorney for patient (§137-J:7); patient and one with his written consent; ombudsman for one maintained by the facility (§161-F:14); no employee may be required to bear cost of any medical exam or record required as condition of employment (§275:3)	Doctor-patient (§329:26) and psychologist-patient privilege recognized (330-A:19)				
NEW JERSEY	Limited right of access for attorneys and next of kin of mental patients in state institutions and attorneys handling personal injury cases (§§30:4-24.3; 2A:82-42)	Privilege with limitations (§30:4-24.3; 2A:82-42)	Child abuse (§9:6-8.30); pertussis vaccine (§26:2N-5); VD (§26:4-41)			

(Continued)

Table 28: Medical Records—Continued

State	Who Has Access	Privilege	Mandatory Reporting	Patient Waiver	Insurance Purposes	AIDS
NEW MEXICO	Ombudsman of patient/resident/client (§28-17-13); child's biological or adopted parent (§40-7-53); mental health client caregiver if necessary, client has access (§43-1-19); worker, employer, and insurer records of any health care service provided the worker (§52-10-1)					
NEW YORK	Patient (Civ. Ser. R. §82.1); anyone patient authorizes (§82.3); medical director of prison in reference to inmate (Corrections §601); youth facility of a juvenile offender (Exec. §515-b); ombudsman (Exec §544); inspector of a mental facility (Men. Hyg. §16.11); physician or hospital must release medical file to another physician or hospital designated by patient; records concerning venereal disease treatment or abortion for minor may not be released, even to parent (NY Pub. Health §17); parent, guardian	Doctors and nurses (Civ. Prac. §4504)				
NORTH CAROLINA	Medical information is privileged except in child abuse cases or when court compels disclosure (§§130-184; 130-95)					
NORTH DAKOTA		Doctor-patient (§31-01-06(3))	Venereal disease and child abuse or neglect (§§23-07-02; 50-25-01 to 05)			
OHIO	Patient or designated representative may request records from employer, physician, health care professional, hospital, or lab (§4113.23)	Doctor-patient (§2317-02(A))	Child abuse (§2151-42.1)			
OKLAHOMA	Patient to non-psychiatric files (Tit. 76 §19); parents may have access to treatment needed or provided to minor; such disclosure does not breach right to privacy (Tit. 63 §2601; Tit. 43A §1-109)	Doctor (Tit. 12 §2503)	Child abuse and confidential reports on venereal disease (Tit. 21 §846; Tit. 63 §1-528(b))			

(Continued)

Table 28: Medical Records—Continued

State	Who Has Access	Privilege	Mandatory Reporting	Patient Waiver	Insurance Purposes	AIDS
OREGON	Institutions are encouraged to permit patient to copy doctor and hospital records (§192.525)	Doctor-patient (§44.040(1)(d))	Suspected violence (in confidence)(§146-750)	Venereal disease data may be reported with consent or in public interest (§44-040)		
PENNSYLVANIA	Mental health records in state agencies must be kept confidential (Tit. 50 §7111)	Privilege only as to derogatory information in civil cases (Tit. 28 §328)				
RHODE ISLAND	Patient (Gen. Laws §5-37.3.3); holders of medical records must keep them confidential (§5-37.3-4)					
SOUTH CAROLINA	No statutory provisions					
SOUTH DAKOTA		Doctor and hospital records (§19-2-3)	Venereal disease; tuberculosis; child abuse			
TENNESSEE	Hospital records property of hospital, upon "good cause" patient may see (§53-1322); medical records of patients in state facilities and those whose care is paid for by state funds are confidential (§10-7-504)	Psychiatrists (§24-1-207); psychologists (§63-1117)				
TEXAS	Medical information identifiable as to individuals is to be kept confidential in state files (Art. 4447d)					State law spells out when AIDS blood tests may be conducted, including when employer can show necessity based upon bona fide occupational qualification; results must be kept confidential (Art. 4419b-1 §9.01)
UTAH	Patient's attorney (§78-25-25)	Doctor-patient (§78-24-8(4))	Suspected child abuse (§55-16-2; 78-3b-3)			
VERMONT		Physician, dentist, or nurse not allowed to testify on information acquired in attending a patient (Tit. 12 §1608)				

(Continued)

Table 28: Medical Records—Continued

State	Who Has Access	Privilege	Mandatory Reporting	Patient Waiver	Insurance Purposes	AIDS
VIRGINIA	Individual medical data in state files exempt from public disclosure (§2.1-342(b)); patient or his attorney to hospital records except for mental records when doctor declares release would be injurious to patient (§8.01-413; 10.413)	Physician (§8.01-399)			Insurance company must provide medical information to customer or his physician (§38.1-52(11)); doctor limited in what s/he may disclose to third party payor re mental health, retardation, substance abuse, or emotional condition; third party payor may not further disclose information without written consent of patient	
WASHINGTON		Physician (§5.60.050)	Child abuse (§26.44.030)			
WEST VIRGINIA			Venereal disease; communicable diseases; tuberculosis (§§16-4-6; 16-2A-5; 26-5A-4)	Physician may testify only with patient's consent (§50-6-10)		
WISCONSIN	Patient may inspect and copy and must be notified of this right (§146.83); records must be kept confidential except for use in health care, processing payments and claims, and research (§146.82)	Physician (§885.21)	Venereal disease; tuberculosis; child abuse (§§143.06; 48.981)			AIDS test results must remain confidential (§146.025)
WYOMING		Doctor may testify only with patient's consent or when patient testifies himself on medical matters (§1-139(1))	Child abuse; venereal disease; communicable disease (§§14-28.8; 35-177; 35-172)			

29. NEGLIGENCE

Negligence is an actionable tort. This means that if one person's carelessness causes another personal injury, the injured party may sue to recover damages (money) for his or her injuries. The idea that a person can sue for negligence is a relatively new phenomenon, only about a century old.

The reason for negligence's late recognition is because common law traditionally recognized only intentional torts; that is, it held parties responsible for injuries that were the result of intentional acts. It was irrelevant that the actor did not intend to injure anyone, much less the injured party, but it only needed to be shown that the actor intended the *action* that caused the injury. In these cases, evidence of who caused what injury was affirmative, direct, and fairly objective.

The concept of permitting someone to recover damages for injuries caused by someone's *lack of action* or *failure to do something* was a revolutionary concept. Since its recognition as an action in tort, negligence has become a major source of very large jury awards. It is the root of all product liability cases. When people complain about our legal system and the outrageous verdicts being awarded nowadays, they are speaking about negligence.

Originally, negligence was recognized by the courts as part of the common law. Over time, as causes of action became more numerous and as damages became larger, various efforts were undertaken to limit the appeal of negligence lawsuits.

Contributory Negligence

When contributory negligence first appeared in the repertoire of personal injury lawyers, the standards of proof needed to succeed were quite high and very severe. Originally, under the doctrine of contributory negligence if it were shown that the plaintiff contributed in any way to his injuries, he was barred from any recovery. This has been modified over time to permit the plaintiff to recover even if he contributed to his injuries, as long as his fault is under 50 percent. In these cases, recovery is relative to fault. For instance, if a jury finds a party's injuries worth $100,000 and holds that the party was 25 percent at fault, the party's recovery would be $75,000. On the other hand, if the jury found the party 60 percent at fault, the party would be barred from any recovery.

Comparative Fault

The doctrine of contributory negligence eventually evolved, in some states, into a system of comparative fault that permitted recovery on a completely relative scale. Thus, in an accident one could be 90 percent at fault for one's own personal injury and still sue to recover the 10 percent of the damages suffered that were caused by the other party.

Contribution Among Tortfeasors

In the doctrine of contribution among tortfeasors, when there are multiple tortfeasors ("guilty" parties), all parties are equally liable for the damages caused to the injured party. This doctrine is quite harsh. For example, if the driver of a truck hits a pedestrian at night and the jury holds that the city is 15 percent responsible because it did not properly maintain the lighting at that portion of the road and the truck driver, who is 85 percent at fault, is uninsured, unemployed, and without assets, the city can be made to pay 100 percent of the damages. In most comparative fault states liability is the proportionate responsibility of each party.

The State of the Law

As can be seen by looking at the table of negligence laws, there is great diversity among the states as to how negligence is handled. As the law of negligence continues to mature and change, courts have led the way in defining the laws and legislatures have in may cases responded with statutes that both recognize the cause of action and often limit it as well.

There have been many attempts over the years to have Congress or state legislatures pass laws that would specifically limit the amount of recovery available to plaintiffs in negligence actions. So far, none has met with much success. Under the general term "tort reform," such acts promise to be proposed in the future.

Table 29: Negligence

State	Code Section	Uniform Act	Comparative Negligence	Contributory Negligence—Limit to Plaintiff's Recovery	Judicial Imposition of Comparative Negligence	Contribution Among Tortfeasors
ALABAMA	None	No	Not recognized. *Godfrey v. Vinson*, 110 So. 13 (1926), was never overruled.	Plaintiff's negligence is a bar to recovery. Contributory negligence is an affirmative defense. ARCP 8 (c)	No.	No. *Gobble v. Bradford*, 147 So. 619 (1933)
ALASKA	23.25.010 (Employer's liability for negligence)	Yes; §09.16.010	Yes, §09.17.060 Contributory fault diminishes proportionately the award based on claimant's fault, but does not bar recovery ("Pure" comparative negligence)	See Comparative Negligence	*Kaatz v. Alaska*, 540 P.2d 1037 (1975); "Pure" form adopted and codified herein	Yes. §09.16.010-060
ARIZONA	12-2505	Yes; §12-2501, *et seq.*	"Pure" comparative negligence			§12-2501, *et seq.*
ARKANSAS	16-64-122	Yes; 16-61-201 to 212	Yes	If Plaintiff's fault is of less degree than defendant's, he may recover amount diminished in proportion to degree of his own fault (§16-64-122); if plaintiff's fault is equal to or greater than defendant, he may not recover at all		Yes; §§16-61-201 to 212
CALIFORNIA	None	No	"Pure" form adopted by *Li v. Yellow Cab Co.*, 532 P.2d 1226 (1975).		*Li v. Yellow Cab Co.*, 543 P.2d 1226 (1975)	No.
COLORADO	13-21-111	Yes. §§13-50.5-101 to 13.50.5-106	Plaintiff's negligence not as great as that of defendant	If plaintiff's percentage of negligence is as great as defendant's, no recovery		Yes; §§13-50.5-101 to 13.50.5-106
CONNECTICUT	52-572h		Plaintiff's negligence not greater than combined negligence of defendants	If plaintiff's negligence is greater than defendant's		Yes; §52-5720(e). Must be brought within one year
DELAWARE	Tit. 10 §8132	Yes; Tit. 10 §§6301 to 6308	Plaintiff's negligence not greater than the combined negligence of defendants; Tit. 10 §8132	If plaintiff's negligence is greater than defendant's		Yes; Tit. 10 §§6301 to 6308

(Continued)

Table 29: Negligence—Continued

State	Code Section	Uniform Act	Comparative Negligence	Contributory Negligence—Limit to Plaintiff's Recovery	Judicial Imposition of Comparative Negligence	Contribution Among Tortfeasors
DISTRICT OF COLUMBIA	None			Plaintiff's negligence is a bar to recovery except the liability of common carriers for injuries to employees, when plaintiff's negligence is slight and employer's is gross. See §44-402		No
FLORIDA	768.81, *et seq.*	Yes; §768.31	Any contributory fault chargeable to claimant diminishes proportionately the amount awarded as economic or uneconomic damages; §768.81	Percentage of own fault	*Hoffman v. Jones,* 280 So. 2d 431 (1973)	Yes; §768.31
GEORGIA	51-11-7	No	Yes; 49 S.E.2d 90 says plaintiff's negligence cannot be equal to or exceed defendant's.	If plaintiff by ordinary care could have avoided defendant's negligence, he is barred		Yes; §51-12-32
HAWAII	663-31	663-11 to 663-17	Plaintiff's negligence not greater than aggregate negligence of defendants; §663-31	If plaintiff's negligence is greater than defendant's		§§663-11 to 663-17
IDAHO	6-801	No	Plaintiff's negligence not as great as defendant's	If plaintiff's negligence is as great as defendant's		Yes; §6-803.
ILLINOIS	735 ILCS 5/2-1116	No	If plaintiff is more than 50% negligible, he is barred from recovery (735 ILCS 5/2-1116; passed 1986 in response to the "insurance crisis")	Over 50% negligence attributed to plaintiff		Yes; 740 ILCS 100/1, *et seq.*
INDIANA	34-4-33-3, 4	No	Plaintiff's fault not greater than defendants' aggregate fault	Plaintiff's fault greater than defendant's		No; §34-4-33-7, but section does not affect indemnity rights
IOWA	668.3; 668.5	No	Barred if claimant's fault is greater than combined fault of defendant (§668.3, enacted 1984)	If claimant's fault is greater than aggregate of defendant's	*Goetzman v. Wichern,* 327 N.W. 2d 742 (1982)	Yes, §668.5

(Continued)

Table 29: Negligence—Continued

State	Code Section	Uniform Act	Comparative Negligence	Contributory Negligence—Limit to Plaintiff's Recovery	Judicial Imposition of Comparative Negligence	Contribution Among Tortfeasors
KANSAS	60-258a	No	Plaintiff's negligence less than causal negligence of defendants	Plaintiff's negligence greater than defendant's		No
KENTUCKY	None	No	No; Failure to put child in safety restraint is statutorily not contributory negligence. (§189.125).	Plaintiff's negligence is a bar to recovery. Contributory negligence will not bar employee's recovery when railroad violated any safety statute (§277.320).		Yes; §412.030
LOUISIANA	La-Civ. Code Art 2323	No	"Pure" comparative negligence (La. Civ. Code Art. 2323)			No
MAINE	Tit. 14 §156	Plaintiff's negligence less than defendant's (Tit. 14 §156)	If plaintiff's negligence is equal to or greater than defendant's, then no recovery			No
MARYLAND	None	Uniform Contribution Among Tortfeasors Act Md. Ann. Code Art. 50 §16-24 (1957)	Not using seatbelt is not contributory negligence (Transp. §§22-412.3 & 4)	Plaintiff's negligence is a bar to recovery		Yes; Md. Ann. Code Art. 50 §16-24
MASSACHUSETTS	Ch. 231 §85	Ch. 231B §§1-4	Plaintiff's negligence not greater than defendant's (Ch. 231 §85)	Plaintiff's negligence greater than defendant's		Ch. 31B §§1-4
MICHIGAN	None		"Pure" comparative negligence	Percentage of his own negligence	*Placek v. City of Sterling Heights*, 275 N.W.2d 511 (1979)	Yes; MCL 600.2925c
MINNESOTA	604.01, *et seq.*		Plaintiff's fault not greater than defendant's, but damages are diminished in proportion to fault	Plaintiff's fault greater than defendant's		No

(Continued)

Table 29: Negligence—Continued

State	Code Section	Uniform Act	Comparative Negligence	Contributory Negligence—Limit to Plaintiff's Recovery	Judicial Imposition of Comparative Negligence	Contribution Among Tortfeasors
MISSISSIPPI	11-7-15	No	"Pure" comparative negligence	Plaintiff's percentage of negligence		Yes; §85-5-5
MISSOURI	None				*Gustafson v. Benda*, 661 S.W. 2d 11 (1983)	Yes; §537.060
MONTANA	27-1-702	No	Plaintiff's negligence not greater than combined negligence of defendants (§27-1-702)	Plaintiff's negligence greater than defendant's		Yes; §27-1-703
NEBRASKA	25-21, 185.03		Plaintiff's award diminishes proportionally with negligence, but negligence equal to or greater than defendant's is a total bar.	Plaintiff's award diminishes proportionally with negligence, but negligence equal to or greater than defendant's is a total bar.		No
NEVADA	41.141	17.225 to 17.305	Plaintiff's negligence not greater than defendant's			Yes; §§17.225 to 17.305
NEW HAMPSHIRE	507:7d	No	Plaintiff's negligence not greater than causal negligence of defendant			Yes; §507.7f
NEW JERSEY	2A:15-5.1, *et seq.*		Plaintiff's negligence not greater than defendant's (§2A: 15-5.1)			Yes; 2A:15-5.3 & 2A:53A-2
NEW MEXICO	None	41-3-1 to 41-3-8	"Pure" comparative negligence		*Scott v. Rizzo*, 634 P.2d 1234 (1981)	Yes; §§41-3-1 to 41-3-8
NEW YORK	N.Y. Civ. Prac. L. & R. §§1411, *et seq.*		"Pure" comparative negligence			Yes; N.Y. Civ. Prac. L. & R. §§1401 *et seq.*
NORTH CAROLINA	None	§1B-1 to 1B-6	Defendant has burden of proving plaintiff was comparatively negligent (§1-139)	Plaintiff's negligence bar to recovery		Yes; G.S. §§1B-1 to 1B-6
NORTH DAKOTA	9-10-07	32-38-01 to 04	Plaintiff's negligence not as great as defendant's (§9-10-07)	Plaintiff's negligence as great as defendant's		Yes; §§32-38-01 to 04

(Continued)

Table 29: Negligence—Continued

State	Code Section	Uniform Act	Comparative Negligence	Contributory Negligence—Limit to Plaintiff's Recovery	Judicial Imposition of Comparative Negligence	Contribution Among Tortfeasors
OHIO	2315.19	2307.31, 2307.33	Plaintiff's negligence no greater than combined negligence of defendants; award diminished proportionately with fault (§2315.19)	Plaintiff's negligence greater than defendant's		Yes; §§2307.31, 33
OKLAHOMA	Tit. 23 §13-14	Tit. 12 §832	Plaintiff's negligence is not of greater degree than defendant's	Plaintiff's negligence greater than defendant's		Yes; Tit. 12 §832
OREGON	18.470	No	Plaintiff's negligence not greater than combined fault of defendants	Plaintiff's negligence greater than defendant's		Yes; §18.440
PENNSYLVANIA	Tit. 42 §7102	Tit. 42 §§8321-8327	Plaintiff's negligence not greater than causal negligence of defendants (§7102)	Plaintiff's negligence cannot be greater than defendant's		Yes; Tit. 42 §§8321-8327
RHODE ISLAND	9-20-4	§§10-6-1 to 11	"Pure" comparative negligence	Only percentage of negligence attributable to plaintiff; award diminished proportionately (9-20-4)		Yes; §§10-6-1 to 11
SOUTH CAROLINA	None	§§15-38-10 to 70	Does not exist in South Carolina except by statute for railroad employer's liability	Plaintiff's negligence bar to recovery		Yes; §§15-38-10 to 70
SOUTH DAKOTA	20-9-2	15-8-11, *et seq.*	Plaintiff's negligence slight in comparison to defendant's; he may then recover in proportion to comparative fault (§20-9-2)	Plaintiff's negligence is found to be more than slight in comparison to defendant's negligence		Yes; SDCL §§15-8-11 to 22
TENNESSEE	None	29-11-101	No; Last Clear Chance Doctrine (*See Street v. Calvert*, 541 S.W. 2d 576 (1976))	Plaintiff's negligence is a bar to recovery (*See Street v. Calvert*, 541 S.W. 2d 576 (1976) for discussion of "remote" contributory negligence.)		Yes; TCA §§29-11-101 to 106
TEXAS	Civ. Prac. & Rem. §33.001	No	Plaintiff's negligence not greater than defendant's; award diminished in proportion to negligence (Civ. Prac. & Rem. §33.001)			Yes; Civ. Prac. & Rem. §32.012

(Continued)

Table 29: Negligence—Continued

State	Code Section	Uniform Act	Comparative Negligence	Contributory Negligence—Limit to Plaintiff's Recovery	Judicial Imposition of Comparative Negligence	Contribution Among Tortfeasors
UTAH	78-27-37, *et. seq.*	No	Plaintiff's negligence not as great as defendant's (§78-27-38)			No; but §78-27-40 will not affect any right to comparative negligence arising from statute, contract, or agreement
VERMONT	Tit. 12 §1036		Plaintiff's negligence not greater than causal total negligence of defendants.			No
VIRGINIA	8.01-58 (Contributory negligence is no bar to recovery in certain employee-railroad disputes.)	No	In an action against a common carrier, comparative negligence will not bar recovery and if carrier violated a safety code, the injured party won't be found comparatively negligent (8.01-58)	Plaintiff's negligence bar to recovery		8.01-34; Contributory negligence may be applied when the wrong results from negligence and involves no moral turpitude
WASHINGTON	4.22.005 to 925	Yes; 4.22.005 to 925	"Pure" comparative negligence (§4.22.005); Amount of reward reduced proportionately with fault			Yes; §4.22.040
WEST VIRGINIA	None	No	Plaintiff's negligence does not exceed or equal defendant's		*Bradley v. Appalachian Power Co.,* 256 S.E.2d 879 (1979), at 885.	Yes; §55-7-13
WISCONSIN	895.045	No	Plaintiff's negligence not greater than defendant's (§895.045)			Yes; common law right based on equitable principles (*State Farm Mutual Auto Ins. v. Continental Cas. Co.,* 59 N.W. 2d 425)
WYOMING	1-1-109	No	Plaintiff's negligence must not be over 50% of the total fault (§1-1-109)	Over 50% fault ascribed to plaintiff		No

30. RIGHT TO DIE

Euthanasia laws, living wills, and the durable power of attorney, often referred to as the "Right-to-Die" laws, are concerned with how an individual who has become incapacitated may exert some influence and control over certain decisions that will be made concerning his or her care. Living wills and the durable power of attorney permit individuals to instruct his or her survivors, guardians, or attending physicians to either administer or withhold life support if they are near death and unable to communicate, such as when in a coma.

The moral questions raised by the right-to-die laws are a direct result of developments in modern technology. From the earliest times, the primary goal of doctors has been to cure the sick and comfort the dying. But modern technology has now allowed them to prolong life beyond the body's natural ability to maintain itself. Machines can artificially breathe for a person; intravenous feeding can artificially supply sustenance. Indeed, technology can keep a patient's body completely alive even when its brain is dead.

A major problem arises in situations such as these when the patient's desires are not known; it is then up to others to decide how long artificial life-sustaining procedures should be administered. Next of kin are nearly always the ones to whom this emotionally difficult decision falls, and the complexity of right-to-die laws reveals just how legally complicated the decision can be as well.

Next of kin are very often the persons most anxious to end their loved one's suffering. But generally physicians, who are trained to prolong life, maintain an ethical and moral, as well as a legal, obligation to sustain life and are loathe to do anything that will end life unless they are protected from all liability stemming from charges of homicide or wrongful death or violations of codes of professional responsibility. In the past, every time the question of "pulling the plug" arose it was "taken care of quietly" or ended up in court, where a judge determined if the doctor should end life support. If the judge ruled that life support could be witheld, the attending physician and the health care provider were completely protected from liability.

Obviously, this was a very inefficient method of dealing with this situation. After one or two high-profile cases, the public generally accepted "pulling the plug" as an option for the terminally ill. Where once medical practitioners and the public looked upon the act as murder, many have come to see it as merciful. This change in attitude has manifested itself, in most states, in a body of rather dark statutes falling into three specific categories, living wills, durable power of attorney, and euthanasia.

Living Wills

A living will is a legal instrument that is executed by a person of sound mind and witnessed in much the same manner as a will. A living will expresses the individual's desires regarding life support should he or she become incapacitated as a result of a terminal illness: specifically, whether or not to administer artificial life-sustaining procedures in the event of an incurable or irreversible terminal condition that would otherwise result in death in a short time.

Durable Power of Attorney

A durable power of attorney is an instrument that is similar to a living will except that it gives authority to a named individual to decide whether or not to begin or discontinue artificial life support. Any decision the holder of the durable power of attorney makes regarding life support is said to have the exact same legal effect as though the patient had made the decision himself or herself.

Euthanasia

No state sanctions euthanasia—also known as mercy killing—assisted suicide, or suicide. However, the terms of these right-to-die statutes are worded such that nearly all states include clauses explicitly stating that nothing in the statutes may be construed to condone suicide.

There is considerable diversity among states regarding the handling of the right-to-die issue, but the variance is entirely in the detail. While every state recognizes some form of durable power of attorney or living will, each has added its own character. Many states require state-sanctioned forms, while some allow as little as "some form of communication" to execute or revoke a durable power of attorney or living will.

Note: Because laws governing the right to die are fast changing, all users of this book are advised to consult local statutes before acting on any information contained in this chapter.

Table 30a: Right to Die: Durable Power of Attorney

State/ Code Section	Specific Powers, Life- Prolonging Acts	Operative Facts	Revocation/Duration	Reciprocity	Transfer of Patient if Physician Unwilling	Immunity for Attending Physician
ALABAMA No statutory provisions						
ALASKA 13.26.332, 335, *et seq.*	Consent or refusal to consent to medical care or relief for the principal from pain but agent may not authorize the termination of life-sustaining procedures	(1) Must contain wording that power-of-attorney becomes effective upon disability of principal; (2) designate health care service decisions to agent	Revocable at any time		A third party shall honor the terms of a properly executed power of attorney, but physician may withdraw after services of another physician have been obtained	A third party who relies on reasonable representations of an attorney-in-fact does not incur a liability to the principal or principal's heirs, assigns, or estate
ARIZONA 36-322, *et seq.*	Power to give or refuse consent to all medical, surgical, hospital, and related health care	(1) Adult; (2) in writing; (3) language clearly indicating intent to create a power of attorney; (4) dated; (5) signed; (6) witnessed by at least one adult or a notary public	Person may revoke health care directive or disqualify a surrogate by (1) written revocation; (2) orally notifying surrogate or health care provider; (3) making new health care directive; (4) any other act demonstrating specific intent to revoke	Health care directive prepared in another state is valid in this state if it was valid where and at the time it was adopted to the extent it does not conflict with the criminal laws of Arizona		Health care provider making good faith decisions in reliance on apparently genuine health care directive or decision of a surrogate is immune from civil, criminal, and professional discipline for that reliance
ARKANSAS 20-17-201, *et seq.*	Any medical procedure or intervention that will serve only to prolong the dying process or to maintain the patient in a condition of permanent unconsciousness	The declaration may appoint a health care proxy as attorney-in-fact to make health care decisions including life-sustaining treatment	Revocable at any time in any manner by the declarant without regard to declarant's mental/physical condition. Effective upon communication to attending physician	A declaration executed in another state in compliance with the laws of that state or Arkansas law is validly executed	Physician shall as promptly as practicable take all reasonable steps to transfer care to another physician	Physician whose actions under this chapter are in accord with reasonable medical standards is not subject to criminal, civil, or professional liability with respect to them

(Continued)

Table 30a: Right to Die: Durable Power of Attorney—Continued

State/ Code Section	Specific Powers, Life-Prolonging Acts	Operative Facts	Revocation/Duration	Reciprocity	Transfer of Patient if Physician Unwilling	Immunity for Attending Physician
CALIFORNIA Civ. §2430	Decisions on any care, treatment, service, or procedure to maintain, diagnose, or treat an individual's physical or mental condition	Durable power of attorney must specifically authorize the attorney-in-fact to make health care decisions; dated; witnessed by 2 attesting to the principal's signature or by a notary public	Anytime while principal has capacity to give a durable power of attorney, he may (1) revoke the appointment of the attorney-in-fact orally or in writing; (2) revoke the agent's authority by notifying the physician orally or in writing; (3) a subsequent durable power of attorney revokes prior one; (4) divorce revokes any designation of former spouse	Enforceable if executed in another state or jurisdiction in compliance with the laws of that state or jurisdiction or of California		Subject to limitations, a physician acting in good faith on decision of attorney-in-fact is not subject to criminal, civil, or professional liability except to the same extent that would be the case if the principal, having had capacity to give informed consent, had made the health care decision on his/her own behalf under like circumstances
COLORADO 15-14-503, *et seq.*	An agent shall have the same power as the principal if the principal did not lack decisional capacity to consent to or refuse medical treatment including artificial nourishment and hydration		Divorce revokes any designation of former spouse as agent	A durable power of attorney executed in another state shall be presumed to comply with this law and may, in good faith, be relied on by a health care provider	Physician must provide for prompt transfer	No criminal or civil liability or regulatory sanction for complying in good faith with an advance medical directive
CONNECTICUT 1-54a	Consent, refuse consent, or withdraw consent to any medical treatment other than that designed solely to maintain physical comfort, the withdrawal of life support systems, or of nutrition or hydration	See statutory form §1-43				

(Continued)

Table 30a: Right to Die: Durable Power of Attorney—Continued

State/ Code Section	Specific Powers, Life-Prolonging Acts	Operative Facts	Revocation/Duration	Reciprocity	Transfer of Patient if Physician Unwilling	Immunity for Attending Physician
DELAWARE 16 §2501, *et seq.*	Grant, refuse, withdraw consent to provision of medical treatment, including right to refuse medical treatment which would extend appointer's life	(1) Adult; (2) written declaration; (3) attending physician judges appointer incapable of making decision to accept or refuse medical treatment due to illness or injury; (4) signed by appointer or another person at his express direction and in his presence; (5) dated; (6) 2 or more adult witnesses	Revocable at any time without regard to declarant's mental state or competency by (1) destruction of declaration with intent to revoke; (2) oral statement in presence of 2 persons 18 yrs. or older expressing intent to revoke; (3) written revocation signed and dated by declarant			No civil or criminal liability
DISTRICT OF COLUMBIA 21-2201	To grant, refuse, withdraw consent to the provision of any health-care service, treatment, or procedure	(1) Competent adult; (2) in writing; (3) must include language clearly communicating the intent for attorney-in-fact to have authority to make health-care decisions; (4) dated; (5) signed; (6) in presence of 2 adult	Revocable at any time principal has capacity to create a durable power of attorney by notifying health care provider or attorney-in-fact orally or in writing. Divorce revokes designation of former spouse			

(Continued)

Table 30a: Right to Die: Durable Power of Attorney—Continued

State/ Code Section	Specific Powers, Life-Prolonging Acts	Operative Facts	Revocation/Duration	Reciprocity	Transfer of Patient if Physician Unwilling	Immunity for Attending Physician
FLORIDA 765.201, *et seq.* Health Care Surrogate Act	All health care decisions, including life-prolonging procedures. Any medical procedure, treatment, or intervention which utilizes mechanical or other artificial means to sustain, restore, supplant a spontaneous vital function and serves only to prolong the dying process of a patient in terminal condition. Does not include medication or medical procedure to alleviate pain	(1) Signed; (2) in presence of 2 adult witnesses	Revocable at any time by principal by (1) signed, dated writing; (2) destruction of declaration; (3) oral expression of intent to revoke; (4) subsequent advance health care directive materially different from the previously executed advance directive; (5) divorce revokes any designation of the former spouse as surrogate	An advance directive executed in another state in compliance with the laws of that state or Florida is validly executed	Physician should make reasonable efforts to transfer to a willing health care provider. Physician unwilling to carry out the patient's wishes because of moral or ethical beliefs must within 7 days: (1) transfer the patient and pay the cost of transporting the patient to another health care provider or (2) carry out the wishes of the patient unless provisions of judicial intervention	Health care facility, provider, or other person acting under their direction is not subject to criminal, civil, or professional liability for carrying out health care decision
GEORGIA 31-36-1, *et seq.*	All powers the individual may have to be informed about and to consent or refuse to consent to any type of health care for the individual including withholding or withdrawal of life-sustaining or death-delaying procedures	(1) In writing; (2) signed by principal; (3) 2 or more competent adult witnesses; (4) statutory form §31-36-10 may be used	Revocable at any time by principal without regard to physical or mental condition by (1) destruction of the document; (2) written revocation signed and dated by the principal; (3) by oral or any other expression of intent to revoke in presence of an adult witness who must sign and date in writing confirming the expression of such intent; (4) divorce revokes agency in former spouse		Physician should promptly inform the agent who is responsible to make the transfer, but physician will continue to afford consultation and care in connection with the pending transfer	No health care provider subject to any civil, criminal, or professional liability solely for complying with decision of agent

(Continued)

Table 30a: Right to Die: Durable Power of Attorney—Continued

State/ Code Section	Specific Powers, Life-Prolonging Acts	Operative Facts	Revocation/Duration	Reciprocity	Transfer of Patient if Physician Unwilling	Immunity for Attending Physician
HAWAII 551D-1, *et seq.* Uniform Durable Power of Attorney Act	Agent authorized to make any lawful health care decisions that could have been made by principal at time of election. Agent may decide that principal's life should not be prolonged through surgery, resuscitation, life-sustaining medicine, or procedures for provision of nutrition or hydration if explicitly appointed	(1) Competent adult; (2) in writing and signed by principal or another in his or her presence at expressed direction; (3) dated; (4) in presence of 2 or more adult witnesses; (5) signature notarized	Effective only during period of incapacity of principal. Not revoked until notice is given			
IDAHO 39-4505, *et seq.*	Health care decisions, meaning consent, refusal of consent, or withdrawal of consent to any care, treatment, services, or procedure to maintain, diagnose, or treat an individual's physical condition. Also includes life-prolonging care decisions (see Living Wills for description of life-prolonging measures)	(1) Signed by principal; (2) dated; (3) signed by 2 witnesses	Revocable at any time by the maker without regard to competence by (1) destruction of the document; (2) by written, signed revocation; (3) by verbal expression of intent to revoke. Divorce revokes former spouse as agent or may be revoked by notary public		Physician may withdraw without civil or criminal liability provided physician makes a good faith effort to assist patient in transferring	No civil or criminal liability for physician acting in accordance with wishes of patient as expressed by statutory procedure
ILLINOIS 45/4-1 Powers of Attorney for Health Care Law	Health care powers may be delegated to an agent and include consent or refusal or withdrawal of any type of health care for individual. May extend beyond principal's death if necessary to permit anatomical gift, autopsy, or disposition of remains	Neither attending physician nor health care provider may act as agent	Revocable at any time by principal without regard to mental or physical condition by (1) written revocation; (2) oral expression in presence of witness; (3) destruction of power of attorney in manner indicating intent to revoke		Agent responsible for transfer after prompt informing by attending physician	No civil, criminal, or professional liability if good faith reliance on any decision or direction by agent not clearly contrary to terms of a health care agency

(Continued)

Table 30a: Right to Die: Durable Power of Attorney—Continued

State/ Code Section	Specific Powers, Life-Prolonging Acts	Operative Facts	Revocation/Duration	Reciprocity	Transfer of Patient if Physician Unwilling	Immunity for Attending Physician
INDIANA 16-8-12-6, *et seq.*	Any care, treatment, service, or procedure to maintain, diagnose, or treat an individual's physical or mental condition including admission to a health care facility	(1) In writing; (2) signed by appointer; (3) witnessed by adult other than representative	Individual capable of consenting to health care may revoke appointment at any time by notifying representative or health care provider orally or in writing. Individual who may consent to his own health care may disqualify others from consenting for the individual			No criminal, civil, or professional liability for a physician acting in good faith in reliance on the agent's direction
IOWA 144B.1, *et seq.* Durable Power of Attorney for Health Care	Consent, refusal of consent, or withdrawal of consent to health care. Attorney-in-fact has priority over court-appointed guardian to make health care decisions	(1) Explicitly authorizes attorney-in-fact to make health care decisions; (2) 2 witnesses; (3) notarized	May be revoked at any time in any manner by which principal is made to communicate intent to revoke. Revocation upon subsequent execution of durable power of attorney or upon dissolution of marriage if spouse was attorney in fact.		Unwilling physician must make provisions to transfer patient	Health care provider not subject to civil or criminal liability if acting in good faith on decision of attorney-in-fact
KANSAS 58-625	Consent, refuse consent, or withdraw consent to any care, treatment, service, or procedure to maintain, diagnose, or treat a physical or mental condition	(1) Writing must have words of intent that principal conferred authority to be exercised notwithstanding principal's subsequent incapacity; (2) dated; (3) signed; (4) 18; (5) in presence of 2 witnesses or notarized; (6) in substantially statutory form of §58-632				

(Continued)

Table 30a: Right to Die: Durable Power of Attorney—Continued

State/ Code Section	Specific Powers, Life-Prolonging Acts	Operative Facts	Revocation/Duration	Reciprocity	Transfer of Patient if Physician Unwilling	Immunity for Attending Physician
KENTUCKY 311.970 Health Care Surrogates	Surrogate may make any decision grantor could make, including withholding or withdrawal of artificial nutrition or hydration if (1) death is imminent; (2) such nutrition or hydration cannot be physically assimilated; (3) burden or providing outweights benefit. Artificial nutrition or hydration not to be withdrawn if needed for comfort or relief of pain. Life sustaining treatment shall be provided to pregnant woman unless attending physician determines such treatment will not permit continuing development and live birth of unborn child or will be physically harmful to woman or prolong severe pain which cannot be alleviated by medication	(1) Grantor with decisional capability; (2) may designate 1 or 2 adults as surrogates; (3) if 2 or more, any decisions must be unanimous; (4) in writing, signed by grantor; (5) 2 witnesses, notarized; (6) document part of grantor's medical record; (7) surrogate may only make decisions when physician has determined grantor has lost decisional capability	(1) May be revoked in whole or in part or surrogate's powers reduced or limited at any time; (2) subsequent executed appointments negate earlier ones unless specifically negated; (3) may be oral or written, or by destruction by grantor or at his or her direction. Such revocation shall be added to medical records if revoked while grantor confined to health care facility		Unwilling physician shall promptly notify grantor and surrogate and shall not impede transfer to another physician or health care facility	Unlawful for any health care facility or licensing agency to discriminate against health care professional that is unwilling to comply with designation of grantor
LOUISIANA 40:1299.58.3(c) (1)	Any medical procedure or intervention, including but not limited to invasive administration of nutrition and hydration, which would serve only to prolong the dying process for a person diagnosed as having a terminal and irreversible condition. Does not include any measure necessary for comfort care	The declaration made under statutory "Declarations Concerning Life-sustaining Procedures" may include designation of another person to make treatment decision for the declarant should s/he be diagnosed with terminal or irreversible condition and be comatose, incompetent or otherwise mentally or physically incapable of communication	Revocable at any time by declarant without regard to mental state or competency by (1) destruction of document; (2) written revocation signed and dated by declarant; (3) oral or nonverbal expression by declarant of intent to revoke. Effective upon communication to physician		Physician shall make reasonable effort to transfer patient to another physician	Any health care facility, physician or other person acting under their direction shall not be criminally, civilly, or professionally liable for withholding life-sustaining procedures in accordance with the provisions of this chapter

(Continued)

Table 30a: Right to Die: Durable Power of Attorney—Continued

State/ Code Section	Specific Powers, Life-Prolonging Acts	Operative Facts	Revocation/Duration	Reciprocity	Transfer of Patient if Physician Unwilling	Immunity for Attending Physician
MAINE 5-501, *et seq.* Durable Health Care Power of Attorney	Consent or withhold consent or approval relating to any medical or other health care treatment including life-sustaining treatment when principal is in terminal condition or persistent vegetative state	(1) Signed by principal or another at principal's direction; (2) 2 witnesses other than designated attorney-in-fact	May be revoked or terminated by a fiduciary of principal only with prior approval of court upon petition by any interested person			
MARYLAND No statutory provisions						
MASSACHU-SETTS Ch. 201D §1, *et seq.* Health Care Proxies	Any and all health care decisions on principal's behalf that principal could make including decisions about life-sustaining treatment, subject to any express limitations in health care proxy	(1) Competent adult; (2) in writing; (3) signed; (4) in presence of 2 adult witnesses; (5) Health care proxy must contain identities of principal and health care agent and indicate principal intends agent to have authority to make health care decisions on his behalf and describe any limitations and indicate agent's authority effective if it is determined that principal lacks decisional capacity	Revocable by (1) notification of agent or health care provider orally or in writing or by any other act evidencing specific intent to revoke the proxy; (2) execution of subsequent health care proxy; (3) divorce or legal separation where spouse was principal's agent	Effective if executed in another state or jurisdiction if in compliance with laws of that state or jurisdiction	Physician should arrange for transfer of patient; if unable to do so, physician shall seek judicial relief or honor agent's decision	No civil, criminal, or professional liability for carrying out in good faith a health care decision by an agent pursuant to a health care proxy

(Continued)

Table 30a: Right to Die: Durable Power of Attorney—Continued

State/ Code Section	Specific Powers, Life-Prolonging Acts	Operative Facts	Revocation/Duration	Reciprocity	Transfer of Patient if Physician Unwilling	Immunity for Attending Physician
MICHIGAN §700.496 Designation of Patient Advocate	Designation may include statement of patient's desires on care, custody, and medical treatment and may authorize patient advocate to exercise 1 or more powers concerning patient's care, custody, and medical treatment that patient could have exercised on own behalf. Patient advocate may make decision to withhold or withdraw treatment which would allow patient to die only if patient has expressed in a clear and convincing manner that patient advocate is allowed to do so	(1) 18 yrs.; (2) sound mind; (3) in writing; (4) 2 witnesses; (5) proposed patient advocate must sign acceptance	(1) Revocable at any time and in any manner sufficient to communicate intent to revoke; (2) patient advocate may revoke acceptance to designation at any time and in any manner sufficient to communicate intent to revoke; (3) subsequent designation prevails; (4) divorce revokes designation of patient advocate in former spouse; (5) death of patient; (6) order of court; (7) occurrence of provision for revocation contained in designation; (8) any current desires of patient are binding on patient advocate		Physician or health care provider is bound by sound medical practice and instructions of patient advocate if patient advocate complies with law	Person providing, performing, withholding, withdrawing medical treatment reasonably relying on decisions of patient advocate is liable in same manner and to same extent as if patient had made decision on his or her own behalf
MINNESOTA 145B.01, *et seq.*	Decisions on whether to begin, continue, increase, limit, discontinue, or not begin care, treatment, services, or procedures to maintain, diagnose, or treat an individual's physical condition when the individual is in a terminal condition. Decisions must be based on reasonable medical practice including (1) continuation of appropriate care to maintain comfort, hygiene, human dignity, and alleviate pain; (2) oral administration of food and water to a patient who accepts it, except for clearly documented medical reasons	(1) Competent adult; (2) signed by declarant; (3) signed by 2 witnesses or notary public; (4) must state preference regarding artificial administration of nutrition and hydration or give decision to proxy; without such statement, decisions will be made on reasonable medical practice; (5) must be in substantially the statutory form	Revocable at any time in any manner by declarant without regard to physical or mental condition. Effective upon communication to physician. Divorce revokes any designation of former spouse as proxy to make health care decisions	Effective when executed in another state if it substantially complies with Minnesota law	Physician must notify competent declarant but has no duty to transfer. If physician received declaration from competent patient and did not so notify him and declarant later becomes incompetent, physician must transfer	

(Continued)

Table 30a: Right to Die: Durable Power of Attorney—Continued

State/ Code Section	Specific Powers, Life- Prolonging Acts	Operative Facts	Revocation/Duration	Reciprocity	Transfer of Patient if Physician Unwilling	Immunity for Attending Physician
MISSISSIPPI 41-41-151 to 183 Durable Power of Attorney for Health Care Act	Consent, refuse consent, or withdraw consent to any care, treatment, service, or procedure to maintain, diagnose, or treat an individual's physical or mental condition	(1) Durable power of attorney must specifically authorize the attorney-in-fact to make health care decisions; (2) dated; (3) witnessed by 2 or notarized; (4) should follow substantially statutory form (§41-41-163)	Unless the document provides a shorter time, it shall be effective until revoked by principal. Durable power of attorney revocable at any time the principal has capacity to give a durable power of attorney for health care by notifying the attorney-in-fact in writing or notifying the health care provider in writing. Wishes of principal supersede the consent of any health care agent			No civil, criminal, or professional responsibility if health care provider relies in good faith on health care decision
MISSOURI 404.800, *et seq.*	May make health care decisions, but no agent may authorize withdrawal of artificially supplied nutrition and hydration which the patient may ingest through natural means	(1) Signed; (2) dated; (3) includes provision that durable power shall not terminate if principal becomes disabled or incapacitated; (4) agent has no duty to exercise authority granted unless he has agreed expressly in writing to act	Revocable at any time in any manner by which patient is able to communicate the intent to revoke. Effective upon communication to agent or to physician		Physician may not impede the attorney-in-fact from transferring patient to another physician or facility	Any third party acting in good faith may rely on the instructions of the attorney-in-fact without liability to the patient or the patient's successors-in-interest

(Continued)

Table 30a: Right to Die: Durable Power of Attorney—Continued

State/ Code Section	Specific Powers, Life-Prolonging Acts	Operative Facts	Revocation/Duration	Reciprocity	Transfer of Patient if Physician Unwilling	Immunity for Attending Physician
MONTANA 50-9-103 Montana Rights of the Terminally Ill Act	Withholding or withdrawal of life-sustaining treatment, defined as any medical procedure or intervention that will serve only to prolong the dying process. Qualified patient may designate another individual to make decisions governing withholding or withdrawal of life-sustaining treatment. Life-sustaining procedures may not be withdrawn when qualified patient is known to be pregnant and when it is likely fetus will result in live birth	(1) 18 yrs. and of sound mind; (2) signed by declarant or another at his request; (3) 2 witnesses; (4) communicated to physician and made part of patient's medical record; (5) declared to be terminal and no longer able to make decisions regarding life-sustaining treatment; (7) declarant may designate another individual, 18 yrs. old and of sound mind, to make decisions regarding life-sustaining treatment	Revocable at any time in any manner without regard to physical or mental condition. Effective upon notice	Declaration made in another state in compliance with that state's laws executed in a substantially similar manner to laws of Montana is effective	Unwilling physician shall take all reasonable steps as promptly as practicable to transfer to another who is willing	Individual appointed under this section not criminally or civilly liable for decisions made pursuant to executed declaration
NEBRASKA 30-3401 Power of Attorney for Health Care	Consent, refusal of consent, withdrawal of consent to health care. Shall not include (1) withdrawal of routine comfort care; (2) nutrition and hydration; (3) withdrawal or withholding of life-sustaining procedures or artificially administered nutrition or hydration except if declarant gives that authority	(1) In writing; (2) identify parties; (3) specifically authorize attorney-in-fact to make decisions; (4) 2 adult witnesses	Revocable at any time by principal; withdrawal at any time by attorney-in-fact. Otherwise, effective until death of principal		Unwilling physician shall inform attorney-in-fact and promptly assist in transferring principal to willing physician	No criminal, civil, or professional liability if acting in good faith

(Continued)

Table 30a: Right to Die: Durable Power of Attorney—Continued

State/ Code Section	Specific Powers, Life-Prolonging Acts	Operative Facts	Revocation/Duration	Reciprocity	Transfer of Patient if Physician Unwilling	Immunity for Attending Physician
NEVADA 449-800 to 860	Attorney-in-fact has power to make health care decisions before or after death including consent, refusal of consent, or withdrawal of consent to any care, treatment, service, or procedure to maintain, diagnose, or treat physical or mental condition except treatment specifically stated, commitment to mental facility, convulsive treatment, psychosurgery, sterilization, or abortion	(1) Signed; (2) notarized or 2 witnesses	Divorce revokes designation of former spouse. Power of attorney remains valid indefinitely unless principal designates shorter period or it is revoked			
NEW HAMPSHIRE 137-J:1 Durable Power of Attorney for Health Care	Any decisions on principal's behalf that principal could make. Artificial nutrition and hydration may not be withdrawn or withheld unless clear expression of such power in document	(1) In writing; (2) substantially statutory form; (3) 2 witnesses	Revocable by (1) notifying attorney-in-fact orally or in writing or in any other way communicating specific intent to revoke; (2) execution of subsequent durable power of attorney; (3) filing of action of divorce if spouse is agent. Revocation effective upon notice to health care provider or to attorney-in-fact	Documents executed in another state are enforceable if they comply with New Hampshire state laws	Unwilling physician or health care provider must inform attorney-in-fact and allow for transfer of patient to another facility	Health care provider with actual knowledge is bound to follow terms of durable power of attorney for health care. No person acting in good faith on the directives in a document shall be subject to criminal or civil liability

(Continued)

Table 30a: Right to Die: Durable Power of Attorney—Continued

State/ Code Section	Specific Powers, Life-Prolonging Acts	Operative Facts	Revocation/Duration	Reciprocity	Transfer of Patient if Physician Unwilling	Immunity for Attending Physician
NEW JERSEY 26:2H-53, *et seq.* A Proxy Directive	Decisions to accept or refuse treatment, service, or procedure including life-sustaining treatment. Includes decisions on use of any medical device or procedure, artificially provided fluids and nutrition, drugs, surgery or therapy that uses mechanical or other artificial means to sustain, restore, or supplant a vital bodily function and thereby increase the expected life span of a patient	(1) Competent adult; (2) signed; (3) dated; (4) 2 witnesses or notarized or other person authorized to administer oaths. May be substituted by video or audio tape recording	Revocable by (1) oral or written notification; (2) execution of subsequent directive; (3) divorce revokes former spouse's designation as representative. Patient's clearly expressed wishes take precedent over any patient's decision or proxy directive	Effective if executed in compliance with New Jersey law or the laws of another state. Effective if executed in a foreign country in compliance with that country's laws or the laws of New Jersey and is not contrary to public policy of New Jersey	Unwilling physician should act as soon as practicable to effect transfer and to assure patient is not abandoned or treated disrespectfully	No civil, criminal, or professional liability for any physician acting in good faith pursuant to this act
NEW MEXICO 45-5-501, *et seq.*	Decisions relating to medical treatment, surgical treatment, nursing care, medication, hospitalization, institutionalization in a nursing home or other facility, and home health care	(1) In writing; (2) contains words "This power of attorney shall not be affected by incapacity of the principal" or similar words showing intent that authority be exercisable notwithstanding principal's incapacity				
NEW YORK Pub. Health Law §2980, *et seq.* Health Care Proxy	Any decision to consent or refuse consent of any treatment, service, or procedure to diagnose or treat an individual's physical or mental condition	(1) Competent adult; (2) signed; (3) dated; (4) 2 adult witnesses; (5) indicate agent and that principal wants agent to make health care decisions for him	Proxy may provide that it expires on a specified date or occurrence of condition; otherwise in effect until revoked. Revocable by (1) notifying agent or health care provider orally, in writing, or any other act evidencing intent to revoke; (2) divorce if former spouse was agent	Effective if executed in another state in compliance with laws of that state		No criminal, civil, or professional liability for acting in good faith pursuant to statute

(Continued)

Table 30a: Right to Die: Durable Power of Attorney—Continued

State/ Code Section	Specific Powers, Life-Prolonging Acts	Operative Facts	Revocation/Duration	Reciprocity	Transfer of Patient if Physician Unwilling	Immunity for Attending Physician
NORTH CAROLINA 32A-15 Health Care Powers of Attorney	Decisions regarding life-sustaining procedures, including those which serve to artificially prolong the dying process and may include mechanical ventilation, dialysis, antibiotics, artificial nutrition and hydration and other forms of treatment which sustain, restore, or supplant vital bodily functions but do not include care necessary to provide comfort or alleviate pain	(1) In writing; (2) 2 witnesses	Revoked on decree of divorce if spouse is agent, except if alternate has been appointed. If all health care attorneys-in-fact are unwilling or unable to act, the health care power of attorney will cease to be effective		Health care power of attorney may contain contingency provisions relating to appointment, resignation, or removal and substitution of health care agent	No person acting on the authority of the health care attorney shall be liable for actions taken pursuant to decision of health care attorney. Withholding or discontinuing life-sustaining procedures shall not be considered suicide or cause of death in criminal or civil matters
NORTH DAKOTA 23-06.5-01	Agent has power to make any health care decisions principal could if he did not lack capacity, including consent, refusal or withdrawal of consent to any care, treatment, service, or procedure to maintain, diagnose, or treat individual's physical or mental condition	(1) Signed; (2) 2 witnesses; (3) agent must accept appointment in writing; (4) statutory form of durable power of attorney is preferred format	Revocable by (1) notification of agent orally, in writing, or any other act evidencing specific intent to revoke; (2) execution of subsequent durable power of attorney; (3) divorce where spouse was principal's agent	Effective if executed in another state in compliance with the law of that state	Physician has duty to inform principal or agent and take all reasonable steps to transfer care to another who is willing to honor agent's directive	No civil, criminal, or professional liability if acting in good faith pursuant to directives of durable power of attorney
OHIO 1337.10, *et seq.*	Medical procedure, treatment, intervention, or other measure that will serve to prolong the process of dying, including right to give informed consent and make other decisions principal could if s/he had capacity	(1) Adult; (2) sound mind; (3) signed; (4) dated; (5) 2 adult witnesses or notarized	Does not expire unless principal specifies an expiration date in the instrument. Revocable at any time in any manner effective when expressed, but if physician had knowledge of the durable power of attorney, revocation is effective on communication to physician	Effective if document substantially complies with the laws of the state where executed or with Ohio law	Physician may not prevent or delay patient's transfer to another physician	No civil, criminal, or professional liability for good faith reliance on agent's health care decisions

(Continued)

Table 30a: Right to Die: Durable Power of Attorney—Continued

State/ Code Section	Specific Powers, Life-Prolonging Acts	Operative Facts	Revocation/Duration	Reciprocity	Transfer of Patient if Physician Unwilling	Immunity for Attending Physician
OKLAHOMA Tit. 58 §1072, *et seq.;* Tit. 63 §3101.2	Under Uniform Durable Power of Attorney Act, agent may make health and medical care decisions but not life-sustaining treatment decisions unless declarant authorizes agent as a "health care proxy" under Oklahoma Rights of Terminally Ill or Persistently Unconscious Act, Tit. 63 §3101.2	(1) Signed; (2) 2 adult witnesses	Revocable in whole or in part in any manner at any time without regard to declarant's mental or physical condition. Effective upon communication to physician	Effective if executed in another state if substantially complies with the Uniform Durable Power of Attorney Act and laws of that state and so long as it does not exceed authorizations allowed under Oklahoma law	Physician shall take all reasonable steps to arrange for care by another physician	No civil, criminal, or professional liability for carrying out the directives of durable power of attorney
OREGON 127.505 Durable Power of Attorney for Health Care	Health care decisions regarding life-sustaining procedures including any medical procedure or intervention that uses mechanical or other artificial means to sustain, restore, or supplant a vital function when principal is terminally ill and such treatment only serves to artificially prolong the moment of death	(1) Must be made part of patient's medical record; (2) must specifically state powers designated; (3) 2 adult witnesses who must make written declaration; (4) agent must accept appointment	Seven years duration, or until revoked. Agent may withdraw up to time of principal's incapacity. Principal may revoke (1) in any manner by which s/he is able to communicate to health care provider or attorney-in-fact intent to revoke; (2) by execution of subsequent durable power of attorney; (3) upon divorce if spouse is agent		Physician must promptly notify agent if unable or unwilling to comply with durable power of attorney	Health care provider acting on a durable power of attorney in good faith is not liable if power was previously revoked but notice not given
PENNSYL-VANIA 20 Pa CSA §5601-5604	Authorize admission to medical facility and enter into agreements for principal's care and to authorize medical and surgical procedures	(1) In writing; (2) signed; (3) filed with clerk of court in county in which principal resides	Durable power of attorney not affected by subsequent disability or incapacity. Agent must have actual notice of revocation for it to be effective			
RHODE ISLAND 23-4.10-1, *et seq.*	Any medical procedure or intervention that will only prolong the dying process; it shall not include intervention necessary to alleviate pain or provide comfort	(1) 18 yrs.; (2) resident of Rhode Island; (3) 2 adult witnesses; (4) only in statutory form set forth in §23-4.10-2	Revocable at any time in any manner declarant is able to communicate intent to revoke, without regard to physical or mental condition. Effective upon communication to physician	Durable power of attorney executed in another state in compliance with laws of that state is valid	Unwilling physician must make necessary arrangements to effect transfer	No civil, criminal, or professional liability when acting in accordance with the statute

(Continued)

Table 30a: Right to Die: Durable Power of Attorney—Continued

State/ Code Section	Specific Powers, Life-Prolonging Acts	Operative Facts	Revocation/Duration	Reciprocity	Transfer of Patient if Physician Unwilling	Immunity for Attending Physician
SOUTH CAROLINA 62-5-501, *et seq.*	Medical procedure or intervention serving only to prolong the dying process, not including medication or treatment for pain alleviation. Principal should indicate whether provision of nutrition and hydration through surgically implanted tubes is desired	(1) Substantially in statutory form; (2) signed; (3) dated; (4) 2 witnesses; (5) state name and address of agent	Revocable by (1) written or oral statement or other act constituting notification to agent or health care provider; (2) principal's execution of subsequent health care power of attorney	Effective if executed in compliance with South Carolina law or laws of another state	Physician must make reasonable effort to transfer the patient to a physician who will follow directive	No civil, criminal, or professional liability for relying in good faith on agent's health care decisions
SOUTH DAKOTA 59-7-2.1, *et seq.*	Any decisions for principal which principal could have made if s/he had decisional capacity including rejection or withdrawal of consent for medical procedures, treatment, or intervention. Agent may not authorize withholding of comfort care, nutrition, or hydration. Artificial nutrition or hydration may be withheld under certain circumstances but never if needed for pain relief	Specific intent must be included in document for durable power of attorney to extend even when principal is disabled	Revocation must be recorded with register of deeds			No civil, criminal, or professional liability for physician acting in good faith reliance on a health care decision by agent
TENNESSEE 34-6-201, *et seq.*	Any procedure, treatment to diagnose, assess, or treat a disease, illness, or injury, including surgery, drugs, transfusions, mechanical ventilation, dialysis, CPR, artificial nourishment, hydration or other nutrients, radiation. Death by starvation or dehydration allowed only if specifically directed	Signed before 2 witnesses and notary public	Revocable by (1) notifying the attorney-in-fact orally or in writing; (2) notifying health care giver orally or in writing; (3) executing subsequent durable power of attorney; (4) divorce if former spouse was designated; (5) principal's current wishes supersede durable power of attorney	Effective if document complies with laws of Tennessee or laws of the state of principal's residence	Prompt transfer required	No criminal, civil, or professional liability for physician acting in good faith

(Continued)

Table 30a: Right to Die: Durable Power of Attorney—Continued

State/ Code Section	Specific Powers, Life-Prolonging Acts	Operative Facts	Revocation/Duration	Reciprocity	Transfer of Patient if Physician Unwilling	Immunity for Attending Physician
TEXAS Civ. Prac. & Rem. Code 135.001, *et seq.*	Decisions regarding consent to health care, treatment, service, or procedure to maintain, diagnose, or treat individual's physical or mental condition. Agent may not consent to voluntary in-patient mental health services, convulsive treatment, psychosurgery, abortion, or neglect of principal through omission of care primarily intended to provide for comfort of principal	(1) Signed; (2) 2 witnesses; (3) substantially statutory form and accompanied by disclosure statement. Principal may designate alternative agents	Effective indefinitely upon execution and delivery of document unless revoked. Revocable orally or in writing by (1) specific declaration; (2) execution of subsequent power of attorney; (3) divorce if spouse is agent. Effective upon receipt and notice to agent and health care provider. Treatment may not be given if principal objects	Durable power of attorney executed in another state valid if it complies with the law of that state or jurisdiction	Physician must notify agent immediately to arrange for transfer	Agent not liable for health care decision made in good faith. Physician not liable for acts or decisions made under durable power of attorney if done in good faith
UTAH 75-2-1101	Any medical procedure or intervention that would serve only to prolong the dying process; does not include medication, sustenance, or any procedure to alleviate pain	(1) 18 yrs.; (2) in writing; (3) signed; (4) if signed by someone other than principal, s/he must be over 18 and must be notarized; (5) dated; (6) 2 witnesses	Current wishes of declarant take precedent over any directive. Revocable at any time by (1) signed revocation; (2) destruction of document; (3) oral expression of intent to revoke in presence of witnesses. Effective on receipt by physician		Unwilling physician required to transfer patient	No civil, criminal, or professional liability for good faith compliance with directive
VERMONT Tit. 14 §3451, *et seq.*	To make health care decisions for principal including withdrawal of consent to any care, treatment, service, or procedure or to maintain, diagnose, or treat an individual's physical or mental condition	(1) Signed; (2) 2 witnesses; (3) signed statement that principal understands a disclosure statement on durable powers of attorney	Principal's current wishes supersede directives at all times. Revocable by (1) notifying agent or health care provider orally or in writing or any other act evidencing specific intent to revoke; (2) executing a subsequent durable power of attorney; (3) divorce, if former spouse was principal's agent	Effective if in compliance with the law of the state in which it was executed	Unwilling physician must inform agent and principal if possible and assist in selecting another physician willing to honor agent's directive	No civil, criminal, or professional liability if physician acts in good faith

(Continued)

Table 30a: Right to Die: Durable Power of Attorney—Continued

State/ Code Section	Specific Powers, Life-Prolonging Acts	Operative Facts	Revocation/Duration	Reciprocity	Transfer of Patient if Physician Unwilling	Immunity for Attending Physician
VIRGINIA 54.1-2984 Advanced Directive	Any medical procedure, treatment, intervention utilizing mechanical or other artificial means to sustain, restore, or supplant a vital function. Includes artificially administered nutrition and hydration but does not include any medication or procedure necessary to alleviate pain. Includes CPR	(1) In writing; (2) 2 witnesses; (3) oral declaration in presence of physician and 2 witnesses. Life prolonging procedures can be withheld without declaration if incapable of communication and there is agreement with physician or specified party	Revocable at any time by (1) signed, dated writing; (2) physical destruction; (3) oral expression of intent to revoke. Effective upon communication to attending physician	Directive executed in another state valid if in compliance with Virginia law or law of state where executed	Unwilling physician must make reasonable effort to transfer patient to another physician, even if physician thinks it medically or ethically inappropriate	No civil, criminal, or professional liability if acting in good faith. It would have to be shown by preponderance of the evidence that the person authorizing life-prolonging procedures acted in bad faith
WASHINGTON 11.94.010, *et seq.*	Appointed attorney-in-fact may make health care decisions on principal's behalf	(1) In writing; (2) principal designates another as his attorney-in-fact	Continues until revoked or terminated by principal, court-appointed guardian or court order			Anyone acting in good faith and without negligence shall incur no liability
WEST VIRGINIA 16-30A-1, *et seq.* Medical Power of Attorney		(1) 18 yrs.; (2) in writing; (3) signed by declarant or someone at his or her directive; (4) dated; (5) 2 witnesses; (6) notarized	Desires of principal at all times supersede effect of medical power of attorney. Revocable at any time by (1) destruction of document; (2) written revocation signed and dated; (3) verbal expression with witnesses present; (4) divorce if former spouse was designated	Valid if in compliance with laws of West Virginia or state where executed an expressly delegates health care decisions		No criminal civil liability for good faith compliance
WISCONSIN 155.01	Any care, treatment, service or procedure to diagnose, maintain, or treat physical or mental condition. Feeding tube may be withheld or withdrawn unless it would cause pain. Agent may not consent to withholding or withdrawing of orally ingested nutrition or hydration unless provision is medically contraindicated	(1) 18 yrs.; (2) in writing; (3) signed; (4) dated; (5) 2 witnesses; (6) voluntarily executed	Revocable at any time by (1) canceling or destroying document; (2) revocation in writing signed and dated; (3) verbal revocation in presence of 2 witnesses; (4) executing a subsequent power of attorney; (5) divorce if former spouse was attorney-in-fact			No civil, criminal, or professional liability if acting in good faith

(Continued)

Table 30a: Right to Die: Durable Power of Attorney—Continued

State/ Code Section	Specific Powers, Life-Prolonging Acts	Operative Facts	Revocation/Duration	Reciprocity	Transfer of Patient if Physician Unwilling	Immunity for Attending Physician
WYOMING 3-5-201, *et seq.*	Consent, refusal of consent, or withdrawal of any medical procedure, intervention, or nourishment by artificial means except for alleviation of pain	(1) Signed; (2) dated; (3) 2 witnesses; (4) notarized; (5) attorney-in-fact authorized to make health care decisions	Principal's wishes if able to give informed consent take precedent over durable power of attorney. Revocable by (1) notifying attorney-in-fact in writing; (2) notifying health care provider in writing; (3) divorce if former spouse was attorney-in-fact			No criminal, civil, or professional liability if acting in good faith

(Continued)

Table 30b: Right to Die: Euthanasia

State	Code Section	Mercy Killing Condoned	Operative Facts
ALABAMA	22-8A-10; 22-8A-9(a)	Euthanasia not condoned or authorized nor is allowed any affirmative act or omission to end life other than to permit the natural process of dying	Withholding or withdrawal of life-sustaining procedures in accordance with this chapter shall not constitute assisting suicide.
ALASKA	18.12.080(F)	Euthanasia or mercy killing not condoned, authorized, or approved by Alaska law.	
ARIZONA	36-3210	Euthanasia, suicide, or assisted suicide not authorized, or approved by Arizona law.	
ARKANSAS	20-17-210(a), (g)	Euthanasia or mercy killing not condoned, authorized, or approved by Arkansas law.	Death resulting from withholding or withdrawal of life-sustaining treatment pursuant to declaration and in accordance with this section does not constitute suicide or homicide.
CALIFORNIA	Civ. Code §2443; H&S §7191.5	Nothing condones, authorizes, or approves mercy killing or permits an affirmative act or omission to end life other than the withholding of health care pursuant to a durable power of attorney so as to permit the natural process of dying. In making health care decisions under a durable power of attorney, an attempted suicide shall not be construed to indicate a decision of the principal that health care treatment be restricted or inhibited.	Death resulting from withholding or withdrawing life-sustaining treatment in accordance with the Natural Death Act does not constitute for any purposes suicide or homicide.
COLORADO	15-14-504; 15-18-111, 112; 15-18.5-101(3); 15-18.6-108	Nothing condones, authorizes, or approves euthanasia or mercy killing or shall be construed as permitting any affirmative or deliberate act to end a person's life except to permit natural death.	Withholding or withdrawing life-sustaining procedures pursuant to a declaration and the law shall not constitute a suicide or homicide.
CONNECTICUT	No statutory provisions		
DELAWARE	16 §2507		Neither execution of declaration nor fact that maintenance medical treatment is withheld from patient in accordance with the declaration shall constitute suicide.
DISTRICT OF COLUMBIA	6-2430; 21-2212	Euthanasia not condoned, authorized, or approved nor is any affirmative or deliberate act or omission to end a human life other than to permit the natural process of dying.	Withholding or withdrawing life-sustaining procedures in accordance with the Natural Death chapter shall not constitute the crime of suicide.
FLORIDA	765.309	Nothing construed to condone, authorize, or approve mercy killing or euthanasia or to permit any affirmative or deliberate act or omission to end life other than to permit the natural process of dying.	The withdrawing of life-prolonging procedures from a patient in accordance with any provision of this chapter does not for any purpose constitute a suicide.

(Continued)

Table 30b: Right to Die: Euthanasia—Continued

State	Code Section	Mercy Killing Condoned	Operative Facts
GEORGIA	31-32-9		The making of a living will pursuant to this chapter shall not for any purpose constitute a suicide.
HAWAII	327D-13	Euthanasia not condoned or authorized by Hawaii law.	Death resulting from withholding or withdrawal of life sustaining procedures does not constitute suicide.
IDAHO	No statutory provisions		
ILLINOIS	35/9(f)	Nothing in this Act shall be construed to condone mercy killing or to permit any affirmative or deliberate act or omission to end life other than to permit natural process of dying.	Withholding or withdrawal of death delaying procedures from a qualified patient or in accordance with terms of a health care agency shall not constitute suicide or homicide.
INDIANA	16-8-11-20; 16-8-12-11	Euthanasia not condoned or authorized by Indiana law.	
IOWA	144A.11.6	Sections of code should not be construed to condone, authorize, or approve mercy killing or euthanasia or permit any affirmative or deliberate act or omission to end life other than to permit the natural process of dying.	
KANSAS	65-28.108(a); 65-28.109	Nothing in this act shall be construed to condone, authorize, or approve mercy killing or to permit any affirmative or deliberate act or omission to end life other than to permit the natural process of dying.	Acting in accordance with the Natural Death Act shall not for any purpose constitute a suicide or the crime of assisting suicide.
KENTUCKY	311.636	Nothing in KRS §§311.622-311.644 shall be construed to condone mercy killing or euthanasia or to permit any affirmative or deliberate act to end life other than to permit natural process of dying.	Withholding or withdrawal of life prolonging treatment shall not constitute suicide.
LOUISIANA	1299.58.10(A), (B)	Nothing in this section shall be construed to condone, authorize, or approve mercy killing or euthanasia or to permit any affirmative or deliberate act or omission to end life other than to permit the natural process of dying.	The withholding of life-sustaining procedures in accordance with this part shall not for any purpose constitute suicide.
MAINE	5-711		Neither the decision to withhold or withdraw or actual withholding or withdrawal of life sustaining treatment which results in death shall be deemed a suicide or homicide.
MARYLAND	Health-Gen. §5-613		Act authorized by this subtitle may not for any purpose be considered to be a suicide or a violation of any criminal law or standard of professional conduct.

(Continued)

Table 30b: Right to Die: Euthanasia—Continued

State	Code Section	Mercy Killing Condoned	Operative Facts
MASSACHUSETTS	Ch. 201D §12	Nothing in this chapter shall be construed to constitute, condone, authorize, or approve suicide or mercy killing or to permit any affirmative or deliberate act to end one's own life other than to permit the natural process of dying.	
MICHIGAN	§700.497	Designation of a patient advocate shall not be construed to condone, allow, permit, authorize, or approve suicide or homicide. Senate Bill No. 211, Act 3, Public Acts of 1993: §7: A person with knowledge that another person intends to commit or attempt to commit suicide and who intentionally either (a) provides the physical means by which the other person attempts or commits suicide, or (b) participates in a physical act by which the other person attempts or commits suicide is guilty of criminal assistance to suicide, a felony punishable by imprisonment for up to 4 yrs. or by a fine up to $2000. This section shall not affect any other laws that may be applicable to withholding or withdrawing medical treatment by a licensed health care professional. A physician who administers, prescribes, or dispenses medications or procedures to relieve a person's pain or discomfort, even if it may hasten or increase the risk of death, is not guilty of assistance to suicide unless the medications or procedures are knowingly and intentionally administered or prescribed to cause death. The Michigan Commission on Death and Dying was created and commissioned to develop and submit to the legislature recommendations concerning the voluntary self-termination of life. Section 7 is repealed 6 months after the date the commission makes its recommendations.	
MINNESOTA	145B:14	Euthanasia, suicide, or assisted suicide not condoned or authorized by Minnesota law.	
MISSISSIPPI	41-41-119		Authorization of withdrawal of life-sustaining mechanisms under the Withdrawal of Life-Saving Mechanisms Act may not for any purpose be considered suicide.

(Continued)

Table 30b: Right to Die: Euthanasia—Continued

State	Code Section	Mercy Killing Condoned	Operative Facts
MISSOURI	404.845; 459.055	Euthanasia not condoned or authorized by Missouri law.	When patient's death results from withholding or withdrawing life-sustaining treatment in accordance with a durable power of attorney, it shall not constitute a suicide or homicide for any purpose.
MONTANA	50-9-205(7)	Montana's Right of the Terminally Ill Act does not condone, authorize, or approve mercy killing or euthanasia.	Under §§50-10-101, *et seq.*, an individual may register and wear a Health & Safety Board certified identification that signifies the possessor has executed a declaration under §50-9-103 and that his or her attending physician has issued a Do Not Resuscitate Order and has documented grounds for the order in the possessor's medical file.
NEBRASKA	20-412(7); 28-308	This Act does not confer any new rights regarding provision or rejection of specific medical care and does not alter laws regarding assisted suicide. Nor does it approve, authorize, or condone assisted suicide. Assisting suicide is a Class IV felony.	
NEVADA	449.670	Euthanasia not condoned or authorized by Nevada law.	
NEW HAMPSHIRE	137-H:10, 13	Euthanasia not condoned or authorized by New Hampshire law.	Withdrawing or withholding life-sustaining procedures from onesself by living will or otherwise or doing so pursuant to instructions in an instrument or at request of terminal patient pursuant to provisions in these code sections is not condoned, authorized, or approved by statute
NEW JERSEY	26:2H-77		Withholding or withdrawing of life-sustaining treatment pursuant to an advanced directive for health care when performed in good faith shall not constitute suicide, assisted suicide, or active euthanasia.
NEW MEXICO	No statutory provisions		
NEW YORK	Pub. Health Law §2989	Statute not to be construed to permit agent to consent to any act or omission to which the principal could not consent under law.	
NORTH CAROLINA	90-320(b)	Provisions in the act do not authorize any affirmative or deliberate act or omission to end life other than to permit natural process of dying.	Withholding life support is not considered cause of death for civil or criminal purposes.
NORTH DAKOTA	23-06.5-01	Euthanasia is not condoned or authorized by North Dakota law, nor is any other act or omission other than to allow the natural process of dying.	

(Continued)

Table 30b: Right to Die: Euthanasia—Continued

State	Code Section	Mercy Killing Condoned	Operative Facts
OHIO	2133.12(A), (D)	Euthanasia is not condoned or authorized by Ohio law.	Death of any patient resulting from withholding life-sustaining treatment does not constitute suicide, murder or any homicide offense for any purpose.
OKLAHOMA	Tit. 63 §§3101.2, 3101.12(A), (F)	Euthanasia is not condoned or authorized by Oklahoma law.	Death from withdrawing life-sustaining treatment shall not constitute homicide or suicide.
OREGON	127.570	Nothing in statute is intended to condone, authorize, or approve mercy killing or permit affirmative or deliberate act or omission to end life, other than to allow the natural process of dying.	
PENNSYLVANIA	No statutory provisions		
RHODE ISLAND	23-4.10-9	Euthanasia is not condoned or authorized by Rhode Island law.	
SOUTH CAROLINA	44-77-110, 130; 62-5-504(m), (o)	Euthanasia is not condoned or authorized by South Carolina law, nor is any act or omission other than to allow the natural process of dying.	Effectuation of health care power of attorney does not constitute suicide for any purpose.
SOUTH DAKOTA	34-12D-14, 20	Euthanasia is not condoned or authorized by South Dakota law.	Death by withdrawing or withholding life-sustaining treatment does not constitute suicide or homicide.
TENNESSEE	32-11-110		Following provisions of a directive does not constitute suicide.
TEXAS	Health & Safety §672.020	Euthanasia is not condoned or authorized by Texas law, nor is any act or omission other than to allow the natural process of dying.	
UTAH	75-2-1116, 1118	Euthanasia is not condoned or authorized by Utah law.	Compliance with a directive is not suicide.
VERMONT	Tit. 18, §526D		Acting pursuant to terminal care document is not suicide.
VIRGINIA	54.1-2990, 2991	Euthanasia is not condoned or authorized by Virginia law, nor is any act or omission other than to allow the natural process of dying.	Acting in accordance with Natural Death Act statute is not suicide.
WASHINGTON	70.122.100	Euthanasia is not condoned or authorized by Washington law, nor is any act or omission other than to allow the natural process of dying.	
WEST VIRGINIA	16-30A-16	Euthanasia is not condoned or authorized by West Virginia law, nor is any act or omission other than to allow the natural process of dying.	
WISCONSIN	154.11; 155.70	Euthanasia is not condoned or authorized by Wisconsin law, nor is any act or omission other than to allow the natural process of dying.	Withholding or withdrawal of life-sustaining procedures or feeding tube does not constitute suicide.

(Continued)

Table 30b: Right to Die: Euthanasia—Continued

State	Code Section	Mercy Killing Condoned	Operative Facts
WYOMING	35-22-105, 109; 3-5-2-209, 211	Euthanasia is not condoned or authorized by Wyoming law, nor is any act or omission other than to allow the natural process of dying.	An incompetent with a terminal condition or irreversible coma may have life-sustaining measures withheld if family members agree in good faith that the patient, if competent, would forego the treatment.

Table 30c: Right to Die: Living Wills

State/Code Section	Specific Powers, Life-Prolonging Acts	Operative Facts	Revocation/Duration	Reciprocity	Transfer of Patient if Physician Unwilling	Immunity for Attending Physician
ALABAMA 22-8A-1 Natural Death Act	Any medical procedure or intervention serving only to prolong the dying process and death will occur whether or not such intervention is utilized; does not include medication or any medical procedure deemed necessary to provide comfort care or pain alleviation	(1) Adult; (2) in writing; (3) signed by declarant; (4) dated; (5) signed in presence of 2 or more witnesses over 19; (6) declaration should be substantially in statutory format	Revocable at any time by (1) destruction of document; (2) execution of written revocation by declarant; (3) oral revocation in presence of adult witness		Physician shall permit the patient to be transferred	No criminal, civil, or professional liability for physician acting in good faith pursuant to reasonable medical standards and pursuant to a declaration
ALASKA 18.12.010 Rights of Terminally Ill	Withholding or withdrawal of procedures that merely prolong the dying process and are not necessary for comfort or to alleviate pain; includes the administration of food and water by gastric tube or IV; declaration may provide declarant does not want nutrition and hydration administered intravenously or by gastric tube	(1) Competent; (2) 18 yrs.; (3) signed; (4) witnessed by 2 or acknowledged by person qualified to take acknowledgments	Revocable at any time and in any manner declarant is able to communicate intent to revoke without regard to physical/mental condition; effective upon communication	Declaration executed in another state in compliance with the law of that jurisdiction is effective	Physician may withdraw after services of another physician have been obtained	Physician causing the withholding or withdrawal of life-sustaining procedures from a qualified patient not subject to civil, criminal, or professional liability
ARIZONA 36-3201 Living Wills and Health Care Directives	Does not include comfort care but may include life-sustaining treatment artificially delaying the moment of death, CPR, drugs, electric shock, artificial breathing, artificially administered food and fluids	(1) Adult; (2) in writing; (3) language clearly indicating intent to create a living will; (4) dated; (5) signed; (6) witnessed by at least one adult or a notary public	Person may revoke health care directive or disqualify a surrogate by (1) written revocation; (2) orally notifying surrogate or health care provider; (3) making new health care directive; (4) any other act demonstrating specific intent to revoke	Health care directive prepared in another state is valid in this state if it was valid where and at the time it was adopted to the extent it does not conflict with the criminal laws of Arizona	Physician must effect prompt transfer to a physician willing to comply	Health care provider making good faith decisions in reliance on apparently genuine health care directive or decision of a surrogate is immune from criminal, civil, and professional discipline for that reliance
ARKANSAS 20-17-201, *et seq.*	Any medical procedure or intervention that will serve only to prolong the dying process or to maintain the patient in a condition of permanent unconsciousness	(1) Sound mind; (2) 18 yrs.; (3) signed by declarant; (4) witnessed by 2	Revocable at any time in any manner by the declarant without regard to the declarant's mental/physical condition; effective upon communication to attending physician	A declaration executed in another state in compliance with the laws of that state or Arkansas law is validly executed	Physician shall as promptly as practicable take all reasonable steps to transfer care to another physician	Physician whose actions under this chapter are in accord with reasonable medical standards is not subject to criminal, civil, or professional liability with respect to them

(Continued)

Table 30c: Right to Die: Living Wills—Continued

State/Code Section	Specific Powers, Life-Prolonging Acts	Operative Facts	Revocation/ Duration	Reciprocity	Transfer of Patient if Physician Unwilling	Immunity for Attending Physician
CALIFORNIA H&S §7185 Natural Death Act	Any medical procedure or intervention that will serve only to prolong the process of dying or an irreversible coma or persistent negative state; nutrition and hydration artificially administered may be withdrawn but not treatment to alleviate pain	(1) Sound mind; (2) over 18; (3) signed by declarant; (4) witnessed by 2; (5) declaration shall contain substantially the information in §7186.5	Revocable at any time in any manner without regard to declarant's mental/physical condition; revocation is effective upon its communication to the attending physician	Declaration executed in another state in compliance with the laws of that state or California law is valid	Physician shall take all reasonable steps as promptly as practical to transfer the patient to a physician who is willing to comply	Physician is not subject to civil, criminal, or professional liability for acting in good faith pursuant to declaration
COLORADO 15-18-102, *et seq.* Future Medical Treatment; 15-18.6-101, Directive Relating to Cardiopulmonary Resuscitation	Any medical procedure or intervention that would serve only to prolong the dying process; it shall not include any medical procedure for nourishment or to provide comfort or alleviate pain; however, artificial nourishment may be withdrawn pursuant to declaration that artificial nutrition (1) not be provided or continued when it is the only procedure being provided; (2) be continued for a specified period when it is the only procedure being provided	(1) Competent; (2) adult; (3) executed before 2 witnesses	Revocable by declarant orally, in writing, or by destruction of the declaration			No hospital or physician acting under direction of physician and participating in the withholding or withdrawal of life-sustaining procedures in compliance with a declaration shall be subject to any civil or criminal liability or licensing sanction therefore
CONNECTICUT 19a-570, *et seq.* Removal of Life Support	Any medical procedure or intervention serving only to postpone the moment of death or maintain individual in a state of permanent unconsciousness including artificial means of nutrition/ hydration, artificial respiration, CPR, but does not include comfort care and pain alleviation	(1) 18 yrs.; (2) signed; (3) dated; (4) presence of 2 witnesses; (5) in substantially form of §19a-515				Physician withholding, removing life-support system of an incapacitated patient shall not be civilly or criminally liable if decision was based on physician's (1) best medical judgment; (2) physician deems patient in a terminal condition; (3) patient's wishes were considered according to an executed document

(Continued)

Table 30c: Right to Die: Living Wills—Continued

State/Code Section	Specific Powers, Life-Prolonging Acts	Operative Facts	Revocation/ Duration	Reciprocity	Transfer of Patient if Physician Unwilling	Immunity for Attending Physician
DELAWARE 16 §2501, *et seq.*	Right to refuse medical or surgical treatment via written declaration instructing any physician to cease or refrain from medical or surgical treatment	(1) Legally adult, competent, of sound mind; (2) written dated declaration; (3) declarant in terminal condition confirmed in writing by 2 physicians; (4) signed by declarant or another person in declarant's presence and at his express direction; (5) dated; (6) 2 or more adult witnesses; (7) not pregnant	Revocable at any time without regard to declarant's mental state or competency by (1) destruction of declaration with intent to revoke; (2) oral statement in presence of 2 persons 18 years or older expressing intent to revoke; (3) written revocation signed and dated by declarant			No civil or criminal liability
DISTRICT OF COLUMBIA 6-2421, *et seq.* Natural Death Act	Any medical procedure or intervention which would serve only to artificially prolong the dying process and where death will occur whether or not such procedures are utilized; does not include medication or any medical procedure necessary to alleviate pain	(1) 18 yrs.; (2) in writing; (3) dated; (4) signed; (5) in presence of 2 or more witnesses over 18; (6) declaration should be in substantially the statutory form of §6-2422	Revocable at any time by declarant without regard to declarant's mental state by (1) destruction of documents; (2) written revocation signed and dated; (3) verbal expression of intent to revoke in presence of an 18 year old witness; desires of patient at all times supersede the effect of the declaration		Physician must effect a transfer and failure to do so shall constitute unprofessional conduct	No civil, criminal, professional liability for physician who acts in good faith pursuant to reasonable medical standard and to a declaration made

(Continued)

Table 30c: Right to Die: Living Wills—Continued

State/Code Section	Specific Powers, Life-Prolonging Acts	Operative Facts	Revocation/ Duration	Reciprocity	Transfer of Patient if Physician Unwilling	Immunity for Attending Physician
FLORIDA 765.101, *et seq.* Advanced Directive	Any medical procedure, treatment, or intervention which (1) utilizes mechanical or other artificial means to sustain, restore, supplant a spontaneous vital function and serves only to prolong the dying process of a patient in terminal condition; does not include medication or a medical procedure to alleviate pain; emergency medical services shall honor a do-not-resuscitate order; consent to CPR presumed absent a do-not-resuscitate order	(1) Competent; (2) adult; (3) signed by principal; (4) in presence of 2 subscribing witnesses	Revocable at any time by principal by (1) signed, dated writing; (2) destruction of the declaration; (3) oral expression of intent to revoke; (4) subsequent advance directive materially different from the previously executed advanced directive; (5) divorce revokes the designation of former spouse as surrogate	An advanced directive executed in another state in compliance with the laws of that state or Florida is validly executed	Physician should make reasonable efforts to transfer to a health care provider who will comply with the declaration; a physician unwilling to carry out the patient's wishes because of moral or ethical beliefs must within 7 days: (1) transfer the patient and pay the cost of transporting the patient to another health care provider or (2) carry out the wishes of the patient unless provisions of judicial intervention apply	Health care facility, provider or other person who acts under the direction of a health care facility, or provider is not subject to criminal prosecution or civil or professional liability for carrying out a health care decision
GEORGIA 31-32-1, *et seq.*	Any medical procedures or interventions which would serve only to prolong the dying process for a patient in a terminal condition or persistent vegetative state; may include the provision of nourishment and hydration but shall not include medication or any medical procedure to alleviate pain	(1) Competent; (2) adult; (3) signed by declarant; (4) in presence of 2 competent adults; (5) any declaration constituting declarant's intent shall be honored regardless of the form or when executed	Revocable at any time by declarant without regard to mental competency by (1) destruction of document; (2) declarant signs and dates a written revocation; (3) any verbal or nonverbal expression by declarant of intent to revoke which clearly revokes the living will as opposed to a will relating to the disposition of property after death			No physician acting in good faith in accordance with the requirements of this chapter shall be subject to any civil liability, criminal, or professional

(Continued)

Table 30c: Right to Die: Living Wills—Continued

State/Code Section	Specific Powers, Life-Prolonging Acts	Operative Facts	Revocation/ Duration	Reciprocity	Transfer of Patient if Physician Unwilling	Immunity for Attending Physician
HAWAII 327D-1, *et seq.*	Execute declaration directing provision, continuation, withholding, or withdrawal of any medical procedure or intervention including artificial provisions of fluids, nourishment, medication that when administered to patient will only serve to prolong dying process; does not include procedure necessary for patient's comfort or relief	(1) Competent person, age of majority; (2) in writing; (3) signed by declarant or another person in his presence and at his expressed direction; (4) dated; (5) signed in presence of 2 or more adult witnesses; (6) all signatures notarized; (7) not pregnant; (8) in terminal condition or permanent loss of ability to communicate concerning medical treatment	Revocable at any time by various methods including: (1) in writing signed and dated by declarant; (2) verbal expression by declarant in front of 2 witnesses; (3) canceling, destroying declaration in declarant's presence and at his direction; (4) verbal expression to attending physician	Document executed in another state is valid if it substantially complies with requirements of this chapter	Physician shall without delay make necessary arrangements to transfer patient and medical records to another physician; transfer without unreasonable delay or good faith attempt to transfer is not abandonment	No criminal prosecution or civil liability or deemed to have engaged in unprofessional conduct as result of withholding or withdrawal of life sustaining procedures unless absence of actual notice of revocation is result of negligence of health care provider, physician, or other person
IDAHO 39-4502 Natural Death Act; 39-4504, *et seq.* Living Will	Any medical procedure or intervention which utilizes mechanical means to sustain or supplant a vital function serving only to artificially prolong the moment of death and where death is imminent whether or not procedures are utilized; does not include the administration of medication or a medical procedure to alleviate pain; patient may choose whether to withhold nutrition and hydration	(1) Of sound mind; (2) voluntarily made; (3) 2 witnesses must sign	Revocable at any time by declarant without regard to competence by (1) destruction of the document; (2) by written, signed revocation; (3) by verbal expression of intent to revoke		Physician may withdraw without civil or criminal liability provided the physician makes a good faith effort to assist the patient in transferring	No civil or criminal liability for a physician acting in accordance with the wishes of the patient as expressed by statutory procedure
ILLINOIS 35/1, *et seq.* Illinois Living Will Act	Individual may execute document directing that if he is suffering from a terminal condition, then death–delaying procedure shall not be utilized for the prolongation of his life	(1) Sound mind and age of majority; (2) signed by declarant or another at declarant's direction; (3) 2 witnesses over 18; (4) not pregnant; (5) notify attending physician; (6) qualified patient	Revocable at any time by declarant (1) in writing signed and dated by declarant or person acting at his direction; (2) by oral expression in presence of witness or attending physician; (3) by destroying declaration in manner indicating intent to cancel; revocation is effective upon communication to attending physician	Declaration executed in another state in compliance with law of that state or Illinois is valid	Patient is responsible to initiate transfer; if patient not able to initiate transfer then attending physician shall without delay notify person with highest priority who is available, able, and willing to make arrangements for transfer	No physician, health care provider, or health care expert who in good faith and pursuant to reasonable medical standards causes or participates in withholding or withdrawal of death delaying procedure from qualified patient per declaration shall be subject to criminal or civil liability or be found to have committed an act of unprofessional conduct

(Continued)

Table 30c: Right to Die: Living Wills—Continued

State/Code Section	Specific Powers, Life-Prolonging Acts	Operative Facts	Revocation/ Duration	Reciprocity	Transfer of Patient if Physician Unwilling	Immunity for Attending Physician
INDIANA 16-8-11-1 Living Wills and Life Prolonging Procedures Act	Living will declarant may ask that life prolonging procedures that would serve only to artificially prolong dying process not be used in case of terminal diagnosis and incapacity, except that appropriate nutrition, hydration, and pain and comfort medication may not be withdrawn. Life Prolonging Procedures declarant may ask that all life-prolonging procedures that would extend life be used.	(1) Person of sound mind, 18 yrs. old; (2) voluntary; (3) in writing; (4) dated; (5) signed in presence of 2 witnesses; (6) notice to declarant's attending physician; (7) presumptive of declarant's intent.	Living will declaration is presumed valid. Revocable at any time by (1) signed writing; (2) physical destruction by declarant or at declarant's direction; (3) oral expression of revocation		Physician who refuses to comply shall transfer to another physician who will comply unless (1) physician believes declaration is invalid and (2) patient is unable to validate declaration	Destroying or falsifying a Living Will Declaration or a Life-Prolonging Declaration is a Class D felony. Destroying, falsifying, or concealing a revocation of a Declaration is a Class C felony. Act of withdrawing or withholding life-prolonging procedures pursuant to an executed living will shall not be construed to be an intervening force to affect the chain of proximate cause between the conduct of any person that placed the patient in a terminal condition and the patient's death
IOWA 144A.2 Life-Sustaining Procedures Act	(1) Declarant may declare desire to not have life-sustaining procedures employed to prolong life; (2) life sustaining procedures are those that utilize mechanical or artificial means to sustain, restore, or supplant a spontaneous vital function and/or when applied to a patient would only serve to prolong the dying process; declaration shall not be in effect when declarant is pregnant as long as fetus can develop to point of live birth	(1) Declarant competent adult; (2) signed in presence of 2 witnesses; (3) physician may presume declaration is valid; (4) actual notice of declaration to attending physician	Revocable at any time in any manner that declarant can communicate intent, without regard to mental or physical condition. Physician shall become part of medical records		Physician shall take reasonable steps to transfer to another physician	Individual or health care provider is not liable civilly or criminally or guilty of unprofessional conduct for complying in good faith with provisions in declaration. Persons complying with provisions in executed declaration may assert these code provisions as absolute defense

(Continued)

Table 30c: Right to Die: Living Wills—Continued

State/Code Section	Specific Powers, Life-Prolonging Acts	Operative Facts	Revocation/ Duration	Reciprocity	Transfer of Patient if Physician Unwilling	Immunity for Attending Physician
KANSAS 68-28, 101 Natural Death Act	Any medical procedure or intervention which would serve only to prolong the dying process and where death will occur whether or not such procedure is utilized. Does not include medication or any medical procedures necessary to alleviate pain	(1) Any adult; (2) in writing; (3) signed by declarant; (4) dated; (5) in presence of 2 or more adult witnesses	Revocable at any time by declarant by (1) destruction of document; (2) written revocation signed an dated by principal; (3) verbal expression in presence of adult witnesses. Effective upon receipt by physician. Desires of patient at all times supersede the declaration		Physician shall effect the transfer	No criminal, civil, or professional liability for acting in good faith pursuant to a declaration
KENTUCKY 311.622, *et seq.* Kentucky Living Will Act	Withholding or withdrawal of any medical procedure, treatment, or intervention which utilizes mechanical or other artificial means to sustain spontaneous vital function or affords no reasonable expectation of recovery from terminal condition and would only prolong dying process. Does not include medication or procedure to alleviate pain or provide nutrition or hydration.	(1) 18 years old; (2) in writing; (3) signed in presence of 2 subscribing witnesses; (4) notify attending physician who shall made declaration part of medical records; (5) diagnosed as having terminal condition; (6) not pregnant	Revocable by (1) written declaration signed and dated by declarant; (2) oral statement of intent to revoke; (3) destruction of declaration with intent to revoke; (4) effective immediately; (5) received by attending physician or health care facility		Physician must immediately inform patient and family or guardian and shall not impede transfer to another physician or health care facility	Not subject to criminal prosecution or civil liability or deemed to have engaged in unprofessional conduct
LOUISIANA 40:1299.58.1, *et seq.* Declarations Concerning Life-Sustaining Procedures	Any medical procedure or intervention, including but not limited to invasive administration of nutrition and hydration, which would serve only to prolong the dying process for a person diagnosed as having a terminal and irreversible condition. Does not include any measure necessary for comfort care	(1) Any adult; (2) written declaration; (3) signed by declarant; (4) in presence of 2 witnesses; (5) oral or nonverbal declaration may be made in presence of 2 witnesses by any non-written means of communication at any time subsequent to the diagnosis of a terminal and irreversible condition	Revocable at any time by declarant without regard to mental state or competency by (1) destruction of document; (2) written revocation signed and dated by declarant; (3) oral or nonverbal expression by the declarant of the intent to revoke. Effective upon communication to physician		Physician shall made a reasonable effort to transfer the patient to another physician	Any health care facility, physician, or other person acting under the direction of a physician shall not be civilly, criminally, or professionally liable for withholding life-sustaining procedures in accordance with the provisions of this chapter

(Continued)

Table 30c: Right to Die: Living Wills—Continued

State/Code Section	Specific Powers, Life-Prolonging Acts	Operative Facts	Revocation/ Duration	Reciprocity	Transfer of Patient if Physician Unwilling	Immunity for Attending Physician
MAINE 18-A§§5-701, *et seq.* Uniform Rights of Terminally Ill Act	Any medical procedure or intervention administered only to prolong process of dying. May include artificially administered nutrition and hydration	(1) Of sound mind and over 18; (2) signed by declarant or another at his direction; (3) witnessed by 2 people; (4) communicated to attending physician; (5) declarant determined to be in terminal condition or persistent vegetative state and no longer able to make or communicate decisions regarding administration of life-sustaining treatment; (6) physician records terms of declaration in medical record	Revocable at any time and in any manner. Revocation effective upon communication to attending physician or health care provider by declarant or witness to revocation	Declaration executed in another state in compliance with laws of that state and Maine is valid	Attending physician or other health care provider who is unwilling shall take all reasonable steps as promptly as practicable to transfer to another physician willing to comply. Willful failure to transfer is Class E crime	Physician or other health care provider whose action is in accord with reasonable medical standards is not subject to criminal or civil liability or discipline for unprofessional conduct
MARYLAND 5-601, *et seq.*	Any medical procedure, treatment, or intervention which uses mechanical or other artificial means to maintain, restore a spontaneous vital function or afford patient no reasonable expectation of recovery from a terminal condition which when applied to terminal patient would secure only a precarious and burdensome prolongation of life. Does not include medication or procedure necessary to alleviate pain or provide comfort care or provision of food or water	(1) Voluntary; (2) dated and in writing; (3) signed by declarant or in declarant's presence on behalf of declarant; (4) executed in presence of 2 adult witnesses; (5) not pregnant; (6) communicated to physician who shall made it part of declarant's medical records	Revocable at any time by (1) written statement signed and dated by declarant or person acting at declarant's direction; (2) expression declaring intent to revoke; (3) destroying the declaration; (4) marking or altering declaration in such a manner to indicate intention to revoke it	Declaration executed out-of-state by nonresident is effective if declaration is in compliance with these provisions	Attending physician shall make every reasonable effort to transfer declarant to another physician	Any person in good faith not subject to civil or criminal liability and may not be found to have committed professional misconduct
MASSACHUSETTS No statutory provisions						
MICHIGAN No statutory provisions						

(Continued)

Table 30c: Right to Die: Living Wills—Continued

State/Code Section	Specific Powers, Life-Prolonging Acts	Operative Facts	Revocation/ Duration	Reciprocity	Transfer of Patient if Physician Unwilling	Immunity for Attending Physician
MINNESOTA 145B.01, *et seq.*	Decisions on whether to begin, continue, increase, limit, discontinue, or not begin care, treatment, services, or procedures to maintain, diagnose, or treat an individual's physical condition when the individual is in a terminal condition. Decisions must be based on reasonable medical practice including (1) continuation of appropriate care to maintain comfort, hygiene, human dignity, and alleviate pain; (2) oral administration of food and water to a patient who accepts it, except for clearly documented medical reasons	(1) Competent adult; (2) signed by declarant; (3) signed by 2 witnesses or notary public; (4) must state preference regarding artificial administration of nutrition and hydration or give decision to proxy; (5) must be in substantially the statutory form	Revocable at any time in any manner by declarant without regard to declarant's physical or mental condition. Effective upon communication to physician. Divorce revokes any designation of the former spouse as a proxy to make health care decisions	Effective when executed in another state if it substantially complies with Minnesota law	Physician must notify competent declarant of unwillingness but has no duty to transfer. If physician received living will from competent patient and did not notify declarant of unwillingness to comply and declarant subsequently becomes incompetent, physician must transfer	
MISSISSIPPI 41-41-101, *et seq.* Withdrawal of Life-Saving Mechanisms	May authorize the withdrawal of life-sustaining mechanisms defined as cessation of use of extraordinary techniques and applications including mechanical devises which prolong life through artificial means	(1) 18 or older; (2) mentally competent; (3) signed by at least 2 witnesses; (4) filed with Bureau of Vital Statistics of the State Board of Health; (5) must be in substantially statutory form, §41-41-107	Revocable if revocation is signed by declarant and at least 2 witnesses in substantially same form as §41-41-109 and shall be filed with bureau of vital statistics of state board of health. If declarant wishes to revoke authorization of life-sustaining mechanisms but is physically unable to execute a revocation in preceding manner, a clear expression by declarant, oral or otherwise, of wish to revoke the authorization is effective as a revocation		Physician has duty to cooperate in the transfer of the patient to another physician	Physician acting in good faith pursuant to a declaration who causes withdrawal of life-sustaining mechanisms is not guilty of a criminal offense, or civil or professional liability

(Continued)

Table 30c: Right to Die: Living Wills—Continued

State/Code Section	Specific Powers, Life-Prolonging Acts	Operative Facts	Revocation/ Duration	Reciprocity	Transfer of Patient if Physician Unwilling	Immunity for Attending Physician
MISSOURI 459.010	Any medical procedure or intervention which would serve only to prolong artificially the dying process where death will occur within a short time whether or not such procedure or intervention is utilized. Does not include medication or procedure to alleviate pain or any procedure to provide nutrition or hydration	(1) Competent person; (2) in writing; (3) signed by declarant; (4) dated; (5) if not wholly in declarant's handwriting, signed in presence of 2 adult witnesses	Revocable at any time in any manner declarant is able to communicate intent to revoke, without regard for mental or physical condition. Directions of declarant shall at all times supersede a declaration		Physician must take all reasonable steps to effect the transfer of a declarant	No criminal, civil, or professional liability for acting in good faith pursuant to a declaration
MONTANA 50-9-101; 50-9-201; 50-10-101 Montana Rights of the Terminally Ill Act	Withholding or withdrawal of life-sustaining treatment, defined as any medical procedure or intervention that will serve only to prolong the dying process. Qualified patient may designate another individual to make decisions governing withholding or withdrawal of life-sustaining treatment. Life-sustaining procedures may not be withdrawn when qualified patient is known to be pregnant and when it is likely fetus will result in live birth	(1) 18 years or more and of sound mind; (2) signed by declarant or another at declarant's direction; (3) witnessed by 2 individuals; (4) communicated to physician and made part of patient's medical record; (5) declared to be terminal and no longer able to make decisions regarding life-sustaining treatment; (6) absent contrary actual notice, physician or health care provider may presume that declaration is valid	Revocable at any time in any manner without regard to physical or mental condition. Effective upon communication to attending physician or health care provider. Health care provider or emergency medical services personnel in receipt of such communication shall act upon revocation an communicate it to attending physician at earliest opportunity. Revocation shall become part of declarant's medical record	Declaration made in another state in compliance with that state's laws executed in a substantially similar manner to laws of Montana is effective	Attending physician or health care provider who is unable or unwilling to comply shall take all reasonable steps as promptly as practicable to transfer to another who is willing	Attending physician or health care provider not subject to civil or criminal liability or guilty of unprofessional conduct
NEBRASKA 20-401, *et seq.* Rights of the Terminally Ill Act	Any medical procedure or intervention that will serve only to prolong the process of dying or maintain the patient in a persistent vegetative act. Does not affect physician's responsibility to provide treatment, including nutrition and hydration for patient's comfort or alleviation of pain. Life-sustaining treatment shall be provided if declarant is pregnant and fetus is likely to develop to the point of live birth	(1) Adult of sound mind; (2) signed by declarant or another at declarant's direction; (3) witnessed by 2 adults or notary public; (4) communicated to attending physician	Revocable at any time in any manner effective upon communication to physician or other health care provider	Declaration executed in another state in compliance with that state or Nebraska is valid	Physician shall take prompt and reasonable steps to transfer to another physician	Not subject to civil, criminal, or professional discipline in the absence of knowledge of revocation or whose action under this Act is in accord with reasonable medical standards. Unjustifiable violation of patient's directions shall be a civil cause of action maintainable by patient or patient's next officer

(Continued)

Table 30c: Right to Die: Living Wills—Continued

State/Code Section	Specific Powers, Life-Prolonging Acts	Operative Facts	Revocation/ Duration	Reciprocity	Transfer of Patient if Physician Unwilling	Immunity for Attending Physician
NEVADA 449.535, *et seq.* Uniform Act on Rights of the Terminally Ill	Any medical procedure or intervention that serves only to prolong the process of dying. Artificial nutrition and hydration by way of gastro-intestinal tract is considered medical procedure or life sustaining treatment	(1) 18 yrs. or older; (2) may designate another to make decisions governing withholding or withdrawing; (3) signed by declarant or another at declarant's direction; (4) 2 witnesses	Revocable at any time and in any manner. Effective upon communication to the attending physician or other provider of health care	Declaration executed in another state in compliance with the law of that state or of this state is valid	Physician shall take all reasonable steps as promptly as possible to transfer care of declarant to another physician	Not subject to civil, criminal liability or professional discipline if acted in good faith
NEW HAMPSHIRE 137-H:1	Qualified patient may instruct physician to provide, withhold, or withdraw life-sustaining procedures in the event the person is in a terminal condition or is permanently unconscious. "Life-sustaining procedures" means any medical procedure or intervention which utilizes mechanical or artificial means to sustain, restore, or supplant a vital function which would only serve to artificially postpone the moment of death, not including medication, sustenance, or performance of any medical procedure to alleviate pain or provide comfort. Procedures that may be withheld include feeding tubes and IV hydration, etc., but shall not include "sustenance," the natural ingestion of food or fluids by eating and drinking	(1) in writing; (2) signed by declarant (3) 2 witnesses; (4) upon request, physician shall made document part of medical record	Revocable by (1) destroying document; (2) oral or written revocation before 2 witnesses. Revocation effective upon notice to attending physician	Documents executed in another state are enforceable if they comply with New Hampshire state laws	Physician unwilling or unable to comply shall notify and inform the patient and/or patient's family. Patient or his family may then request transfer to another physician	Physician or health care professional is immune from civil or criminal liability for good faith actions in keeping with reasonable medical standards pursuant to the living will. Withholding or withdrawing of life-sustaining procedures pursuant to executed living will shall not be construed to be suicide "for any legal purpose."

(Continued)

Table 30c: Right to Die: Living Wills—Continued

State/Code Section	Specific Powers, Life-Prolonging Acts	Operative Facts	Revocation/ Duration	Reciprocity	Transfer of Patient if Physician Unwilling	Immunity for Attending Physician
NEW JERSEY 26:2H-53, *et seq.* An instruction directive	Decisions to accept or refuse any treatment, service, or procedure used to diagnose, treat, or care for a patient's physical or mental condition including life-sustaining treatment. Includes decisions on use of any medical device or procedure, artificially provided fluids and nutrition drugs, surgery, or therapy that uses mechanical or other artificial means to sustain, restore, or supplant a vital bodily function and thereby increase the expected life span of a patient	(1) Competent; (2) adult; (3) signed; (4) dated; (5) in presence of 2 witnesses or in front of a notary public, attorney, or another person authorized to administer oaths. May be substituted by video or audio tape recording	Revocable by oral or written notification or execution of subsequent directive. Divorce revokes former spouse's designation as the health care representative. Patient's clearly expressed wishes take precedent over any patient's decision or instruction directive	Effective if executed in compliance with New Jersey law or the laws of another state. Effective if executed in a foreign country in compliance with that country's laws or the laws of New Jersey and is not contrary to the public policy of New Jersey	Physician should act as soon as practicable to effect an appropriate, respectful, and timely transfer of care and to assure that patient is not abandoned or treated disrespectfully	No civil, criminal, or professional liability for any physician acting in good faith pursuant to this act
NEW MEXICO 24-7-1, *et seq.*	May refuse maintenance medical treatment designed solely to sustain the life processes	(1) Of sound mind; (2) age of majority; (3) document must be executed with the same formalities as required of a valid will under the Probate Code. If a minor has been certified under the Right to Die Act as suffering a terminal illness or irreversible coma, an adult spouse or parent/guardian may execute the document on his behalf	Revocable at any destruction of the document or a contrary indication expressed in the presence of an adult witness. A minor may also revoke in the same ways		Physician must take appropriate steps to transfer the patient to another qualified physician	No civil or criminal liability for acting pursuant to statute in good faith
NEW YORK No statutory provisions						
NORTH CAROLINA 90-320, *et seq.* Right to Natural Death	Declarant may instruct attending physicians to withhold extraordinary means to keep declarant alive which would only serve to postpone artificially the moment of death by sustaining, restoring, or supplanting a vital function	(1) Signed; (2) 2 witnesses; (3) dated; (4) notarized or proved before a clerk	Revocable in any manner by which declarant is able to communicate without regard for mental or physical state			Withholding or discontinuing of extraordinary means shall not be considered cause of death for civil or criminal purposes. These provisions may be asserted as a defense to any civil or criminal suits or charges filed against a health care provider

(Continued)

Table 30c: Right to Die: Living Wills—Continued

State/Code Section	Specific Powers, Life-Prolonging Acts	Operative Facts	Revocation/ Duration	Reciprocity	Transfer of Patient if Physician Unwilling	Immunity for Attending Physician
NORTH DAKOTA 23.06.4-01, *et seq.*	Any medical procedure, treatment, or intervention that serves only to prolong the process of dying. Does not include the provision of the appropriate nutrition and hydration or any medical procedure to alleviate pain	(1) Sound mind; (2) 18 yrs.; (3) signed by declarant; (4) witnessed by 2 persons	Revocable at any time in any manner as long as declarant is competent, including (1) by signed, dated writing; (2) destruction of document; (3) oral expression of intent to revoke. Effective upon communication to physician or other health care provider	Effective if executed in another state by a resident of that state in compliance with the laws of that state or of North Dakota	Physician must take all reasonable steps to transfer patient to physician willing to comply with statute	No civil, criminal, or professional liability for actions authorized by statute unless done in a grossly negligent manner
OHIO 2133.01, *et seq.*	Any medical procedure, treatment, intervention, or other measure that will serve principally to prolong the process of dying. Declarant may authorize withholding hydration and nutrition	(1) Adult; (2) of sound mind; (3) signed by declarant; (4) dated; (5) in presence of 2 witnesses or a notary public	Revocable at any time and in any manner effective when expressed and communicated to a witness or physician	Effective if executed in another state in compliance with that law or in substantial compliance with Ohio law	Physician may not prevent or unreasonably delay a transfer	No civil criminal or professional liability for physician acting in good faith within the scope of their authority
OKLAHOMA Tit. 63 §3101.13; §3081.1	Any medical procedure or intervention that will serve only to prolong the dying process including artificial administration of nutrition and hydration if declarant has specifically authorized its withdrawal. Does not include treatment to alleviate pain or the normal consumption of food and water	(1) 18 yrs.; (2) of sound mind; (3) signed by declarant; (4) witnessed by 2 adults	Revocable in whole or in part in any manner at any time without regard to declarant's mental or physical condition. Effective upon communication to physician	Effective if complies with Oklahoma law or in compliance with law of another state so long as it does not exceed authorizations allowed under Oklahoma law	Physician shall take all reasonable steps to arrange for care by another physician	No civil, criminal, or professional liability for carrying out the advance directive pursuant to statute
OREGON 127.605, *et seq.* Directive to Physician	Life-sustaining acts means mechanical or other artificial means to sustain, restore, or supplant a vital function that is used to maintain life of a person suffering from a terminal condition and serves only to prolong artificially the moment of death	(1) In writing; (2) signed by two witnesses	Revocable by declarant or someone in his presence destroying document; by written revocation; duration until declarant revokes or regains consciousness after a comatose condition			No liability if in good faith has acted on fully executed directive
PENNSYLVANIA No statutory provisions						

(Continued)

Table 30c: Right to Die: Living Wills—Continued

State/Code Section	Specific Powers, Life-Prolonging Acts	Operative Facts	Revocation/ Duration	Reciprocity	Transfer of Patient if Physician Unwilling	Immunity for Attending Physician
RHODE ISLAND 23-4.11-2, *et seq.*	Any medical procedure or intervention serving only to prolong the dying process. Does not include anything necessary to alleviate pain	(1) 18 yrs.; (2) signed; (3) in presence of 2 witnesses	Revocable at any time in any manner by which declarant is able to communicate the intent to revoke without regard to physical or mental condition. Only effective upon communication to physician by declarant or one witnessing the revocation	Declaration executed in another state in compliance with the laws of that state is valid.	Physician must effect a transfer	No civil, criminal, or professional liability for acting in accordance with requirements of the statute
SOUTH CAROLINA 44-77-10, *et seq.*	Medical procedures or intervention serving only to prolong the dying process; does not include treatment for comfort care or pain alleviation; declarant should indicate whether nutrition and hydration through surgically implanted tubes is desired	(1) Declaration must set out intent for no life-sustaining procedures; (2) signed; (3) dated; (4) in presence of officer authorized to administer oaths; (5) presence of 2 witnesses	(1) Destruction of document when communicated to physician; (2) written revocation signed and dated upon communication to physician; oral expression of intent to revoke when communicated to physician; communication of oral revocation may be made by someone present when evocation made, if communicated within reasonable time and declarant is physically or mentally able to confirm		Physician must make a reasonable effort to locate a physician who will effectuate patient's declaration	No criminal or civil liability for acting in good faith
SOUTH DAKOTA 34-12D-1, *et seq.*	Any medical procedure or intervention that will serve only to postpone death or maintain person in state of permanent unconsciousness. Does not include comfort care, hygiene and human dignity, oral administration of food and water, or medical procedure to alleviate pain	(1) Competent adult; (2) signed by declarant; (3) witnessed by 2 adults; (4) may be in presence of notary public	Revocable at any time in any manner without regard to declarant's physical or mental condition. Effective upon communication to physician or other health care provider		Unwilling physician must make a reasonable effort to transfer patient to a physician who will honor the declaration	No civil, criminal, or professional liability for giving effect to a declaration

(Continued)

Table 30c: Right to Die: Living Wills—Continued

State/Code Section	Specific Powers, Life-Prolonging Acts	Operative Facts	Revocation/ Duration	Reciprocity	Transfer of Patient if Physician Unwilling	Immunity for Attending Physician
TENNESSEE 32-11-101, *et seq.*	Any procedure, treatment to diagnose, assess, or treat a disease, illness, or injury. Includes surgery, drugs, transfusions, mechanical ventilation, dialysis, CPR, artificial nourishment, hydration or other nutrients, radiation. Death by starvation or dehydration allowed only if specifically directed	(1) Competent adult; (2) signed; (3) in presence of 2 witnesses	Revocable at any time by declarant regardless of mental state if effectively communicated to the physician by written revocation dated and signed or oral statement made to physician	Effective if in compliance with Tennessee law or the law of the state of declarant's residence	Unwilling physician must make every reasonable effort to assist in a transfer. Failure to do so will subject him to civil and professional liability	No civil, criminal, or professional liability if acting in accord with reasonable medical standards
TEXAS Health & Safety Code §672.001, *et seq.* Natural Death Act; Written Directive	May designate a person to make treatment decisions in the event declarant becomes comatose or otherwise incompetent. Medical procedure or intervention that uses mechanical or other artificial means to sustain, restore, or supplant a vital function. Does not include administration of medication or performance of procedure to provide comfort or alleviate pain	(1) Competent adult; (2) 2 witnesses; (3) may be oral with 2 witnesses; (4) written directive shall become a part of medical record of declarant	Revocable at any time without regard to declarant's mental state or competency. May be revoked by declarant or someone in presence destroying document; by signed written revocation; orally stating intent to revoke. Effective when delivered or mailed to attending physician, or when physician notified of oral revocation. Directive effective until revoked. Desire of qualified competent patient supersedes directive		Unwilling physician must make reasonable effort to transfer patient to another physician	Immune from effects of revocation if not adequately notified. No criminal or civil liability for failing to effectuate a directive. By complying with legal directive, one does not commit act of criminally aiding suicide. It is Class A misdemeanor to destroy or conceal directive without declarant's consent. A person is guilty of homicide if they procure directive by forgery or deception
UTAH 75-2-1101; Directive	Any medical procedure or intervention that would serve only to prolong the dying process; does not include medication, sustenance, or any procedure to alleviate pain	(1) 18 yrs.; (2) in writing; (3) signed by declarant or at his directive; (4) dated; (5) signed in presence of 2 or more witnesses	Current wishes of declarant take precedent over any directive. Revocable at any time by signed revocation or destruction of document or oral expression of intent to revoke in presence of witnesses. Effective on receipt by physician		Unwilling physician required to transfer patient	No civil, criminal, or professional liability for good faith compliance with a directive

(Continued)

Table 30c: Right to Die: Living Wills—Continued

State/Code Section	Specific Powers, Life-Prolonging Acts	Operative Facts	Revocation/ Duration	Reciprocity	Transfer of Patient if Physician Unwilling	Immunity for Attending Physician
VERMONT Tit. 18 §§5251, *et seq.* Terminal Care Document	Any medical procedure or intervention utilizing mechanical or other artificial means to sustain, restore, supplant a vital function serving only to postpone the moment of death and where patient is in a terminal state according to judgment of physician	(1) 18 yrs.; (2) of sound mind; (3) in presence of 2 or more witnesses	Revocable orally in presence of 2 or more witnesses or by destroying the document		Unwilling physician must assist in selecting another physician willing to honor patient's directive	No civil or criminal liability for physician acting pursuant to the terminal care document
VIRGINIA 54.1-2981, *et seq.* Natural Death Act of Virginia; Written Advanced Directive	Any medical procedure, treatment, intervention, utilizing mechanical or other artificial means to sustain, restore, or supplant a vital function. Includes artificially administered hydration and nutrition but does not include any medication or procedure to alleviate pain. Includes CPR	(1) Written declaration; (2) signed in presence of 2 witnesses; (3) oral declaration in presence of physician and 2 witnesses; (4) witness cannot be spouse or blood relative. Life-prolonging procedures can be withheld without declaration if incapable of communication, and there is agreement with physician or specified party	Revocable at any time by (1) signed, dated writing; (2) physical cancellation by destruction of declaration; (3) oral expression of intent to revoke. Effective upon communication to attending physician	Directive executed in another state valid if in compliance with Virginia law or law of state where executed	Unwilling physician shall make reasonable effort to transfer patient to another physician, even if physician thinks it medically or ethically inappropriate	No civil, criminal, or professional liability if acting in good faith. It would have to be shown by preponderance of the evidence that the person authorizing life-prolonging procedures acted in bad faith
WASHINGTON 70.122.010, *et seq.*	Withdrawal or withholding of any medical or surgical procedure or intervention which utilizes mechanical or other artificial means to sustain, restore, or supplant a vital function which would serve only to artificially prolong life. Shall not include administration of medication to alleviate pain	(1) Any adult; (2) signed by declarant; (2) presence of 2 witnesses	Revocable at any time by defacing or destroying document; written revocation signed and dated and communicated to attending physician; oral revocation to physician by declarant or one acting on behalf of declarant			No civil, criminal, or professional liability if acting in good faith unless otherwise negligent
WEST VIRGINIA 15.30-2, *et seq.*	Any medical procedure or intervention which should serve solely to artificially prolong the dying process; does not include medication or other medical procedure necessary for comfort or to alleviate pain	(1) 18 yrs.; (2) in writing; (3) executed by declarant or at his direction; (4) dated; (5) in presence of 2 witnesses; (6) in front of notary public	Revocable at any time without regard to declarant's mental state by destruction of document, written revocation effective on delivery or verbal expression in presence of a witness	Valid in West Virginia if executed in compliance with West Virginia law or the law of state where executed	Unwilling physician must effect a transfer	No criminal or civil liability if acting in good faith

(Continued)

Table 30c: Right to Die: Living Wills—Continued

State/Code Section	Specific Powers, Life-Prolonging Acts	Operative Facts	Revocation/ Duration	Reciprocity	Transfer of Patient if Physician Unwilling	Immunity for Attending Physician
WISCONSIN 154.01, *et seq.*	Includes assistance in respiration, artificial maintenance of blood pressure and heart rate, blood transfusion, kidney dialysis, and similar procedures but does not include pain alleviation or provision of nutrition or hydration	(1) 18 yrs.; (2) signed; (3) in presence of 2 witnesses	Revocable at any time by destruction of document, written revocation signed and dated, or verbal expression of revocation effective upon notifying physician			No criminal, civil, or professional liability when acting in good faith
WYOMING 35-22-101 to 109	Any medical procedure, intervention, or nourishment by artificial means not including medication or procedure necessary for comfort or alleviation of pain	(1) adult; (2) in writing; (3) signed and dated; (4) in presence of 2 or more adult witnesses	Revocable by destruction of document, written revocation, verbal expression of intent to revoke. Patient's immediate desires at all times supersede the document		Unwilling physician must transfer patient	No criminal or civil liability for physician acting in good faith

31. WILLS

The purpose of a will is to permit the living to provide for those who come after him or her. By "willing" their estates, individuals can control the way their property is distributed after their deaths. If an individual dies without a will and without heirs or relatives, however, the estate escheats to the state. A will is thus a way to keep the estate in the hands of family and/or loved ones, and out of the hands of the state.

Over the years, the law of wills developed into a very mechanical, strict set of rules generally uniform among states that safeguard against unscrupulous heirs who may forge or tamper with wills for financial gain. Virtually all states require the testator (the person making the will) to be over eighteen or "an adult," the will must be typed or printed, and the only writing permitted on the document is the signature of the testator and witnesses.

Some noteworthy types of wills are nuncupative wills and holographic wills. Nuncupative wills are oral wills with a very special, very limited purpose. Typically, the oral will has the power to dispose of only a limited amount of personal property. The original purpose of this type of will was to permit mortally injured soldiers or sailors to give gifts of personal property to their comrades-in-arms. This provision is still reflected in many of the nuncupative statutes; it permits a dying individual to grant specific bequests to friends who may have cared for him during his last injury.

Holographic wills are wills that are entirely handwritten instead of being typed or printed. They are generally not as formal as typed wills and are therefore more suspect by law, for a greedy heir may more easily be able to persuade the testator to hastily write out a will without the proper amount of counsel or reflection. It is for these reasons that holographic wills are looked upon with general disfavor, are subject to closer scrutiny than other wills, and are less commonly recognized than other wills.

Table 31: Wills

State	Code Section	Age of Testator	Number of Witnesses	Nuncupative (Oral Wills)	Holographic Wills
ALABAMA	43-8-130, *et seq.*	18 years or older and of sound mind	Signed by at least two persons, each of whom witnessed either the signing or testator's acknowledgment of signature or of will	Not recognized	Not recognized because of statutory requirement that every will must be witnessed and attested by at least two people; will in handwriting of testator and attested to by two witnesses is not considered holographic will
ALASKA	13.11-150, *et seq.*	18 years or older and of sound mind	Signed by at least two persons, each of whom witnessed either the signing or testator's acknowledgment of signature or of will	Valid for mariner at sea or soldier in the military service for personal property as he would have done by common law or by reducing the same to writing; proof must be made within 6 months of words spoken or reduced to writing within 30 days	Recognized as valid if signature and material provisions are in handwriting of testator; does not need to be witnessed
ARIZONA	14-2501, *et seq.*	18 years or older and of sound mind	Signed by at least two persons, each of whom witnessed either the signing or testator's acknowledgment of signature or of will	Not recognized	Valid if signature and material provisions are in handwriting of testator; does not need to be witnessed
ARKANSAS	28-25-101, *et seq.*	18 years or older and of sound mind	Signed by at least two witnesses	Not mentioned	Valid if entire body and signature is in handwriting of testator and evidence of three disinterested witnesses
CALIFORNIA	Prob. §§6100, *et seq.*	18 years or older and of sound mind	At least 2 persons present at the same time, witnessing either signing of will or testator's acknowledgment and must understand that it is testator's will	Not recognized	Valid if signature and material provisions are in handwriting of testator; does not need witnesses
COLORADO	15-11-501, *et seq.*	18 years or older and of sound mind	Signed by at least two persons, each of whom witnessed either the signing or testator's acknowledgment of signature or of will	Not recognized	Valid whether or not there are witnesses if signature and material provisions are in handwriting of testator

(Continued)

Table 31: Wills—Continued

State	Code Section	Age of Testator	Number of Witnesses	Nuncupative (Oral Wills)	Holographic Wills
CONNECTICUT	45-160, *et seq.*	18 years or older and of sound mind	Two witnesses, each of whom must subscribe in presence of testator; unnecessary that witnesses should subscribe in each other's presence	Invalid if executed in Connecticut	Executed in Connecticut is not admissible but valid if properly made outside the state
DELAWARE	12-201, et seq.	18 years or older and of sound mind	Attested and subscribed in testator's presence by two or more credible witnesses; need not be signed in presence of witnesses	Statutory authorization repealed	Must meet requirements of all wills
DISTRICT OF COLUMBIA	18-102, *et seq.*	18 years or older and of sound mind	Attested and subscribed in presence of testator by two credible witnesses	Void except for soldiers in active service and marine at sea during their last sickness if oral will is proved by two witnesses and reduced to writing within 10 days	Valid if executed and attested in accordance with statute
FLORIDA	FL Statutes §§732.501, *et seq.*	18 years and of sound mind	Signed in presence of two attesting witnesses; witnesses must sign in presence of each other and testator	Not recognized	Not recognized; properly executed will in testator's handwriting is not considered holographic will
GEORGIA	O.C.Ga §§53-2-20, *et seq.*	14 years	Must be subscribed and attested in testator's presence by two or more competent witnesses; testator must sign/ acknowledge signature in presence of two witnesses	Can be made only during last illness and must be proved by oath of at least two witnesses present at making; must be reduced to writing within 30 days of speaking; application for probate made within 6 months of death	Not recognized
HAWAII	HI Revised Statutes §§560:2-501, *et seq.*	18 years or older and of sound mind	Signed by at least two persons, each of whom witnessed either the signing or testator's acknowledgment of signature or of will	Must be in writing	Not recognized; however, foreign holographic wills valid where executed may be admitted to probate

(Continued)

Table 31: Wills—Continued

State	Code Section	Age of Testator	Number of Witnesses	Nuncupative (Oral Wills)	Holographic Wills
IDAHO	I.C. §§15-2-501, *et seq.*	18 years or older or any emancipated minor	Signed by two or more persons, each of whom witnessed either the signing or testator's acknowledgment of the signature or of the will	Not recognized	Valid if signature and material provisions are in handwriting of testator; does not need witnesses
ILLINOIS	Ill. Ann. Stat. 755 ILCS 5/4-1, *et seq.*	18 years or older and of sound mind	Attested in presence of testator by two or more credible witnesses (not necessarily in each other's presence)	Not valid	Not valid
INDIANA	Burns Ind. Stat. §§29-1-5-1, *et seq.*	18 years or older; under 18 OK if member of armed forces or merchant marine	Must be signed and acknowledged in presence of two or more witnesses; witnesses must sign in presence of testator and each other	Valid only if made in imminent peril of death and testator dies from such peril; need two disinterested witnesses, reduced to writing within 30 days after declaration and submitted to probate within 6 months after death; may only dispose of personal property not exceeding $1,000 in value; person in active military service in time of war can dispose of personal property not exceeding $10,000 in value	No statutory provisions
IOWA	Code of Iowa §§633.264, *et seq.*	Any person of full age and sound mind	Witnessed, at his request, by two competent witnesses who must sign in presence of testator and each other	Not authorized	Not valid unless executed as stated in §633.279
KANSAS	K.S.A. §§59-601, *et seq.*	Anyone of sound mind and possessing rights of majority	Must be attested and subscribed in presence of testator by two or more competent witnesses who saw testator subscribe or heard him acknowledge same	Made in last sickness, oral will is valid in respect to personal property if reduced to writing and subscribed by two disinterested witnesses within 30 days after speaking it	Not recognized

(Continued)

Table 31: Wills—Continued

State	Code Section	Age of Testator	Number of Witnesses	Nuncupative (Oral Wills)	Holographic Wills
KENTUCKY	Ky. Rev. Stat. §§394.020, *et seq.*	18 years or older and of sound mind.	If will is not wholly written by testator, subscription must be made or will acknowledged by testator in presence of at least two credible witnesses; witnesses must sign in presence of testator and each other; not absolutely necessary witnesses sign in front of each other if acknowledged by testator upon witnesses signing (223 Ky. 23, 24 S.W. 2d 902)	Provisions recognizing validity for personal property for soldiers in actual service or marines at sea repealed effective June 16, 1972	Recognized
LOUISIANA	LSA Civ. Code §§1476, *et seq.*	Minor over 16 can make will as though a person of full age	Different numbers of witnesses required for different classifications of wills	Valid by: (1) Public Act: must be received by notary public in presence of 3 witnesses residing in place of execution or 5 not residing in place; must be written by notary as dictated and read to testator in presence of witnesses; must be signed by testator or expressly mentioned why he cannot and signed by at least one witness; (2) Act Under Private Signature: written by testator or another from dictation and presented in front of 5 witnesses who reside in place of execution or 7 who do not	Valid if entirely written, dated, and signed by testator without its being subject to any other formality
MAINE	Tit. 18A §§2-501, *et seq.*	18 years or older and of sound mind	Signed by at least two persons, each of whom witnessed either the signing or testator's acknowledgment of signature or of will	Not recognized	Valid if signature and material provisions are in handwriting of testator; does not need to be witnessed

(Continued)

Table 31: Wills—Continued

State	Code Section	Age of Testator	Number of Witnesses	Nuncupative (Oral Wills)	Holographic Wills
MARYLAND	Estates & Trusts §§4-101, *et seq.*	18 years or older	Must be attested and signed in presence of testator by two or more credible witnesses	Not mentioned	Valid if made outside U.S. by person serving in U.S. Armed Forces but is void after one year after testator's discharge unless testator has died or does not then possess testamentary capacity
MASSACHUSETTS	Ann. Laws §§191-1, *et seq.*	18 years or older and sound mind	Attested and subscribed in testator's presence by two or more competent witnesses	Soldiers in actual service or mariner at sea may make nuncupative will of personal property	Not recognized
MICHIGAN	MSA §§700.121, *et seq.*	18 years or older and sound mind	Signed by at least two persons, each of whom witnessed either the signing or testator's acknowledgment of signature or of will	Not recognized	Valid if testator's signature appears at end of will and material provisions are in testator's handwriting; does not need witnesses
MINNESOTA	Minn. Stat. Ann. §§524.2-501, *et seq.*	18 years or older and of sound mind	Signed by at least two persons, each of whom witnessed either the signing or testator's acknowledgment of signature or of will	Not recognized	Not recognized
MISSISSIPPI	91-5-1, *et seq.*	18 years or older and of sound and disposing mind	Attested to by two or more credible witnesses in testator's presence	Can be established if made during last illness of testator; must be proved by two witnesses that testator called on some person present to take notice that such is his will	Recognized
MISSOURI	474.310, *et seq.*	18 years or older and of sound mind	Must be attested by two or more competent witnesses subscribing their names to the will in presence of testator	Valid only if made in imminent peril of death and death results, declared to be his will before two disinterested witnesses, reduced to writing within 30 days and submitted for probate within 6 months of death; can only dispose of personal property of no more than $500 and does not change or revoke existing will	No statutory or judicial pronouncement of validity

(Continued)

Table 31: Wills—Continued

State	Code Section	Age of Testator	Number of Witnesses	Nuncupative (Oral Wills)	Holographic Wills
MONTANA	72-2-31, *et seq.*; UPC adopted except Arts. VI and VII and 1975 and 1977 official amendments	18 years or older and of sound mind	Signed by at least two persons, each of whom witnessed either the signing or testator's acknowledgment of signature or of will	Not recognized	Valid, whether or not witnessed, if signature and material provisions are in testator's handwriting
NEBRASKA	UPC adopted as NPC at §§30-2326, *et seq.*	18 years or older or anyone not a minor and of sound mind	Signed by at least two individuals, each of whom witnessed either the signing or testator's acknowledgment of signature or of the will	Not recognized	Valid, whether or not witnessed, if signature, material provisions, and an indication of the date of signing are in handwriting of testator; in absence of such indication of date, if instrument is the only such instrument or contains no inconsistency with any like instrument or if date is determinable from contents, from extrinsic circumstances, or from any other evidence
NEVADA	133.020, *et seq.*	18 years or older or any married person and of sound mind	Attested by at least two competent witnesses subscribing their names to the will in presence of testator	Valid if estate does not exceed $1000 in value, if proved by two witnesses present at making, during last sickness, and must be proved within 6 months and reduced to writing within 30 days after spoken.	Valid if entirely written, dated, and signed in handwriting of testator. Can be made in or out of state and need not be witnessed.
NEW HAMPSHIRE	551-1, *et seq.*	18 years or older or married	Attested and subscribed in testator's presence by two or more credible witnesses	Not valid where property exceeds in value $100, unless declared in presence of three witnesses, in last sickness, and in his usual dwelling (except where taken sick away from home and died before his return), or unless memo was reduced to writing within 6 days and presented to probate court within 6 months after making	Not recognized

(Continued)

Table 31: Wills—Continued

State	Code Section	Age of Testator	Number of Witnesses	Nuncupative (Oral Wills)	Holographic Wills
NEW JERSEY	3B:3-1, *et seq.*	18 years or older and of sound mind	Signed by at least two people who witnessed signing or testator's acknowledgment of the signature or of the will	Not recognized	Valid whether or not witnessed if signature and material provisions are in testator's handwriting
NEW MEXICO	Chap. 45 §§2-501, *et seq.*	Anyone who has reached age of majority and of sound mind	Must be signed or acknowledged in presence of two or more credible witnesses; witnesses must sign in presence of testator and each other	Not recognized	Not recognized
NEW YORK	Estates, Powers & Trusts §§3-1.1, *et seq.*	18 years or older. and of sound mind and memory	Signed by testator or acknowledged in presence of two attesting witnesses; witnesses must attest to testator's signature within 30 days, signing their names and residence addresses	Valid only if made by members of armed forces while in actual military or naval service during a war or other armed conflict, person who serves with or accompanies an armed force engaged in such activity, or mariner at sea	Same provisions as for nuncupative wills and written entirely in testator's handwriting
NORTH CAROLINA	Ch. 31 §§1, *et seq.*	18 years or older and of sound mind	Attested by at least two competent witnesses, each of whom must sign will in presence of testator but need not sign in presence of each other	Made by person in his last sickness or in such imminent peril of death and who does not survive sickness or peril and declared to be his will before two competent witnesses simultaneously present and specially requested by him to bear witness thereto	Written entirely in testator's handwriting and subscribed by testator and found after testator's death among his valuable papers or in safe deposit box or other safe place or with some person under his authority for safekeeping; no witness required
NORTH DAKOTA	30.1-08-01, *et seq.*	Any adult who is of sound mind	Signed by at least two persons, each of whom witnessed either signing or testator's acknowledgment of signature or of will	Not recognized	Signature and material provisions are in handwriting of testator, need not be witnessed

(Continued)

Table 31: Wills—Continued

State	Code Section	Age of Testator	Number of Witnesses	Nuncupative (Oral Wills)	Holographic Wills
OHIO	2107.02, *et seq.*	18 years or older and of sound mind and memory	Attested and subscribed in presence of testator by two competent witnesses who saw testator subscribe or heard him acknowledge signature	Valid if made in last sickness as to personal estate if reduced to writing and subscribed by two competent disinterested witnesses within 10 days after speaking and if testator is of sound mind, memory, and not under restraint and if called upon there is someone to bear testimony that it is his will; must be offered to probate within 6 months after death; not valid if beneficiary named is witness	Not recognized
OKLAHOMA	Tit. 84,. 41, *et seq.*	18 years or older including married woman	Two attesting witnesses signed in presence of testator	Valid with following requirements: (1) no more than $1000; (2) must be proved by two witnesses present at making, one of whom was asked by testator to bear witness as such; (3) testator must have been in actual military service in field or duty at sea and in actual contemplation, fear, or peril of death or testator must have been in expectation of immediate death from injury received same day	Must be entirely written, dated, and signed by testator's hand; need not be witnesses
OREGON	112.225, *et seq.*	18 years or older or lawfully married and of sound mind	At least two witnesses who see testator sign will or hear him acknowledge signature and attest by signing name to it	Not recognized	Not recognized
PENNSYLVANIA	20-2501, *et seq.*	18 years or older and of sound mind	Two witnesses signing will in presence of testator; testator must declare instrument to be his will in presence of witnesses	Not valid; provisions of §20-2503 repealed effective July 1, 1972	Not recognized

(Continued)

Table 31: Wills—Continued

State	Code Section	Age of Testator	Number of Witnesses	Nuncupative (Oral Wills)	Holographic Wills
RHODE ISLAND	33-5-2, *et seq.*	18 years or older and of sane mind	Must be signed or acknowledged by testator in front of two or more witnesses present at same time who must attest and subscribe will in presence of testator and each other	Not recognized except any soldier or airman in actual military service or any mariner or seaman at sea can dispose of his personal estate as he might have done under common law	Not recognized except any soldier or airman in actual military service or any mariner or seaman at sea can dispose of his personal estate as he might have done under common law
SOUTH CAROLINA	62-2-501, *et seq.*	18 years or older or married and of sound mind	Signed by at least two persons who witnessed either signing or testator's acknowledgment of signature or of will	No statutory recognition of soldiers' and mariners' wills of personalty nor nuncupative wills of personalty	Impliedly forbidden by statute unless specifically recognized by valid out-of-state execution or out-of-state probate
SOUTH DAKOTA	29-2-3, *et seq.*	18 years or older and of sound mind	Two attesting witnesses must sign name and place of residence at testator's request and in his presence	Valid if: (1) value less than $1000; (2) proved by two witnesses present at its making and one of whom asked by testator to bear witness; (3) must have been in actual military service in field or on shipboard at sea and in actual contemplation, fear, or peril of death, or in expectation of immediate death from injury received same day	Valid if entirely written, dated, and signed by hand of testator; subject to no other form, may be made in or out of state and need not be witnessed

(Continued)

Table 31: Wills—Continued

State	Code Section	Age of Testator	Number of Witnesses	Nuncupative (Oral Wills)	Holographic Wills
TENNESSEE	32-1-102, *et seq.*	18 years or older and of sound mind	Two or more attesting witnesses must sign in presence of testator and each other	Must be made only by person in imminent peril of death and valid only if testator dies as result of peril; must be declared to be his will before two disinterested witnesses, reduced to writing by or under direction of one of the witnesses within 30 days and submitted to probate within 6 months after death of testator; only valid for personal property not exceeding $1000 unless person is in active military, air, or naval service in time of war, then $10,000; neither revokes nor changes existing written will	Signature and material provisions must be in handwriting of testator and handwriting must be proved by two witnesses
TEXAS	Probate §§57, *et seq.*	18 years or older or lawfully married or member of U.S. Armed Forces and of sound mind	Attested by two or more credible witnesses above age of 14 subscribing names in presence of testator	Must have been made during last sickness, at residence of at least 10 days before date of will unless taken sick and dies away from home; when value is more than $30, must be proved by three credible witnesses that testator called upon someone to bear testimony that such is his will	Will wholly written by testator needs no attesting witnesses and may be self-proved by testator attaching affidavit that it is his last will; if not self-proved, it can be proved by testimony of two witnesses as to handwriting
UTAH	Tit. 75-2-501, *et seq.*	18 years or older and of sound mind	Signed by at least two persons, each of whom witnessed either signing or testator's acknowledgment of signature or of will and who sign in presence of testator and each other	Not recognized	Will which does not comply with §75-2-502 is valid whether or not witnessed if signature and material provisions are in handwriting of testator

(Continued)

Table 31: Wills—Continued

State	Code Section	Age of Testator	Number of Witnesses	Nuncupative (Oral Wills)	Holographic Wills
VERMONT	14-1, *et seq.*	"Of age" (18 years) and of sound mind	Attested and subscribed by three or more credible witnesses in presence and at request of testator and in presence of each other	Shall not pass personal estate over $200; not proved unless memo made in writing (by person present at making) within 6 days from making of will and presented for probate within 6 months from death of testator; soldier in actual military service or seaman at sea may dispose of personal property as he would at common law	Not recognized unless statutory formalities are satisfied (§14-5)
VIRGINIA	64.1-46, *et seq.*	18 years or older and of sound mind	Two or more competent witnesses present at same time who must subscribe will in presence of testator	Valid for soldier in actual service or mariner or seaman at sea to dispose of personal property	If will is wholly in handwriting of testator and signed by him, neither acknowledgment nor witnesses are necessary; proof of handwriting must be by at least two disinterested witnesses
WASHINGTON	11.12.010, *et seq.*	18 years or older and of sound mind	Attested by two or more competent witnesses who must sign in presence and at request of testator	No real estate; personal property not more than $1000; members of U.S. Armed Forces and persons employed on U.S. Merchant Marine vessels may dispose of unlimited wages and personal property; must be made with two witnesses present at time of making that testator requested person to bear witness to will and that it was made at time of last sickness; must be reduced to writing, proof offered within 6 months of words spoken, and citation issued to widows and heirs-at-law that they might contest	Not valid if executed without witnesses

(Continued)

Table 31: Wills—Continued

State	Code Section	Age of Testator	Number of Witnesses	Nuncupative (Oral Wills)	Holographic Wills
WEST VIRGINIA	41-1-1, *et seq.*	18 years or older and of sound mind	Two witnesses present at same time when will is signed or acknowledged by testator must sign in presence of testator and each other	Soldiers in actual military service and mariners or seamen at sea may dispose of personal estate as he would at common law	If will is wholly in handwriting of testator and signed by him, does not need acknowledgment or witnesses
WISCONSIN	853.01, *et seq.*	18 years or older and of sound mind	Signed by two or more competent witnesses in presence of testator and each other	Not valid	Without witnesses, not recognized under Wisconsin law unless executed in accordance with law of place where executed or law of state of domicile at time of execution
WYOMING	2-6-101, *et seq.*	Legal age and of sound mind	Two competent witnesses and signed by testator or by some person in his presence and by his express direction	Not recognized	Valid if entirely in handwriting of testator and signed by him

VII.   REAL ESTATE LAWS

32. ADVERSE POSSESSION

The doctrine of "adverse possession" is one of the most interesting in the field of real property law. The character of the law reflects the pioneer spirit of a growing world in both North America and Europe over the last few centuries.

If a person moves into possession of property, improves it and possesses it in a public manner, then after a certain amount of time he will acquire title to the property even though it is actually owned by someone else. The idea for adverse possession has at its root that land should not lie idle. If it does, it is wasted to the community. Therefore, if someone moves onto the land and makes it productive, that person may earn the right to claim it as his or her own. It is also reflective of the imprecise nature of ancient land sales: a person who believes he owns land, establishes himself on it in public, and is not hindered after a period of time, that person is entitled to own the land.

Requirements

The basic requirement for adverse possession is that the claiming party must take exclusive possession of the property. This type of possession is called "open and notorious" or proactive and absolutely not secretive possession. Some states require that the possession be "under color of title," or that the person must believe that he has the *right* to possess it *and* has some form of document or is relying on some fact that while not actually *conveying* title, appears to do so. In addition, many states require concurrent the payment of property taxes for a specified period of time, and a few states also require that improvements be made upon the land. Eventually, the possessor is required to file for title with the county recorder. The actual owner then has a limited amount of time in which to challenge the newcomer's title. Essentially, the owner's only argument is to claim some sort of disability; such as age, mental instability, or imprisonment. The owner is not required to do much in order to stop the possessor from acquiring title; merely sending the possessor a note granting permission to be there will usually suffice. Various rules exist regarding the continuousness of the possession and the ability to "tack" various periods of possession together in order to satisfy the time of possession requirement; see your state codes or the code of the state in which you are interested for more detailed information.

Table 32: Adverse Possession

State	Code Section	Prescriptive Period	Occupation	Time to Challenge	Improve-ments	Payment of Taxes	Title from Tax Assessor
ALABAMA	6-5-200		and Color of Title: 10 yrs. and Payment of Taxes: 10 yrs.				
ALASKA	09.25.050		and Color of Title: 7 yrs.				
ARIZONA	12-523 to 528	2 yrs. (if occupied with no claim to title)	and Color of Title: 3 yrs.		Taxes plus cultivation: 5 yrs.; Cultivation only: 10 yrs.		
ARKANSAS	18-61-101, 106	7 yrs.		After disability lifted: 3 yrs.			
CALIFORNIA	Civ. Proc. §§318, 325, 328		and Payment of Taxes: 5 yrs.	With disability: 20 yrs.; After disability lifted: 5 yrs.			
COLORADO	38-41-101, *et seq.*	18 yrs.	and Color of Title/ Payment of Taxes: 7 yrs.	After disability lifted: 2 yrs.			
CONNECTICUT	52-575	15 yrs.		After disability lifted: 5 yrs.			
DELAWARE	Tit. 10 §§7901, *et seq.*	20 yrs.		After disability lifted: 10 yrs.			
DISTRICT OF COLUMBIA	12-301; 16-1113, 16-3301	15 yrs.		With disability: 22 yrs.; After disability lifted: 2 yrs.			
FLORIDA	95.16, 18; 191, 192		and Color of Title: 7 yrs. and Payment of Taxes: 7 yrs.				4 yrs.
GEORGIA	44-5-163, 164, 170	20 yrs.	and Color of Title: 7 yrs.	Prescriptive period does not run until disability removed.			
HAWAII	657-31.5, 34; 669-1	20 yrs.		After disability lifted: 5 yrs.			
IDAHO	5-203 to 213		and Color of Title: 5 yrs. and Payment of Taxes: 5 yrs.	After disability lifted: 5 yrs.		Required	
ILLINOIS	735 ILCS 5/ 13-101, *et seq.*	20 yrs.	and Color of Title: 7 yrs. and Color of Title/Payment of Taxes: 7 yrs.	After disability lifted: 2 yrs.			7 yrs.

(Continued)

Table 32: Adverse Possession—Continued

State	Code Section	Prescriptive Period	Occupation	Time to Challenge	Improvements	Payment of Taxes	Title from Tax Assessor
INDIANA	32-1-20-1; 34-1-2-2, 3	10 yrs. (15 yrs. if cause of action arose before Sept. 1, 1982)		After disability lifted: 2 yrs.		Required	
IOWA	614.8, 17	Within 1 year (after 7/1/80)		After disability lifted: 1 yr.			
KANSAS	60-503, 507, 508	15 yrs.		With disability: 23 yrs.; After disability lifted: 2 yrs.			
KENTUCKY	413.010, 060, 20, 30	15 yrs.	and Color of Title: 7 yrs.	With disability: 30 yrs.; After disability lifted: 3 yrs.			
LOUISIANA	Civ. Art. 3655, *et seq.*	30 yrs.	and Color of Title: 10 yrs.				
MAINE	Tit. 14 §§801, *et seq.*	20 yrs.		After disability lifted: 10 yrs.		Required on uncultivated lands in unincorporated areas	
MARYLAND	Cts. & Jud. Proc. §5-103, 201	20 yrs.		After disability lifted: 3 yrs.			
MASSACHUSETTS	260§21	20 yrs.					
MICHIGAN	MCL §600. 5801, 5851	15 yrs.		After disability lifted: 1 yr.			10 years
MINNESOTA	541.02, 15	15 yrs.		With disability: 5 yrs. (except for infancy); After disability lifted: 1 yr.			
MISSISSIPPI	15-1-7, 13, 15	10 yrs.		With disability: 31 yrs.; After disability lifted: 10 yrs.			3 yrs. Must occupy for 2 yrs. after tax sale.
MISSOURI	516.010, 030	10 yrs.		With disability: 21 yrs.; After disability lifted: 3 yrs.			

(Continued)

Table 32: Adverse Possession—Continued

State	Code Section	Prescriptive Period	Occupation	Time to Challenge	Improve-ments	Payment of Taxes	Title from Tax Assessor
MONTANA	70-19-401, 411, 413	5 yrs.	and Payment of Taxes: 5 yrs. and Color of Title/ Payment of Taxes: 5 yrs.	After disability lifted: 5 yrs.		Required	
NEBRASKA	25-202, 213	10 yrs.		With disability: 20 yrs.; After disability lifted: 10 yrs.			
NEVADA	11.070, 110, 150, 180	5 yrs.	and Color of Title: 5 yrs. and Color of Title/Payment of Taxes: 5 yrs.	After disability lifted: 2 yrs.		Required	
NEW HAMPSHIRE	508:2, 3	20 yrs.		After disability lifted: 5 yrs.			
NEW JERSEY	2A:14-30 to 32; 2A:62-2	30 yrs. or 60 yrs. if woodland	and Color of Title: 30 yrs. and Payment of Taxes: 5 yrs.	After disability lifted: 5 yrs.			
NEW MEXICO	37-1-22		and Color of Title/ Payment of Taxes: 10 yrs.	After disability lifted: 1 yr.		Required	
NEW YORK	Real Prop. Acts §511		and Color of Title: 10 yrs.				
NORTH CAROLINA	1-38, 40	20 yrs.	and Color of Title: 7 yrs.	After disability lifted: 3 yrs.			
NORTH DAKOTA	28-01-04, 08, 14; 47-06-03	20 yrs.	and Color of Title: 20 yrs. and Color of Title/Payment of Taxes: 10 yrs.	After disability lifted: 10 yrs.			
OHIO	2305.04	21 yrs.		With disability: 21 yrs.; After disability lifted: 10 yrs.			
OKLAHOMA	12§93, 94	15 yrs.		After disability lifted: 2 yrs.			5 yrs.
OREGON	12.050, 160	10 yrs.		With disability: 5 yrs.; After disability lifted: 1 yr.			
PENNSYLVANIA	Tit. 42§5530	21 yrs.					
RHODE ISLAND	34-7-1	10 yrs.		After disability lifted: 10 yrs.			
SOUTH CAROLINA	15-67-210	10 yrs.	and Color of Title: 10 yrs.				

(Continued)

Table 32: Adverse Possession—Continued

State	Code Section	Prescriptive Period	Occupation	Time to Challenge	Improve-ments	Payment of Taxes	Title from Tax Assessor
SOUTH DAKOTA	15-3-1, 2, 14 to 16	20 yrs.	and Color of Title: 20 yrs. and Color of Title/Payment of Taxes: 10 yrs.	With disability: 20 yrs.; After disability lifted: 10 yrs.			
TENNESSEE	28-2-101, 102, 109, 110	7 yrs.	and Payment of Taxes: 20 yrs.	After disability lifted: 3 yrs.			
TEXAS	Civ. Prac. & Rem. §16.024, *et seq.*		and Color of title: 3 yrs.	With disability: 25 yrs.	Taxes plus cultivation: 5 yrs.; Cultivation only: 10 yrs.		
UTAH	78-12-7, 12	7 yrs.	and Color of Title/ Payment of Taxes: 7 yrs.			Required	
VERMONT	Tit. 12 §501	15 yrs.					
VIRGINIA	8.01-236, 237	15 yrs.		With disability: 25 yrs.			
WASHINGTON	7.28.050, 070, 090		and Color of Title: 7 yrs. and Color of Title/Payment of Taxes: 7 yrs.	Without disability: 3 yrs.		Required	
WEST VIRGINIA	55-2-1, 3	10 yrs.		After disability lifted: 5 yrs.			
WISCONSIN	893.16, 25 to 27	20 yrs.	and Color of Title: 10 yrs. and Color of Title/Payment of Taxes: 7 yrs.	With disability: 5 yrs., except when due to insanity or imprisonment. After disability lifted: 2 yrs.			
WYOMING	1-3-103, 104	10 yrs.		After disability lifted: 10 yrs.			

33. HOMESTEAD

Homestead laws are designed to protect small individual property owners and ordinary folks from the ravages of economic climates and conditions that are often harsh and out of their control. Homestead laws allow an individual to register a portion of his real and personal property as "homestead," thereby making that portion of the individual's estate off-limits to most creditors. The idea behind these homestead laws is the preservation of the family farm, home, or other assets in the face of severe economic conditions.

The items and amounts of money that can be set aside as a homestead are varied. The rules governing which property can be registered in this fashion seem to adhere to regional patterns. Real property that may be subject to the homestead exemptions vary in value from a $300 exemption from judgments in Pennsylvania to a $200,000 exemption for persons over age sixty-two in Massachusetts. They vary in character from the District of Columbia's allowable homestead of $200 worth of tools, $300 worth of furniture, and $300 in clothes per person to Colorado's unlimited acreage or Texas's 200 acres. In each case, the property that may be homesteaded is designed to perpetuate the family's estate and improve its chances for survival in hard times.

Limitations

The homestead is a back-up and a type of insurance against unexpected catastrophe; it will not ordinarily protect you from a bad business deal or from ordinary bankruptcy. Nonetheless, because an unscrupulous person could manipulate the homestead protections as a shield from living up to his legal obligations, there is much case law on homesteads. Indeed, ordinary business and commercial creditors ordinarily may penetrate property set aside as homestead.

Table 33: Homestead

State	Code Section	Maximum Value Of Property	Maximum Acreage (Urban)	Maximum Acreage (Rural)
ALABAMA	§6-10-2; Const. Art. X, §205	Const.: $2,000; Stat.: $5,000	Const.: Lot	Const.: 80 acres; Stat.: 160 acres
ALASKA	09.38.010	$54,000		
ARIZONA	33-1101	$100,000		
ARKANSAS	16-66-210; Const. Art. IX, §4	$2,500. All homesteads less than $1,000 assessed valuation are exempt from all state taxes referred to in art. XVI, §18 of Ark. Constitution. If homestead's value exceeds $1,000, exemption shall apply to first $1,000 of valuation (CONST. amend. XXII §1).	1 acre but not less than ¼ acre (without regard to valuation)	160 acres but not less than 80 acres (without regard to valuation)
CALIFORNIA	Civ. Proc. §704.710	$100,000 if either spouse is over 65 or disabled and unable to engage in substantial employment; $100,000 if person is 55 or older with gross income of not more than $15,000 and sale is involuntary; $100,000 if debtor 55 years old or older is married and couple's combined income not more than $20,000 and sale is involuntary; $75,000 if head of family is under 65; $50,000 for all others		
COLORADO	38-41-201	$30,000	No limits to acreage	No limits to acreage
CONNECTICUT	12-81(21); 12-1296	$10,000 if disabled veteran; $3,000 maximum income if unmarried and over 65; $5,000 maximum income if married and over 65; $6,000 maximum income for all others--combined adjusted gross income and tax exempt interest		
DELAWARE	Tit. 10 §4902 (personal property); Tit. 22 §1002	$75 trade, business in New Castle, Sussex County; $50 trade, business in Kent County; homestead exemption for persons 65 and older to be determined by local ordinance		
DISTRICT OF COLUMBIA	15-501 (personal property)	$200 for tools, $300 for furniture, $300 for clothes per person in value		
FLORIDA	§196.031; Const. Art. X, §4	$10,000 if person is over 65; $9,500 if totally disabled and is a permanent resident for 5 consecutive years prior to claim; $25,000 for taxes levied by governing bodies of school districts; $5,000 for all others	½ acre (Art. X, §K)	160 acres (§222.03; Art. X, §K)
GEORGIA	44-13-1; 51-101	$5,000		
HAWAII	651-92	$30,000 if head of family is 65 years old; $20,000 for all others		

(Continued)

Table 33: Homestead—Continued

State	Code Section	Maximum Value Of Property	Maximum Acreage (Urban)	Maximum Acreage (Rural)
IDAHO	55-1001, 1003	Lesser of $50,000 or total net value of lands, mobile home, or improvements. Net value means market value minus all liens and encumbrances.		
ILLINOIS	735 ILCS 5/12-901	$7,500		
INDIANA	34-2-28-1	$7,500 for residential; $4,000 for other real estate or tangible personal property; $100 for intangible personal property; total value of property may not exceed $10,000		
IOWA	561.1, *et seq.*	$500	½ acre	40 acres
KANSAS	60-2301		1 acre	160 acres
KENTUCKY	427.010, .080	$5,000 plus $3,000 in any property		
LOUISIANA	Const. Art. VII, §20	$7,500	160 acres	160 acres
MAINE	Tit. 14 §4422	$60,000 if debtor or dependent is either 60 or older, disabled, or unable to engage in gainful employment; $7,500 plus $400 in any other property except itemized personal property for all others		
MARYLAND	Cts. & Jud. Proc. §11-504	$3,000 plus an additional $2,500 in a Title 11 bankruptcy		
MASSACHUSETTS	Ch. 188 §1	$200,000 if 62 or over or disabled, meeting the federal requirements of SSI; $100,000 for all others		
MICHIGAN	600.6023	$3,500	Lot	40 acres
MINNESOTA	510.01, *et seq.*		½ acre	160 acres
MISSISSIPPI	85-3-21	$30,000		160 acres
MISSOURI	513.475	$8,000		
MONTANA	70-32-101, 104	$40,000		
NEBRASKA	77-3502; 40-101	$10,000	1 acre (77-3502); 2 lots (40-101)	160 acres
NEVADA	115.010	$95,000		
NEW HAMPSHIRE	480: 1	$5,000		
NEW JERSEY	54: 4-8.57, *et seq.*; 2A: 17-19 personal property	$1,000 personal property; Homeowner, $150 rebate if income is less than $70,000; Renter, $500 rebate if income is $70,000 to $100,000	None	None
NEW MEXICO	42-10-1, 10; 40-10-9	$20,000 or in lieu thereof, $2,000 in any property		

(Continued)

Table 33: Homestead—Continued

State	Code Section	Maximum Value Of Property	Maximum Acreage (Urban)	Maximum Acreage (Rural)
NEW YORK	N.Y. Civ. Prac. L. & R. §5206	$10,000		
NORTH CAROLINA	Const. Art. X, §2	$1,000		
NORTH DAKOTA	47-18-01	$80,000		
OHIO	2329.66	$5,000		
OKLAHOMA	Tit. 31 §2		1 acre or maximum value of $5,000, but not less than ¼ acre without regard to valuation	160 acres
OREGON	23.240	$15,000 or $20,000 if more than one debtor is subject to liability	1 block	160 acres
PENNSYLVANIA	Tit. 42 §8123; Tit. 72 §4751-3	$300 monetary exemption from judgment only; for senior citizens, a formula based on a sliding scale of income up to $15,000		
RHODE ISLAND	9-26-4	$500 for tools $1,000 for furniture	Allows for real property to be exempted but no limitation given in acreage	Allows for real property to be exempted but no limitation given in acreage
SOUTH CAROLINA	15-41-30	$5,000 up to a maximum of $10,000 if there are multiple exemptions on same living unit		
SOUTH DAKOTA	43-31-4		1 acre; mineral lands: 1 acre	160 acres; mineral lands: 40 acres placer claim; 5 acres lode mining
TENNESSEE	26-2-301	$5,000 or $7,500 if more than one debtor is subject to liability		
TEXAS	Const. Art. XVI, §51		1 acre	200 acres
UTAH	78-23-3	$8,000 if head of family; $2,000 for spouse; $500 for each dependent		
VERMONT	Tit. 27 §101	$30,000		
VIRGINIA	34-4	$5,000		
WASHINGTON	6.13.010, 030	$30,000		
WEST VIRGINIA	§38-9-1; Const. Art. VI, §43	$5,000		
WISCONSIN	815.20; 990.01 (14)	$40,000	Not less than ¼ acre or more than 40 acres	
WYOMING	1-20-101	$10,000		

34. LEASES AND RENTAL AGREEMENTS

When an individual agrees to rent or lease real estate property, he, the tenant, signs either a lease or a rental agreement with the owner of the property outlining the terms of the agreement. The difference between rentals and leases is that the terms of leases are generally for at least one year, though lease payments are usually paid by the month. Terms for rentals are generally month-to-month, although they are occasionally paid on a weekly term. Virtually all states recognize that at the end of a lease, the term converts to a month-to-month rental unless a new lease is signed and the landlord continues to accept monthly payments.

Many states have imposed limits on the size of security deposits safeguarding against damage to the property that may be collected by landlords. The highest deposit stated in a statute is three months' rent for a furnished property, but generally the limit is one month's rent. A number of states require landlords holding deposits to add interest when it is returned. Landlords are also required by most states to itemize any deductions taken from deposits and return them within set time periods after the lease is terminated.

Most states have statutes limiting discrimination by landlords. Under these statutes, landlords are prohibited from not renting to certain classes of people, for example, those with young children and pets. State legislatures generally ensure equal access to housing to the broadest range of citizens.

Table 34: Leases and Rental Agreements

State	Code Section	Terms of Leases	Deposits	Discrimination	Uniform Residential Landlord & Tenant Act Adopted?
ALABAMA	24-8-7; 35-9-4	Renting for an unspecified term is presumed to be made for the length of time the parties adopted for estimation of the rent, in absence of agreement respecting length of time for rent, hiring is presumed to be monthly		No discrimination on basis of race, color, religion, sex, familial status, national origin; municipal corporations may zone/regulate as to different classes of inhabitants, but not to discriminate against or favor any class of inhabitants; housing for older persons exempted	No
ALASKA	18.80.210; 34.03.020, 070, 290	Unless otherwise agreed, rent is payable monthly and shall be term of month-to-month	Limit of 2 months rent, interest on deposit not required; deposit must be returned within 14 days of termination	No discrimination on basis of sex, physical/mental disability, marital status, changes in marital status, pregnancy, parenthood, race, religion, color, national origin	Yes
ARIZONA	9-462.01(11); 33-303, 342, 1321; 41-1491.14	Lease does not automatically renew but is converted into a tenancy from month–to–month	Limit 1½ months' rent; interest on deposit not required; deposit must be returned within 14 days of termination	No discrimination on basis of race, color, religion, sex, familial status, national origin; any municipality may establish age –specific community zoning and may restrict residency to head of household or spouse of specific age or older and prohibit minors; housing for older persons exempted	Yes
ARKANSAS	18-16-304	When rent accepted by a landlord of a holding-over tenant, the term becomes a tenancy from year-to-year. (*Jonesboro Trust Co.* v. *Harbough,* 244 S.W. 455, 456 (Ark. 1922))	Limit of 2 months' rent; interest on deposit not required; deposit must be returned within 30 days of termination		No

(Continued)

Table 34: Leases and Rental Agreements—Continued

State	Code Section	Terms of Leases	Deposits	Discrimination	Uniform Residential Landlord & Tenant Act Adopted?
CALIFORNIA	C.C. §51.2, 1945, 1950.5; Govt. Code §§12920, 12955	If tenant remains in possession and landlord accepts rent, parties are presumed to have renewed lease on same terms and for same time, never to exceed 1 year renewal	Limit 2 months rent for unfurnished, 3 months rent for furnished; interest on deposit not required; deposit must be refunded within 2 weeks of termination	No discrimination based on race, color, religion, sex, marital status, national origin, ancestry; special accommodations for senior citizen housing	No
COLORADO	13-40-104; 24-32-502; 38-12-102, *et seq.*		Interest on deposit not required; any damages subtracted must be itemized and balance returned within 1 month of termination unless otherwise agreed, but never over 60 days.	No discrimination on basis of age, sex, marital, status, handicap, race, religion, creed, color, national origin, but does not prohibit compliance with local zoning ordinance provisions concerning residential restrictions on marital status	No
CONNECTICUT	46a-64c; 47a-3d; 47a-21	Holdover not evidence of a new lease; converts to month-to-month	Tenant under 62: limit 2 months rent; tenant over 62: limit 1 month rent; interest on deposit required at 5.25%	No discrimination on basis of race, creed, color, national origin, ancestry, sex, marital status, age, lawful source of income, familial status; may refuse to rent to people not blood related who are not married; public or private programs allowed to assist persons over 64 as long as there is no discrimination on basis of age among those eligible	No
DELAWARE	Tit. 6 §4602; 25 §5511, 6503	Tenant remains in possession and landlord accepts rent, creation of new tenancy from year-to-year is inferred (*Makin* v. *Mack,* 336 A.2d 230 (1975)	Limit 1 month rent; interest on deposit not required; deposit must be returned within 15 days of termination; if deposit not returned within 30 days, tenant entitled to double the amount of security deposit	No discrimination on basis of race, age, marital status, creed, color, sex, handicap, national origin; landlord may reserve 10 or more units exclusively for rent by senior citizens (anyone over 62)	No

(Continued)

Table 34: Leases and Rental Agreements—Continued

State	Code Section	Terms of Leases	Deposits	Discrimination	Uniform Residential Landlord & Tenant Act Adopted?
DISTRICT OF COLUMBIA	1-2515; 45-2555 Security Deposit Act 2/20/76, D.C. Law 1-48	Receipt of rent for new term or part thereof amounts to waiver of landlord's right to demand possession)*Shapiro* v. *Christopher,* 195 F.2d 785 (D.C. Cir. 1952); *Byrne* v. *Morrison,* 25 App. D.C. 72 (1905))	Interest on deposit required at 5% annually for all deposits after 2/20/76, only for deposit on tenancy for 12 months or more; deposit returned within 45 days of termination	No discrimination on basis of race, color, religion, national origin, sex, age, marital status, personal appearance, sexual orientation, family responsibilities, physical handicap, matriculation, political affiliation, source of income, place of residence or business; also illegal to discriminate against families receiving or eligible to receive Tenant Assistance Program assistance; up to $5000 fine per violation; repeat offenders up to $15,000 per violation	No
FLORIDA	83.04, 49; 760.23	Mere payment of rent is not construed as a renewal for the term; but if tenant holding over does so with written consent of landlord then it becomes a tenancy at will	No limits on deposits; landlord may elect to (1) put deposit in non-interest bearing account; (2) hold in interest bearing account at either 75% of average rate or 5%; or (3) post a surety bond and pay tenant interest at 5%; landlord must tell tenant in 30 days which he's doing	No discrimination on basis of race, color, national origin, sex, handicap, or religion; same as Fair Housing Act §760.23	Yes
GEORGIA	8-3-201, 202; 61-602, 605	Rent accepted after expiration of 1 year lease implies renewal of lease for another year (*Allen* v. *Montgomery,* 105 S.E. 33)	Deposit must be deposited in escrow account and held in trust for tenant; any damages subtracted must be itemized and deposit must be returned within 30 days of termination	No discrimination on basis of race, color, religion, sex, handicap, familial status, or national origin; allowable housing for "older people" included in statutes	No

(Continued)

Table 34: Leases and Rental Agreements—Continued

State	Code Section	Terms of Leases	Deposits	Discrimination	Uniform Residential Landlord & Tenant Act Adopted?
HAWAII	515-3, 4; 521-44, 71	Landlord accepting rent in advance after First month of holdover creates a month-to-month tenancy absent contrary agreement; absence of any agreement makes term equal to that at which the rent is computed; notice to quit must give 25 days	Limit 1 month rent; no interest on deposit required; deposit must be returned within 14 days of termination	No discrimination on basis of HIV infection, race, sex, color, marital status, parental status, ancestry, handicapped status; section regarding parental status does not apply to housing for older persons as defined in 42 USC §2607(b)(2)	Yes
IDAHO	6-321; 67-5909	Whether landlord waives right to give notice to quit the tenancy is question of intent; intent to waive must clearly appear; each case to be judged on case-by-case basis (*Riverside Dev. Co. v. Ritchie,* 650 P.2d 657, 663)	No limit on deposit; no interest on deposit required; deposit must be returned within 21 days or within 30 days after surrender of possession by tenant	No discrimination on basis of race, color, religion, sex, national origin, with exceptions	No
ILLINOIS	65 ILCS 5/11-11-1.1; 775 ILCS 5/3-105, 106; 765 ILCS 715/1	Tenant holds over and landlord receives rent, presumed that new year-to-year tenancy created, absent express intent otherwise. (*Demerath* v. *Schennum,* 59 N.E.2d 348)	No limits on deposit; interest required on deposit at 5% per year if held for over 6 months and if lessor owns 25 units or more in one building or complex of buildings	No discrimination on basis of race, color, religion, sex, creed, ancestry, national origin, physical/mental handicap; statute repealed prohibiting discrimination against children; provisions for senior citizen housing	No
INDIANA	22-9.5-3-4; 22-9.5-5-1; 32-7-5-12	Holding over from a year tenancy and paying rent creates year-to-year tenancy (*Alleman* v. *Vink,* 62 N.E. 461)	No limits on deposit; interest on deposit not required; any damages subtracted must be itemized and returned within 45 days of termination	No discrimination on basis of race, color, religion, sex, familial status, handicap, or national origin; housing for older persons exempted	No

(Continued)

Table 34: Leases and Rental Agreements—Continued

State	Code Section	Terms of Leases	Deposits	Discrimination	Uniform Residential Landlord & Tenant Act Adopted?
IOWA	562A.34; 562A.9(4); 562A.12; 601A.12(5)	Holding over converts to month-to-month tenancy	Limit 2 months rent; interest on deposit not required; any interest earned on deposit for first 5 years of tenancy is landlord's property	No discrimination on basis of race, color, creed, sex, religion, origin, disability, or family status; housing for older persons exempted	Yes
KANSAS	44-1016; 44-1019; 58-2571; 58-2545; 58-2550	Holdover converts to month-to-month tenancy	Limit 1 month rent; special rules for pets and furnishings; interest on deposit not required unless renting from municipal housing authority	No discrimination on basis of race, religion, color, sex, disability, familial status, national origin; housing for older persons exempted	Yes
KENTUCKY	344.360, 362; 383.565(3), 580, 695	Holdover converts to month-to-month tenancy	No limit on deposit; interest on deposit not required; landlord must send notice to last known/ determinable address that tenant has a refund due; if tenant does not respond within 60 days, it becomes landlord's property	No discrimination on basis of race, color, religion, national origin, sex, familial status, disability; housing for older persons exempted; landlord may refuse to rent to unmarried couple	Yes
LOUISIANA	9:3251; 51:2602, 2605	Landlord's right to eject is waived when he accepts rent from holdover tenant (*Canal Realty & Improvement Co.* v. *Pailet,* 46 So.2d 303 (1950))	No limit on deposit; interest on deposit not required; deposit must be returned within one month of termination	No discrimination on basis of race, color, religion, sex, handicap, familial status, national origin; housing for older persons exempted	No
MAINE	Tit. 5§4552; 14§6031, *et seq.*		Limit 2 months rent; interest on deposit not required; deposit must be returned within 30 days	No discrimination on basis of race, color, sex, physical or mental disability, religion, ancestry, national origin, familial status; housing for older persons exempted.	No

(Continued)

Table 34: Leases and Rental Agreements—Continued

State	Code Section	Terms of Leases	Deposits	Discrimination	Uniform Residential Landlord & Tenant Act Adopted?
MARYLAND	Real Prop. 8-203, 402; MD Code (1957) Art 49B §20, *et seq.*	Holdover tenancy becomes week-to-week if weekly before and month-to month in all other cases	Limit greater of $50 or 2 months rent; interest on deposit required at 4% simple interest per year; landlord must return deposit within 45 days of termination	No discrimination on basis of race, religion, color, sex, national origin, marital status, handicap. If owner maintains personal residence in dwelling which has 5 or less units, owner may discriminate on sex or marital status. May rent to elderly exclusively only if dwelling planned specifically for specified age group	No
MASSACHUSETTS	Ch. 151B §4; Ch. 186 §15, 16	Payment and acceptance of rent create tenancy at will (*Staples* v. *Collins,* 73 N.E.2d 729 (1947)); certain acts/conduct may negate this presumption (*Corcoran Management Co., Ins.* v. *Withers,* 513 N.E.2d 218)	Limit 1 month rent; interest on deposit required at 5% from first day of tenancy if landlord has held deposit for one year	No discrimination on basis of race, religious creed, color, national origin, sex, sexual orientation (unless orientation is for minor child), age, ancestry, marital status, member of armed forces, handicapped in any multiple dwelling, contiguously located housing accommodations or publicly assisted dwellings	
MICHIGAN	37.2102; 37.2502; 37.2503; 554.134; 554.601, *et seq.*	Holdover converts to year-to-year tenancy (*Faraci* v. *Fassvio,* 212 Mich. 216)	Limit 1 ½ months rent; interest on deposit not required	No discrimination on basis of religion, race, color, national origin, age, sex, height, weight, marital status. Housing programs for elderly exempted; children may be restricted to certain areas of complex (*Dept. of Civil Rights* v. *Beznos Co.,* 421 Mich. 110))	No

(Continued)

Table 34: Leases and Rental Agreements—Continued

State	Code Section	Terms of Leases	Deposits	Discrimination	Uniform Residential Landlord & Tenant Act Adopted?
MINNESOTA	363.02, 03; 504.07, 20	Period of the shortest interval between times of payment of rent under expired lease shall be implied	No limit on deposit; interest on deposit required at 5.5% simple interest	No discrimination on basis of race, color, creed, religion, national origin, sex, marital status, disability, familial status; housing for older persons exempted; landlords may advertise "adults only"	No
MISSISSIPPI	89-8-19, 21; 43-33-723	Holdover converts to month-to-month tenancy unless tenant pays weekly	No limit on deposit; interest on deposit not required; deposit must be returned within 45 days of termination	No discrimination on basis of race, religious principles, color, sex, national origin, ancestry, handicap, age, families because of children; housing for older persons exempted	No
MISSOURI	108.470; 213.040; 441.060; 535.300	All tenancies not made in writing and signed by parties shall be held as month-to-month	Limit 2 months rent; interest on deposit not required; deposit must be must be returned within 30 days of termination	No discrimination on basis of race, color, religion, national origin, ancestry, sex, handicap; may not discriminate on marital status for housing loans	No
MONTANA	49-2-305; 70-24-201(2), 429; 70-25-201, *et seq.*	Holdover converts to month-to-month tenancy unless tenant pays weekly, then week-to-week	No limit on deposit; interest on deposit not required; before any damages are subtracted from deposit, landlord must give tenant an itemized list and provide an opportunity for tenant to clean or fix the problem; deposit must be returned within 10 days of termination	No discrimination on basis of sex, marital status, race, creed, religion, age, familial status, physical/mental handicap, color, national origin; housing for older persons exempted; landlord may discriminate against children in duplex in which owner resides in half	Yes

(Continued)

Table 34: Leases and Rental Agreements—Continued

State	Code Section	Terms of Leases	Deposits	Discrimination	Uniform Residential Landlord & Tenant Act Adopted?
NEBRASKA	6-1401, *et seq.*; 18-1724; 76-1414, 76-1416	Holdover converts to month-to-month tenancy unless tenant pays weekly, then week-to-week	Limit 1 month rent plus ¼ of 1 month rent pet deposit; deposit must be returned within 14 days after demand and designation of location to be mailed	No discrimination on basis of race, color, creed, religion, ancestry, sex, marital status, national origin, familial status, handicap	Yes
NEVADA	118.010, *et seq.*; 118A.240; 118A.470; 207.300	Holdover converts to month-to month tenancy unless tenant pays weekly, then week-to-week	Limit 3 months rent; interest on deposit not required; deposit must be returned within 30 days of termination	No discrimination on basis of race, religious creed, color, national origin, disability, ancestry, familial status, sex	No
NEW HAMPSHIRE	354-A:1; 540:1; 540-A:6, 7	Every tenancy shall be deemed to be at-will and rent payable on demand absent contrary contract shown	Limit 1 month rent or $100, whichever is greater. Interest on deposit required at 5% if landlord he holds the deposit for one year or longer	No discrimination on basis of age, sex, race, creed, color, marital status, physical/mental disability, national origin, familial status; retirement communities exempted	No
NEW JERSEY	2A:42-101; 10:5-4; 46:8-10; 46:8-21.1, 2; 55:14A-39.1	Holdover converts to month-to-month tenancy absent agreement to the contrary	Limit 1 ½ months rent; interest on deposit required; any damages subtracted from deposit must be itemized and balance of deposit must be returned within 30 days of termination	No discrimination on basis of race, creed, color, national origin, ancestry, age, marital status, affectionate or sexual orientation or sex, subject only to conditions and limitations applicable alike to all persons; retirement communities exempted; landlord may discriminate against children in owner-occupied house with 2 dwelling units; housing opportunity declared to be a civil right	No

(Continued)

Table 34: Leases and Rental Agreements—Continued

State	Code Section	Terms of Leases	Deposits	Discrimination	Uniform Residential Landlord & Tenant Act Adopted?
NEW MEXICO	28-1-7(G); 47-8-15C, 18, 37	Holdover converts to month-to-month tenancy unless tenant pays weekly, then week-to-week	If term is under one year, then limit is 1 month rent; interest on deposit required if landlord demands deposit in excess of 1 month rent; deposit must be returned within 30 days of termination or departure, whichever is later	No discrimination on basis of race, religion, color, national origin, ancestry, sex, or physical or mental handicap	Yes
NEW YORK	Real Prop. §§232-G 236-237; Exec. §296(5)(A); Rent & Evict. Regs. §2105.5; Gen. Oblig. §§7-103, 105	Holdover converts to month-to-month tenancy absent agreement otherwise	Limit 1 month rent; interest on deposit required at 1%	No discrimination on basis of race, creed, color, national origin, sex, age, disability, marital status, familial status; exception for housing accommodations exclusively for those 55 and older; landlord may discriminate against children in senior citizen housing, 1 or 2 family homes, mobile homes parks for those 55 or older	No
NORTH CAROLINA	41A-6(e); 42-26; 42-50, *et seq.*	Landlord may treat tenant as trespasser and eject or may recognize him as tenant with presumption of year-to-year tenancy. *(Murrill* v. *Palmer,* 80 S.E. 55); this presumption is rebuttable and will yield to the actual intention of the parties (*Gurtis* v. *City of Sanford,* 197 S.E. 2d 585 (1973)	Limits: week-to-week, 2 weeks rent; month-to-month, 1 ½ months rent; over month-to-month, 2 months rent; interest on deposits not required; deposit must be returned within 30 days of termination	No discrimination on basis of race, religion, color, sex, national origin, handicap, or familial status; housing for older persons exempted	No

(Continued)

Table 34: Leases and Rental Agreements—Continued

State	Code Section	Terms of Leases	Deposits	Discrimination	Uniform Residential Landlord & Tenant Act Adopted?
NORTH DAKOTA	14-02.4-12; 47-16-06, 07.1	Lease renews on holdover for same time and terms as previous one but not exceeding one year	Limit 1 month rent; interest on deposit required unless occupancy less than 9 months	No discrimination on basis of race, color, religion, sex, national origin, age, physical or mental handicap, or status in marriage or public assistance	No
OHIO	4112.02(4); 5321, *et seq.*	Presumption that holdover converts to year-to-year term but it is rebuttable (*Bumiller* v. *Walker,* 116 N.E. 797 (1917))	Limit greater of $50 or 1 month rent. Interest on deposit required at 5% per year if tenant remains in possession 6 months or more; deposit must be returned within 30 days of termination	No discrimination on basis of race, color, religion, sex, ancestry, handicap, national origin, familial status	No
OKLAHOMA	41 §§35, 115; 25 §1452, 1453	Parties presumed to have renewed lease for same terms and time, not exceeding 1 year	No limit on deposit; interest on deposit not required; deposit must be returned within 30 days of termination	No discrimination on basis of race, color, religion, gender, national origin, age, familial status, handicap; housing for older persons exempted	No
OREGON	90.240(4), 300, 900; 659.033	Holdover converts to month-to-month tenancy	No limit on deposit; interest on deposit not required; deposit must be returned within 30 days after termination	No discrimination on basis of race, color, sex, marital status, familial status, religion; housing for older persons exempted	Yes
PENNSYLVANIA	Tit. 43 §955; Tit. 68 §250.511	Holdover converts to same term as original lease if it was for 1 year or less	Limit 2 months rent; interest on deposit required if deposit held over 2 years	No discrimination on basis of race, color, familial status, age, religious creed, ancestry, sex, national origin, handicap, disability; housing for older persons exempted	No

(Continued)

Table 34: Leases and Rental Agreements—Continued

State	Code Section	Terms of Leases	Deposits	Discrimination	Uniform Residential Landlord & Tenant Act Adopted?
RHODE ISLAND	34-37-2; 34-18-19, 39	Parties may agree to a term, otherwise month-to-month unless tenant pays weekly, then week-to-week	Limit 1 month rent; interest on deposit not required; deposit must be returned within 20 days of termination	No discrimination on basis of race, color, religion, sex, marital status, ancestral origin, handicap, age or familial status. Right to equal housing opportunities for all individuals in the state declared a civil right; housing specifically for older persons exempted; landlord may discriminate against children if house is 2 units, one of which is occupied by owner, or 4 units and one unit is owner-occupied and one occupied by senior citizen/infirm person for whom children would be a hardship	Yes
SOUTH CAROLINA	27-40-10, *et seq.*; 27-40-310, 27-40-410, 27-40-770; 31-21-10	Holdover converts to month-to-month tenancy unless tenant pays weekly, then week-to-week	No limit on deposit; interest on deposit not required; deposit must be returned within 30 days of termination	No discrimination on basis of race, color, religion, sex, familial status, or national origin; housing for older persons exempted; landlord may discriminate against children in single family dwellings and certain other small unit buildings	Yes
SOUTH DAKOTA	20-13-20, *et seq.*; 43-32-6.1, 14, 24	Holdover converts to rental on same terms and same time as original lease	Limit 1 month rent, unless otherwise agreed because special conditions pose a danger to premises maintenance; interest on deposit not required; deposit must be returned within 2 weeks of termination	No discrimination on basis of race, color, creed, religion, sex, ancestry, disability, familial status or national origin; housing for older persons exempted; landlord may discriminate against children in duplexes where one unit is owner-occupied	No

(Continued)

Table 34: Leases and Rental Agreements—Continued

State	Code Section	Terms of Leases	Deposits	Discrimination	Uniform Residential Landlord & Tenant Act Adopted?
TENNESSEE	4-21-601; 66-28-201, 301, 512	Holdover converts to month-to-month tenancy or upon agreement, apportionable day-to-day	No limit on deposit; interest on deposit not required	No discrimination on basis of race, color, creed, religion, sex, handicap, familial status, national origin; housing for older persons exempted	Yes
TEXAS	Prop. §§92.101, *et seq.*; Tex. Rev. Civ. Stat. Ann. Art. 1f §1.01, *et seq.*	Holdover implies an agreement between landlord and tenant; normally lease for 1 year will be implied absent express or implied contrary agreement (*Barragan* v. *Munoz,* 525 S.W. 2d 559 (1975))	No limit on deposit; interest on deposit required; deposit must be returned within 30 days of termination	No discrimination on basis of race, color, religion, sex, familial status, national origin; housing for older persons exempted	No
UTAH	57-17-1, *et seq.*; 57-21-1, *et seq.*	Holdover tenant is bound to covenants previously agreed to and binding in first term (*Cottonwood Mall Co.* v. *Sine,* 767 P.2d 499, 503.)	No limit on deposit; interest on deposit not required; deposit must be returned within 30 days of termination	No discrimination on basis of race, color, religion, sex, national origin, familial status, source of income, disability; housing for older persons exempted; no discrimination against children unless in adults-only apartment complex, condo, or other housing not violating federal law	No
VERMONT	Tit. 9 §4461, 4503	Holdover may convert into year-to-year tenancy; result of legal consequence of conduct of parties and does not depend on tenant's intention (*Manlatty* v. *Carroll Co.,* 41 A.2d 144 (Vt. 1945))	No limit on deposit; interest on deposit not required; deposit must be returned within 14 days of termination or landlord forfeits right to withhold any of it.	No discrimination on basis of race, sex, age, marital status, religious creed, color, national origin, handicap, recipient of public assistance, or because person intends to occupy with children; housing for older persons exempted	No

(Continued)

Table 34: Leases and Rental Agreements—Continued

State	Code Section	Terms of Leases	Deposits	Discrimination	Uniform Residential Landlord & Tenant Act Adopted?
VIRGINIA	36-96, *et seq.*; 55-248	Holdover converts to month-to-month or any lesser term	Limit 2 months rent; interest on deposit held longer than 13 months required at 5% accrued every 6 months; deposit must be returned within 30 days of termination	No discrimination on same bases as 42 U.S.C. §§3601, *et seq.*; special provisions for housing for elderly	Yes
WASHINGTON	49.60.010; 59.04.010, 020; 59.18.260, *et seq.*	When term of tenancy is indefinite, period becomes that on which rent is payable	No limit on deposit, but no deposit may be collected unless rental agreement is in writing; interest on deposit not required; deposit must be returned within 14 days of termination	No discrimination on basis of race, creed, color, national origin, sex, marital status, age, or any sensory, mental, or physical handicap	No
WEST VIRGINIA	5-11A-5, 9; 37-6-5	Holdover converts to year-to-year tenancy upon terms of original lease (*Allen* v. *Bartlett*, 20 W. Va. 46)		No discrimination on basis of race, color, religion, ancestry, familial status, blindness, handicap, or national origin; housing for older persons exempted	No
WISCONSIN	101.22; 704.25	Landlord may elect to hold tenant to month-to-month basis on holdover, unless the lease for weekly or daily rent		No discrimination on basis of race, sex, color, sexual orientation (including owner-occupied single-family dwellings), disability, religion, national origin, marital status, family status, income source (lawful), age, ancestry; housing for older persons exempted	No
WYOMING	6-9-102; 34-2-128, 129	Accepting rent on holdover does not imply renewal, constitutes only tenancy by sufferance		No discrimination based on race, color, sex, creed, or national origin	No

VIII. TAX LAWS

35. CONSUMER TAXES

The taxation system in the United States is very complicated due, in part, to the attempt by governing bodies to make taxation, across the board, appear reasonable and invisible.

Overall, there are two types of consumer taxes. Some are meant merely to raise revenues while others are designed to inhibit certain behavior. (In the income tax arena, however, which is significantly in the domain of the federal government, taxes and deductions and exemptions are used to actually promote certain behavior, such as saving money or buying a house.) In many cases, the behavioral control aspect of the tax has outweighed the particular tax's revenue-raising function. For example, tobacco-producing states do not have cigarette taxes that are as high as those in states that, for various reasons, attempt to inhibit smoking.

Market forces also influence consumer taxes. For example, the tax on wines produced in California is low compared to taxes on wines produced in other states. If California taxes were close to the national average, then California wines sold in other states would have artificially inflated prices, thus hurting its marketability.

The taxes treated in this chapter are not exhaustive. Rather, they are representative of the most common and significant consumer taxes levied by states.

Table 35: Consumer Taxes

State	Sales Tax	Cigarette Tax	Gasoline Tax	Use Tax	Liquor Tax	Gambling Tax
ALABAMA	4% §40-23-2	16.5¢ §40-25-2	16¢ §§40-17-31, 220	4% §§40-23-61, 63	Liquor monopoly state; Beer 9.875¢/12 oz. (§§28-3-184, 190); Wine and spirits 10% wholesale price (§28-3-200) + 46% (§§28-3-201 to 205); Table wine 45¢/liter (§28-7-16)	NA
ALASKA	None	29¢ §43.50.190	8¢ §43.40.010	None	Beer 35¢/gal.; Wine and spirits ≤21% alcohol 85¢/gal., >21% $5.60/gal. §43.60.010	NA
ARIZONA	5% §42-1317	18¢ §§42-1204, 1231	18¢ §28-1501	Same as sales for same type of activity §42-1408	Beer 16¢/gal.; Wine <24% 84¢/gal., >24% $4.00/gal.; Spirits $3.00/gal. §42-1204	NA
ARKANSAS	4.5% §§26-52-301, 302	22¢ §26-57-208	18.5¢ §§26-55-205, 1002	4.5% §§26-52-302; 26-53-106, 107	Beer 20¢/gal.; Light wine 25¢/gal.; Wine 75¢/gal.; Spirits $2.50/gal. §3-7-104	NA
CALIFORNIA	6% Rev. & Tax §§6051 to 6051.5	35¢ Rev. & Tax §§30101, 30123	17¢; 18¢ effective 1/1/94; Rev. & Tax §7351	6% Rev. & Tax §§6201 to 6201.5	Beer $6.20/barrel; Still wines 20¢/gal.; Sparkling wine 30¢/gal.; Spirits $3.30/gal. Rev. & Tax §§32151, 32201, 32220	NA
COLORADO	3% §39-26-106	20¢ §39-28-103	22¢ §39-27-102	3% §39-26-202	Beer 8¢/gal.; Wine 8.33¢/liter (12.33¢/liter Colorado wines); Spirits 60.26¢/liter §§12-46-111, 127	Not to exceed 40% of adjusted gross profits §12-47.1-601
CONNECTICUT	6% §§12-408, 411	45¢ §12-296	29¢; 30¢ effective 1/1/94; 31¢, 7/1/94; §12-458	6% §§12-408, 411	Beer $6.00/barrel; Still wine <21% 60¢/gal., >21% and sparkling wine $1.50/gal.; Spirits $4.50/gal. §12-435	NA
DELAWARE	None	24¢ Tit. 30 §5305	19¢ Tit. 30 §5110	2% Tit. 30 §4302	Beer $4.85/barrel; Wine 97¢/gal.; Spirits <25% $3.64/gal., >25% $5.46/gal. Tit. 4 §§581, 709	NA

(Continued)

Table 35: Consumer Taxes—Continued

State	Sales Tax	Cigarette Tax	Gasoline Tax	Use Tax	Liquor Tax	Gambling Tax
DISTRICT OF COLUMBIA	6% §47-2002	50¢ §47-2402	20¢ §47-2301	6% §47-2202	Beer $2.79/barrel; Wine <14% 30¢/gal, >14% 40¢/gal.; Sparkling wine 45¢/gal.; Spirits $1.50/gal. §§25-124, 138	NA
FLORIDA	6% §§212.03, *et. seq.*	33.9¢ §210.02	4¢ §206.487, 877	6% §§212.03, *et seq.*	Beer 48¢/gal.; Wine <17.259% $2.25/gal., >17.259% $3.00/gal.; Sparkling wine $3.50/gal.; Spirits 17.259% to 55.78% $6.50/gal., >55.78% $9.53/gal. §§563.05; 564.06; 565.12	NA
GEORGIA	4% §48-8-30	12¢ §48-11-2	7.5¢ §48-9-3	4% §48-8-30	Beer $10/barrel, in bottles or cans 4.5¢/12 oz.; Wine 40¢/liter (11¢/liter Georgia wines); Spirits 50¢/liter, $1.20/liter imported §§3-5-60; 3-6-50; 3-4-60	NA
HAWAII	4% §237-13	40% of wholesale price §245-3	16¢ §243-4, 5	4% §238-2	Draft beer 50¢/gal.; Bottle beer 89¢/gal.; Still wine $1.30/gal.; Sparkling wine $2/gal.; Spirits $5.75/gal. §244D-4	NA
IDAHO	5% §§63-3619, 3621	18¢ §63-2506	21¢ §§63-2402, 2405, 2416, 2417	5% §§63-3619, 3621	Liquor monopoly state; Beer $4.65/barrel; Wine 45¢/gal.; 15% of price per unit on all goods sold in state dispensary	
ILLINOIS	6.25% 35 ILCS 120/2-10	30¢ 35 ILCS 130/2	19¢ 35 ILCS 505/2	6.25% 35 ILCS 105/3-10	Beer 7¢/gal.; Wine <14% 23¢/gal., §14% 60¢/gal.; Spirits $2.00/gal. 235 ILCS 5/8-1	Riverboat gambling tax $2 per person admitted; wagering tax 20% adjusted gross receipts 230 ILCS 10/12, 230 ILCS 10/13

(Continued)

Table 35: Consumer Taxes—Continued

State	Sales Tax	Cigarette Tax	Gasoline Tax	Use Tax	Liquor Tax	Gambling Tax
INDIANA	5% §§6-2.5-2-2, 6-2.5-3-3	15.5¢ §6-7-1-12	15¢ §6-6-2.1-201	5% §§6-2.5-2-2, 6-2.5-3-3	Beer 11.5¢/gal.; Wine <21% 47¢/gal., >21% $2.68/gal.; Spirits $2.68/gal. §§7.1-4-2-1; 7.1-4-3-1; 7.1-4-5-1	NA
IOWA	5% §422.43	36¢ §98.6	20¢ §324.3	5% §423.2	Liquor monopoly state; Beer $5.89/barrel; Wine $1.75/gal. §§123, 123.22, 136, 183	Excursion boat gambling tax: 5% on first $1 million; 10% next $2 million; 20% over $3 million
KANSAS	4.9% §79-3603	24¢ §79-3310	18¢ §§79-34, 141	4.9% §79-3703	Beer 18¢/gal.; Wine <14% 30¢/gal., >14% 75¢/gal.; Spirits $2.50/gal. §§41-501(2); 79-3818, 4101, 41a02	NA
KENTUCKY	6% §§139.200, 310	3¢ §138.140	15¢ (9% of average wholesale price plus supplementary highway user motor fuel tax, computed quarterly) §138.220	6% §§139.200, 310	Beer $2.50/barrel; Wine 50¢/gal.; Spirits $1.92/gal. §§243.680, 690, 710, 720	NA
LOUISIANA	4% §§39:2006; 47:302, 331	20¢ §47:841	20¢ §§47:711, 820.1	4% §§39:2006; 47:302, 331	Beer $10/barrel; Still wine <14% 3¢/liter, >14% 6¢/liter; Sparkling wine 42¢/liter; Spirits 66¢/liter §§26:341, 342	NA
MAINE	5% Tit. 36 §§1811, 1861	37¢ §4365	17¢ Tit. 36 §2903	5% Tit. 36 §§1811, 1861	Liquor monopoly state; Beer 85¢/gal.; Wine 60¢/gal.; Sparkling wine $1.24/gal.; Spirits: Commission must sell at price that will produce state liquor tax of at least 75% of carload cost plus $1.25/ proof gal. Tit. 28-A §§1651, 1652, 1703	NA

(Continued)

Table 35: Consumer Taxes—Continued

State	Sales Tax	Cigarette Tax	Gasoline Tax	Use Tax	Liquor Tax	Gambling Tax
MARYLAND	5% Tax-Gen. §11-104	36¢ Tax-Gen. §12-105	23.5¢ Tax-Gen. §9-305	5% Tax-Gen. §11-104	Beer 9¢/gal.; Wine 40¢/gal.; Spirits $1.50 gal.; Tax-Gen. §5-201	NA
MASSACHUSETTS	5% Ch. 64H §2	26¢ Ch. 64C §20	21¢ (19.1% of average price, but minimum cannot be less than 21¢/gal.) Ch. 62C§3A; Ch. 64A§1; Ch. 64E§4; Ch. 64F§3	5% Ch. 64I §2	Beer $3.30/barrel; Still wine 55¢/gal.; Sparkling wine 70¢/gal.; Spirits <15% $1.10/proof gal., 15-50% $4.05/proof gal., >50% $4.05/proof gal. Ch. 138 §21	NA
MICHIGAN	4% §205.52	25¢ §§205.507, 507a	15¢ §§207.102; 259.203	4% §205.93	Liquor monopoly state; Beer $6.30/gal.; Wine <16% 13.5¢/liter, >16% 20¢/liter; Spirits offsale 13.85% of retail selling price, onsale 12% of retail selling price §§436.16a, 40, 101, 121	NA
MINNESOTA	6% §§297A.02, 14	48¢ §297.03	20¢ §296.02	6% §§297A.02, 14	Beer 3.2% $2.40/barrel, >3.2% $4.60/barrel; Wine 14% 30¢/gal., 14-21% 95¢/gal., 21-24% $1.82/gal., >24% $3.59/gal.; Sparkling wine $1.82/gal.; Spirits $5.03/gal. §297C.02	Horseracing 6% of net receipts plus 1% of gross bets §240.15; Bingo 10% §349.212
MISSISSIPPI	7% §§27-65-15, *et seq.*	18¢ §27-69-13	18¢ §27-55-11	Same rate as sales tax 27-67-5	Liquor monopoly state; Beer, light wine 42.68¢/gal.; Wine 5¢/gal.; all other vitis rotundifolia grapes 35¢/gal.; Sparkling wine $1/gal.; Spirits $2.50/gal. A 27.5% markup is imposed on all alcoholic beverages sold by the Alcoholic Beverage Control Division §§27-71-7, 5, 201, 307, 335; 67-1-41	4% <$50,000/mo., 6% $50,000-134,000/mo.; 8% over $134,000/mo. §75-76-177

(Continued)

Table 35: Consumer Taxes—Continued

State	Sales Tax	Cigarette Tax	Gasoline Tax	Use Tax	Liquor Tax	Gambling Tax
MISSOURI	4.225% §144.020; Mo. Const. Art. IV §§43(a) and 47(c)	13¢ §149.015	13¢ (15¢ effective 4/1/94) §142.025	Same rate as sales tax §144.610	Beer $1.86/barrel; Wine 30¢/gal.; Spirits $2/gal. §§311.550; 312.320, 520	5% on first million dollars; 12% on next two million dollars; 20% over 3 million dollars; L. 1991, H.B. No. 149, §10 (approved 11/3/92)
MONTANA	None	18¢ §16-11-111	20¢ §15-70-204	None	Liquor monopoly state; Beer $4.30/barrel; Wine 28¢/liter; Spirits 22.4% retail selling price for companies <200,000 gal./year nationwide, 26% for >200,000 gal./year §§16-1-401, 404, 406, 408, 411; 16-2-301	NA
NEBRASKA	5% (Legislature is required to set rate each year) §§77-2701.02, 2715.01	27¢ §77-2602	23.6¢ §§66-4, 105; 66-4,144; 66-4,145; 66-4,146; 66-489	5% §§77-2701.02, 2715.01	Beer 23¢/gal.; Wine <14% 75¢/gal., >14% $1.35/gal.; Spirits $3.00/gal. §53-160	NA
NEVADA	6.5% §§372.105, 185; 374.110, 190; 377.040	35¢ §370.165	20.75¢ §§365.170, 180, 190, 192	6.5% §§372.105, 185; 374.110, 190; 377.040	Beer 9¢/gal.; Wine <14% 40¢/gal., 14-22% 75¢/gal., >22% $2.05/gal. §369.330	Gross revenues <$50,000/mo. 3%; $50,000-134,000 4%; >$134,000 6.25% §§463.320,370
NEW HAMPSHIRE	None	25¢ §78:7	18¢ §260:32	None	Liquor monopoly state; 30¢/gal. on all beverages sold at retail §§177:1; 178:6, 28, 30	NA
NEW JERSEY	6% §54:32B-3	40¢ §54:40A-8	10.5¢ §54:39-27	6% §54:32B-6	Beer 12¢/gal.; Wine 70¢/gal.; Spirits $4.40/gal. §54:43-1	8% of gross revenues §5:12-144
NEW MEXICO	5% §7-9-4	15¢ §7-12-3	16¢ §7-13-3	5% §7-9-7	Beer 18¢/gal.; Wine 25¢/liter; Spirits $1.04/liter §7-17-5	NA

(Continued)

Table 35: Consumer Taxes—Continued

State	Sales Tax	Cigarette Tax	Gasoline Tax	Use Tax	Liquor Tax	Gambling Tax
NEW YORK	4% Tax §§1105, 1110	39¢ §471	8¢ §§284, *et seq.*	4% §§1105, 1110	Beer 21¢/gal.; Sparkling wine 15¢/liter (artificial), 25¢/gal. (natural); Wine and spirits <24% 67¢/gal.; other $1.70/liter Tax Ch. 60 §424	NA
NORTH CAROLINA	4% §105-164.4	5¢ §105-113.5	21.9¢ §105-434	4% §105-164.4	Liquor monopoly state; Beer 48.387¢/gal. in barrels, 53.376¢/gal. in containers <7.75 gal.; Wine 21¢/liter unfortified, 24¢/liter fortified; Spirits 28% retail §§105-113.80; 18A-15(3)(c)	NA
NORTH DAKOTA	5% §§57-39.2-02.1, 03.2	29¢ §§57-36-06, 27	17¢ §57-43.1-02	5% §§57-40.2-02.1, 57-40.2-03.2	Beer 8¢/gal. in barrels, 16¢/gal. in bottles; Wine <17% 50¢/gal.; 17-24% 60¢/gal.; Sparkling wine $1.00/gal.; Spirits $2.50/gal. §5-03-07	NA
OHIO	5% §5739.025	18¢ §§5743.02, 023, 32, 322	21¢ §§5728.16; 5735.05, 25, 29, 011	Same rate as sales tax §5741.02	Liquor monopoly state; Beer $3.50/barrel; bottled: .14¢/oz. <12 oz.; .84¢/6oz. in containers >12 oz.; Wine 4-14% 26¢/gal., 14-21% 62¢/gal.; Vermouth 77¢/gal.; Sparkling wine $1.27/gal.; Spirits $2.25/gal. §§4301.10, 12, 42, 43, 4305.01, 09; 4307.02; 4309.04	NA
OKLAHOMA	4.5% Tit. 68 §§1354; 1362	23¢ Tit. 68 §§302	16¢ Tit. 68 §§502; 516; 522	4.5% §1402	Beer 3.2% $11.25/barrel, >3.2% $12.50/barrel; Wine <14% 19¢/liter, >14% 37¢/liter; Sparkling wine 55¢/liter; Spirits $1.47/liter Tit. 37 §§163.3; 553; 576	NA

(Continued)

Table 35: Consumer Taxes—Continued

State	Sales Tax	Cigarette Tax	Gasoline Tax	Use Tax	Liquor Tax	Gambling Tax
OREGON	None	28¢ §323.030	24¢ §319.020	None	Liquor monopoly state; Beer $2.60/barrel; Alcoholic beverages <14% 67¢/gal., 14-21% 77¢/gal.; Oregon Liquor Control Commission fixes prices §§471.725, 730; 473.010, 030	NA
PENNSYLVANIA	6% Tit. 72 §§7202, 7210	31¢ Tit. 72 §8206	12¢ Tit. 72 §§2611d, 2612.1; Tit. 75 §9511.1	6% Tit. 72 §§7202; 7210	Liquor monopoly state; Beer 8¢/gal.; Wine.5-24%.005/ unit proof/gal.; Spirits $1.00/gal. Tit. 47 §§301, 746, 747, 795	NA
RHODE ISLAND	7% §§44-18-18, 20	37¢ §44-20-12	26¢ §31-36-7	7% §44-18-20	Made in state: Beer .097¢/gal., $3.00/barrel; Still wine 60¢/gal. (from Rhode Island grapes 30¢); Sparkling wine 75¢/ gal.; Spirits $3.75/gal. Imported into state: Beer .065¢/gal., $2.00/barrel; Still wine 40¢/gal.; Sparkling wine 50¢/ gal.; Spirits $2.50/gal. §3-10-1	NA
SOUTH CAROLINA	5% §§12-36-910, 2620	13¢ §12-21-620	16¢ §§12-27-230, 240, 510, 520, 1210, 1220	5% §§12-36-1310, 2620	Beer <5% .006¢/gal.; Wine <21% 90¢/gal.; All other alcoholic beverages 12¢/8oz. or 50.7¢/liter; Wholesalers are subject to additional tax; Additional excise tax on sale of wine §§12-21-1020, 1030, 1040, 1310; 12-33-230, 240, 410, 425, 460	NA

(Continued)

Table 35: Consumer Taxes—Continued

State	Sales Tax	Cigarette Tax	Gasoline Tax	Use Tax	Liquor Tax	Gambling Tax
SOUTH DAKOTA	4% §10-45-2	23¢ §§10-50-3; 10-50A-10	18¢ §10-47A-39	Same general rates as sales tax §§10-46-2	Beer $8.50/barrel; Wine 3.2-14% 93¢/gal., 14-20% $1.45/gal., 21-24% (except sparkling) $2.07/gal.; All other $3.93/gal.; Additional 2% imposed on all but malt beverages by wholesaler from distiller, manufacturer, or supplier §§35-5-3; 35-5-6.1	8%; May be decreased or increased by Commission on Gaming from 5-15% §42-7B-28
TENNESSEE	6% 67-6-202, 205, 209, 221	13¢ §§67-4-1004, 1005	14¢ 67-3-1103	6% 67-6-202, 205, 209, 221	Beer <5% $3.40/barrel; Wine <21% $1.10/gal.; Spirits $4/gal., <7% $1.10/gal. §§57-3-302, 303; 57-5-201	NA
TEXAS	6.25% Tax §§151.051, 101	41¢ Tax §154.021	20¢ Tax §153.102	6.25% Tax §§151.051, 101	Beer $6.00/barrel; Malt liquor >4% 19.8¢/gal.; Still wine <14% 20.4¢/gal., >14% 40.8¢/gal.; Sparkling wine 51.8¢/gal.; Spirits $2.40/gal. (minimum tax 5¢/pkg. <2 oz., 12.2¢/pkg 8 oz.) Tax §§203.01, *et seq.*	Bingo Enabling Act 5% gross receipts (state); 2% gross receipts (local); 3% facility rental; 3% prize Civ. Stat. Art. 179d
UTAH	5% §59-12-103	23¢ §§59-14-204, 302	19¢ §59-13-201	5% §59-12-103	Liquor monopoly state; Beer $11/barrel; 13% retail purchase price all other §§32A-2-101; 59-15-101; 59-16-100	NA
VERMONT	Tit. 32 §9771	20¢ §7771	15¢ Tit. 10 §§1942, 3106; Tit. 32 §9773	Tit. §9773	Beer 26.5¢/gal.; Wine 55¢/gal.; Spirits and fortified wine 25% of gross revenues Tit. 7 §§421, 422	NA

(Continued)

Table 35: Consumer Taxes—Continued

State	Sales Tax	Cigarette Tax	Gasoline Tax	Use Tax	Liquor Tax	Gambling Tax
VIRGINIA	3.5% §§58.1-603, 604	2.5¢ §§58.1-1001, 1018	17.5¢ §58.1-2105	3.5% §§58.1-603, 604	Liquor monopoly state; Beer $.95/barrel, 2¢/bottle <7 oz., 2.65¢/bottle 7-12 oz., 2.22 mills/oz./bottle >12 oz.; Wine 40¢/liter §§4-128; 4-22.1	NA
WASHINGTON	6.5% §82.08.020	34¢ §§82.24.020, 027	23¢ §82.36.025	6.5% §82.12.020	Liquor monopoly state; Beer $2.60/barrel; Wine <14% 21.50¢/liter, >14% 43.94¢/liter; Additional tax on sales of wine and beer at 7% of basic tax rates §§66.08.050; 66.24.210, 220, 290; 82.02.030	NA
WEST VIRGINIA	6% §11-15-9	17¢ §11-17-3	15.5¢ §11-14-3	6% §11-15A-2	Nonintoxicating beer $5.50/barrel; Intoxicating liquor 5% of purchase price §11-16-13 60-3A-21	NA
WISCONSIN	5% §§77.52, 53	38¢ §139.31(1)	22.2¢ §§78.01, 015, 40, 405, 017, 407	5% §77.52, 53	Beer $2/barrel; Wine <14% 6.605¢/liter, 14-21% 11.89¢/liter; All other 85.86¢/liter; administrative fee on all beverages >21% 3¢/gal.; §§139.02, 03, 06	NA
WYOMING	3% §39-6-404	12¢ §39-6-103	9¢ §39-6-209	3% §39-6-504	Liquor monopoly state; Beer .5¢/liter; Wine .75¢/ml.; Spirits 2.5¢/100 ml. §12-2-101-301	NA

36. PERSONAL INCOME TAX

If you live in Alaska, Florida, Nevada, South Dakota, Texas, Washington, or Wyoming, you may not be aware that most of the rest of the country has to file two tax returns every April. Every other state, aside from these lucky seven, requires income tax—over and above federal taxes—from its citizens.

Deductions and exemptions available to the taxpayer vary greatly from state to state. Tennessee claims one of the more interesting exemptions: the income of a prisoner of war is not taxed. There is also a provision to exempt all income of estates of individuals who perished in Operations Desert Storm and Desert Shield. Wisconsin has a "recycling tax surcharge" for all people or entities filing returns; the only exemption is for entities engaged in farming. The surcharge lasts until 1999 and carries a maximum of $9,800 per year.

North Dakota has the highest percentage tax rate at 12 percent of taxable income over $50,000. Massachusetts taxes interest, capital gains, and dividends at 12 percent. California and Montana are next with 11 percent rates. Hawaii has a 10 percent rate, and after that states tend to group together. Most rates in the higher brackets are in the 5 percent to 8 percent range.

It is interesting to note also that California has the highest income brackets: $300,000 to $400,000 and over $400,000. The intent here is clearly to have the rich pay taxes at higher rates and shoulder more of the load for maintaining the revenue base; a pragmatic view, however, is that higher brackets protect those in the middle from the higher rates at the top. Arizona is the only other state with an income tax bracket over $150,000, with one of $300,000. Most states have an upper bracket that is below $60,000.

Five states have had their income tax schemes challenged in court: Illinois, Louisiana, Michigan, Nebraska, and Ohio. All of these tax codes have been "certified" constitutional by federal courts.

The chart in this chapter deals only with the general principles of state personal income tax. The tax tables are accurate but are very much consolidated and generalized in order to give the reader a broad basis for comparison. The rates listed are, for the most part, for married couples filing jointly or for heads of households. Where this is not the case, the rate is noted. Slightly different rates and tables will apply in most states for couples filing separately or for single individuals. Also, there are countless deductions and exemptions available to the taxpayer that are similar to those available in the federal income tax code. Included here are only the general deductions and exemptions for determining state taxable income. See your state codes or the code of the state in which you are interested for detailed information.

Table 36: Personal Income Tax

State	Code Section	Who is Required to File	Rate	Federal Income Tax Deductible	Federal Income Used as Basis
ALABAMA	40-18-1, *et seq.*	Resident natural persons, fiduciaries, estates and trusts, and nonresidents receiving income from property owned or business transacted in the state	First $1,000, 2%; Next $5,000, 4%; Over $6,000, 5%	Yes	Yes
ALASKA	Income tax repealed 1/1/79, Alaska Laws 1980, 2d Sp. Sess. §9, ch. 2	Individual may file at his or her option to obtain certain tax credits for political donations or expenses for child care necessary for employment. (Note: Provisions suspended until 1/1/93)			
ARIZONA	43-1010, *et seq.*	All Arizona residents and nonresidents that derive income from activity or ownership of property within the state; Partnerships are not taxable	$20,001 to $50,000 = $760 plus 4.4% of excess over $20,000; $50,001 to $100,000 = $2,080 plus 5.25% of excess over $50,000; $100,001 to $300,000 = $4,705 plus 6.5% of excess over $100,000; $300,001 and over = $17,705 plus 7% of excess over $300,000	No	Yes
ARKANSAS	26-51-201, *et seq.*	Resident individuals, estates and trusts, and nonresidents deriving income from local property or activity	First $2,999, 1%; Next $3,000, 2.5%; Next $3,000, 3.5%; Next $6,000, 4.5%; Next $10,000, 6%; $25,000 or over, 7%; general rate for all taxpayers; special reduced rates available for low income	No	No

(Continued)

Table 36: Personal Income Tax—Continued

State	Code Section	Who is Required to File	Rate	Federal Income Tax Deductible	Federal Income Used as Basis
CALIFORNIA	REV. & TAX CODE §§17041, *et seq.*	Resident persons, including estates and trusts; nonresidents and part-year residents are liable for pro-rata share	$0 to $9,104 = 1%; $9,104 to $21,578 = $91.04 plus 2% of excess over $9,104; $21,578 to $34,054 = $340.52 plus 4% of excess over $21,578; $34,054 to $47,274 = $839.56 plus 6% of excess over $34,054; $47,274 to $59,746 = $1,632.76 plus 8% of excess over $47,274; $59,746 to $207,200 = $2,630.52 plus 9.3% of excess over $59,746; $207,200 to $414,400 = $16,343.74 plus 10% of excess over $207,200; $414,400 and over = $37,063.74 plus 11% of excess over $414,400	No	Yes
COLORADO	39-22-104, *et seq.*	Every individual, estate, and trust that is required to file federal return; non- and part-year residents are liable for pro-rata share; Partnerships are not subject to tax	5% of federal taxable income; general rate for all taxpayers; alternative rates may apply	No	Yes
CONNECTICUT	51, *et seq.*, act 3, Laws (1991), 1st sp. sess.	Each resident individual, trust, and estate with Connecticut taxable income; Nonresident individuals, estates, and trusts on Connecticut income	4.5% of Connecticut taxable income; general rate for all resident taxpayers	No	Yes
DELAWARE	1102, *et seq.*	Individuals, estates, and trusts with Delaware taxable income	$2,001 to $5,000, 3.2%; Next $5,000, 5%; Next $10,000, 6%; Next $5,000, 6.6%; Next $5,000, 7%; Next $10,000 7.6%; Over $40,000 7.7%; general rate for all resident taxpayers	No	Yes

(Continued)

Table 36: Personal Income Tax—Continued

State	Code Section	Who is Required to File	Rate	Federal Income Tax Deductible	Federal Income Used as Basis
DISTRICT OF COLUMBIA	47-1806, *et seq.*	Any individual domiciled in the district, any resident of 183 days or more, and estates and trusts	$10,001 to $20,000 = $600 plus 8% of excess over $10,000; over $20,000 = $1,400 plus 9.5% of excess over $20,000; general rate for all resident taxpayers	No	Yes
FLORIDA	No personal income tax				
GEORGIA	48-7-20, *et seq.*	Resident and non-resident individuals with taxable net income and estates and trusts	First $1,000 = 1%; $1,000 to $3,000 = $10 plus 2% of amount over $1,000; $3,000 to $5,000 = $50 plus 3% of amount over $3,000; $5,000 to $7,000 = $110 plus 4% of amount over $5,000; $7,000 to $10,000 = $190 plus 5% of amount over $7,000; Over $10,000 = $340 plus 6% of amount over $10,000	No	Yes
HAWAII	235, *et seq.*	Resident individual, estate or trust nonresidents, estates and trusts on income derived from Hawaii sources	First $3,000 = 2%; $3,000 to $5,000 = $60 plus 4% of excess over $3,000; $5,000 to $7,000 = $140 plus 6% of excess over $5,000; $7,000 to $11,000 = $260 plus 7.25% of excess over $7,000; $11,000 to $21,000 = $550 plus 8% of excess over $11,000; $21,000 to $31,000 = $1,355 plus 8.75% of excess over $21,000; $31,000 to $41,000 = $2,225 plus 9.5% of excess over $31,000; Over $41,000 = $3,175 plus 10% of amount over $41,000	No	Yes

(Continued)

Table 36: Personal Income Tax—Continued

State	Code Section	Who is Required to File	Rate	Federal Income Tax Deductible	Federal Income Used as Basis
IDAHO	63-3024, *et seq.*	Resident individuals, estates and trusts with taxable income and nonresident or part-year resident individuals, estates and trusts from Idaho sources	$1,000 but less than $2,000 = $20 plus 4% of excess over $1,000; $2,000 but less than $3,000 = $60 plus 4.5% of excess over $2,000; $3,000 but less than $4,000 = $105 plus 5.5% of excess over $3,000; $4,000 but less than $5,000 = $160 plus 6.5% of excess over $4,000; $5,000 but less than $7,500 = $225 plus 7.5% of excess over $5,000; $7,500 but less than $20,000 = $412.50 plus 7.8% of excess over $7,500; Over $20,000 = $1,387.50 plus 8.2% of excess over $20,000; for couples filing joint return, tax is twice tax imposed on half of aggregate taxable income	No	Yes
ILLINOIS	35 ILCS 5/201, *et seq.*	Individuals, estates, and trusts; Partnerships are not taxable	3% of taxable net income imposed on all taxpayers; tax rate is reduced to 2.75% for tax years beginning after June 30, 1993. An additional personal property replacement tax of 1.5% of net income is imposed on partnerships, trusts, and S corporations.	No	Yes
INDIANA	6-3-1, *et seq.*	Resident individuals, estates and trusts, and nonresidents on adjusted gross income derived from Indiana sources	3.4% of adjusted gross income; general rate for all resident taxpayers	No	Yes

(Continued)

Table 36: Personal Income Tax—Continued

State	Code Section	Who is Required to File	Rate	Federal Income Tax Deductible	Federal Income Used as Basis
IOWA	422, *et seq.*	Residents, part-year residents, nonresidents, estates and trusts	$1,060 to $2,120 = $4.24 plus 0.8% of excess over $1,060; $2,120 to $4,240 = $12.72 plus 2.7% of excess over $2,120; $4,240 to $9,540 = $69.96 plus 5% of excess over $4,240; $9,540 to $15,900 = $334.96 plus 6.8% of excess over $9,540; $15,900 to $21,200 = $767.44 plus 7.2% of excess over $15,900; $21,200 to $31,800 = $1,149.04 plus 7.55% of excess over $21,200; $31,800 to $47,700 = $1,949.34 plus 8.8% of excess over $31,800; Over $47,700 = $3,348.54 plus 9.98% of excess over $47,700; general rate for all taxpayers; an alternative minimum tax is imposed equal to 75% of the maximum state individual income tax rate for the tax year of the state alternative minimum taxable income	Yes	Yes
KANSAS	79-32; 110, *et seq.*	Resident and nonresidents, estates, trusts and fiduciaries	First $30,000 = 3.5%; $30,000 to $60,000 = $1,050 plus 6.25% of excess over $30,000; Over $60,000 = $2,925 plus 6.45% of evcess over $60,000	No	Yes
KENTUCKY	141.020, *et seq.*	Residents, nonresidents on net income from businesses, trade, professions or other activities carried on in the state or tangible or intangible property located in the state	First $3,000, 2%; Next $1,000, 3%; Next $1,000, 4%; Next $3,000, 5%; $8,000 and over 6%; general rate for all taxpayers	No	Yes

(Continued)

Table 36: Personal Income Tax—Continued

State	Code Section	Who is Required to File	Rate	Federal Income Tax Deductible	Federal Income Used as Basis
LOUISIANA	47:200, *et seq.*	Residents and nonresidents on Louisiana income; Individuals permanently domiciled in the state are taxed on all income from whatever source; All others are taxed on Louisiana income; Partnerships are not taxable	First $10,000, 2%; Next $40,000, 4%; Over $50,000, 6%; (Maximum tax rates for individuals)	No	Yes
MAINE	Title 36 §§5111, *et seq.*	Every resident on entire taxable income and nonresidents on adjusted gross income, estates, and trusts	Less than $4,150 = 2.1%; $4,150 to $8,250 = $87 plus 4.725% of excess over $4,150; $8,250 to $16,500 = $281 plus 7.35% of excess over $8,250; $16,500 to $37,500 = $887 plus 8.925% of excess over $16,500; $37,500 or more = $2,761 plus 9.89% of excess over $37,500; (single individuals and married persons filing separately); For 1993 and thereafter, the upper bracket is repealed	No	Yes
MARYLAND	Tax-Gen. 10-102, *et seq.*	Residents and nonresidents on taxable net income. Partnerships are not taxed.	First $1,000, 2%; Second $1,000, 3%; Third $1,000, 4%; Over $3,000, 5%	No	Yes
MASSACHUSETTS	Ch. 62, generally	Individuals, including fiduciaries, estates of deceased Massachusetts inhabitants, and nonresidents earning income in Massachusetts; Partnerships are not taxed; A "corporate trust" engaged in business in Massachusetts is taxed	Interest, dividends, net capital gains, 12%; All other income 5.95%	No	Yes
MICHIGAN	206.51	Individuals, estates, and trusts; Each person with business activity in Michigan allocated or apportioned to Michigan is subject to the single business tax	4.6% of taxable income	No	Yes

(Continued)

Table 36: Personal Income Tax—Continued

State	Code Section	Who is Required to File	Rate	Federal Income Tax Deductible	Federal Income Used as Basis
MINNESOTA	290.01, *et seq.*	Resident and nonresident individuals and estates and trusts; Partnerships are not taxed; Individual partners subject to their share of income	$0 to $20,960, 6%; $20,961 to $83,300, 8%; Over $83,301, 8.5% (married individuals filing jointly and surviving spouses)	No	Yes
MISSISSIPPI	27-7-5, *et seq.*	Resident individuals, trusts and estates on entire net income from property owned or sold and business trade or occupation carried on in Mississippi by nonresident individuals, partnerships, trusts and estates	First $5,000, 3%; Next $5,000, 4%; Over $10,000, 5%	No	No
MISSOURI	143.010, *et seq.*	Resident individuals and nonresidents with income derived from Missouri sources, and estates and trusts; Partnerships are not taxable	First $1,000 = 1.5%; $1,000 to $2,000 = $15 plus 2% of excess over $1,000; $2,000 to $3,000 = $35 plus 2.5% of excess over $2,000; $3,000 to $4,000 = $60 plus 3% of excess over $3,000; $4,000 to $5,000 = $90 plus 3.5% of excess over $4,000; $5,000 to $6,000 = $125 plus 4% of excess over $5,000; $6,000 to $7,000 = $165 plus 4.5% of excess over $6,000; $7,000 to $8,000 = $210 plus 5% of excess over $7,000; $8,000 to $9,000 = $260 plus 5.5% of excess over $8,000; Over $9,000 = $315 plus 6% of excess over $9,000	Yes	Yes

(Continued)

Table 36: Personal Income Tax—Continued

State	Code Section	Who is Required to File	Rate	Federal Income Tax Deductible	Federal Income Used as Basis
MONTANA	15-30-100, *et seq.*	Residents on entire net income; Nonresidents on net income from property owned and business carried on in Montana; Estates and trusts are taxed during administration except if for educational, charitable, or religious purposes; Partnerships are not taxed	First $1,699 = 2%; $1,700 to $3,400 = 3% less $17; $3,400 to $6,800 = 4% less $51; $6,800 to $10,200 = 5% less $119; $10,200 to $13,600 = 6% less $221; $13,600 to $17,000 = 7% less $357; $17,000 to $23,700 = 8% less $527; $23,700 to $33,900 = 9% less $764; $33,900 to $59,400 = 10% less $1,103; Over $59,400 = 11% less $1,697	Yes	Yes
NEBRASKA	77-2701, *et seq.*	Residents on entire income and nonresidents on income derived from Nebraska sources; Estates and trusts are taxable; Partnerships are not taxable	First $3,000, 2.37%; Next $25,000, 3.63%; Next $17,000, 5.62%; Over $45,000, 6.92%	No	Yes
NEVADA	No personal income tax				
NEW HAMPSHIRE	77.1, *et seq.*	Inhabitants and part-year residents, partnerships, associations and trusts, and fiduciaries with income of more than $1,200 per year	5%, limited to interest and dividends	No	No
NEW JERSEY	54A:1, *et seq.*	Individuals, estates and trusts, residents and nonresident taxed on gross income; Nonresidents are only taxed on income derived from New Jersey sources; Partnerships are not taxable	First $20,000 = 2%; $20,000 to $50,000 = $400 plus 2.5% of excess over $20,000; $50,000 to $70,000 = $1,150 plus 3.5% of excess over $50,000; $70,000 to $80,000 = $1,850 plus 5% of excess over $70,000; $80,000 to $150,000 = $2,350 plus 6.5% of excess over $80,000; Over $150,000 = $6,900 plus 7% of excess over $150,000	No	No

(Continued)

Table 36: Personal Income Tax—Continued

State	Code Section	Who is Required to File	Rate	Federal Income Tax Deductible	Federal Income Used as Basis
NEW MEXICO	7-7-2, *et seq.*	Residents on net income and nonresidents deriving income from business or property in New Mexico, including estates and trusts	Not over $8,000 = 2.4%; $8,000 to $16,000 = $192 plus 3.8% of excess over $8,000; $16,000 to $24,000 = $496 plus 4.8% of excess over $16,000; $24,000 to $36,000 = $880 plus 5.9% of excess over $24,000; $36,000 to $48,000 = $2,416 plus 6.9% of excess over $36,000; $48,000 to $64,000 = $2,416 plus 7.7% of excess over $$64,000; Over $64,000 = $3,648 plus 8.5% of excess over $64,000	No	Yes
NEW YORK	TAX 601, *et seq.*	Individuals, estates and trusts, and nonresidents on income derived from New York sources; Partnerships are not taxable; New York City taxes resident individuals, estates, and trusts on their city taxable income; Partnerships are not taxable (§§11-1701, *et seq.*)	Not over $11,000 = 4%; $11,000 to $16,000 = $440 plus 5% of excess over $11,000; $16,000 to $22,000 = $690 plus 6% of excess over $16,000; $22,000 to $26,000 = $1,050 plus 7% of excess over $22,000; Over $26,000 = $1,330 plus 7.875% of excess over $26,000	No	Yes
NORTH CAROLINA	105-134, *et seq.*	Every individual on North Carolina taxable income, and income of estates and trusts.	Up to $21,250, 6%; Next $78,750, 7%; Over $100,000, 7.75%	No	Yes
NORTH DAKOTA	57-38-02, *et seq.*	Residents and nonresidents on property owned or business carried on in North Dakota; Individuals, estates, and trusts have optional tax available (§57-38-30.3); Partnerships are not taxed	First $3,000, 2.67%; Next $2,000, 4%; Next $3,000, 5.33%; Next $7,000, 6.67%; Next $10,000, 8%; Next $10,000, 9.33%; Next $15,000, 10.67%; Over $50,000, 12%	Yes	Yes

(Continued)

Table 36: Personal Income Tax—Continued

State	Code Section	Who is Required to File	Rate	Federal Income Tax Deductible	Federal Income Used as Basis
OHIO	5747.01, *et seq.*	Every individual and estate residing in or earning or receiving income in Ohio	First $5,000 = 0.743%; $5,000 to $10,000 = $37.15 plus 1.486% of excess over $5,000; $10,000 to $15,000 = $111.45 plus 2.972% of excess over $10,000; $15,000 to $20,000 = $260.05 plus 3.715% of excess over $15,000; $20,000 to $40,000 = $445.80 plus 4.457% of excess over $20,000; $40,000 to $80,000 = $1,337.20 plus 5.201% of excess over $40,000; $80,000 to $100,000 = $3,417.60 plus 5.943% of excess over $80,000; $100,000 to $200,000 = $4,606.20 plus 6.9% of esxcess over $100,000; Over $200,000 = $11,506.20 plus 7.5% of excess over $200,000	No	Yes
OKLAHOMA	Title 68 §2355, *et seq.*	Resident and nonresident individuals, estates, and trusts on taxable income	First $2,000, 0.5%; Next $3,000, 1%; Next $2,500, 2%; Next $2,300, 3%; Next $2,400, 4%; Next $2,800, 5%; Next $6,000, 6%; Remainder 7%	Yes	Yes
OREGON	316.037, *et seq.*	Every Oregon resident on entire taxable income and every nonresident or part-year resident on a prorated amount of their entire taxable income; Estates and trusts are taxable; Partnerships are not taxable	First $2,000 = 5%; Next $3,000 = $100 plus 7% of excess over $2,000; Over $5,000 = $310 plus 9% of excess over $5,000	Yes	Yes
PENNSYLVANIA	Tit. 72 §§7301, *et seq.*	Resident and nonresident individuals, estates, or trusts; Nonresidents only pay for portion of income derived from Pennsylvania sources	2.8%	No	No

(Continued)

Table 36: Personal Income Tax—Continued

State	Code Section	Who is Required to File	Rate	Federal Income Tax Deductible	Federal Income Used as Basis
RHODE ISLAND	44-30-1, *et seq.*	Resident and nonresident individuals, estates, and trusts on Rhode Island income; Partnerships are not taxed	If federal income tax liability is greater than $15,000: 27.5% of federal income tax liability up to $15,000 and 32% of federal income tax liability over $15,000	No	Yes
SOUTH CAROLINA	12-7-210, *et seq.*	Individuals, estates, and trusts; Partnerships are not subject to tax; Part-year and nonresidents are subject to special tax	First $2,160 = 1.5%; $2,160 to $4,320 = $54 plus 3% of excess; $4,320 to $6,480 = $119 plus 4% of excess; $6,480 to $8,640 = $205 plus 5% of excess; $8,640 to $10,800 = $313 plus 6% of excess; Over $10,800 = $443 plus 7% of excess	No	Yes
SOUTH DAKOTA	No personal income tax				
TENNESSEE	67-2-101, *et seq.*	Resident persons, partnerships, associations, trusts, estates, and corporations	6%, limited to interest and dividends	No	No
TEXAS	No personal income tax				
UTAH	59-10-104, *et seq.*	Resident individuals, estates and trusts, and nonresidents on state taxable income derived from Utah sources; Partnerships are not taxable	First $1,500 = 2.55%; $1,500 to $3,000 = $38.25 plus 3.5% of excess over $1,500; $3,000 to $4,500 = $90.75 plus 4.4% of excess over $3,000; $4,500 to $6,000 = $156.75 plus 5.35% of excess over $4,500; $6,000 to $7,500 = $237.00 plus 6.25% of excess over $6,000; Over $7,500 = $330.75 plus 7.2% of excess over $7,500	Yes	Yes
VERMONT	Tit. 32 §§5822, *et seq.*	Residents, nonresidents, estates, and trusts on Vermont income	28% of federal income tax	No	Yes
VIRGINIA	58.1-320, *et seq.*	Individuals, estates, and trusts; Partnerships are not taxable; Estates and trusts are subject to tax on their Virginia taxable income	First $3,000, 2%; Next $2,000, 3%; Next $12,000, 5%; Over $17,000, 5.75%	No	Yes

(Continued)

Table 36: Personal Income Tax—Continued

State	Code Section	Who is Required to File	Rate	Federal Income Tax Deductible	Federal Income Used as Basis
WASHINGTON	No personal income tax				
WEST VIRGINIA	11-21-4e	Every individual, estate, and trust; Special tax on nonresidents with West Virginia income; Partnerships are not taxable	First $10,000 = 3%; $10,000 to $25,000 = $300 plus 4% of excess over $10,000; $25,000 to $40,000 = $900 plus 5% of excess over $25,000; $40,000 to $60,000 = $1,575 plus 6% of excess over $40,000; Over $60,000 = $2,775 plus 6.5% of excess over $60,000	No	Yes
WISCONSIN	71.02, *et seq.*	Individuals, fiduciaries, and trusts on net income; nonresident individuals and trusts on income derived from Wisconsin sources; nonresident's and part-year resident's tax liability is prorated according to amount of income derived from Wisconsin sources; Special "recycling surcharges" apply to all Wisconsin individuals, estates, trusts, businesses, and partnerships except those engaged solely in farming	$0 to $10,000, 4.9%; $10,001 to $20,000, 6.55%; $20,001 and over 6.93%	No	Yes
WYOMING	No personal income tax				

APPENDIX

STATUTORY COMPILATIONS USED IN THIS BOOK

The code section numbers used in this book refer to sections within the statutory compilations listed below. In those states where multiple compilations are available, the one preferred by **The Blue Book, A Uniform System of Citation,** 15th ed., 1991 (Harvard Law Review Association: Cambridge, Mass.) is used. Occasionally the preferred code was not available; every effort, however, was then made to verify the accuracy of the citations and/or convert section numbers to the preferred system.

Some states do not use a universal system of numeration but separately number individually named codes. For these states the individual code names and the abbreviations used in the book are listed.

Table 37: Statutory Compilations

State	Statutory Compilation	Abbrevation
ALABAMA	Code of Alabama	
ALASKA	Alaska Statutes	
ARIZONA	Arizone Revised Statues Annotated	
ARKANSAS	Arkansas Code of 1987 Annotated	
CALIFORNIA	West's Annotated California Code	
	The following are the named codes in the California codification:	
	Business & Professions	Bus. & Prof.
	Civil	Civ.
	Civil Procedure	Civ. Proc.
	Commercial	Com.
	Corporations	Corp.
	Education	Educ.
	Election	Elec.
	Evidence	Evid.
	Financial	Fin.
	Fish and Game	Fish & Game
	Food and Agricultural	Food & Agric.
	Government	Gov't
	Harbors and Navigation	Harb. & Nav.
	Health and Safety	Health & Safety
	Insurance	Ins.
	Labor	Lab.

(Continued)

Table 37: Statutory Compilations—Continued

State	Statutory Compilation	Abbrevation
	Military and Veterans	Mil. & Vt.
	Penal	Pen.
	Probate	Prob.
	Public Contract	Pub. Cont.
	Public Resources	Pub. Res.
	Public Utilities	Pub. Util.
	Revenue and Taxation	Rev. & Tax
	Streets and Highways	Sts. & High.
	Unemployment Insurance	Unemp. Ins.
	Vehicle	Veh.
	Water	Wat.
	Welfare and Institutions	Welf. & Inst.
COLORADO	West's Colorado Revised Statutes Annotated	
CONNECTICUT	Connecticut General Statutes Annotated (West)	
DELAWARE	Delaware Code Annotated	
DISTRICT OF COLUMBIA	District of Columbia Code Annotated	
FLORIDA	Florida Statutes Annotated (West)	
GEORGIA	Code of Georgia Annotated (Harrison)	
HAWAII	Hawaii Revised Statutes	
IDAHO	Idaho Code	
ILLINOIS	West's Smith-Hurd Illinois Compiled Statues Annotated	
INDIANA	Burns Indiana Statutes Annotated Code Edition	
IOWA	Code of Iowa (1991); Iowa Code Annotated (West)	
KANSAS	Kansas Statutes Annotated	
KENTUCKY	Kentucky Revised Statues Annotated, Official Edition (Michie/Bobbs-Merrill)	
LOUISIANA	West's Louisiana Revised Statutes Annotated	
	West's Louisiana Civil Code Annotated	
MAINE	Maine Revised Statutes Annotated (West)	
MARYLAND	Annotated Code of Maryland	
	The following are the named codes in the Maryland codification:	
	Agriculture	Agric.
	Alcoholic Beverages	Alco. Bev.
	Business Occupations and Professions	Bus. Occ. & Prof.
	Commercial Law I	Com. Law I
	Commercial Law II	Com. Law II
	Constitutions	Const.

(Continued)

Table 37: Statutory Compilations—Continued

State	Statutory Compilation	Abbrevation
	Corporations and Associations	Corps. & Ass'ns.
	Courts and Judicial Proceedings	Cts. & Jud. Proc.
	Criminal Law	Crim. Law
	Economic Development	Econ. Dev.
	Education	Educ.
	Elections	Elec.
	Environment	Envir.
	Estates and Trusts	Est. & Trusts
	Family Law	Fam. Law
	Financial Institutions	Fin. Inst.
	General Provisions	Gen. Prov.
	Health-Environmental	Health-Envtl.
	Health-General	Health-Gen.
	Health Occupations	Health Occ.
	Insurance	Ins.
	Local Government	Local Gov't
	Natural Resources	Nat. Res.
	Public Safety	Pub. Safety
	Real Property	Real Prop.
	Social Services	Soc. Serv.
	State Finance and Procurement	State Fin. & Proc.
	State Government	State Gov't
	State Personnel	State Pers.
	Tax-General	Tax-Gen.
	Tax-Property	Tax-Prop.
	Transportation	Transp.
	Annotation Code of Maryland (1957)	__§__
MASSACHUSETTS	Annotated Laws of Massachusetts	
MICHIGAN	Michigan Statutes Annotated (Callaghan)	
MINNESOTA	Minnesota Statues Annotated (West)	
MISSISSIPPI	Mississippi Code Annotated	
MISSOURI	Vernon's Annotated Missouri Statutes	
MONTANA	Montana Code Annotated	
NEBRASKA	Revised Statutes of Nebraska	
NEVADA	Nevada Revised Statutes	
NEW HAMPSHIRE	New Hampshire Revised Statutes Annotated	
NEW JERSEY	New Jersey Statutes Annotated (West)	

(Continued)

Table 37: Statutory Compilations—Continued

State	Statutory Compilation	Abbrevation
NEW MEXICO	New Mexico Statutes Annotated	
NEW YORK	McKinney's Consolidated Laws of New York Annotated	
	Consolidated Laws Service.	
	The following are the named codes in the New York codification:	
	Abandoned Property	Aband. Prop.
	Agricultural Conservation and Adjustment	Agric. Conserv. & Adj.
	Agriculture and Markets	Agric. & Mkts
	Alcoholic Beverage Control	Alco. Bev Cont
	Alternative County Government	Alt County Gov't
	Arts and Cultural Government	Arts & Cult.
	Aff.	
	Banking	Banking
	Benevolent Orders	Ben. Ord.
	Business Corporations	Bus. Corp.
	Canal	Canal
	Civil Practice Law and Rules	N.Y. Civ. Prac. L.&R.
	Civil Rights	Civ. Rights
	Civil Service	Civ. Serv.
	Commerce	Com.
	Cooperative Corporations	Coop. Corp.
	Correction	Correct.
	County	County
	Criminal Procedure	Crim. Proc.
	Debtor and Creditor	Debt. & Cred.
	Domestic Relations	Dom. Rel.
	Education	Educ.
	Election	Elec.
	Eminent Domain Procedure Law	Em. Dom. Proc.
	Employers' Liability	Empl'rs Liab.
	Energy	Energy
	Environmental Conservation	Envtl. Conserv.
	Estates, Powers and Trusts	Est. Powers & Trusts
	Executive	Exec.
	General Association	Gen. Ass'ns
	General Business	Gen. Bus.
	General City	Gen. City
	General Construction	Gen.Constr.

(Continued)

Table 37: Statutory Compilations—Continued

State	Statutory Compilation	Abbrevation
	General Municipal	Gen. Mun.
	General Obligations	Gen. Oblig.
	Highway	High.
	Indian	Indian
	Insurance	Ins.
	Judiciary	Jud.
	Labor	Lab.
	Legislative	Leg.
	Lien	Lien
	Local Finance	Local Fin.
	Mental Hygiene	Mental Hyg.
	Military	Mil.
	Multiple Dwelling	Mult. Dwell.
	Multiple Residence	Mult. Res.
	Municipal Home Rule	Mun. Home Rule
	Navigation	Nav.
	Not-for-Profit Corporation	Not-for-Profit Corp.
	Optional County Government	Opt. County Govt.
	Parks, Recreation and Historic Preservation	Parks, Rec. & Hist. Preserv.
	Partnership	Partnership
	Penal	Penal
	Personal Property	Pers. Prop.
	Private Housing Finance	Priv. Hous. Fin.
	Public Authorities	Pub. Auth.
	Public Buildings	Pub. Bldgs.
	Public Health	Pub. Health
	Public Housing	Pub. Hous.
	Public Lands	Pub. Lands
	Public Officers	Pub. Off.
	Public Service	Pub. Serv.
	Racing, Pari-Mutuel Wagering and Breeding	Rac. Pari-Mut. Wag. & Breed.
	Railroad	R.R.
	Rapid Transit	Rapid Trans.
	Real Property	Real Prop.
	Real Property Actions and Proceedings	Real Prop. Acts.
	Real Property Tax	Real Prop. Tax
	Religious Corporations	Rel. Corp.

(Continued)

Table 37: Statutory Compilations—Continued

State	Statutory Compilation	Abbrevation
	Retirement and Social Security	Ret. & Soc. Sec.
	Rural Electric Cooperative	Rural Elec. Coop.
	Second Class Cities	Second Class Cities
	Social Services	Soc. Serv.
	Soil and Water Conservation Districts	Soil & Water Conserv. Dist.
	State Administrative Procedure Act	A.P.A.
	State Finance	State Fin.
	State Law	State L.
	State Printing and Public Documents	State Print. & Pub. Doc.
	Statute of Local Governments	Stat. Local Gov'ts
	Surrogate's Court Procedure Act	Surr. Ct. Proc. Act
	Tax	Tax
	Town	Town
	Transportation	Transp.
	Transportation Corporations	Transp. Corp.
	Uniform Commercial Code	U.C.C.
	Uniform Commercial Code Appendix	U.C.C. App.
	Unconsolidated	Unconsol.
	Vehicle and Traffic	Veh. & Traf.
	Village	Vill.
	Volunteer Firefighters' Benefit	Vol. Fire. Ben.
	Workers' Compensation	Work. Comp.
NORTH CAROLINA	General Statues of North Carolina	
NORTH DAKOTA	North Dakota Century Code	
OHIO	Ohio Revised Code Annotated (Anderson)	
OREGON	Oregon Revised Statutes	
PENNSYLVANIA	Purdon's Pennsylvania Consolidated Statutes Annotated (by title)	
RHODE ISLAND	General Laws of Rhode Island	
SOUTH CAROLINA	Code of Laws of South Carolina 1976 Annotated (Law. Co-op.)	
SOUTH DAKOTA	South Dakota Codified Laws Annotated	
TENNESSEE	Tennessee Code Annotated	
TEXAS	Vernon's Texas Codes Annotated	
	The following are the named codes found in the Texas codification:	
	Agriculture	Agric.
	Alcoholic Beverage	Alco. Bev.
	Business and Commerce	Bus. & Com.

(Continued)

Table 37: Statutory Compilations—Continued

State	Statutory Compilation	Abbrevation
	Civil Practice and Remedies	Civ. Prac. & Rem.
	Corporations and Associations	Corps. & Ass'ns
	Criminal Procedure	Crim. Proc.
	Education	Educ.
	Election	Elec.
	Family	Fam.
	Financial	Fin.
	Government	Gov't
	Health and Safety	Health & Safety
	Highway	High.
	Human Resources	Hum. Res.
	Insurance	Ins.
	Labor	Lab.
	Local Government	Local Gov't
	Natural Resources	Nat. Res.
	Occupations	Occ.
	Parks and Wildlife	Parks & Wild.
	Penal	Penal
	Probate	Prob.
	Property	Prop.
	Resources	Res.
	Tax	Tax
	Utilities	Util.
	Vehicles	Veh.
	Water	Water
	Welfare	Welf.
	Vernon's Texas Revised Civil Statues Annotated	
	Vernon's Texas Code of Criminal Procedure Annotated	
UTAH	Utah Code Annotated	
VERMONT	Vermont Statues Annotated	
VIRGINIA	Code of Virginia Annotated	
WASHINGTON	Revised Code of Washington Annotated	
WEST VIRGINIA	West Virginia Code	
WISCONSIN	West's Wisconsin Statues Annotated	
WYOMING	Wyoming Statutes Annotated (Michie)	

For Reference

Not to be taken from this room